MUSEUMS, OBJECTS AND COLLECTIONS

FOR MY STUDENTS

Museums, Objects and Collections: A Cultural Study

SUSAN M. PEARCE

Leicester University Press
Leicester and London

© Susan M. Pearce 1992

First published in Great Britain in 1992 by Leicester University Press (a division of Pinter Publishers Limited)

Editorial offices
Fielding Johnson Building, University of Leicester, Leicester, LE1 7RH, England

Trade and other enquiries
25 Floral Street, London, WC2E 9DS

British Library Congress Cataloguing in Publication Data
A CIP catalogue record for this book is available from the British Library

ISBN 0 7185 1320 0

Typeset by BookEns Ltd., Baldock, Herts.
Printed and bound in Great Britain by Billing & Sons Ltd, Worcester

Contents

List of plates   vi
List of figures   viii
Preface   x
1.   Museums, Objects and Collections   1
2.   Objects Inside and Outside Museums   15
3.   Collecting: Body and Soul   36
4.   Collecting: Shaping the World   68
5.   Museums: the Intellectual Rationale   89
6.   Making Museum Meanings   118
7.   Meaning as Function   146
8.   Meaning as Structure   166
9.   Meaning in History   192
10.   Objects in Action   210
11.   Problems of Power   228
12.   Projects and Prospects   256
Appendix: Models for object study   265
Bibliography   274
Index   288

List of Plates

1. Macdonald of Keppoch's sword, National Museums of Scotland. 25
2. Stuffed and mounted British magpie, Leicestershire Museum Service. 32
3. Gold neck ornament, later Bronze Age, Yeovil, Somerset. 34
4. Two Yoruba figures, Exeter City Museum. 40
5. Metal badge showing Daniel Lambert of Leicestershire, Leicestershire Museum Service. 58
6. Col. C. Peel and his trophies, Exeter City Museum. 70
7. Etching by Max Pollack of Freud at his desk, Freud Museum, London. 74
8. Front cover of *Miller's Magazine*, Vol. 1, No. 1, 1991. 77
9. Poster advertising *The People's Show*, Walsall, 1990. 80
10. Rotunda proposal for Pitt Rivers Museum, Oxford, 1960s. 86
11. Tradescant Room, Ashmolean Museum, Oxford. 96
12. Engraved frontispiece, *Musei Wormiani Historia*, Leiden, 1655. 97
13. Old Ashmolean Museum building, Oxford. 98
14. Cabinets for John Woodward's collection, Sedgwick Museum, Cambridge. 102
15. Poster for exhibition *Artificial Curiosities*, 1978, Bernice Pavahi Museum, Honolulu, Hawaii. 104
16. Kensington Case at Exeter City Museum, 1931. 106
17. Cases at Weston Park Museum, Sheffield, 1938. 107
18. The Harris Museum, Preston, Lancashire. 108
19. The Natural History Museum, South Kensington, London. 109
20. Stag Cases at Manchester University Museum, 1938. 111
21. Inuit with kayak, 1961, Pelly Bay, North-West Territories, Canada. 148
22. Exhibition on life of John Hodges, Abbey Barn, Glastonbury, Somerset. 181
23. Reconstruction of Thomas Hardy's study, Dorset County Museum, Dorchester. 199
24. *Armada 1588–1988* exhibition, National Maritime Museum, Greenwich, London. 204
25. Tureen and cover in shape of a rabbit, Chelsea, FitzWilliam Museum, Cambridge. 218
26. Reliquary châsse showing martyrdom of St Thomas Becket, Burrell Collection, Glasgow. 225

27. Central feature of *Evolution*, Royal Museum of Scotland.   243

28. Poster for exhibition *Celtic Britain: Life and Death in the Iron Age 500 BC–AD 50*, 1990, British Museum.   246

29. Poster for exhibition *Museum of the Iron Age: Danebury*, Andover, Hampshire.   247

30. Poster for exhibition *Warriors, Druids, Slaves*, Museum of the North, Llanberis.   250

31. Poster for exhibition *Treasures and Trinkets*, 1992, Museum of London.   251

32. Poster for exhibition *Tudor London*, 1991, Museum of London.   252

33. Poster for exhibition *Useful and Beautiful: Museums in the Six Towns*, Stoke-on-Trent.   254

List of Figures

1.1	Relationship between museum theory and practice.	10
1.2	Nineteeth-and-twentieth-century traditions of thought and critical theory.	12
2.1	Duality in the Western tradition.	18
2.2	Semiotic analysis of Macdonald of Keppoch's sword.	28
2.3	Extended semiotic analysis of Macdonald of Keppoch's sword.	29
2.4	Analysis of magpie as sign and symbol.	31
3.1	Semiotic analysis of collecting process.	39
3.2	Analysis of the making of a collection.	41
3.3	Cognitive processes underlying collection-making.	42
3.4	Strategies for collection closure.	54
3.5	'Simple stimulus' and 'activating stimulus'.	60
3.6	Contrasts between Mouse Cottage and Fire Museum.	62
3.7	Masculine and feminine images and characters in collection.	64
3.8	Plan of Pinto Gallery, Birmingham City Museum, 1970.	67
4.1	Analysis of the significance of animal trophies.	71
4.2	Analysis of contents of first issue of *Miller's Magazine*.	76
4.3	Advertisement for *Collectamania* exhibition, Stevenage Museum.	79
5.1	Genesis and history of museums.	90
6.1	Beds: classification according to yes : no answers.	123
6.2	Furniture: taxonomic structure in daily speech.	125
6.3	Natural history: Linnaean structure.	125
6.4	Bronze Age material: typological structure.	126
6.5	Part of Welsh Folk Museum classification system.	130
6.6	Stylistic change in silver candlesticks, 1660–1800.	133
6.7	Exhibitions: the organization of space.	138
6.8	Plan of ground floor, Natural History Museum, London.	140
6.9	Semiotic analysis of exhibition.	142
7.1	Factor score plot for differentiation in Beaker pottery.	152
7.2	Factor score plot for differentiation in school uniform.	153
7.3	Social system and subsystems.	154
7.4	Late Roman Somerset AD 300–450.	156
7.5	Simple systems analysis for late Roman east Somerset.	157
7.6	Simple systems analysis for late Roman west Somerset.	158
7.7	Post-Roman Somerset AD 450–600.	160

7.8	Simple systems analysis for post-Roman Somerset.	161
7.9	Model for the collapse of civilization.	162
8.1	*Langue, parole* and trousers.	169
8.2	Sets of clothes.	171
8.3	Binary pairs drawn from sets of clothes.	172
8.4	Structuralist plot of clothes.	173
8.5	Binary pairs drawn from terraced house.	173
8.6	Internal arrangement of Pirà-paranà longhouse, and model of house as body.	175
8.7	Terraced house as body.	176
8.8	Semiotic analysis of tea drinking.	177
8.9	Association between pottery and major social variables in an Indian village.	178
8.10	Structuralist plot of traditional social life of Central Inuit.	179
8.11	Binary pairs drawn from bull and cow.	182
8.12	Binary pairs drawn from traditional English cattle processing.	182
8.13	Structuralist plot of traditional dairy farm.	183
8.14	Analysis of traditional dairy farm.	184
8.15	Binary pairs drawn from willow pattern plate – 1.	185
8.16	Binary pairs drawn from willow pattern plate – 2.	186
8.17	Functionalist analysis of southern English nineteenth-century dairy farm.	190
9.1	Plan of Hardy exhibition, Dorset County Museum.	200
9.2	Opposed pairs showing nature of historical exhibition.	206
10.1	Behavioural action: young woman and clothes.	215
10.2	Braudel's scales in the historical process.	223
11.1	Grants under Victoria and Albert Museum grant fund, 1985–6.	239
App.1.1	Model for object study by Panofsky.	266
App.1.2	Model for object study by Fleming.	267
App.1.3	Model for object study based upon Prown.	268
App.1.4	Model for object study by Elliott *et al.*	269
App.1.5	Model for object study based upon Batchelor.	271
App.1.6	Model for object study by Pearce.	272

Preface

This book has been written from one clear perspective, that of a curator who believes that collections, and the objects and specimens within them, will always be, and should always be, at the heart of the museum operation. This is not to deny the crucial role of interpretation to the public in the broadest sense, but it is to express the conviction that only through an understanding of our museums and our material can the special experiences which we have to offer the visitor be developed, with all the warmth and skill at our command. We should, therefore, bring to our understanding of museums and museum material not only the study proper to our various disciplines, and the techniques of collection and resource management, indispensable though these are, but also the effort to understand the nature of museums, of their material, and of curatorship, as cultural expressions in their own right, and to develop theoretical perspectives which help in this understanding. With this goes the need to recognize that theory and practice in museums are indivisible, and that both come into play every time we choose an object for display, or give a gallery talk.

If there are still those in the museum world for whom the discussion of theory is 'not relevant' then I suggest that they read no further, for this book is not for them. It is offered to the growing number of people, inside and outside museums, who recognize the unique significance of museums and collections in the European cultural tradition, and believe that this significance is a proper subject for study. This is as true for the scientific collections as it is for human history material, and the bias towards human history in this book represents my own areas of experience rather than anything else. I hope that the natural history museum community will continue the work which they have started in developing our understanding of the significance of the scientific collections in cultural history and interpretation.

Many conversations with museum people and others over the years have helped me to write this book. I should particularly like to record the helpful and enjoyable discussions I have had with my graduate students. Singling out individuals is always difficult, but I owe particular debts to Kevin Moore, Harriet Purkis, Sarah Harbidge, Ann Nicol, Jo Bailey, Liz Sobell (all for giving me references and details of museum projects) and Karen Goldstein (who put me in touch with work done in the USA). To all these, and many others, I am very grateful. A number of people have helped with illustrative material for the book, especially Dave Bolton, Roger Peers, David Dawson, Yolande Courtney, Julia Holberry, A. C. Edmonds, Dale Idiens and Tim Schadla-Hall.

Some of the material which appears in Chapter 4 has already appeared in a chapter in *Museum Languages: Objects and Texts* (ed. G. Kavanagh), Leicester University Press, 1991. I acknowledge that some may find the use of language in this book sexist, but I assure them that this relates to the lack of suitable English pronouns and suggest that they turn their attention to this difficult matter.

My grateful thanks go to Ann Sarson who typed the manuscript with great care and skill. My warmest thanks go to Jim Roberts who produced the figures. Finally, as always, my thanks go to my husband.

SUSAN PEARCE
Leicester, March 1992

1 Museums, Objects and Collections

When you are looking at an artefact you are looking at a person's thoughts.
(Leader board label, exhibition of collections of human history, Newfoundland
Museum (Government of Newfoundland and Labrador), Canada)

Introduction

Museums are a characteristic part of the cultural pattern of modern Europe, and of
the European-influenced world. Numbers are difficult to judge but Europe has at
least 13,500, of which perhaps 5,000 are in Britain, and there are roughly another
12,000 throughout the rest of the world. Museums are by nature institutions
which hold the material evidence, objects and specimens, of the human and natural
history of our planet. The Natural History Museum, London, numerically one of
the largest collections in the world, holds some 67 million specimens, and the
overall figure across the world must run into hundreds of millions. All of these
museum holdings were assembled, with some degree of conscious intention, by
collectors (some of whom were also curators) whose collections found their way
into a holding museum, where they are curated and interpreted by museum staff.
Museums, objects and collections are the three faces of this cultural triangle, each
showing different features to the world but together making up the whole. The
purpose of this book is to explore the nature of the triangle, and of its cultural and
social significance.

Each of these assertions needs some amplification.

Museums in Modern Europe

Notwithstanding the fact that the collection-forming habit can be traced far back
into European prehistory, that the word 'museum' comes to us from the classical
past, or that material has been assembled and displayed in many other parts of the
world (see Clunas 1991; Yamaguchi 1991; Goswamy 1991), it is nevertheless true
that in the very broad sense the museum as a modern institution came to birth
around the middle of the fifteenth century in the Renaissance cities and courts of
Italy and has continued in a linear development in Europe since that time, spreading

to the rest of the world along with all the other characteristically European institutions. Those who wish may stray through the grey maze of definition-making, but I take as a simple starting point the view that in the past and the present, a museum (or an art gallery) is constituted by its collections, however large or small, and by a broadly institutional purpose which relates to this material and which is likely to be expressed by a building (whole or part), staff (not necessarily paid), visitors, and most crucially, by a cultural perspective which underwrites the whole and upon which, in their turn, museums themselves exercise some influence. This has been succinctly expressed by the definition adopted by the Museums Association in 1984 which reads: 'A museum is an institution which collects, documents, preserves, exhibits and interprets material evidence and associated information for the public benefit' (Museums Association 1991: 13). We should remember that the line between private and public (in the sense of 'open to the public') museums is now, and historically has always been, a thin one, and that 'for the public benefit' should be interpreted in the most general sense to include broad contributions to knowledge and appreciation in the material sphere.

Museums are a typical part of modern European cultural expression, and although Europe as a term can be allowed to speak for itself, 'modern' needs to be examined more closely (Harvey 1989; Habermas 1987). The nature and origins of modern European society have been a matter of intense debate (Giddens 1991; Jameson 1991; Hall and Gieben 1992), resulting in some confusion of terms and their detailed meanings. Broadly, modern Europe can be seen to begin with the break-up of the feudal system and to have experienced an early phase of modernity running roughly from the mid fifteenth to the mid seventeenth centuries. The period of classic modernity followed, running up to about 1950, to be succeeded by what is variously called 'late modernity' or post-modernity, depending upon whether modernity itself is seen as essentially a condition of change, or whether the break with the past around the mid twentieth century is seen to be extreme enough to warrant a separate term. Here the words post-modernity or post-modern will be used to describe the current phase, although it is clear that in museums, as elsewhere, even its immediate origins lie well back in the late nineteenth century. Naturally enough, as we shall see in Chapter 5, the progress of the museum idea has reflected and enhanced the wider cultural pattern.

Modernity was a complex bundle of characteristic modes of thinking and acting which gradually gathered momentum. In essence, modernity was concerned with the development of meta-narratives, overarching discourses through which objective realities and eternal truths could be defined and expressed. At bottom this rested on the belief – and it *was* a belief – that objective reality existed and that human beings as essential individuals shared in it and could therefore appreciate it. This gave rise to the discourse of scientific knowledge and understanding arrived at by the operation of human reason upon the observed phenomena of the natural world, for which museums and their collections were perceived as the principal repositories of primary evidence. Linnaeus's scheme of taxonomy or Darwin's theory of evolution were typical meta-narratives of this kind. With this went a moral stance closely associated with the Northern European work ethic which supposed the existence of absolute ethical values of a broadly Judaeo-Christian kind (but not necessarily of Christian theology) linked with the virtues of industry and self-reliance. To these moral qualities art, held and publicly displayed in museums, gave tangible and visible forms.

The same Judaeo-Christian tradition contributed the idea of linear time (in contrast to the cyclical time of most other traditions), which sharpened into a universal feeling of historical forward movement and chronological purposefulness in the later seventeenth century, with Newton's concept of mathematical time as a straight geometric line, and with the development of accurate time-keeping. The historical discourse, child of ideas about the nature of scientific evidence translated into human history material and of the belief in the essential individual, spoke about great men (mostly) who had contributed to the growth of knowledge and experience by expressing its ideals. Museums held the tangible relics of the great, and especially, the works of art created by the great painters and sculptors.

The modern world has also been a world of things, of objects and material goods. The economic discourse, which matched the scientific, ethical and historical ones, was the interrelated market system of production, consumption, credit and interest, usually called capitalism, and implicit in this is an ever-increasing demand for more goods, which continually feeds upon itself. The modern world came to define itself, both communally and individually, largely in terms of ownership of goods, which correspondingly came to be its most characteristic expression. In written literature, as the extracts at the heads of the chapters of this book show, objects share with people the parallel life of the text, and modern fiction, itself a most typical modern genre, would be as unthinkable without them as real life. Our complex relationship with objects – as producers, owners and collectors – is itself a characteristic modern meta-narrative, and so, in its way, is our effort to understand material culture and our interest in it. The important point here is that in a materially-orientated world of goods, modern museums, which grew up and grew old with the capitalist system, are equally material-orientated in the most fundamental sense.

An essential link between all these propositions was the idea of progress, in which the process of history in the hands of the great, the rational grip on objective knowledge harnessed to technological improvement, and the moral qualities of Enlightened man – good sense, tolerance, enlightened self-interest – would combine to produce a world of steady environmental and ethical improvement. As McCarthy has put it: 'Since the beginning of the modern era the prospect of a limitless advance of science and technology, accompanied at each step by moral and political improvement has exercised a considerable hold over Western thought' (McCarthy 1984: 105). In their different ways, the ideas of Rousseau, of the British utilitarians and of Marx are all meta-narratives of this kind.

The role of museums in this is clear. Museums served an educational purpose which gathered strength and social breadth as the modern period progressed. They were seen as playing their part in the development of the reliable and orderly citizens which the Victorian establishment desired to see. Henry Cole, writing in 1857 about what was to become the Victoria and Albert Museum, said:

The working man comes to this museum from his one or two dimly lighted, cheerless dwelling rooms, in his fustian jacket, with his shirt collars a little trimmed up, accompanied by his threes and fours, and fives of little fustian jackets, a wife in her best bonnet, and a baby, of course, under her shawl. The looks of surprise and pleasure on the whole party when they first observe the brilliant lighting inside the museum show what a new, acceptable, and wholesome excitement this evening affords them all. Perhaps the evening opening of public museums may furnish a powerful antidote to the gin palace.

(Cole, 1884: 293)

The tone is affectionate, if patronizing, but the social implications are clear.

The sum of museum participation in these characteristically modern discourses adds together into a crucial role in cultural expression, and this explains why so many early collections were brought together in the sixteenth and seventeenth centuries, why so many museums were founded in the eighteenth and increasingly during the nineteenth and early twentieth centuries, why nearly every British city or large town, and many European cities, felt they must have one, and why such relatively large resources were expended on buildings. Civic pride is not the reason, because we must ask ourselves why civic pride took this form. The answer lies in the unique characteristic of museums to hold the real objects, the actual evidence, the true data as we would say, upon which in the last analysis the materialistic meta-narratives depended for their verification. With this is linked the other side of the unique museum mode, the ability to display, to demonstrate, to show the nature of the world and of man within it by arranging the collected material in particular patterns which reflect, confirm and project the contemporary world view. With this go the modes of curatorial care, study and interpretation which, in themselves, make up elements in the constituting modern discourses. These three museum characteristics will haunt this book.

Museum Objects

It will be helpful to clear some paths through the undergrowth by picking out some of the key words relating to museum material, and taking a closer look at them. One group comprises those words which are used to describe an individual piece, or in general terms a number of pieces, and this group includes 'object', 'thing', 'specimen', 'artefact', 'good' usually used in the plural as 'goods', and the term 'material culture' used as a collective noun. All of these terms share common ground in that they all refer to selected lumps of the physical world to which cultural value has been ascribed, a deceptively simple definition which much of this book will be devoted to discussing, but each carries a slightly different shade of meaning because each comes from a distinguishably different tradition of study.

One problem common to them all, and one which throws up the characteristic cleft between philosophical speculation and the everyday meanings attached to words, revolves around the scope to be attributed to them. Strictly speaking, the lumps of the physical world to which cultural value is ascribed include not merely those discrete lumps capable of being moved from one place to another, which is what we commonly mean when we say 'thing' or 'artefact', but also the larger physical world of landscape with all the social structure that it carries, the animal and plant species which have been affected by humankind (and most have), the prepared meals which the animals and plants become, and even the manipulation of flesh and air which produces song and speech. As James Deetz has put it in a famous sentence: 'Material culture is that segment of man's physical environment which is purposely shaped by him according to a culturally dictated plan' (Deetz 1977: 7).

This is to say, in effect, that the whole of cultural expression, one way or another, falls within the realm of material culture, and if analytical definition is pushed to its logical conclusion, that is probably true. It is also true that the material culture held today by many museums falls within this broader frame, like the areas of industrial landscape which Ironbridge exhibits. However, for the purposes of study, limits must be set, and this book will concentrate upon those movable pieces, those 'discrete lumps' which have always formed, and still form, the bulk of museum holdings and which museums were, and still are, intended to hold.

This brings us to a point of crucial significance. What distinguishes the 'discrete lumps' from the rest – what makes a 'movable piece' in our sense of the term – is the cultural value it is given, and not primarily the technology which has been used to give it form or content, although this is an important mode of value creation. The crucial idea is that of selection, and it is the act of selection which turns a part of the natural world into an object and a museum piece. This is clearly demonstrated by the sample of moon rock which went on display in the Milestones of Flight hall at the National Air and Space Museum, Washington, DC:

> The moon rock is an actual piece of the moon retrieved by the Apollo 17 mission. There is nothing particularly appealing about the rock; it is a rather standard piece of volcanic basalt some 4 million years old. Yet, unlike many other old rocks, this one comes displayed in an altar-like structure, set in glass, and is complete with full-time guard and an ultrasensitive monitoring device (or so the guards are wont to say). There is a sign above it which reads, 'You may touch it with care.' *Everyone touches it.*
>
> (Meltzer 1981: 121)

The moon rock has been turned into material culture because through its selection and display it has become a part of the world of human values, a part which, evidently, every visitor wants to bring within his own personal value system.

What is true of the moon rock is equally true of the stones which the Book of Joshua tells us Joshua commanded the twelve tribes of Israel to collect from the bed of the River Jordan and set up as a permanent memorial of the crossing of the river, and of all other natural objects deliberately placed within human contexts. It is also equally true of the millions of natural history pieces inside museum collections for which 'specimen', meaning an example selected from a group, is our customary term. It is clear that the acquisition of a natural history specimen involves selection according to contemporary principles, detachment from the natural context, and organization into some kind of relationship (many are possible) with other, or different, material. This process turns a 'natural object' into a humanly-defined piece, and means that natural history objects and collections, although like all other collections they have their own proper modes and histories of study, can also be treated as material culture and discussed in these terms. The development of contemporary epistemology suggests that no fact can be read transparently. All apparently 'natural' facts are actually discursive facts, since 'nature' is not something already there but is itself the result of historical and social construction. To call something a natural object, as Laclau and Mouffe say (1987: 84), is a way of conceiving it that depends upon a classificatory system: if there were no human beings on earth, stones would still be there, but they would not be 'stones' because there would be neither mineralogy nor language with which to distinguish and classify them. Natural history specimens are therefore as much social constructs as spears or typewriters, and as susceptible to social analysis.

'Thing' is our most ordinary word for all these pieces, and it is also used in everyday speech for the whole range of non-material matters (a similarly elusive word) which have a bearing on our daily lives. 'Object' shares the same slipperiness both in ordinary speech and in intellectual discourse, where it is generally the term used. The ways in which we use these terms, and the implications of this usage for the ways in which our collective psyche views the material world are very significant, and are further pursued in the next chapter. The term 'artefact' means 'made by art or skill' and so takes a narrow view of what constitutes material objects, concentrating upon that part of their nature which involves the application of human technology to the natural world, a process which plays a part in the creation of many, but by no means all, material pieces. Because it is linked with practical skills, and so with words like 'artisan', 'artefact' is a socially low-value term, and one which is correspondingly applied to material deemed to be humble, like ordinary tables and chairs, rather than paintings and sculptures. In this book 'thing' and 'object', and sometimes 'artefact', will be used to refer to material pieces without any particular distinction being made between them, and 'material culture' will be used in the same general sense.

'Goods' comes to us from the world of economics and production theory and relates to that aspect of material pieces which embraces the market-place value which is set upon them, and their exchange rate in relation to other similar or different goods and services. This is the treatment of material culture as commodity, and the work of social anthropologists, particularly Douglas and Isherwood (1979), has shown how shallow the purely economic discussion of material is until social or cultural dimensions of value are added to it, and the word will be generally avoided in this book unless objects in their commodity aspect are specifically intended.

Museum Collections: Some Preliminary Points

All museum collections have three things in common: they are made up of objects within the definition given in the previous section; the objects within them come to us from the past; and they have been assembled with some degree of intention (however slight) by an owner or curator who believed that the whole was somehow more than the sum of its parts.

Three points are particularly important. Firstly, all the material within collections participates in the nature of objects which has already been touched upon and will be explored further in Chapter 2. Secondly, only a very small proportion of the available material ever finds its way into a collection. The process of selection lies at the heart of collecting, and as we shall see, the act of collecting is not simple; it involves both a view of inherited social ideas of the value which should (or should not) be attached to a particular object and which derive from the modern narratives we have been considering, and impulses which lie at the deepest level of individual personality. Finally, some collections, but by no means all, find their way into an established museum, although all museum material has (one way or another) been collected. A second process of selection, then, lies at the heart of the museum operation or, to put it another way, museum objects are created by the act of collecting, usually twice over – firstly through the choices of the individual collector, and secondly, by the willingness of a museum to take the collected assemblage for reasons which have to do with its perceived aesthetic, historic or scientific value. It is upon this basis that museum interpretation of material is erected.

The Critical Tradition

The title of this section is something of a misnomer in that the critical study of the museum as an institution, of the nature of its collections, and of material culture (rather than of museum material according to the views and methods of the academic discipline to which it belongs) is still relatively in its infancy. In general terms the critical tradition within museum studies mirrors that within other related cultural fields, although until recently it has shown a distinct tendency to lag behind.

The earliest paradigm of study was that of the traditional historian and biographer concerned with the choice of 'important' men and 'significant' collections and with the sequential assemblage of facts guaranteed by the normal procedures of historical evidence. Since the middle of the nineteenth century, this has produced a steady stream of museum histories and biographies of major collectors, with which should be linked the steady publication of museum and special exhibition catalogues. These are usually discipline-based but contribute considerably to our understanding of what museums hold and how they came by it. Important contributions to the history of collecting have been made by Frank Herrmann (1972) and by Oliver Impey and Arthur MacGregor (1985) and the Oxford *Journal of the History of Collections*. From the contemporary critical point of view all this provides indispensable raw material with which to work.

Curiously enough,the paradigm of study aimed at a critical elucidation of the meaning of objects, and of the relationship of collecting and collections to this, also began well back in the nineteenth century with the published ideas of Pitt Rivers, whose collecting drive was linked with an overarching philosophy of man and material culture in which Darwinian ideas, applied to objects, yielded a scheme whereby artefact types developed one from another according to a process of natural selection. The resulting historical sequences could, Pitt Rivers thought, be reconstructed, using actual objects to show the different cultural levels achieved by different human groups and to illustrate the notion of progress. Pitt Rivers hoped that the establishment of his collection at Oxford would encourage the development of a research community devoted to extending his ideas, but it did not because anthropological interest was turning away from the study of material culture, in which Pitt Rivers' grand designs were looking increasingly fragile, and towards the study of whole communities in the field, matched in museums by the life-style display scenes mounted in Washington by Franz Boas (Stocking 1974; Jacknis 1986).

Meanwhile, archaeologists were beginning to accumulate large museum collec-tions, backed by interpretative ideas about typological relationships derived from Pitt Rivers and ultimately from eighteenth-century biology, and about the relation-ship between material evidence and human 'cultures' derived from Gordon Childe. Conceptually, material culture studies, and museums, languished in the doldrums for most of the middle decades of this century, until around 1975 when ideas about the meanings of objects and how they can be studied underwent a radical shift as the broadly structuralist and post-structuralist ideas developed earlier in the century in Central Europe, Paris, Moscow and North America were applied to them. In Britain, a milestone was marked with the publication of Ucko's work on penis sheaths (1969). While there is a limit to what can be got out of a penis sheath, material culture studies were much extended by key work done at Cam-bridge by Ian Hodder (Hodder 1982a; 1982b; 1989) and his colleagues (Miller 1985, 1987; Shanks and Tilley 1987a and 1987b).

Important contributions, particularly on the social significance of objects tra-ditionally seen merely as commodities, have been made by Douglas and Isherwood (1979), Appadurai (1986) and Csikszentmihalyi and Rochberg-Halton (1981). In North America, where the tradition of material culture study concentrates upon what in British museums would be called social history, important work is represented in the collections of essays edited by Schlereth (1982), Bronner (1985) and Pocius (1991). One exhibition has been mounted which was specifically concerned with material culture and its history and social role: *A Material World*, put on by the National Museum of American History in 1988. From this exhibition has emerged a volume of papers entitled *History from Things* (Kingery and Lubar 1992). The editors conclude their Introduction by suggesting that mate-rial culture studies has now 'all the intellectual and emotional content necessary to establish new relationships, to develop what is, in essence, a peer group of its own' (1992: 9).

Contemporary ideas about material culture studies marry up with concepts drawn from the same broadly post-modern thinking about the nature of museums and of collectors and collecting to give us our contemporary paradigm of museum studies: the critical evaluation of the whole museum phenomenon as an important element in social theory and practice, matching similar critical studies in literary theory, the media, and the idea of the past, inside and outside the heritage movement (see Eagleton 1983; Silverstone 1981; Walsh 1992). Study is now being actively pursued at a number of centres, chiefly the Universities of Brno and Zagreb in Eastern Europe, the University of Leicester in Western Europe, and in North America at the Smithsonian Institution (Karp and Levine 1991) and the University of Utah, where the studies on contemporary collecting carried out in Consumer Behavior Odyssey organized by Russell Belk and his colleagues should be singled out for special mention. Important material is also produced by a still relatively small number of individuals, whose published work is cited throughout this volume.

The relationship between the critical tradition, which analyses the nature and operation of museums, and of museum work – between (in a nutshell) museum theory and practice – is an important one and deserves thought. It is, of course, true that theoretical stances are implicit in every action, and that therefore the writing of every label or the filling of every show-case is a theory-laden activity underpinned by a wide range of conceptual stances which we should try to understand. But the relationship between theory and practice is more complicated than this would suggest, because the development of theory takes place in a number of modes which bear different relationships to work practice.

Figure 1.1 sets out one model for expressing these relationships, and this suggests a structure in which a number of cycles are operating simultaneously. A starting-point is the effort to expand knowledge and appreciation, which will draw on past and present interpretative philosophies like those which have already been identified as within the modern meta-narrative, those which regard these narratives with a critical eye, and more specifically, those associated with particular writers, like Marx and his successors. From this climate of opinion will come both discipline-based study of museum material, and study of the history and nature of museums, their collections and their operation; both these two studies, in their turn, will exercise some influence upon how the climate of opinion develops – in particular, the study of museum material plays its own part in the developing philosophy of knowledge proper to each discipline, and so to knowledge as a whole. All three of these endeavours go towards shaping the development of critical museum theory as a part of cultural study, and this, too, has its effect upon the broader climate.

This critical museum theory feeds into theory-making at the level of specific museum operation, in the drafting of management plans, or the framing of visitor surveys and exhibition briefs. These in their turn issue as museum practice, as actual staff structures, research projects and operating stores. Empirical understanding drawn from the experience of practice has its influence upon both museum theory and the whole climate of opinion. We can see that there are three modes of theory, all of which feed off each other, and all of which are part of the seamless garment of interacting theory and practice. This book fits somewhere

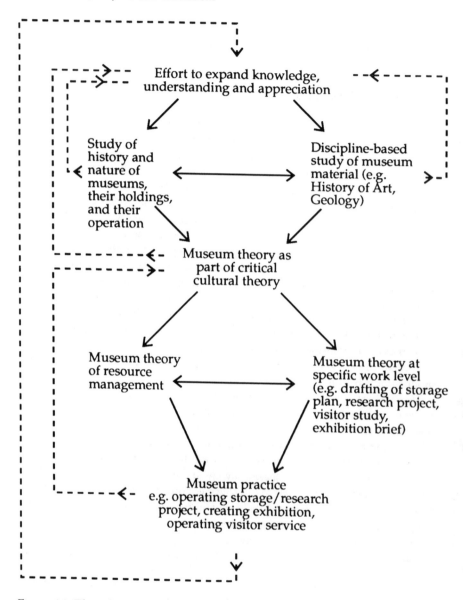

Figure 1.1 The relationship between theory and practice in museums

around the middle of the model in Figure 1.1. It is concerned with the development of critical museum theory as a part of broader social theory.

The Shape of This Study

This study intends to explore the philosophies and cultural traditions which underlie museums, their collections, and the objects which make them up, and to see how meaning is created amongst them. It endeavours to get behind the traditional academic disciplines amongst which museum work is usually divided, and to look at the nature of the museum and its material as a whole. It will be concerned with the historical context from which museums and their material have come – a part, as we have seen, of the European modern tradition; with how museums appear in the critical post-modern gaze; and with the symbolic nature of objects, collections and exhibitions. It intends to open up for discussion areas like the nature of collecting, the presumptions and problems implicit in curatorial work, the philosophical stances which are used to make meaning in the interpretation and exhibition of objects, and the post-modern dilemmas which museums face. In considering these things, it will draw upon nineteenth- and twentieth-century traditions of thought and contemporary critical theory, the main features of which are expressed in simple form in Figure 1.2. It will also draw on my own experience of museum work and on the broad mass – largely descriptive rather than critical – of literature which museums have produced.

This study is not primarily concerned with the broad field of museum visiting, or with questions like who goes to museums and why – an area in which more good work (e.g. Merriman 1991; McManus 1988) has been done than in most others in museum studies. Equally, it is not concerned with the problems of exhibition evaluation in the formal sense, an area which has also seen excellent published work (e.g. Miles 1986). It is not concerned with the problems of museum management as such. It is not an analysis of the broad contemporary heritage movement of the kind written by Hewison (1987) or Walsh (1992), although questions with a bearing on the nature of heritage arise within it. Still less is it concerned with the nature of museum work or research in particular museum disciplines; analyses of specific areas like archaeological or biological field work, or the oral recording of contemporary society, are outside its scope. It is written in the passionately-held conviction that in museums, as in everything else, theory and practice are indistinguishable: every time we take a museum decision, we are carrying out a philosophical act which arises from a cultural context and has cultural implications, and the more we understand about this, the better for all concerned. Museums and their collections are a part of the wider world of society and its material culture, and so a cultural study of museums must take a range of important broader issues into account, and this I have endeavoured to do.

I have tried to write in a user-friendly style, believing that there is no virtue in mystification, but accepting the risk of over-simplifying complex arguments which this approach entails. For this reason I have often drawn arguments from early

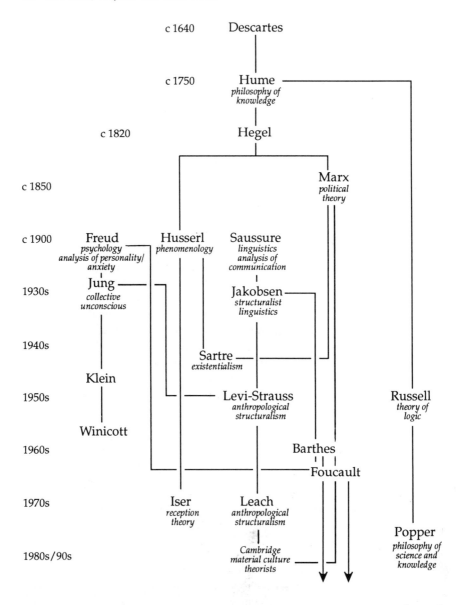

Figure 1.2 A simple chart showing some important points in nineteenth- and twentieth-century traditions of thought and critical theory

practitioners in their particular fields, like Saussure or Clarke, who set out some first principles. For the same reason, I have in places made considerable use of specific case-histories, trying to draw these from a mixture of traditional discipline-based material, but recognizing my own limitations here as a museum archaeologist and anthropologist.

As befits an examination, this book is arranged according to broad topics, rather than as a linear chronological narrative. The first section comprises this introductory chapter (1) which is intended to set out the parameters of the study, to describe the position of museums in the history of European culture, and to clarify some notions about museum objects and collections. The next group of chapters concentrates upon the interrelationship between objects, collections and museums in order to show the nature of the internal structure of museum content. This starts with an analysis of material culture in Chapter 2, an analysis which applies to the vast range of material both inside and outside museums, but which also concentrates on those aspects of objects which are particularly relevant to their collected lives. The next two chapters (3 and 4) consider the nature of the collecting process which selects out from the broad mass some objects for special consideration, and here we are primarily interested in the inward or private reasons for this activity. Chapter 5 discusses how, over the last five centuries or so, museums have consti- tuted themselves through the collections which they contain, the ways in which these have been treated and housed, and the relationship of this to the public and explicit intellectual and social tradition.

The subsequent chapters are concerned with how museum workers make meaning with the objects in their care in terms of the ways in which they are curated, studied and displayed. Chapter 6 discusses the curatorial tradition and analyses the nature of the inheritance and the ways in which meaning is made through documentation and research, through policies of collection management, and through the exhibition viewed as a medium in its own right with its own proper history and nature. The next three chapters look in turn at the principal theo- retical positions from which meaning in objects is generated in study and display, considering objects viewed as functional artefacts (Chapter 7), objects as symbolic structures (Chapter 8) and objects as historical evidence (Chapter 9).

The next part of the book looks at the implications of the making of museum meanings. Chapter 10 considers the active role of both objects (on and off dis- play) and the individual who experiences them, and analyses the nature of this interreaction by drawing on phenomenological and behavioural theory. Chapter 11 examines the underside, the ideological nature of museums and their collections in the power-broking world of European capitalism, and in the nihilistic response to this world made in post-structuralist thought. Finally, the last chapter draws together the threads of the discussion, and suggests ways in which museum workers may be able to reconcile their pasts and their presents in a project for the future.

I have already referred to my belief that theory and practice are indistinguishable and must be developed together. This book is intended to contribute to that development. I hope that it will link up with similar endeavours across the museum world, still as yet few in number but growing, to create, for museum workers and others, the cultural and critical investigation of museums as a field in its own right, a fitting complement to the social significance which museums command.

2 Objects Inside and Outside Museums

Most of the marks that man has left on the face of the earth during his career as a litterbugging, meddlesome and occasionally artistic animal have one aspect in common: they are things, they are not deeds, words or ideas.

(Isaac 1971: 123)

Even the humblest material artefact, which is the product and symbol of a particular civilization, is an emissary of the culture out of which it comes.

(Eliot 1948: 46)

Consider the solid silver cigarette cases of forty to fifty years ago, which, no longer carried, have not yet joined the display of Georgian snuff-boxes in the curiosity cabinet, but lie instead stacked in attics, awaiting a decision as to their value – antiques or just their weight in silver.

(Douglas and Isherwood 1979: 99)

Introduction: Material Things

The expression 'material things' suggests something of our essentially ambiguous relationship to material, which on the one hand we regard as merely the physical means of living, and on the other as setting the vitally relevant parameters by which we live. This opaqueness runs through the language. 'Matter' carries a feeling of boring formlessness, but phrases like 'What is the matter?' or 'the heart of the matter' suggest something of crucial importance. This chapter will single out for discussion some of the characteristics of objects which give them the problematic character which we experience as living people and, specifically, as curators.

Let us then start with a statement of the glaringly obvious, and hope to proceed to more complicated matters as the argument unwinds. Objects are lumps of the material world. They share this nature with all living things, including ourselves, and this materiality distinguishes all that share it from insubstantial creations like tunes, poems, or the idea of marriage. Like ourselves, objects can only be in one place at any given time. Objects are three-dimensional, and the quantity of space they take up depends upon their height and breadth and the air-displacing effect of their individual contours, together with their density and the extent to which this allows them to be compressed or to expand as circumstances dictate. The materiality of objects means that they occupy their own space, and this is how we experience them. Whether we bark our shins against them or put them in our pockets, we understand that where one of them is, nothing else can be. The physicality which we and objects share creates a relationship between us, of which we have to take account as we move around in our lives, and their lengths, breadths, volumes, degrees of hardness or softness, and their differing abilities to absorb light which means that we see them as multi-coloured, define this relationship.

We apprehend objects chiefly through sight and touch, and an important part of our childhood learning revolves around the understanding of how gravity acts upon things, what can be climbed, what can be safely brushed aside, and so on. We learn that we cannot walk through walls or expect big, heavy objects to stay put on top of small, frail ones. We cannot cut stones with a table knife, or have our cake and eat it. The very obviousness of these facts is why they need stressing. We tend to take them for granted, and yet they shape the fabric of our lives in the most fundamental way to an overwhelming extent.

There is also an important principle of determinism here. We have to accept that the physical nature of materials as we experience them is given, and we have to work with them as best we can. The curse of Adam comes into play, and sheer hard work is required, of human or animal muscle or of devised machinery, to cut large timbers or move quantities of pig iron. It takes time to weave a basket, and any skills or social implications which are involved in the making of the basket have to take this into account. Each kind of material has its own range of things which it can and cannot do: textile containers will not usually hold liquids, and wooden implements cannot be used in the fire. Social practice usually tells us that it is taking notice of these basic facts by letting miraculous reversals of nature – the anvil that can float, the glove which the flames cannot consume – slip into myths and fairy stories, where their strangeness makes its own play upon our imaginations and contributes to the construction of social poetry; but the anchorage of all this in experienced external reality must not be ignored.

The fact that objects always have to be in one specific place at any given time has generated its own range of analytical techniques, intended to promote the analysis of objects in their locational relationships, and this is an important part of developing an understanding of context – itself a crucial part of the curatorial process. Equally, the materials from which objects are made must take a specific size and shape. They must be made to a particular intentional conformation so that a number of such pieces can be joined together in a range of ways to make what is regarded as a complete piece. The surfaces of which this piece is composed can be dressed or decorated with a variety which is almost infinite. These physical facts, also, are the starting points for curatorial investigation.

Objects, like ourselves, have a finite life-span, although their lives are frequently much longer than ours are. There is a moment when each object is 'finished', that is, when the manufacturing processes necessary to its creation have been completed. As it moves through time, it acquires (to a greater or lesser extent) a history of its own, passing from one possessor to another, perhaps from one kind of use to another, and from one place to another. Some objects, especially those to which special values are attributed, have very long and complex life cycles. Other objects, especially some of the mass production material of our time (like packaging) is discarded immediately, to be taken away in the next rubbish collection and buried or burned at the corporation dump. Objects can have complicated life cycles in which part of their time is passed in enjoying some kind of regard, part as garbage or semi-garbage in discard dumps or junk heaps, and part resurrected by archaeological processes or by shifts in taste, to be reinstated in museum collections and the like. Ultimately, however, they die, suddenly in accident, war or act of God, or gradually through the slow processes of decay. Their remaining and disjointed parts become again raw material, sometimes to be deliberately reused, like crushed ceramic utilized as grog in the making of new pots, and sometimes coming to degradation so complete that only elaborate scientific analysis could recognize in the residue the object that once was. The lives which objects lead generate biographical studies, carried out according to what we may call the normal techniques of the historian.

This materiality of objects and the physicality of their anchorage in time and space gives them some special characteristics which I wish to single out for discussion: their social life; their power of physical survival which gives them a unique relationship to past events that moves curators and others to call them 'the real thing'; and their particular susceptibility to possession and valuation. But before we explore these areas, we must consider some implications of materiality itself.

Subject and Object: Mind and Matter

Modern Western thought places a low value on the material world and its products, paralleling traditional Christian morality: both are at odds with modern Western capitalism, which places an inordinately high value upon the possession of material. This is one of the fundamental paradoxes of Western life, and museum collections are part of the heart of it. Here we are concerned with the role Western philosophy has allotted to material culture, a role which can be described as subordinate or secondary, in which objects are seen as merely the outcome or the product – or even the detritus – of primary thinking, feeling and acting which is carried out elsewhere. They are regarded always as the means through which to achieve an end predetermined without reference to them: the creator puts down his tools and stands aside cleaning his finger nails, in H. G. Wells' phrase, while the created object slots into its appointed place in the scheme of things. This lowly significance attributed to material culture is, of course, the fundamental reason why, in general, it has been considered less worthy of study than literature, or politics, and why in the economic sphere the concern has been with production rather than consumption as a social phenomenon.

This view has proved extremely stubborn because it is part of the entrenched duality of Western (and in some respects also non-Western) thought, which can be traced back in written texts to Plato, and which formed part of the world-view from which he drew his philosophical concepts. This duality can be simply

creator	:	created
think	:	thing
subject	:	object
action	:	reflection
pure	:	impure
good	:	bad
ideal	:	actual
presence	:	absence
normal	:	abnormal/deviant
positive	:	negative
true	:	false
logical	:	illogical
superior	:	inferior
essence	:	accidents
original	:	imitation
reality	:	representation
utterance	:	report

Figure 2.1 Set of opposed pairs, expressing the duality in the Western tradition

expressed in the set of pairs, laid out in Figure 2.1. The left hand column gives us the image of the god-like creator, possessed of the power of logical thought, whose utterance, real, true and original, works upon the actual world to make created things which can only be imitative, representational and reflective objects. In many cosmological traditions, including that of Judeo-Christianity, the naming of things marks the final moment of their creation. The report of the utterance, in artefacts or writing, is always an inferior and flawed account of the utterance itself.

The material world is located firmly in the depressed right hand side of the column, and in moral terms its associations are bad, impure and so on, which reminds us again of the low value ascribed to material in traditional Christian ethics. The essential superiority of the non-material world is expressed in our use of the word 'physical' to describe much of what is listed on the right, and 'metaphysical' to describe much of that on the left. In fact, this dual view of the cosmos is deeply embedded in the character of all the languages of the Indo-European family, which are typified by the possession of a strong verbal structure which render very clearly (and logically) the relationships between past, present and future, perceived as essentially sequential, and which locate action and effect, subject and object, in as clear a relationship to these verbs as possible.

One pair was deliberately omitted from the list just given, and this is male : female, to the implications of which we must now turn. The traditional 'maleness' of the left hand group, and 'femaleness' of the right hand group needs no elaboration, but is interesting in relation to the material world. The words 'material' and 'matter' derive from 'mother' and express the mythological principle that the material from which the cosmos is made is feminine. Alan Watts quotes from the Book of Genesis:

In the beginning God created the heaven and the earth
And the earth was without form, and void; and darkness was upon the face of the keep.
And the Spirit of God moved upon the face of the waters.

He continues, 'the "heaven and earth" which God first created was a formless mass. Before he made anything else he made matter – *materia, matrix, mater,* – as the material womb of the universe, for it is a general principle in mythology that material is the feminine component and spirit the masculine, their respective symbols being water or earth and air or fire' (Watts 1954: 46). Every new creation is from matter and spirit as the sacred texts of Christianity make clear:

The Spirit of God moved upon the face of the waters.

(Genesis 1: 1–2)

Who for us men and for our salvation came down from heaven, and was incarnate by the Holy Spirit of the Virgin Mary.

(Nicene Creed)

O God, whose Spirit in the very beginning of the world moved over the waters, that even then the nature of water might receive the virtue of sanctification . . . render the water fruitful for the regeneration of men, to the end that those who have been sanctified in the immaculate womb of this divine font, being born again a new creature may come forth a heavenly offspring.

(*Roman Missal*, Prayer for Blessing of the Font, Liturgy for Holy Saturday)

In the beginning, once God had created *Prima Materia*, he could go on to create the whole universe in the next six days, and each cosmological act of fresh creation, like the incarnation of Christ in the Virgin Mary (who was the *Prima Materia* prior to its division into the multiplicity of created things when she became the Virgin Mother), or the making of a new soul by baptism, followed the same pattern.

The same theme had already appeared in the Babylonian creation myth:

> When in the height heaven was not named
> And the earth beneath did not yet bear a name,
> And the primeval Apsu, who begat them,
> And Chaos, Tiamat, the Mother of them both, –
>
> Their waters were mingled together,
> And no field was formed, no marsh was to be seen;
> When of the gods none had been called into being,
> And none bore a name, and no destinies were ordained . . .
>
> The Lord stood upon Tiamat's hinder parts,
> And with his merciless club he smashed her skull . . .
>
> Then the Lord rested, gazing upon her dead body,
> While he divided the flesh . . . and devised a cunning plan.
> He split her up like a flat fish into two halves;
> One half of her he stablished as a covering for heaven.
>
> (quoted in Watts 1954: 108–9)

The Primeval Mother of Middle Eastern and Christian tradition is matched by the concept of Maya in the Indian tradition, where Maya is the female consort of God and the finite manifestation of the infinite. *Maya* is an Indo-European (Sanskrit) word linked with the root *matr*, to measure, to which are also linked the Greek *meter* (mother), Latin *mater* (mother), 'matter' and associated words, and a range of words like *metre* (the measurement), and *to meter* (to make measurements). At the heart of the image lies the idea of measuring, dividing and cutting up by means of which unformed feminine material chaos is turned into the separate and individual, but still feminine, world of things. This creation of the physical world is brought about by the male Divinity who 'divided the light from the darkness' (Genesis 1.4), created the firmament to 'divide the water from the waters' (Genesis 1.6) and who 'set a compass on the face of the deep' (Proverbs 8.27). Creation is seen as a type of sexual act in which masculinity is active, and the female world of material things the passive recipient.

This cosmological or mythological view of mind and matter dominated European medieval thought, where the mental side was refined into the concept of *intellectum*, the capacity of the human mind to think and understand within the overarching truth of a revealed reality. The internal contradiction here is clear, between on the one hand an aprioristic commitment to truth as Revelation mediated through the authority of the Church, on the other an equally irreducible commitment to the revelations which human reason can offer. As Wernick has pointed out, the intellectual survival of Catholicism in France for two centuries beyond Luther's time in Germany prolonged the influence of the scholasticism that the Counter-Reformation had revived, and left an imprint on the reconstructive attempts of the secular intelligentsia who emerged when clerical Christianity was consumed in the fires of Enlightenment and Reform (Wernick 1984: 133). For our purposes, a principal result of this was the transference of the cosmological view of passive, receptive materiality into the reconstructed view of human reason associated with Descartes.

One small quotation may help to make this more clear. At one point in his *Meditations* Descartes says:

> But it may be said, perhaps, that although the senses occasionally mislead us respecting objects minute and those so far removed from us as to be beyond the reach of those observations, yet there are many other presentations of the truth of which it is impossible to doubt; as for example, that I am in this place, seated by the fire, clothed in a winter dressing gown, that I hold in my hands a piece of paper, with such other intimations.
>
> (quoted in D'Amico 1984: 166–7)

Here we have the famous *ego* of *cogito ego sum*, the knowing subject possessed of the powers of thought, logical reason and deductive understanding, which is able to experience empirically the heat of fire and the nature of the winter dressing gown (as opposed to a summer dressing gown or a shirt), and to draw conclusions from these observations which, ultimately, are firm enough to bear the superstructure which we call modern rational science. In this, we note, the material world is still measured and divided, and classifications are still created by the naming of things. The ancient duality of creator and created is translated into the scientific idiom of mind and matter. This has been taken for granted by traditional social scientists, political economists, anthropologists and historians, with the result that the world of material things has almost never been their prime concern, since that world is by its very materiality deprived of any independence, primary reality or possibility of active intervention.

From the standpoint of much post-modern thought, this blind belief in human reason appears arrogant and insubstantial. More significantly for our present purpose, its view of the workings of the material world is naive and wishful: these brutally concrete lumps are not as tame or as ineffectual as traditional thought would like them to be. In the next section we shall discuss some important aspects of their social role.

The Social Life of Objects

Objects are all-pervasive in human social life, and society as we understand it could not exist without them. Their very commonness is one reason why they are so slippery and tend to drop out of traditional philosophical discourse. One way of putting their social centrality is to say that they are intentional inscriptions on the physical world which embody social meaning; a simpler way of putting much the same is to say that social ideas cannot exist without physical content, but physical objects are meaningless without social content. Idea and expression are not two separable parts, but the same social construct. It would be impossible to say which came first: the abstract idea of, for example, hammering, or the mental image of a hammer-shaped thing doing its job. 'Think' and 'thing' are not sequential because our thinking can only be explicit, and no matter how abstract this may appear to be, in fact it inevitably takes material form: beauty must have something to be beautiful, even if we wish to criticize every example known to us as falling short of perfection. Without the actual buses (or hope of them), the devising of a bus timetable is a meaningless business.

One of the implications of this is to reveal the role which objects play in social reproduction, that is, in the continuous process which enables each society to go on being itself (and also to change more or less subtly, an area explored in Chapter 10). This role is usually, in social and philosophical studies, given to language, which is perceived as the principal medium of social communication and of socialization. Language is seen to embody the traditions of the group into which individuals are born, as they are into their mother tongue, and both are learnt as an inseparable whole. Each language will include the names for all the objects which the society possesses. Some of these will be generic names like 'wallet', 'television', 'spear' or 'paddle', and some will be differentiated by descriptive additions like 'John's wallet', 'the broken television', 'the battle-tried spear' or 'the black paddle', which gives each of them a unique persona in a range of different ways which needs no labouring. As we have seen, modern study here matches traditional imagery which sees the naming of things as the crucial act which brings them into being, and which retains power over them by acting as the referent to which objects relate. The primacy given to language partly reflects, and is partly the result of, the considerable academic effort which has been put into the study of linguistics by figures like Saussure (see Humphrey 1971) and Chomsky (see Faris 1972). The distinctive insights and analytical techniques which these men have developed can be applied to objects as to languages because both operate as communication systems, but this does not imply a necessary superiority for language.

In fact, reflection shows a crucial way in which material culture does not match language in a one-to-one sense, still less in a one-in-relation-to-one sense, but has an independent social existence of its own which contributes to social reproduction. Let us take some simple examples. Imagine trying to describe the difference between two shirts, similar in cut and each in two different shades of blue, or between the appearance of two different kinds of box files, or the design of a flower pattern on curtain material. We are all acutely aware how inadequate language is to encompass this kind of detailed materiality and how frustrating it is to try and make it serve the purpose. We also know that one glance at the actual object will solve the problem and create immediate understanding, because we are capable of making fine perceptual discriminations between one object and another. This quality of material discrimination, presumably a combination of eye, sometimes hand, and culture stored in the memory, is immensely significant in the construction of the social world. It is one of the most important factors which governs our view or choice of our material surroundings and so of the form our social life takes, but we are hard put to get it into coherent words and hence the inarticulateness which overtakes most conversations in which material detail arises.

It seems that perceptions about colour, shape and decoration are not part of our linguistic inheritance, but part of our material tradition in the strict sense. This is why curators have to use such specialized and cumbersome sets of words to speak to each other about matters like the design of eighteenth-century silver or Bronze Age axes, and also why we will not give identification opinions over the telephone: objects are independent of words and we must see them and perhaps touch them to understand them. It is probably also a related reason why objects have not loomed large in academic study for this is, as Miller has suggested (1987: 100), dominated by linguistic modes of communication which find it difficult to appreciate the significance of material culture, just as they do in other areas fundamental to what Miller calls 'the operation of the unconscious' (1987: 100).

This huge gulf between our ability to perceive material and our capacity to express what we see linguistically suggests that objects play a larger part in the processes which produce social structure than we are usually prepared to admit: suggests, indeed, that our ability to produce a world of things is a fundamental part of our ability to create social lives and to feel 'at home' in them. Miller calls this fundamental ability 'the unconscious', and relates its operation to the role of play in the development of the young child, for whom artefacts precede language as the 'principal means of articulating feelings and desires' (1987: 99). In some ways this particular emotional relationship to objects never leaves us: in a bereavement, grief is most acutely stirred by the sight of the raincoat the dead person always used to wear. If 'unconscious' is used in a relatively untechnical sense, and is allowed to stand for that central but essentially ambiguous or ambivalent spring of perception and feeling through which individuals create societies and societies create individuals, then the word is a useful one to describe the source of the object world.

The phrase 'at home' leads us to the next important point, and this revolves around the way in which objects create our familiar frames of reference. The frame in question may be quite literal: in his book *The Sense of Order* (1979), Gombrich discusses the nature of design as opposed to that of art and uses the picture frame as an example of design. He suggests that while the picture endeavours to command our attention and stimulate our feelings and critical faculties, the picture frame should do almost exactly the opposite, in that its task is to draw attention away from itself and towards the content which it surrounds. It is, however, also true that the work of art needs its frame, and by extension the larger frame of gallery and museum building, in order to succeed in drawing our attention to itself and to clarify its character as a 'work of art'. The frame is not merely a technical necessity to protect the edge of the picture, or provide a place for the mirror plates; it is a particularly suitable example of how relatively unimportant objects work to create our understanding and response – in a word, our social selves.

Gossman, in his book *Frame Analysis* (1975), extended the example used by Gombrich by emphasizing how objects create a range of frame-clues which enable us to understand what kind of context we are in and so how we should or should not behave. He suggests that these object clues operate in areas like the theatre or the church, which simplify more general categories such as drama or religion, so providing appropriate settings for specific attitudes or modes of behaviour. The same principle applies to much humbler objects in much more ordinary settings, and the fact that most objects *are* humble in ordinary settings must not be allowed to deceive us about their significance. Each of our homes is a unique collection of objects which constitutes our framework for living (or for a large and important part of our living). We recognize that standing in an empty house and hearing a tape-recorded voice describing what had been there would constitute a completely different form of experience, and probably a much less happy one. Our rooms, once arranged more or less to our liking, constitute an important self-defining statement in a way which is paralleled only by the clothes which we choose to wear. Conversely, we immediately sum up the owners of rooms which we have never seen before by reference to the choice of upholstery, wallpaper and shelving, just as we form an impression of a newly-met individual on the strength of appearance: rightly so, since character is what these things constitute.

The Real Thing

Objects, we have noted, have lives which, though finite, can be very much longer than our own. They alone have the power, in some sense, to carry the past into the present by virtue of their 'real' relationship to past events, and this is just as true for casts, copies and fakes as it is for more orthodox material, for all such copies bear their own 'real' relationship to the impulse which created them, and have their own place in the history of perception and taste (Jones 1990). This 'reality' is fundamental to the impulses which we know as the collecting process, and equally fundamental to both the process of curatorial effort and of exhibition. The point of collections and museums, it is no exaggeration to say, revolves around the possession of 'real things' and, as we have seen, it is essentially this which gives museums their unique role. We must, therefore, try to understand how it is that objects can operate both in the past and in the present, how they work to create the present, what the nature of that relationship is, and why it has such profound significance for us. These questions are crucial, and need to be considered at corresponding length. They are best explored by way of a concrete object which exists in a contemporary collection, and around which clusters enough historical information to enable us to draw out the point of the argument.

Let us then take as a point of departure a basket-hilted broadsword which was carried by Alistair Macdonald of Keppoch at the battle of Culloden, the climax of the '45 Jacobite Rebellion, in north-eastern Scotland on Wednesday, 16 April 1746 (see Plate 1). Keppoch led his Highlanders in the charge and received wounds from which he died. His son, Angus Ban, took his father's sword and dirk and hid them in marshy ground, from which they were afterwards retrieved, and after passing through a number of hands, they finally came into the possession of the National Museums of Scotland (Peeble 1967; Tomasson and Buist 1962; information National Museums of Scotland).

A number of points should be noticed about this because they are of importance in the discussion which follows. The historical circumstances of time, place and

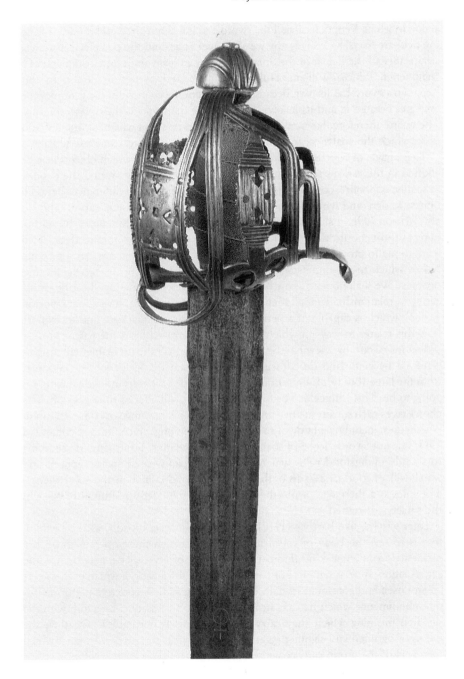

Plate 1.   Sword carried at the battle of Culloden by Macdonald of Keppoch. National Museums of Scotland (photo: National Museums of Scotland).

action in which Keppoch carried the sword and it was retrieved and removed from the field are 'facts' as 'real' as any we shall ever have, and the perceived historical significance of the defeat of the Stuart Prince by an army under the command of a Hanoverian Prince, William, Duke of Cumberland, is not in doubt. In this Keppoch's sword has its part, because it was a genuine element of the action of the time and because it, and its fellows, alone survive the battle in their physical reality. The sword, therefore, has a relationship to past and present which is complex, and upon which the analytical techniques of semiotics may shed some useful light.

There have, of course, been fierce debates about the role which objects may be allotted in the various schools of semiotic thought, revolving around their ability to signify, symbolize, connote, denote and so on, and over the differences between objects as signs and symbols, for which Lyons (1977) gives a useful survey (and see also Jackson 1991). I shall not give here a replay of all these difficulties, but rather here, as throughout this book, make a judicious selection of semiotic ideas which seem to me to provide a helpful frame (however irritating the terms can sometimes be) by which to aid understanding of how this aspect of an object's significance operates. We shall hope to show how the sword works as a message-bearing entity, acting in relationship to Culloden both as an intrinsic sign and as a metaphorical symbol, which is capable of a very large range of interpretations; and to explore how this relates to ways in which the present is created from the past.

We may start by viewing the sword in terms of the fundamental insights achieved by Ferdinand de Saussure. It may be said that each society 'chooses', from the large (but not infinite) range of possibilities, what its individual nature is going to be. This 'choice' is not forever fixed, but will alter as time goes on. The choice gives each society at any particular moment a large range of communication possibilities, including a body of material culture among which, in the Scotland of 1745, was our sword. To be of social use, this range must be structured according to socially understood rules which command broadly-based social support, and which will, of course, be a part of the local system of domination and subservience. The rules and the range of possibilities make up the deep structure, or *langue* of the society concerned.

Later writers, like Barthes (1977), identify the *langue*, broadly, as the *signified*, that is to say, the body of social understanding which must operate through a social action of some kind. From the *langue* of society issues *parole*, that is the actual action, spoken sentence or performed deed, by means of which each society creates itself and continues its daily life. For Barthes, these concrete performances or embodiments, which he calls *signifiers*, have no necessary connection with the signified meaning which they carry (although this is debatable). Together, the union of signified and signifier gives us a *signe*, that is the social construct which members of the group can recognize and understand.

The position in all this of the sword seems quite clear. The *langue* of society within the island of Britain in 1745 held a range of human and material possibilities, which included the production of edged weapons, firearms and cannon, textiles of different weaves and colours, horse gear and so on. Its rules included a desire to define fighting forces and, within these, different ranks and groups.

Keppoch wore the tartan plaid and kilt appropriate to a Highland chief (although *not*, it should be noted, any Macdonald 'set' or 'tartan' which in 1745 belonged in a world yet to come), and carried the broadsword which marked his rank as a Highland gentleman: the sword is then a *signe* in Barthes' sense, uniting the message (the signified) and the physical embodiment (the signifier) (Figure 2.2: A).

We may take the discussion an important stage further by employing the analysis of communication devised by Leach (1976: 12). The message-bearing entity (sword as signifier) stands for the message (the signified) as a result of human choice. At this point, Leach makes a crucial distinction between his sign and his symbol, which is very helpful in enabling us to understand better how the sword works (confusingly, Leach and Barthes use the same word to describe different things; here the French spelling will be used when Barthes' meaning is intended, and the English when Leach's is). Objects (and other messages) operate as a *sign* when they stand for the whole of which they are an intrinsic part, as sword does for the actual events of Culloden, and in this case the relationship between the different parts of the whole is said to be metonymic. They operate as a *symbol* when they are brought into an arbitrary association with elements to which they bear no intrinsic relationship.

This analysis of distinctions gives us a framework for expressing how the sword carries meaning about Culloden into the future. Past *parole* continuously becomes a part of contemporary *langue*, which is continuously restructured to issue as contemporary *parole* in a never-ending spiral. But in this process objects, like the sword, are associated with elements with which they had no original or intrinsic or metonymic relationship and in relation to which they are, therefore, acting as symbols (Figure 2.2: B). Consequently, these new sets of associations bear an interpretative, called in semiotic language a metaphorical, relationship to the original Culloden set. But because the material survival power of the sword means that it always does retain its intrinsic or 'real' relationship with Keppoch and the battle, it is also always working as a sign. It is the ability of objects to be simultaneously signs and symbols, to carry a true part of the past into the present, but also to bear perpetual symbolic reinterpretation, which is the essence of their peculiar and ambiguous power.

It would not be difficult for so emotive a piece as the sword to suggest what, over the last two-and-a-half centuries since the battle, have been some of the newly-created *paroles* in which the sword took part. We might, for example, single out the immediate aftermath of the battle as this was experienced in London, where William, Duke of Cumberland, attended a thanksgiving service for which Handel wrote his *The Conquering Hero*, and a pretty flower was renamed Sweet William. In this set the sword would symbolize barbarity and defeat in the face of civilized enlightenment. This *parole* passed into the *langue* of about 1840, by which time Scott's novels had appeared and the Highlanders had become noble (if savage still) and romantic, and the sword a desirable piece of genuine antiquity. A century later the Highlands and their history, including the site of Culloden, had become a huge tourist park and the sword part of a museum display (Figure 2.3).

These are merely a few of the more obvious and public moments in the sword's

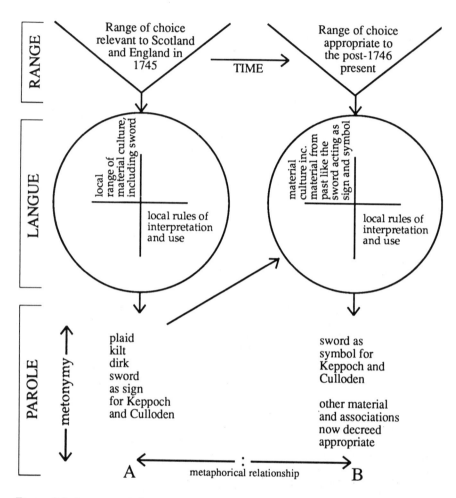

Figure 2.2 Semiotic analysis of Macdonald of Keppoch's sword

symbolic history. Throughout, while it survives physically, it will retain its metonymic relationship to the battle itself; of Culloden, whatever meaning may be attached to it, the sword remains *not* in Leach's terms a 'symbol' (however much it may be so described in ordinary speech) but, in his terms, a 'sign', an intrinsic part. So we have a sign available for constant symbolic reuse in the strict sense, in the creation of fresh sets of signifiers. The cycle of signified – signifier – *signe* (= sign : symbol) is constantly repeating itself throughout the span of an individual's consciousness, and in the course of social action. The sword as the sign which carries meaning is able to do so because, unlike we ourselves who must die, it bears an 'eternal' relationship to the receding past, and it is this that we experience as the power of 'the actual object'. It also plays its part in influencing the nature of

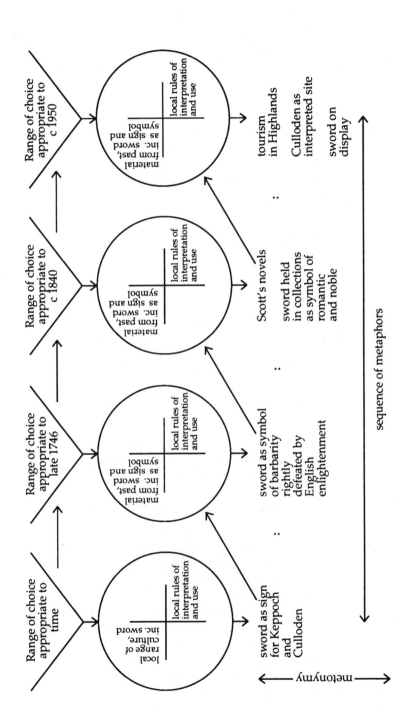

Figure 2.3 Extended semiotic analysis of Macdonald of Keppoch's sword

each freshly-created meaning, so helping to bring about the changes which each successive *parole* represents.

What is true of Keppoch's sword in its relationship to Culloden is true of all objects in our collections, whether they relate to a famous event which forms part of 'national' history, or whether they come from a context of local or popular culture. Equally, it makes no difference if the object is a one-off piece of some craft or artistic merit, or if it is one of many from a modern mass-production line. A moment's thought will show that the same thinking and the same diagram could be equally well applied to a group of pottery fragments excavated from a Roman villa, a late medieval Nottingham alabaster, or a 1950s gym shoe manufactured by Dunlop Ltd.

The same kind of thinking proves illuminating when it is applied to natural history material.

One for Sorrow

Let us take as our example that most characteristic type of museum natural history display piece, a stuffed and mounted British magpie (see Plate 2). This bird, which serves as a typical example of its kind and so stands for all the others, has been the subject of at least two distinctive constructions, one scientific and the other popular and traditional, which create their own *paroles*, and which are metaphorical to each other and to the wild creature living its unregarded natural life (Figure 2.4).

As with the sword, the creature in its habitat is living as a sign, metonymically at one with its intrinsic surroundings. When it is translated into the scientific construction of taxonomy and museum life, it becomes part of a system which bears a metaphorical relationship to nature, and the creature within it acts as a symbol, while the whole construction forms a metonymy of its own. Similarly, it can be constructed into the popular/traditional view of magpies, mirroring human life in their life cycle (as do birds generally), but also possessing human-type characteristics in their thieving and collecting habits (magpie-collecting is an image often upon curators' lips) and a traditional ability to convey information about the future ('One for sorrow, Two for joy', etc.). Here the bird is also acting as a symbol, and this set also forms a metonymy of its own which is metaphorical to the other two.

A number of significant points arise from this. The first is that, like the sword, the actual physical bird is always present as both sign and symbol: a symbol in its interpretation, but a sign in its true and perpetual relationship to the natural world. All natural history material in museums shares this nature, and never ceases to bear a real relationship to the natural world, no matter how, or how frequently, it is reinterpreted. All interpretations, however, are 'readings'; they are metaphorical constructions which, although they arise from observations of the natural world, run in a reality which is parallel to it, not continuous with it. And all the metaphorical constructions are 'true' in their fashion, although their fashions may be very different.

The set of relationships which we have worked out here for the sword and the

creature	:	magpie
(magpie) as SIGN		(creature) as SYMBOL

living creature		one of many birds, all
of this kind		of whom mirror human life
in wild		(two-legged, pair mating,
taking part		home building, brood raising,
in normal		'talking' to each other)
cycles		

thieving magpie
'magpie collecting'
message-bearing magpie
('One for sorrow' etc)

. .

	:	magpie as SYMBOL

Species   *Pica Pica*

Family   Corvidae

Museum accession number
taxidermed and mounted specimen
display in reconstructed habitat

Figure 2.4 Analysis of a magpie as sign and symbol

magpie, and for all the museum material which they represent, as we shall see, creates the character of the collection-forming process and, at the next remove, that of exhibitions which put the collected objects on display.

Possession and Valuation

A further immensely important consequence flows from the materiality of objects in all the aspects already discussed: their physical character means that they can be possessed. Land and buildings are also capable of being possessed, and it is possible to own rights in a song or a ritual, but none of these bring quite the direct and tangible ownership which objects allow. Indeed, we can turn the matter the other way. Ownerless objects, unless they are universally rejected as rubbish (which never happens outside the Western world), are something of a contradiction, and even in the least possession-minded societies, artefacts which have lost their owners for one reason or another rapidly acquire new ones. Museums, of course, are themselves one of the principal object-possessing institutional modes.

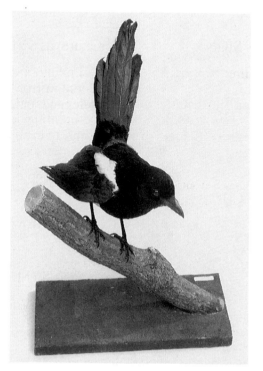

Plate 2.   Stuffed and mounted specimen of *Pica pica*, British magpie, in Leicestershire Museum Service School Loans (photo: University of Leicester).

The physical character of objects means that they are capable of being owned, stored, and handed from one person to another, but the reasons why these things happen to them, that is their desirability, rests in the value that is ascribed to them by the community concerned. The notion of value has always been a difficult one. Superficially it would seem that an object carries whatever exchange value is judged to be appropriate by the community as a body of understanding and will-possessing subjects, and is never an inherent property of the object. However, it is coming to be admitted that the realm in which object value emerges and works, lies, like so much to do with objects, on the uneasy border between the not wholly subjective and the not quite objective, but in that area of human consciousness which operates, quite easily in actual practice, across the two. Georg Simmel, whose writings have been very influential among English writers following the translation of his *Philosophy of Money* in 1978, discusses the subjective nature of object value, but goes on to say that 'subjectivity is only provisional and actually not very essential' (Simmel 1978: 73). We are, in other words, always perceiving the given value of any object, but we are always, also, modifying this value in the light of taste and circumstance, and it is impossible to say whether the individual is altering the value of the object, or the object is making him change his ideas of value. The fluctuations of the art market make this point in a particularly transparent way.

Object value can be constituted in a number of ways. The physicality of objects means that we can do things with them which affect our physical surroundings, and so achieve survival, and it is clear that this is a source of object value. Inherent in social survival is, of course, social organization, and this, it seems, cannot be achieved without the intervention of objects which relate to social identity. The accumulation which objects permit can be important here, and so is the fact that some kinds of objects seem to strike our human nature as desirable in the simplest sense. Most communities ascribe considerable value to artefacts made from bright and flashing or somehow intrinsically attractive materials like gold, pearl shell, colourful feathers or ivory, and this value rests as much in the lust of the eye as it does in the comparative rarity of the materials concerned.

Rarity is, nevertheless, in itself a source of value, and so is the degree of difficulty which surrounds the winning of the raw material, especially if it is exotic and has to be brought some distance. Gold is, geologically, a relatively rare material on earth and occurs only in specific places which are remote from most other places. No doubt it is true that many societies, and the individuals which compose them, need something like gold to serve their own ends, but it is also true that what we might call the goldness of gold stimulates and influences the social response; and the apt conjunction of the two groups of features helps to explain why gold has been so significant in, for example, European society since the Bronze Age (see Plate 3).

An additional factor helps to create value in a material like gold, and that is the level of craftsmanship which it can accept and which is deemed worthy of so intrinsically beautiful a material. Craftsmanship comes expensive because the training is long, and because even once a man has become a master, he usually has to be provided by society with the bulk of his raw materials, food, clothing and shelter. An object upon which much skill has been expended, therefore, carries an additional kind of frozen investment, of which society must, in various ways, take account. These are all deceptively simple notions which start to develop the implications of objects in ownership. As Appadurai (1986: 3) has put it: 'Focusing on the things that are exchanged, rather than simply on the forms or functions of exchange, makes it possible to argue that what creates the line between exchange and value is *politics*', and 'politics' here should be understood as the social web of relationships within which values emerge, of whatever kind these values may be.

However, notions of value developed purely in relation to ideas about the nature of exchange are of limited use where museum material is concerned, because museum objects have (at least in theory) been lifted out of the market-place where commodities are exchanged and have become something else, to which a word like 'heritage' is often attached. Museum objects, like a Turner picture, may be enormously valuable in the market-place, or, like fossil ammonites, they may be worth relatively little, but this is not the point; whatever their monetary exchange value, they share a perceived spiritual or intellectual worth and are guarded as such in a way which puts them in a special 'otherworld' category.

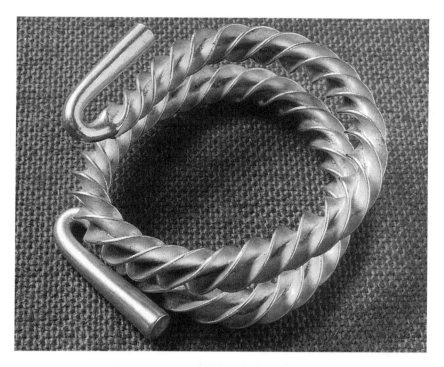

Plate 3.   Gold neck ornament of the later Bronze Age from Yeovil, Somerset. Pieces like this have always attracted a high valuation. Somerset County Museums (photo: Nigel Chaffers-Heard).

In Thompson's useful analysis (1979), objects divide into three broad categories: 'rubbish', to which no value attaches; 'transients', the goods of the capitalist system which are bought and sold in the market-place for the price of the day and which, like used cars, steadily decline in value the more second-hand they become; and 'durables', to which are attracted spiritual, scientific or psychological values which place them above the market-place, and which, one way or another, form the touchstones against which goods and rubbish are evaluated. Museums perform the social function of housing (in the broadest sense) the durables, and also of exercising very considerable influence over the choice of which category any individual object should be placed within, through collecting and purchasing policies and the operation of expertise. Douglas and Isherwood make a point about the nature of strong corporate groups to which class established museums have traditionally been seen to belong: 'Because its legal existence is eternal, it can make its demands in the name of unborn generations . . . No individual acting on his or her own behalf can entertain dreams of such a long-term future. Only the group can develop a full-fledged otherworldly morality, for the group outlives its members' (Douglas and Isherwood 1979: 37). This is why the archetype of the sacred, the temple, the secular cathedral, runs through so much museum imagery in speech and architecture. It is also why the disposal, destruction or sale of collections is such a difficult issue for museum people because such de-accessioning procedures involve the demotion of material from the durable class to one of the other two, and so undercut not merely the meaning of 'museum' as institution, but also the traditional structure of values and judgements in their tangible material form.

In practice, the ways in which objects move from one class to another are extremely complex, a part both of the whole interlocking world of social practice and material culture, and of specific worlds like the legitimate market and the black market. But in terms of social action, the point at which an object passes from 'rubbish' or 'transient' to 'durable' lies in the act of collecting; it is this which produces the transformation of material into the heritage mode. As we actually experience it, collecting is as messy and chancy as all human activities, full of false starts, changes of heart and unforeseeable disasters, which mean that objects take their chances of success just as we do ourselves, and for all kinds of reasons, many once-collected objects fall back into the two other groups. But no object or specimen achieves museum status without passing through some kind of selecting and collecting barrier, and if in some cases this is pretty casual, in most it has been the focus of considerable thought and care. Collecting seems to operate in that obscure zone between cultural ideas of value and the deepest levels of individual personality, and it is to this second aspect that we will turn in the next two chapters.

3 Collecting: Body and Soul

One by one, he lifted the characters of the Commedia from the shelves, and placed them in the pool of light where they appeared to skate over the glass of the table, pivoting on their bases of gilded foam, as if they would forever go on laughing, whirling, improvising. And I realised, as Utz pivoted the figure in the candlelight, that I had misjudged him; that he, too, was dancing; that, for him, this world of little figures was the real world.

(Chatwin 1988: 113–14).

PROFESSOR CLAIMS HE 'DREAMED UP' MYSTERIOUS VICTORIANA COLLECTION FOUND IN CARMEL
by Fred X. Vaterman
A collection of Victorian objects worth, possibly, hundreds of thousands of dollars, has mysteriously appeared in a parking lot behind the Sea Winds Motel, Bluff Road, in Carmel-by-the-Sea. An avalanche of inquiries and world-wide interest yesterday followed an announcement by Professor Anthony Maloney of McGill University, Montreal, Canada, on local Monterey station KCBC, that he . . .

(Moore 1975: 47)

Many of the items are incredibly rare and very old and represent my entire life from childhood to adulthood.

(Walsall Collector, quoted Mullen 1991: 47)

Introduction

Museums, as we have seen, hold the stored material culture of the past, and this material culture, object by object, carries the characteristics discussed in the previous chapter. But the material has not arrived in museums in a steady, single-state flow, one piece at a time. Characteristically, much of it comes in groups which have been gathered together by a single individual, or sometimes a closely associated pair or group of individuals. We are accustomed to call each of these groups 'a collection' and to refer to the whole assemblage as 'the collections'. The notion, then, of group identity and personal association is deeply embedded in the material itself and in museum language.

This chapter and the next are intended to open up discussion of the nature of collections and of the reasons why people collect, particularly the more obscure psychological or social reasons. It is, of course, true that a great deal of collecting does, and for the last five centuries or so, always has, gone on outside the context of any institution which by even the broadest definition could count as a museum, but it is also true that, provided that a collection remains stable and reaches a relatively substantial size (itself a highly subjective judgement), it is likely to find itself eventually in some sort of museum context. The transformation from formally private to formally public, which can be quite an extended process, is an important aspect of collection-making. The collecting processes analysed here seem to hold true regardless of which field in the disciplinary sense the collected material belongs within. Equally, they seem to have been characteristic of collectors over the last five centuries or so, and to be themselves part of the modern European relationship with the world of objects. The making of a collection is one way in which we organize our relationship with the external physical world of which collections are a part. Collection-forming is part of the relationship between the subject, conceived as each individual human being, and the object, conceived as the whole world, material and otherwise, which lies outside him or her. Collections are a significant element in our attempt to construct the world, and so the effort to understand them is one way of exploring our relationship with the world.

This whole area of collecting activity, like the study of museums and material culture in general, has only just begun to attract the serious attention it deserves, apart from a flurry of early-twentieth-century interest in children as collectors (Burk 1900; Whitley 1929), and some other honourable exceptions like Frank Herrmann (1972), although collecting has always featured in a wide range of popular literature. The 1980s, however, have seen a sudden spurt of interest and from a variety of angles: Belk, Wallendorf and their associates in the field of consumer research (1988; 1989; 1990); Stewart (1984) on the interface between acquired objects and values of popular culture; Dannefer (1980; 1981), Olmsted (1988) and Moulin (1987) in sociology; Saisselin (1984) in art history, and Clifford (1988) in anthropology. In addition to this, there have been three data-collecting projects: that of Czikszentmihalyi who gathered information about domestic objects from middle-class Chicago (1981), that of Danet and Katriel who conducted interviews with some 165 collectors in Israel (1989), and that of Belk and his colleagues in the Odyssey Project who did the same in the United States. This gives us a basis from which to discuss the making of collections.

In the pages which follow I shall first endeavour to arrive at a workable idea of the nature of collection-making. I shall then discuss the psychological roots of our fascination with objects and how this generates an urge to collect. I shall look at the nature of collecting as it is pursued by the collectors themselves in the two sections entitled 'Collections as Play' and 'Close of Play'. The succeeding pages will explore the notion of collection as the extended self, pursuing this idea through to the striving for immortality which collections represent.

Thinking About Things

[handwritten: Collections – part of many in which construct our world]

We may make a start by taking up the point just made, that collections are an important part of the way in which we construct our world. We may approach this by applying to collections the semiotic ideas already in part advanced to disentangle the way in which 'real things' work (pp. 24–30), and by looking at collectors in terms of notions about the operation of the cognitive process which they seem to go through.

[handwritten margin note: COLLECTION = SELECTION]

[handwritten margin note: metonymic]

The crucial semiotic notion is that of metaphor and metonymy, a key which helps us to unlock one fundamental aspect of the nature of collections. Everything which goes into a collection of whatever kind has done so as a result of selection. The selection process is the crucial act of the collector, regardless of what intellectual, economic or idiosyncratic reasons he may have when he decides how his selection will work, what he will choose and what he will reject. What he chooses bears an intrinsic, direct and organic relationship, that is a metonymic relationship, to the body of material from which it was selected because it is an integral part of it. But the very act of selection adds to its nature. By being chosen away and lifted out of the embedding metonymic matrix, the selected collection now bears a representative or metaphorical relationship to its whole. It becomes an image of what the whole is believed to be, and although it remains an intrinsic part of the whole, it is no longer merely a detached fragment because it has become imbued with meaning of its own.

Figure 3.1 puts this in concrete terms. The anthropologist collects from the mass of material in Yoruba society what seems to him to be good according to the anthropological theories he espouses; the biologist trawls up from the Indian Ocean and retains a selection of fish according to his intellectual principles; and the social historian works with a range of traditional southern English dairy equipment which the present farmer's grandmother thought it right to keep. In each case the collection is genuinely of real Indian Ocean fish or Yoruba artefacts (see Plate 4) and so it retains its intrinsic or metonymic character, but the process of selection has given it also a metaphorical relationship to the material from which it came. The same idea can be expressed using the broad Saussurian framework already applied to demonstrate the historical reality of Macdonald's sword (p. 28). Here Figure 3.2 shows both how the personality and social situation of the collector have worked upon the Yoruba material, and how that material nevertheless retains a 'real' relationship to Yoruba society. Another way of saying much the same thing is to draw vocabulary from writers like Barthes (1977) and say that collected objects are both the signifier, that is the medium that carries the message, and the signified, the message itself. This dual nature of the collection is at the heart of its significance. It explains why it carries the emotional resonance which comes from its 'real' relationship – the fish in the museum did once really swim off the Seychelles – and the intellectual interest which derives from its metaphorical content, which is not static but can go on carrying fresh interpretations.

[handwritten margin note: Barthes]

The cognitive process which the collector goes through links up with this. In his discussion on fetishism, to which we shall return, Ellen (1988) identifies four general

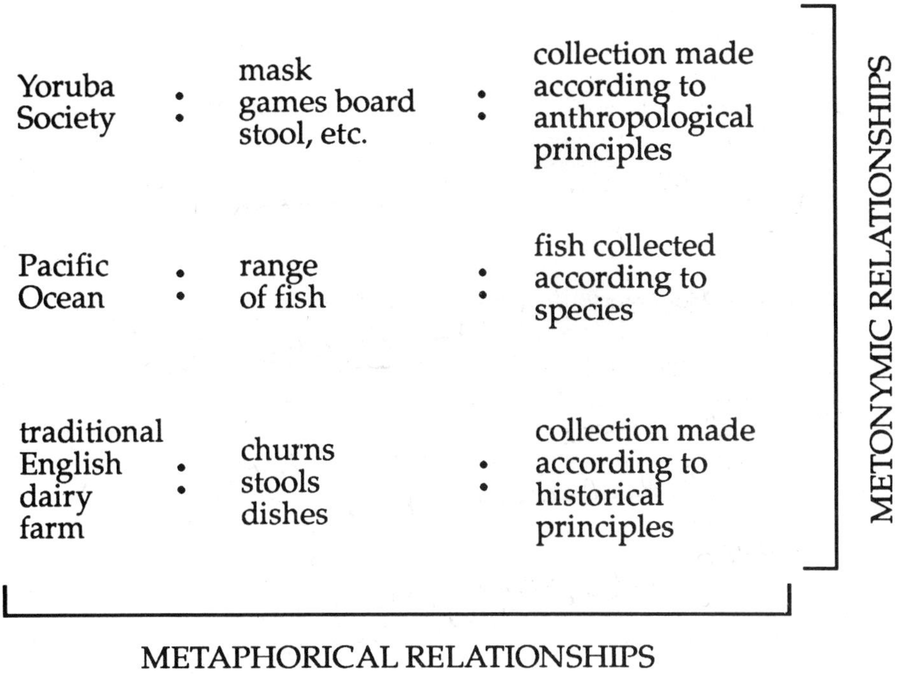

Yoruba Society	•	mask games board stool, etc.	• collection made according to anthropological principles
Pacific Ocean	•	range of fish	• fish collected according to species
traditional English dairy farm	•	churns stools dishes	• collection made according to historical principles

METONYMIC RELATIONSHIPS

METAPHORICAL RELATIONSHIPS

Figure 3.1 Semiotic analysis of the collecting process

underlying cognitive processes at work in the generation of this kind of cultural representation. These are:

1. the recognition of a concrete existence or the concretization of abstractions;
2. a state of mind in which the signifier and signified are conflated;
3. the attribution of qualities of living organisms to the object, often (though not exclusively) human;
4. an ambiguous relationship between control of object by people, and of people by object.

This is a helpful way to order thinking about the genesis of all forms of object accumulation, and particularly that of collection-making with which we are here concerned. The four principles can be organized as the significant moments in a linear process (Figure 3.3). The collector begins with his sensory experience of natural and cultural discontinuities, that is, his perception that things are different one to another and that these differences can be the basis for ideas about what to select and what to reject (Figure 3.3: A). This perception becomes understanding, called by Ellen 'percept', in which natural or social things or parts of things are allotted attributes and so a place in our interlocking web of relationships (B). The abstract percepts are conceptualized as things, a process known as reification ('thingy-making'), which means giving them names so that, for example, they can

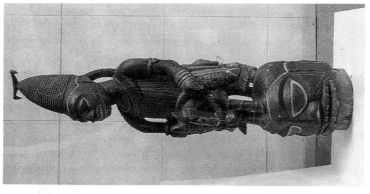

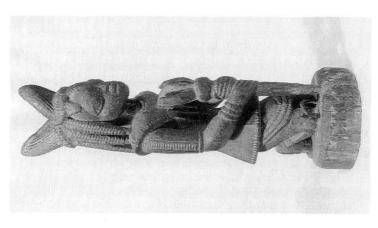

Plate 4.   Two Yoruba figures carved in wood. On the left: One of a pair of male figures that stood at the door of Chief Okabunna as protection against witchcraft. The figure represents Ere Eshu, the Trickster God. Abeokuta, Nigeria. Collected by Rev. H. Townsend, 1868. On the right: Mask showing chief on horseback, used in the Epa cult of north-east Nigeria. Collected by Mrs. F. Pinkett, c.1920. Both these figures are very typical collection pieces, and both were acquired by equally typical collectors. Exeter City Museum Service (photo: Committee for South West Arts).

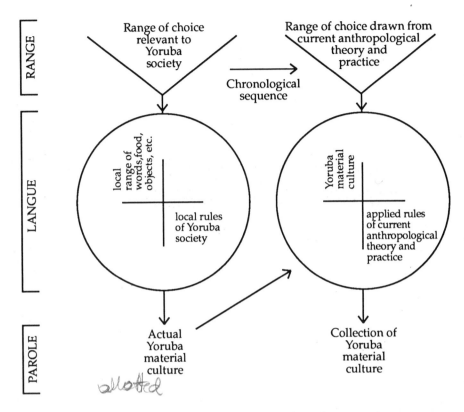

RANGE

Range of choice
relevant to
Yoruba
society

Range of choice drawn from
current anthropological
theory and
practice

Chronological
sequence

LANGUE

local
range of
words, food,
objects, etc.

local rules
of Yoruba
society

Yoruba
material
culture

applied rules
of current
anthropological
theory and
practice

PAROLE

Actual
Yoruba
material
culture

allotted

Collection of
Yoruba
material
culture

Figure 3.2 Analysis of the making of a collection of Yoruba material

REIFACTS

be put on paper as descriptive diagrams or explained in words (C). The reifacts are
then represented as material objects known as 'icons', which are the collections
themselves (D). The physical material in a collection is chosen out in terms of this
process: starfish or Roman Samian ware are seen (A). They are allotted their own
attributes and the attributes get their own descriptive names in the contemporary
scheme of things (B). The actual physical objects are recognized as answering to
the names and descriptions (C), and are selected to become parts of the collection
(D). In practice the actual objects and the cognitive process which makes sense of
them are never separated in our minds. This is because we are dealing with the
material world in which, as we have just seen, objects are always both 'really' or
metonymically within their own world and the subjects of our metaphorical
image-making.

However, and this is very important, the metaphor (or signified or message) has
been added to the original material (the signifier or medium) by the perceiving
humans, from whose human experience come the perceptions and understanding
which is imposed upon the world at any given moment. But the human mind
seems very reluctant to recognize this distinction, and always tends to assume that,

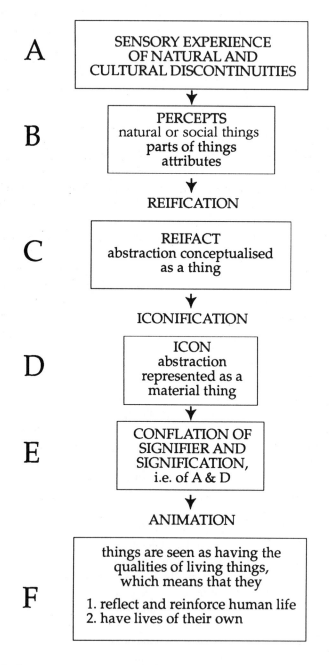

Figure 3.3 Cognitive processes underlying collection-making (based on Ellen 1988, fig. 1)

because the object belongs to a 'real' world, the metaphorical interpretation belongs there also, a piece of self-deception in which the signifier and the signified are conflated (E). Since this comes from us, it must be of us: we model the world in terms of direct experience of our own minds and bodies, for we have no other way of doing it. Among other things, this explains why scientific models of explanation or classic structuralist theories like those of Lévi-Strauss invariably take the human body as their basic paradigm: the ecology of a pond for example, is seen as a network of interdependent parts operating successfully together like a set of bodily organs; the computer works on a yes : no model like we do, and the layout of an African village is seen in terms of head and arms. Collections share in this animation, as we shall see in more detail in a moment (pp. 55–63).

Meanwhile, it is important to make one further point in this discussion. With this quality of animation, collections and the individual objects within them immediately acquire what we are accustomed to call a life of their own, the ambiguous relationship of control by objects of people and people of objects. Objects acquire a kind of power for good or evil. In one sense, this is a simple matter of everyday experience in which we know that the collection can bring the collector prestige and satisfaction, but can leave him alienated from friends and family, impoverished and embroiled in lawsuits. In another sense the psychological power of objects-endowed-with-life is at the roots of our experience of the material world.

Magical Talismans

Then Hervor spoke:

> Wake, Angantyr
> wakes you Hervor
> Svafa's offspring
> your only daughter;
> the keen-edged blade
> from the barrow give me,
> the sword dwarf-smithied
> for Sigrlami.

Angantyr answered:

> Fool you are, Hervor,
> in your heart's daring,
> with eyes open
> to enter the fire!
> The blade from the barrow
> I will bring, rather;
> O young maiden,
> I may not refuse you.

(Tolkien 1960: 14–19)

In this Old Norse poem, we learn how Hervor seeks out her dead father Angantyr in his grave mound in order to take from him the magic sword Tyrfing. Around the barrow burn the cold blue corpse fires, and as Hervor calls for the sword the mound opens and her father warns her of the ruin which the sword will bring. She tells him that, if need be, she will draw the weapon with her own hand from beneath her father's corpse, so he yields to her stubborn resolve and she gains Tyrfing for her own. We are in a world at once strange and deeply familiar in which objects are possessed of their own transforming power, in which they act as if they had wills and characters of their own, acknowledged by the proper names which are given to them.

The intense emotional excitement which some kinds of objects can arouse in us has been an acknowledged and enduring feature of European culture as far back as we can see, and shows no signs of abating. It is at the heart of the Arthurian cycle, constantly told and retold. Here is the description of the Holy Grail as it first appeared, told in the twelfth-century *Quest of the Holy Grail*:

> the Holy Grail appeared, covered with a cloth of white samite; and yet no mortal hand was seen to bear it. It entered through the great door, and at once the palace was filled with fragrance as though all the spices of the earth had been spilled abroad. It circled the hall along the great tables and each place was furnished in its wake with the food its occupants desired.
>
> (Matarasso 1969: 44)

It is at the heart of much legend and mythology, now transposed into the kind of modern fantasy fiction which mingles travel in time and space with barbaric weaponry. It conveys its power in poetry as in prose, and as representative of all this modern fiction let us quote from its prime begetter, Tolkein's *Lord of the Rings*:

> Three Rings for the Elven-Kings under the sky,
> Seven for the Dwarf-lords in their halls of stone,
> Nine for Mortal Men doomed to die,
> One for the Dark Lord on his dark throne
> In the Land of Mordor where the Shadows lie.
> One Ring to rule them all, One Ring to find them,
> One Ring to bring them all and in the darkness bind them
> In the Land of Mordor where the Shadows lie.
>
> (Tolkien 1962: Frontispiece)

The power of sword, cup and ring clings about many objects in our museum collections, especially those, like prehistoric weapons or gold ornaments, which were probably believed to have such powers by their original holders. The finds from Sutton Hoo in the British Museum, the Great Clare Find of Bronze Age gold ornaments in the National Museum of Ireland, the grave goods from Mycenae in the National Museum of Athens: all these reach out to us from behind their glass cases in ways which we cannot deny. This is true, also, of things which we greatly wish to add to our collections (both personal and museum) and of highly-prized objects for which such possession has been achieved. It belongs with the jealous exclusiveness which is itself part of the urge to possess and the sense of power which the act of possessing powerful objects brings.

This power is by no means necessarily benign; at best it is two-faced and double-edged. Objects are a bridge between this world and the Other World, from which they sometimes have power to summon ghosts and revenants. Such evil objects achieve a powerful hold over our imaginations in stories like those of M. R. James, who as a Director of the FitzWilliam Museum at Cambridge knew what he was talking about. In *Oh, Whistle and I'll Come to You My Lad*, the protagonist finds a whistle on the site of a Templar's Preceptory, and when he blows the whistle its call raises a strange bedfellow (James 1953: 109–34). Such dark objects are the misshapen bastard brothers of objects-for-good. Many of them, especially those that have explicit sexual overtones, carry an off-colour taint, the suggestion of abnormal attachment and 'closet' devotion. These, as Browne (1980: 1) says, are not quite an open subject. They are to straight religious or benign objects as devil worship is to religious practices – a cousin blocked from polite society by a bar sinister. They hold the same power, the same strength, the same valid reason for existence as the benign object, but they are not as respectable: they are the illegitimate, the left hand side of the family tree.

Objects with this talismanic character are not, of course, confined to myths, major museums or closet devotion: they are part of common experience. Most of us have things like St Christopher medals, luck pieces and amulets of all kinds which, even now at the very end of the twentieth century, we still half believe will operate magically on our behalf. Cars in particular attract this kind of special devotion. They too, like the swords, are given names of their own, and how many of us cherish a half-guilty conviction that the car itself once took evading action by which an accident was avoided and the driver delivered from evil? Cars attract latter-day mythology. Belk quotes a story told by a car collector who recalled searching for years for the pickup truck that he and his dead father had once repaired. The field notes ran:

> He had looked for it for much of the 11 years since he got rid of it, but with no luck. They had lost a son and had some other difficulties, so they had despon-dently gone to his father's grave. He and his father had done a lot of racing together and were close. He told his father that if he was alright to give him a sign. Shortly after that, a friend told him about a Cameo, and they went to see it. When he saw the 'R & R Racing' on it, he knew it was his old truck and bought it. Ron's wife said they weren't very religious, but that made believers of them.
>
> (Belk *et al.* 1990: 39)

The objects are, in the language of the older anthropology, external souls: external because physically distinct and separate, but souls because the meaning projected on to them brings them into the interior of our personal lives. A number of theories have been advanced to account for this curious aspect of our relationship with the objects which we own and collect. Melanie Klein constructed an object-relations theory in which the interaction of the infant's body with the external world establishes 'object relations', through the processes of Projection whereby states of feeling and unconscious wishes are expelled from the self and attributed to another person or thing, and Interjection whereby qualities that belong to an external object are absorbed and unconsciously regarded as belonging to the self. These 'objects' include both things and persons, and also part-objects, which the child invests with powerful fantasies pleasing and frightening, or indeed both, for at the core of Klein's theory is the awareness that good and bad alternate or coexist within the same object. For the infant the primary object is the breast, which is therefore experienced in turn as 'good' breast, that is one which supplies milk, and 'bad' breast, one which is empty. In the Kleinian view the infant first experiences the 'paranoid-schizoid' position in which it alternately hates and loves the breast, and then, as it learns to perceive its mother as a person, it takes up the 'depressive' position in which, because it fears it has injured its mother, it is filled with guilt and regret (Klein 1977). The movement from one position to the other involves identifying the fantasy with symbol, and hence the ambivalent power, and powerful ambivalence, with which we invest suitable objects. It is worth underlining that what we see as 'suitable' brings us back again to the brute materiality of objects. Swords really do have the power to kill, or cars to move us from place to place, and bright, shiny materials like gold and satin are attractive to our eyes.

Adrian Stokes continued the development of Klein's ideas by concerning himself with the sensations aroused when the body relates to the object world, either through contemplating its separateness, or in attempting to merge with and absorb what is before it. He expressed this as:

> Our relationships to all objects seem to be describable in terms of two extreme forms, the one a very strong identification with the object, whether projective or introjective, whereby a barrier between self and not-self is undone, the other a commerce with a self-sufficient and independent object at arm's length . . . the work of art is *par excellence* a self-sufficient object as well as a configuration that we absorb or to which we lend ourselves as manipulators.
>
> (Stokes 1978, III, pp. 151–2)

This broad line of theoretical development was sustained by D. W. Winnicott (1974), who understood the role of fantasy in the young child as leading to illusion and a certain structure of play. He designates an 'intermediate area of experience' in which a child begins to tell the difference between body parts and non-body parts and in so doing creates 'transitional' phenomena and objects: so, for example, a soft toy which can be sucked and cuddled up to can take the place of a breast, although the child knows that it is not one. What is important about this experience is the capacity to play with illusion, to use imagination working on an external object to create something for which a need is felt. For Julia Kristeva (1980) also, play begins at the meeting place of culture and nature, and play, which is a form of bodily experience, is productive of all objects and persons.

All these interrelated positions tend to make the same presupposition: the object, however viewed, is considered to be already discrete, with clear boundaries. As Wright puts it, 'If the transitional object is to be taken as a paradigm of some sort for art and culture in general, this unexamined premise will, for all the emphasis on play, import into all forms of creativity and interpretation a prejudice for objects assumed to be really for human interpretation' (1982: 95). In other words, the child somehow already seems to know what in theory it should only be able to discover through the course of play, and this pre-knowledge somehow influences the course and outcome of the play. Presumably, it would be possible to advance an answer to the difficulty by talking about common humanity leading inevitably to common appreciations, linked with the subtle effect of adult influence on the playing child; but mercifully this need not concern us. For us, the important point is twofold. The emotional relationship of projection and internalization which we have with objects seems to belong with our very earliest experience and (probably therefore) remains important to us all our lives. Equally, this line of thought brings us back to the intrinsic link between our understanding of our own bodies and the imaginative construction of the material world, which was touched upon in the previous section.

Genesis of our emotional relationship with objects infant experiences may be, but as our lives proceed objects, especially those wrought upon by art, are capable of carrying more profound symbolism. The idea of treasure is one of the ancestors of modern collecting and museum establishment, and figures in literature like the German and Scandinavian versions of the *Nibelungenlied* which is, among other things, the story of a great treasure. It is a story which has haunted European imagination, and in the hands of Richard Wagner became the cycle of operatic dramas in which Ring of the Nibelungs takes a central position and gives its name to the whole. Robert Donnington has argued that the ring, as a continuous flow with no beginning and no end and which stands for perfection, refers to the totality which includes all aspects of the psyche and is, therefore, an archetype of the self. Ring symbols make an insistent appearance in dream imagery, and elsewhere according to Jungian findings, when a person is developing towards wholeness. As Donnington says, 'Symbols for the self, whatever their form, point towards an integration of our opposing tendencies, and in particular of our conscious with our unconscious tendencies. They are uniting symbols' (1963: 92). The primary symbolism of the ring is the self. The gold from which it was forged, taken from the waters of the Rhine, represents unfocused power and energy, and the ring stands for this power sharply defined as the self-aware individual. Life, says Donnington, will offer some kind of meaning to everyone in so far as he can find his own way towards selfhood. The self includes both our conscious and our unconscious components, but its working seems to involve an increase of consciousness, and as we progress through life we become more aware of life's inherent opposites and manage to integrate them better into our personalities, and come closer to being whole persons, truly integrated and truly individual (1963: 67–8). For all this, the ring is the symbol.

The potential inwardness of objects is one of their most powerful characteristics, ambiguous and elusive though it may be. Objects hang before the eyes of the imagination, continuously re-presenting ourselves to ourselves, and telling the stories of our lives in ways which would be impossible otherwise.

prequinue [raled

The Urge to Collect

In a world of objects, different people will take different things into their hearts and minds, and so objects cross the threshold from the outside to the inwardness of collection. A number of definitions of what makes a collection have been attempted, and although definition-making is an arid affair at best, with each definition inevitably open to a variety of niggling objections based on specific examples, definitions are a useful way of gaining a perspective on the subject, both of itself and of the way in which it has been regarded. In 1932 Durost, one of the earliest students of collecting, offered:

> A collection is basically determined by the nature of the *value* assigned to the objects, or ideas possessed. If the *predominant* value of an object or idea for the person possessing it is intrinsic, i.e., if it is valued primarily for use, or purpose, or aesthetically pleasing quality, or other value inherent in the object or accruing to it by whatever circumstances of custom, training, or habit, it is not a collection. If the predominant value is representative or representational, i.e., if said object or idea is valued chiefly for the relation it bears to some other object or idea, or objects, or ideas, such as being one of a series, part of a whole, a specimen of a class, then it is the subject of a collection.
>
> (Durost 1932: 10)

This holds the valuable distinction between objects held for use, with a helpfully wide idea of what constitutes 'use', and objects held as part of a sequence: it is the idea of series or class which creates the notion of the collection. Probably Durost had in mind collections, like those of butterflies or cigarette cards, in which the notion of series is particularly clear, but in an extended form in which sequence is a largely subjective creation of the collector, the idea has a potentially wide application.

Alsop has offered a refreshingly simple approach. He says: 'To collect is to gather objects belonging to a particular category the collector happens to fancy . . . and a collection is what has been gathered' (Alsop 1982: 70). The stress here is laid on the mentality of the collector, for essentially a collection is what he believes it is, provided there are at least some physical objects gathered together. This expresses the essentially subjective element in collecting very well. The late 1980s have produced two further efforts at definition. Aristides offers: 'collection . . . [is] "an obsession organized." One of the distinctions between possessing and collecting is that the latter implies order, system, perhaps completion. The pure collector's interest is not bounded by the intrinsic worth of the objects of his desire; whatever they cost, he must have them' (Aristides 1988: 330). This recognizes the subjective element in its use of the word 'obsession', and suggests that the crucial difference between 'possessing' and 'collecting' is the order and possibility of completion which collecting possesses. This is open to a number of objections: a group of working tools, for example, will have order and may be complete, but they do not hold the place in the imagination which a collection would occupy.

Belk and his colleagues have arrived at the following: 'We take collecting to be the selective, active, and longitudinal acquisition, possession and disposition of an interrelated set of differentiated objects (material things, ideas, beings, or experiences) that contribute to and derive extraordinary meaning from the entity (the collection) that this set is perceived to constitute' (Belk *et al.* 1990: 8). This definition takes on board the idea of the interrelated set, Durost's series or class, and adds to it the notion that the collection as an entity is greater than the sum of its parts, an important contribution to the discussion. It brings in the actively selecting collector, with his personal or subjective slant on what he is doing, and it recognizes that collecting is a prolonged activity, extending through time. We might take issue with the unglossed use of the word 'active'. The study of collectors makes clear that collections can creep up on people unawares until the moment of realization: it suddenly dawns on a woman that the old clothes at the back of the wardrobe constitute an important group of Mary Quant or Carnaby Street dresses, which then in her mind becomes a collection to which she may actively add. Even more difficult to bring into Belk's and the other definitions are the collections of personalia or memorabilia: the little group of German helmet, bayonette, piece of shrapnel and shell case cigarette lighter which represent somebody's memories of the Somme, or the lifetime's accumulation of an important figure like Thomas Hardy. Perhaps the real point is that a collection is not a collection until someone thinks of it in those terms.

A good deal of ink has been spilt in the effort to pin down the difference between 'collecting' and 'accumulating' or 'hoarding'. Baudrillard suggests:

> Le strade inférieur est celui de l'accumulation de matières: entassement de vieux papiers, stockage de nourriture – à mi-chemin entre l'introjection orale et la retention anale – puis l'accumulation sérielle d'objets identiques. La collection, elle, émerge vers la culture . . . sans cesser de renvoyer les uns aux autres, ils incluent dans ce jeu une extériorité sociale, des relations humaines.
>
> (Baudrillard 1968: 147–8)

Perhaps notions of anal retention should be taken with a dose of salts, but 'accumulating' is usually seen as the simple magpie act, the heaping-up of material without any kind of internal classification, often covered by some pretence at a utilitarian purpose. Belk quotes the case of a man in his seventies who had accumulated three garages full of miscellaneous possessions and was facing pressure from his family to begin to discard these things so that they were not faced with the burden of doing so after his death (Belk 1988: 13). Nevertheless, the line between collecting and accumulating is a very fine one, which individual groups of material can cross in each direction, depending upon the view taken by their owner at different points in his life. Motive is all-important, and motives change. Hoarding is more difficult. In everyday use it means the gathering of material like Baudrillard's old papers or tins of food, sometimes carried to miserly excess, which comes within the accumulation mode just discussed. However, to archaeologists it means the deliberate gathering of selected materials for clearly social purposes, even if we do not know for certain what these purposes were: this kind of hoarding in ancient

Europe is best regarded as an ancestor of modern collecting. The term is therefore liable to confusion and, except in relation to the ancient past, it will be avoided in this book.

From this discussion we glean that ideas like non-utilitarian gathering, an internal or intrinsic relationship between the things gathered – whether objectively 'classified' or not – and the subjective view of the owner are all significant attributes of a collection, together with the notion that a collection is more than the sum of its parts. At some point in the process the objects have to be deliberately viewed by their owner or potential owner as a collection, and this implies intentional selection, acquisition and disposal. It also means that some kind of specific value is set upon the group by its possessor, and with the recognition of value comes the giving of a part of self-identity. But collecting is too complex and too human an activity to be dealt with summarily by way of definitions. In the rest of this chapter we will hope to tease out some of these complexities.

Collections as Play . . .

In modern times collecting is inextricably entangled with capitalist society, and one of the prime characteristics of this society is a sharp distinction between occupation and pleasure, work and play, in which play has come to assume a philosophical dimension of its own. The fruitful idea of play offers valuable insights into the collecting process (Huizinga 1955; Gombrich 1984; Danet and Katriel 1989), provided we remember that play can be extremely serious, and that it is not only the English who take their pleasures sadly.

For collectors, collecting is characteristically a leisure-time activity which happens at a different time and in a different place to that of the working day (one good reason why curators, for whom collections are work, are discussed not in this chapter, but in a later one). The distinction between the economic activity of working to make a living, and collecting, is usually very clear in the collector's mind: collecting is voluntary and the collection is separate and distinct; it will not be sold or dispersed except in serious necessity. It is set aside from daily life, like all the fenced-off enclosures in which games are played, and acquires a sacred character of apartness from the profane world, enshrined in its display shelves and cabinets. Collecting, like all sport, has the character of ritual activity which is carried out for its own sake with all the social and emotional quality which this implies. It is part of what Bourdieu has called 'the aesthetic disposition' in which: 'The aesthetic disposition, a generalized capacity to neutralize ordinary urgencies and to bracket off practical ends, a durable inclination and aptitude for practice without a practical function, can only be constituted within an experience of the world freed from urgency and through the practice of activities which are an end in themselves' (Bourdieu 1984: 54).

As we have seen, many collectors report that their collections did not begin purposefully, for it was not until they realized that they already had the beginnings of a collection that they began to take themselves seriously as collectors: so, notoriously, we are gradually drawn into play. Contest is another feature of play which has often been discussed (Huizinga 1955). Competition has always been a clearly-marked feature of collecting from its early practitioners to the present day, and runs from a desire to be at the head of the queue when the village fête white elephant stall opens, to the tension which gathers in Sotheby's sale room when an important item is going under the hammer. Chanciness too, the thrill of the chase in acquisition, and the prowess required to take chances and make the most of them, is both important and beguiling. Collections lend themselves to make-believe and the construction of fantasies: adults who collect teddy bears (and many do) are presumably playing out a dream of golden Edwardian childhood, while those who collect Japanese swords are preoccupied with rather different images. In our imaginations, collections make other times and other places open to us. As Rheims has put it:

> An object's date is of prime importance to a collector with an obsession for the past. He values it for its associations, that it once belonged to and was handled by a man he can visualize as himself. The object bears witness: its possession is an introduction to history. One of a collector's most entrancing day-dreams is the imaginary joy of uncovering the past in the guise of an archaeologist.
>
> (Rheims 1980: 211)

In the playing of games, separateness from the world is not loneliness, because for the time all players suspend other differences and unite to create for each other an identity and a security. Collectors, who sometimes feel that their possessive streak is excessive or childish, value this reassuring sense of community, and have always used the devices of correspondence, discussion, visits and formal meeting places to establish it. This is matched by the willingness of the European world in general to accord to collecting and collectors a legitimacy which would not be given to simple acquisitiveness, although a sharp and traditional system of values is applied here, and 'important' collections, usually those of fine and applied art in their broadest sense, are rated higher than others and given correspondingly larger degrees of legitimacy and prestige. Prestige is, of course, a major collecting motive here, especially where the collection can serve to give public legitimacy to fortunes amassed in trade and commerce: this was true of the Medicis, and it was true of most of the Great American nineteenth-century merchant prince collectors. Many modern collectors, however, cherish the hope that their collections will eventually achieve this kind of honour when their contributions are 'recognized': another way of hoping that the world will one day come to share the collector's view of his own material, and so of himself. Collecting is seen, or at the very least aspires to be seen, as a moral activity which, like games and love, ennobles the player.

Like love and play, however, collecting does not lack its dark side. As Tuan (1988) has shown, our apparently most harmless activities, like gardening or keeping pets, are all arenas for the play of will and the exercise of domination. Collections are objects of love, but they are also objects of dominance and control. Danet and Katriel (1989: 263) quote a stamp-collector who makes this clear: 'It's mine [the collection]. I can do with it what I want. I can arrange it in the album the way I want. I can display it in exhibits.' Rarity is an important element in the play of dominance. A story is told which is now part of the folklore of collecting, related originally by William Walsh and reported by Maurice Rheims, Baudrillard and Stewart:

> There is a story of a wealthy English collector who long believed that a certain rare book in his possession was a unique. One day he received a bitter blow. He learned that there was another copy in Paris. But he soon rallied, and, crossing over the Channel, he made his way to the rival's home. 'You have such and such a book in your library?' he asked, plunging at once *in medias res*. 'Yes.' 'Well, I want to buy it.' 'But, my dear sir – ' 'Two thousand!' 'On my word, I don't care to dispose of it.' 'Ten thousand!' and so on, till at last twenty-five thousand francs was offered; and the Parisian gentleman finally consented to part with this treasure. The Englishman counted out twenty-five thousand-franc bills, examined the purchase carefully, smiled with satisfaction, and cast the book into the fire. 'Are you crazy?' cried the Parisian, stooping over to rescue it. 'Nay,' said the Englishman, detaining his arm. 'I am quite in my right mind. I, too, possess a copy of that book. I deemed it a unique.'
>
> (Stewart 1984: 160)

In its rather laboured way, this history makes its point.

Danet and Katriel suggest that ownership, and the instant access which control brings is essential also for another reason: the sensuous aspects of collecting – handling, touching, playing with, caring for the collection – are made possible by it. One of their informants said, 'the most important thing is that you are able to handle it, because once it's in a museum you can't – this way you can take it and feel it and look at it' (Danet and Katriel 1989: 263). From this it is a short step to suppose that these are objects of love in a more specific sense, and as psychologists have not failed to point out, collectors often compare their feelings of longing for a piece to sexual desire. This, Baekeland suggests, means that objects are confused in the unconscious with ordinary sex objects, an idea that gets some confirmation from the fact that many collectors like to fondle or stroke the objects they own, for the only other context in which looking, fondling and caressing loom so large is in sexual foreplay (1988: 51). Even if we are tempted to reply that a chimney pot is sometimes just a chimney pot, we cannot deny that, for good and ill, objects live with us at the deepest levels of our personality.

Important and illuminating though these ideas can be, they skirt around the central fact of collecting, in which, to pick up Bourdieu's phrase, the collector's aesthetic disposition engages in an artist's play with his world. The kind of object collected is not important: what matters is the reframing of the object within the collection, as an act of formal admission from one state to another. In a certain sense, objects have rites of passage as do we, and for them this comes when they enter the classification system, the dividing, comparing and contrasting of whatever kind which for each collection constitute the rules of the game. The nature of the rules are equally unimportant – they can be rational or idiosyncratic – for all of them truly contribute a transformation, and the resulting collection runs beside the world of everyday life but does not reflect it in a direct way.

This notion of 'parallel but not exactly the same' is one way of approaching how art works, and collections similarly show the idea of unity-in-diversity which Gombrich has picked out as a general aesthetic principle (1984). The characteristic rule of the collecting game, and one which constitutes collecting as a whole, is the idea that objects or specimens belong within the same broad class but show detailed differences, even though (as in some modern bric-a-brac collections) both the unifying principle and the perceived variation within it may be highly subjective. It is the occurrence of repetition, of sameness-in-difference which here creates that particular feeling of satisfaction which we call beauty.

Following Gerard Manley Hopkins (1959), Humphrey has made the interesting suggestion that the paradigm for the experience of beauty in sameness-within-difference is rhyme, and that just as a poem rhymes, so may an object collection:

> Consider the nature of a typical collection, say a stamp collection. Postage stamps are, in structuralist terms, like man-made flowers: they are divided into 'species,' of which the distinctive feature is the country of origin, while within each species there exists tantalizing variation. The stamp-collector sets to work to classify them. He arranges his stamp in an album, a page for the species of each country. The stamps on each page 'rhyme' with each other, and contrast with those on other pages.
>
> (Humphrey, 1984: 132)

What is true for the stamps, Humphrey's structuralist man-made flowers, is equally true for real flowers and any other group of natural history specimens, and the principle of rhythm remains true for collections of Roman pottery, Renaissance bronzes or glass frogs. The assonance and dissonance, the endless theme and variation, the sacred sticks marking out the ritual ground within which the rhyming game of similarity and difference will be played out according to the rules: in collections these are given their material expression, and we take our corresponding satisfaction.

. . . And Close of Play

Games have endings, precincts have boundaries and collections must have limits, and this closure contributes hugely to the sense of rightness and so to our aesthetic pleasure. Danet and Katriel (1989: 264) draw attention to the suggestion made by Krietler and Krietler of the importance of tension and tension release in our experience, and suggest that by intentionally creating an agenda for the production and reduction of manageable tension, collectors toy with, pursue, and sometimes achieve a sense of completeness and perfection. As Gombrich has put it:

> we must ultimately be able to account for the most basic fact of aesthetic experience, the fact that delight lies somewhere between boredom and confusion; if monotony makes it difficult to attend, a surfeit of novelty will overload the sys-

tem and cause us to give up . . . It is different with hierarchies which we can master and reconstruct . . . The very ease of reconstruction allows us to go on and to enjoy that unity in complexity that has always appealed to paviors and other pattern-makers.

(Gombrich 1984: 9)

Unity in complexity would itself become boring if the pattern had no chance of achieving a satisfactory conclusion.

Danet and Katriel have identified five types of strategies which collectors can follow to produce a satisfactory sense of closure and have organized these in table form in which the strategies and examples speak for themselves (Figure 3.4). In reality, of course, collectors have to live with the fact that most of these routes to satiety and satisfaction are likely to be very difficult or impossible to complete, but this is inherent in the tension, and implies a recognition of the real and difficult

Strategies to Pursue Closure/Completion/Perfection

	Strategy	Example
1.	Completing a series or set	Completing a series of stamps
	Acquiring all of something	Acquiring all editions ever published of a book
	Assembling exemplars of sub-categories	Collecting examples of pipes made by different manufacturers
	Putting together items that 'go together'	Furnishing a room
2.	Filling a space	Filling a wall with a displayed collection of plates
3.	Creating a visually pleasing, harmonious display	Attending to the composition created by a display of plates
4.	Manipulating the scale of objects	
	Collecting very small objects	Collecting miniatures, e.g., dollhouse furniture
	Collecting very large objects	Collecting vintage cars
5.	Aspiring to perfect objects	
	Acquiring items in mint condition	Acquiring a mint condition vintage car
	Restoring items to mint condition	Restoring a vintage car
	Acquiring aesthetically perfect objects	Acquiring an exquisite painting
	Improving the physical quality of items	Replacing a rusted stamp with one in better physical condition
	Improving the aesthetic quality of items	Trading a painting for one of superior aesthetic quality

Figure 3.4 Strategies for collection closure/completion/perfection (after Danet and Katriel 1989, Table 1)

world outside the collection confines. In his study of biology, behaviour and the arts, Peckham (1967) suggested that art is an expression of 'man's rage for chaos' and went on to say that:

> Man desires above all a predictable and ordered world . . . and this is the motivation behind the role of the scientist. But because man desires such a world so passionately, he is very much inclined to ignore anything that intimates that he does not have it . . . Only in protected situations, characterized by high walls of psychic insulation, can he afford to let himself be aware of the disparity between his interests . . . and the data his interaction with the environment actually produces.
>
> (Peckham 1967: 313)

Collecting is one way of living within chaos and transforming it, briefly, into sense.

predictive

Collections as the Extended Self

We have seen that, in a very real sense, we and our collections are one. William James set this out as early as 1890:

> a man's Self is the sum total of all that he can call his, not only his body and his psychic powers, but his clothes and his house, his wife and children, his ancestors and friends, his reputation and works, his lands and yacht and bank account. All these things give him the same emotions. If they wax and prosper, he feels triumphant; if they dwindle and die away, he feels cast down, – not necessarily in the same degree for each thing, but in much the same way for all.
>
> (James 1890: 291)

Rochberg-Halton makes the same point in modern terms: 'Valued material possessions . . . act as signs of the self that are essential in their own right for its continued cultivation, and hence the world of meaning that we create for ourselves, and that creates our selves, extends literally into the objective surroundings' (Rochberg-Halton 1984: 335).

A number of studies carried out in America unite to demonstrate how significant possessions are to the self-image (e.g. McClelland 1951; Prelinger 1959; Furby 1978), and interestingly these tend to suggest that the critical factor is the extent to which we believe we possess or are possessed by an object: control, one way or another, is what makes an object become more a part of the self. Ellis (1985: 115–17) found evidence of human possessiveness in relation to (not listed in any hierarchical order) 1. one's body; 2. personal space; 3. food and drink; 4. territory; 5. home; 6. lovers; 7. children; 8. friends; 9. tools; 10. objects of aesthetic appeal, play and amusement and souvenirs. All such 'objects' act as reminders and confirmers of our identities, and probably our idea of our identity resides more in such objects than it does in any idea of ourselves as individuals. They also seem to ease our movement through life, and to act as a medium of passage. Rochberg-Halton (1984; 1986) found that the kinds of things people describe as special change through life, culminating in old age as those things, like gifts or photographs, which symbolize other people. Equally, the deliberate dispersal of possessions by gift or will seems to be a helpful part of our preparation for death.

It is clear that the acquisition of objects is an important part of selfhood, whether they are intended as additions to a collection or simply as part of a shopping expedition. Ames, when discussing the nineteenth-century purchase of a parlour organ says:

> Buying a prominent object like a parlor organ might initiate a new chapter in a set of lives, not only by providing a new way to use time but also a new tool to measure time. In later years the object would serve to remind its owners of the day it first entered their home and of the time that had passed since then. It would not only structure their present but also their perceptions of their own past. They knew from experience that purchasing a major object could be a significant and momentous occasion in itself, a time of heightened positive emotions and feelings of well-being and importance . . . a major purchase would transform them in their own eyes and in the eyes of others. They would become worth more . . . and acquire greater status. By so doing they would receive more respect and deference from others which would, in turn, make them feel better about themselves. Buying a parlor organ would make them something they were not before.
>
> (Ames 1984: 30–31)

We might add that a curator feels much the same when an important acquisition is made to the museum collection. Czikszentmihalyi and Rochberg-Halton (1981) have provided an explanation by suggesting that we invest 'psychic energy in an object or group of objects to which we have directed effort and time. The energy is part of self, an expenditure of self, and so its products are, equally, regarded as a return of the self.' In his most important work, *Being and Nothingness* (1943), Sartre suggested that doing is merely a transitional state or manifestation of the more fundamental desires to have or to be. Sartre maintains that we want things in order to enlarge our sense of self, and that the only way in which we can know what we are is by observing what we have. Acquisition is an important way of 'having' the object, and purchase is an important form of acquisition. Sartre says: 'Stop before a showcase with money in your pocket; the objects displayed are already more than half yours' (1943: 753).

Clearly, the ultimate in self-definition through having is the devoted accumulation of a collection. We can control our own collection in a way in which we can control little else in the world, and the collection can then take on anthropomorphic features. As Goldberg and Lewis have put it (1978: 64), 'Many collectors who are inhibited and uncomfortable in social interaction, surround themselves with favoured objects upon which they project humanlike qualities. They practically talk to these objects; they find comfort in being with them and regard them as friends!'

The notion of collections as our extended selves accounts for the way in which we use the metaphor of the body for collections in ordinary curatorial speech. So we talk about 'the body of the collection' meaning what is perceived as its main content or 'corpus', and the 'heart of the collection', meaning those pieces which are seen as central to its meaning. This has a number of interesting implications which revolve around the idea of the body as model and referent, and these we will explore in turn.

The Body as Model and Referent

Our own bodies are the primary mode through which we have a sense of scale and an idea of what constitutes the normal. One way of discovering what a past age believed to be normal is to look in art and literature at what it considered to be freakish, since normal and abnormal exist together, defining each other. The normal body becomes the microcosm of the world, so that the body is metaphoric to the larger body of the universe. This corporeal relationship is the root reason why people are attracted to the bizarre and the freakish, and why museums hold material about which they are often nowadays shamefaced. Within this grouping comes human material associated with abnormality or death, like Egyptian mummies, some human skeletons, material like shrunken heads, and freakish animal material, either that which is naturally so, or that which has been treated to make perverted copies of human life, like mice turned by taxidermy and dressing into a copy of human life. Such material on display is both shocking and still often hugely popular, notwithstanding the changes in moral taste which have happened over recent decades (for a discussion of some important issues see Green 1984).

Stewart quotes from a sales pitch at the end of the giant and half-lady show at Strate's Carnival, Washington, DC, in 1941. The giant, Mr Tomainey, says:

> And notice the size of the hands – watch the hand please – and the size of the ring I have here, so large you can pass a silver half a dollar right through the center of the ring . . . Watch this, a silver half a dollar right through the giant lucky ring, believe it or not . . . Right through the center of the ring. Now each one of these rings have my name and occupation engraved on them, and I'm going to pass them out now for souvenirs, and this is how I do it.
>
> (Stewart 1984: 134)

The rings, of course, were only passed out free if the viewer also purchased a booklet about the giant and his life, and as we are all aware, examples of both ring and booklet are very likely to end up in museum collections. The display relating to Daniel Lambert in Newarke Houses Museum, Leicester, strikes a similar note (see Plate 5). Lambert was a giant who lived in the Midlands between 1770 and 1809, and who eventually grew to a weight of 52 stone 11 lb. He served as Leicester city gaoler, and the display includes his shirt, waistcoat, gloves and stockings, together with his chair and walking stick, all of which authenticate the narrative of his great size, and the keys and lantern which he used as a gaoler. In his own day Lambert was a popular local figure, whose size, strength and gentle nature were seen as the epitome of noble British qualities in contrast to those of revolting France, but this aspect of his existence has now been dropped from popular con-

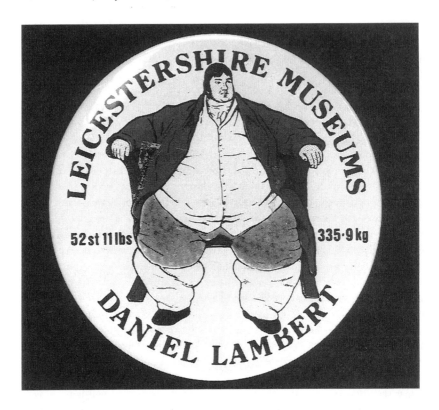

Plate 5.   Metal badge on sale in Leicestershire Museum Service shops, showing
Daniel Lambert, whose belongings are on show in the Newarke Houses
Museum, Leicester (photo: University of Leicester).

sciousness, and he now appears simply as somebody who is interesting because he
is different.

The urge towards miniaturization belongs within the same nexus of feelings.
The taxidermed human-like mice have already been mentioned. With them, if
much less offensively, belong the collections made up of miniature objects, like
dolls, doll's houses and furniture, china cottages, tiny versions of domestic
artefacts like jugs and baskets, and the whole world of miniaturized toys when
these are collected by adults. In part, this is a product of late capitalism in which
production is turned into spectacle (consider the number of factories and farms it
is now possible to 'go round', and the popularity of watching craftsmen at work in
all the open-air folk museums), and for which it is necessary to provide convenient
souvenirs, often in the shape of small versions of what is on show. But miniaturization
is not particularly convenient: small size and mode of manufacture means that the
objects are useless for all utilitarian purposes, and can serve only as collection
items, whether for the purchaser or the recipient of a gift.

The same is true of the freak animals which many museums possess. The Carnegie Museum, Melton Mowbray has the preserved specimen of a two-headed calf which was born around 1895. The calf lived for only a few hours and was immediately skinned and stuffed. It was exhibited as a peep-show in various local cattle markets, and used during both world wars as a money-raising exhibit. It was not donated to the Museum until 1981, and was placed on display soon after, where it has attracted some attention, not all of it favourable.

A number of theories have been developed to account for why this kind of material has such a horrible fascination, all of which involve the idea of reference to the normal body. Stewart argued (1984: 109) that these are not 'freaks of nature' but 'freaks of culture' through which the viewer is able to form his own idea of the normal and aberrant, and so is confirmed in his reassuring view of himself as normal, average and (relatively) beautiful. Monte (1977) picks up Freud's idea of the conflict within us between life instinct and death wish, and suggests that this can lead to a seeking out of things associated with death, including freaks and other morbid matters. This certainly goes some way towards explaining the perennial popularity of Egyptian mummies and such like on display; our death wish leads to intimations of mortality, but at the same time our life instinct is repelled at the idea. Humphrey (1984) proposes that humans and animals seek out experiences through which they learn to classify the objects in the world about them, in order to understand what is, and is not, useful for survival. This trait is so important that it becomes enjoyable in itself, and so eventually leads to curiosity about something which fits into a category ('cow') but is in some way different ('double-headed'). The intriguing nature of theme and variation may be very important, and relates this particular aspect of our relationship to the physical world to collecting activity as a whole.

Fromm (1977) offers a rather different perspective. He suggests that humans need stimulus and excitation, but this can be of two kinds – simple and activating. As Figure 3.5 shows, contemporary life offers much in the way of simple stimulus, and one problem with this is that such stimuli, repeated beyond a certain threshold, no longer register and lose their effect. Consequently, in order to remain powerful such stimuli must intensify or change, and hence our insatiable appetite for fresh crimes, wars, and, in material culture, freaks, peep-shows, morbid remains and black jokes.

Engendering Collections

If collections are the extended self, it follows that they must have the capacity to take on a male or female identity: collecting, collectors and collectable objects are all potentially gendered (Belk and Wallendorf 1992). Gender can be linked to the collecting process through the gendered meaning of collecting as such; through the gender associations of the objects collected; and through the gendered use of collections.

Not surprisingly, until relatively recently, the view taken of the nature of male

SIMPLE STIMULUS	ACTIVATING STIMULUS
provokes a reaction	stimulates a person to be active
produces a drive	causes person to strive towards a goal
requires little effort	requires a lot of effort - person has to think and become involved
easy to feel satiated	never feel satiated until physical fatigue occurs
e.g. tabloid newspapers, some films, magazines, chat shows, etc.	e.g. some novels, poems, "sophisticated" films, landscapes, a loved person

Figure 3.5 'Simple stimulus' and 'activating stimulus' (after Fromm 1977)

and female collectors and their essential characteristics reflected the view taken about men and women in society as a whole. In 1944 Rigby and Rigby were able to write:

> grand scale collecting almost always calls for aggressive and material ambition to a degree uncharacteristic of women, aside from women's historic economic position. Those who came within hailing distance of collecting giants were women who seemed to exhibit the masculine strain of a highly developed competitiveness, although this in no way detracts from the position of women as amateurs.
>
> (Rigby and Rigby 1944: 326–7)

In similar vein, Saisselin suggested:

> By 1880 in France, women were perceived as mere buyers of bibelots, which they bought as they did clothing, in their daily bargain hunting. Men, of course, collected too, but their collecting was perceived as serious and creative. Women were consumers of objects; men were collectors. Women bought to decorate and for the sheer joy of buying, but men had a vision for their collections, and viewed their collections as an ensemble with a philosophy behind it.
>
> (Saisselin 1984: 68)

The historical fact that, by and large, women have not collected on the grand scale is here linked just as much with 'essential' female characteristics of non-aggression and domestic limitation as it is with restricted access to funds, space and the male world of meeting places, all of which would now be regarded as different ways of expressing the same central fact of female deprivation. In terms of gender it seems that, traditionally at least, collecting partakes of the same broad character as society in general.

Given this high degree of cultural determinism, it is likely that the kinds of material which members of the two sexes choose to collect will reflect the same gender stereotypes, and will themselves appear as gender-related collections. The process is in many ways a circular and self-fulfilling prophecy, and so it seems that much actual collecting, including that being undertaken by contemporary collectors, has a gender character. To take an obvious example, gun collecting, which is extremely popular in both Britain and North America, is an almost exclusively male activity. Whether or not guns really do have an explicit phallic symbolism scarcely matters, because everybody knows that they are supposed to have it and this specifically gendered appeal and power unquestionably runs through the collecting activity which guns attract. The language of firearms and firing is so heavily laden with sexual innuendo that *double entendres* are well nigh impossible to avoid, as anybody who has tried (as I have) to write gun labels well knows.

In 1931, Witty found that American girls were more likely to collect flowers, pictures, jewellery, personal items like souvenirs or Valentines, dolls and their accoutrements, and school objects. Boys were more likely to collect animal and insect parts, tobacco souvenirs, objects to do with fighting and hunting, game objects like marbles and kites, and repair and maintenance materials like oil cans, nails and padlocks (1931). The surveys by Whitely (1929) and Durost (1932), carried out at much the same time, also in the United States, bore out Witty's findings. The collecting habits of adults were in general much the same, and all the available evidence suggests that in broad terms this pattern is maintained in contemporary collecting.

Belk and Wallendorf quote a particularly clear and interesting example of modern gender-associated collecting carried out by a husband and wife, and each housed in its own museum. Mouse Cottage contains the wife's collection of mouse replicas. Its brochure invites the visitor to:

> Enter the Mouse Cottage and you'll squeak with delight! Once upon a time, in the early 1920s, there was a little girl so clever and charming in character and petite in stature that her mother quite naturally called her 'mouse'. The childhood name inspired the little girl's imagination with a life long passion for collecting mice of every description.
>
> (Belk and Wallendorf 1992: 5)

The mouse replicas (rather like those of the taxidermed mice referred to earlier) are displayed around pseudo-antique golden oak furniture in a home-like setting. The display is cluttered and chaotic. It includes mouse ornaments hung on a Christmas tree, and a similar miniature Christmas tree in the mouse doll's house. Belk and Wallendorf draw attention to the 'theme of subservience in the mice's diminutive and miniaturized nature – traits which reflect the powerlessness associated with women and children' (1992: 6).

By contrast, the Fire Museum houses the husband's collection of fire equipment, advertised in its brochure as: 'See the world's largest exhibit of fire-fighting equipment. Over 100 fully restored pieces dating from circa 1725 to 1950 . . . Learn about the history of the American fire-fighter – America's most dangerous profession – from

Ben Franklin's Philadelphia volunteers to the modern era.' The display is much larger, the material is well restored and importantly exhibited, and the whole tone is that of a professional, historical museum of some significance. The oppositions which these two establishments embody are well expressed in the table of opposed pairs which Belk and Wallendorf have drawn up (Figure 3.6).

Close kin to this gendered association of collected objects is a gendered use of collections. Belk and Wallendorf (1992) quote two collectors, both of whom show this sexual character of collections very clearly. Both Flo (female) and Brent (male) collect Barbie dolls, a major form of collecting activity in the USA which carries its own structure of magazines, meetings and conferences. Flo has been collecting Barbie dolls for some fifteen years, but a few years ago her collecting was interrupted when she had to undergo major surgery involving radical mastectomy. Flo is very generous with her duplicate items, giving pieces away to fellow collectors, and enacting what Belk and Wallendorf call 'the feminine quality of generosity'. She herself possesses a complete collection of the sets of clothes manufactured by Mattel for Barbie and at least one example of all Barbie models ever produced. The authors draw the inevitable conclusion that

> her use of the collection to demonstrate completeness resonates deeply when contrasted with her difficulties following the removal of her breasts. Though

---

MOUSE COTTAGE IS TO FIRE MUSEUM AS...

X is	to Y
Tiny	Gigantic
Weak	Strong
Chaos	Order
Home	World
Nature	Machine
Art	Science
Playful	Serious
Inconspicuous	Conspicuous

Figure 3.6 Contrasts between Mouse Cottage and Fire Museum (after Belk and Wallendorf 1992, Table 1)

owning a complete set of Barbies, she is able to restore a sense of completeness. Not only does Barbie possess the kind of figure Flo no longer has, collecting allows Flo to possess a complete set of these voluptuous dolls.

(1992: 9)

Brent collects exactly the same objects, but makes his own, very different use of them. Brent is a hairdresser, gay, and with a former history as an exotic dancer and male prostitute. The authors suggest that Brent uses his Barbies to mediate three types of gender images: real life images, worldly images, and otherworldly images, all of which intermingle as Brent uses his collection to construct and confirm his personal myth. Brent's relationship with his mother was poor, so in his collection there are no mother dolls, but he has an oversize Barbie doll to which he has added extremely heavy make-up. He describes this doll as 'a whore', and places her next to a Miss Piggy doll in order to make a deliberate connection between whore and swine. Similarly, he dresses one doll in a silver lamé evening dress put on back to front in order to show more cleavage, and then verbally disparages the doll's supposed desire to show off her breasts. The most vivid image of evil in his collection is that of the 'Ice Queen', a woman beautiful, cold and rejecting of males. Brent says that all the other dolls in the collection hate and fear this particular doll, which seems to represent his simultaneous fascination with, and contempt for, women.

It is possible to put together the inferences from the Mouse Collection, the Fire Collection and the two Barbie Doll collections to create a plot of feminine and masculine images and characters, structured around the ideas of Otherworldly, Worldly and Real Life, as Belk and Wallendorf have done (Figure 3.7). This contains nothing unexpected, but perhaps this is the most important point: these (admittedly in some cases rather extreme) examples show that collecting is shot through with the same kind of gender-related activity that characterizes all our constructions of the world. Gender is itself constructed through collecting and collections as it is through everything else, for material culture has here, as everywhere, an active as well as a passive stance. Collecting does its share to create the gender distinctions which govern social life.

A Kind of Immortality

The extended self which collections represent is intended to extend beyond the grave. In a general study of strategies of identity preservation, Unruh (1983) found, unsurprisingly, that people attempt solidification of identity firstly through letters, journals, memos and poems which are meant to be left behind; secondly, they accumulate objects like photographs and jewellery; finally, they distribute these things to persons who are believed to be willing to care for them and in so doing honour and remember the donor, acts which are accomplished by pre-death gifts, wills and promises.

This brings us to the notion of collected family property, or single pieces of

FEMININE IMAGES AND CHARACTERS

	OTHERWORLDLY	WORLDLY	REAL LIFE
GOOD	Angel	Virgin Bride	
		Little Girl	Self ("Mouse")
	Madonna	Mother	
	Fairy Godmother	Babysitter	Babysitter
EVIL	Witch	Whore	Prostitute
		Temptress	Mother
		Maid	
		Voyeur	
		Ice Queen	Mother

MASCULINE IMAGES AND CHARACTERS

	OTHERWORLDLY	WORLDLY	REAL LIFE
GOOD	King	Businessman	
	Hero	Soldier,Sailor	
		Athlete	
		Cowboy	
	Saviour	Rescuer, Fireman	
		Boy	
EVIL	Devil	Nazi Soldier	Self (Brent)
	Snake	Wild Beasts	Father
		Slave, servant	

Figure 3.7 Masculine and feminine images and characters (after Belk and Wallendorf, Table 2)

property, as heirlooms. Stewart (1984: 137) quotes the plot of John P. Morquand's novel, *The Late George Apley: A Novel in the Form of a Memoire* in which a bitter family quarrel develops over the disputed possession of a 'badly worn square of carpet upon which General Lafayette inadvertently spilled a glass of Madeira during his visit to Boston!' Possessions like this are statements of member-ship, not in the event itself, whether this be a part of more general history or of family history like the accumulation of a collection, but of the prestige generated by the event. Veblen (1899) has suggested that anything which bears witness that wealth has been in a family for several generations has particular value to the leisure class. Rochberg-Halton quotes a Chicago informant who said (1984: 171):

> This [painting] is my great, great grandfather. I've had it since childhood. It's more than just a portrait – it's a person! I'd grab it right away in a fire. [Without it] my life would be lessened. I'd go on living, but it would deplete my secure 'lump.' It would mean that I wouldn't be able to hand it down to my children. The kids already say, 'I'm gonna inherit this and that.' . . . It's part of the continuity of who I am, where I came from, where I'm going.

The function of the heirloom is to sustain a prestigious narrative of genealogy, to elevate the significance of the blood link above that of a larger and more objective view of the past.

The more substantial the collection, and the more of himself the collector has put into it, the greater the significance of final disposal, and correspondingly, the more serious the problems which will surround this disposal. Collectors are char-acteristically extremely anxious that a collection will not be split up, which normally means the sale of the most valuable pieces and the casual distribution or destruction of the rest, and this fear, understood by all curators, has been documented by Rheims (1961), Johnson and Beddow (1986) and von Holst (1967). For this reason a collector quite often singles out a particular member of his family, often quite a young member, and attempts to encourage interest in the collection on the part of this young person. Belk quotes a collector of elephant replicas who plans to leave his collection to his granddaughter, now only a year old, to whom he is making a point of giving elephant toys and an elephant print dress. He does not want to leave the collection to his daughter or wife, because he knows that they will not continue it; but he wants to believe that the collection is historically important and will one day be recognized as a significant achievement (Belk *et al.* 1988: 551).

This urge for long-term recognition on the part of the collector is, of course, the motive for the donation of many collections to museums, and for the founding of museums specifically intended to have and display a particular collection. Museums of this kind are invariably explicit memorials, called after the name of the collector. In the same way, donations to existing museums often contain a requirement to keep the collection together, to document it under the collector's name, and to display all or part of it together in one gallery so that its integral nature is clear to the visitor; sometimes the gallery itself will be given the collector's name.

There are hundreds of such collections in museums throughout Britain. A happy example is the Pinto Collection of Treen, now in Birmingham City

Museum. On 16 July 1964 a national newspaper published an appeal by Mr and Mrs Edward Pinto for a public museum to offer to acquire their world-famous collection of wooden domestic objects at a nominal price. The collection, which had been on informal display in the Pinto's house at Northwood, Middlesex, was acquired by Birmingham City Museum in 1966, and, in accordance with the wish of the collectors, as much of it as possible was to be displayed in one gallery. This implied the decision that the Pinto Collection would be treated as a visible reference and study collection, and the Pinto Gallery was planned with this in mind (Figure 3.8). Accordingly, a series of units based on an octagonal plan were constructed, which would allow a good view of a maximum number of objects, and these were positioned in a meander pattern in order to entice the visitor within (Barnett, Klein and Thomas 1970).

The negotiations involved in such donations or bequests are often delicate and difficult, particularly if the museum does not wish to take the whole of the material on offer, and does need to apply professional standards of curation which clash with a collector's frequently idiosyncratic view of how the material should be treated: and this quite apart from questions of cash value and purchase price. Nevertheless, the collector's desire for immortality is so strong, and the curator's desire to acquire interesting material so fierce, that a fairly satisfactory agreement is reached surprisingly frequently. If entry into a collection is an object's first rite of passage, then entry into a museum is its second – a passage which marks its translation into the class of heritage material, of sacred durables.

Collections, then, come about because individuals select objects and specimens out from all the available material of the world, and put them together in a way which renders the meaning of the group more than the sum of its individual parts. The objects, being material, retain their link with the 'real' world from which they come, but the collection is a metaphor for this 'reality', a dream, an inscription on the world. Collections spring from existing individual and social constructions, but they also underwrite and perpetuate these constructs. Collections are endowed with a life of their own, which bears the most intimate relationship to that of their collector, so that the collector sees them, in the most literal sense, as parts of himself. But at the heart of this relationship is an ambiguity of control; sometimes the collector shapes the collection and sometimes it shapes him – another way of saying that objects are always both active and passive.

Collections are the artistic creation of self out of self, part of the connection of past and present and the hope of a future. Collectors who seek out what they love are involved in an effort of self-discovery and self-affirmation which is characteristically human and so, no matter how trivial others may perceive the material to be, is itself never trivial.

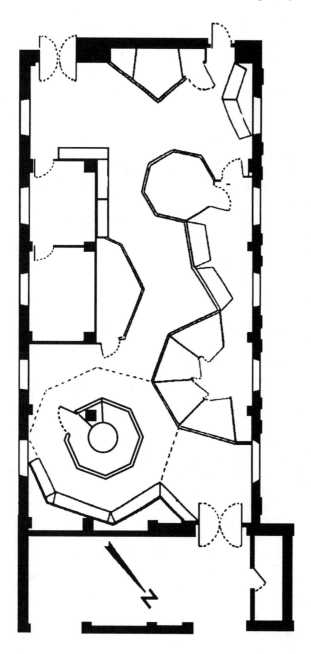

Figure 3.8 Plan of the Pinto Gallery, Birmingham City Museum, 1970 (after Barnett, Klein and Thomas 1970)

4 Collecting: Shaping the World

I met a traveller from an antique show,
His pockets empty, but his eyes aglow.
Upon his back, and now his very own,
He bore two vast and trunkless legs of stone.
Amid the torrent of collector's jargon
I gathered he had found himself a bargain,
A permanent conversation piece post-prandial,
Certified genuine Ozymandial,
And when I asked him how he could be sure
He showed me P. B. Shelly's signature!

(Nash, 'The Collector', 1972)

[My material] is not for the purpose of surprising anybody, either by the beauty or the value of the objects exhibited, but solely with a view to instruction. For this purpose ordinary and typical specimens rather than rare objects have been selected and arranged in sequence.

(General Pitt Rivers, quoted in Daniel 1950: 171)

Outdated
Though the cultural anthropological system be
The lonely and unpopular
Might find the landscapes of their childhood marked out
Here, in the chaotic piles of souvenirs.
The claw of a condor, the jaw-bones of a dolphin . . .

(Fenton, 'The Pitt Rivers Museum' 1983: 82)

Introduction

The discussion so far has endeavoured to throw light on the reasons why collections are made, and the part-conscious, part-unconscious way in which collections relate to our bodies and souls. But beyond this, collecting is a complex activity in which several modes can be detected, each of which represents a particular way of constructing a relationship with the world. It is to these collecting modes that we must now turn.

I shall try to distinguish three modes of collecting, to which it seems to me most of our collections belong, and these may be called collections as 'souvenirs', as 'fetish objects' and as 'systematics'. I shall try to draw out the characteristic features of each mode, using as a framework some of the ideas usually described as phenomenological and associated originally with Hegel, and especially the concept of 'objectification' abstracted by Miller (1987) from Hegel's ideas, which supposes a dual relationship of process between subject and object. 'Process' is an important word to which we shall return. These will be linked with concepts of the romantic, an important group of ideas which are now being applied to the history of collecting (Wainwright 1989) and which have been greatly developed over the last few decades.

These Foolish Things

Let us make a start with that material which can be characterized as souvenir, and do so under the title of a popular song from the thirties, that decade of adult emotions, because souvenirs are the yesterdays of us all, the kind of accumulation from which none of us are entirely free. Souvenirs are the objects which take their collection unity only from their association with either a single person and his or her life history, or a group of people, like a married couple, a family or, say, a scout troop, who function in this regard as if they were a single person. They cover a huge range of possible objects. Examples chosen at random include children's toys in the York Castle Museum, a sampler in the Victoria and Albert Museum, a piece of patchwork in Exeter City Museum, a powder compact in the Leicestershire Museum Service. The range of such pieces formally accessioned into museums is, of course, only a tiny fraction of the number which actually exists out in the world, but they are, nevertheless, very characteristic types of museum accession.

There is one particular kind of souvenir of which our museums are inordinately full and which deserves a few paragraphs of special discussion. This is the wild animal hunted, and then preserved, in part or whole, as trophy. The Peel Collection, held by Exeter City Museum, is typical of many (see Plate 6). It contains the stuffed and mounted heads of a wide range of African and other species shot by Col. Peel in the course of his career as a big game hunter around the turn of the century. The country houses, public houses, and museum services in counties like Leicestershire and Somerset are full of English trophies of the chase, mounted stag heads and antlers, mounted fox masks, paws and brushes.

Much distaste is now felt for such material which is out of step with the new ethic of conservation and respect for the natural world. In consequence this kind of collection often forms part of that *sub fusc* world of material never displayed, unless it can be used in relation to conservation projects or perhaps to help children appreciate the diversity of the natural world, like the *Noah's Ark* exhibition at the Hancock Museum, Newcastle. But viewed as trophy, as souvenir which encapsulates a particular view of our relationship with the natural world, these pieces are illuminating. We must remember that hunting for food is not in question; when the unspeakable chases the inedible, prestige alone is at stake. But it is prestige of a particularly fundamental kind, achieved through the enactment of ritual, which

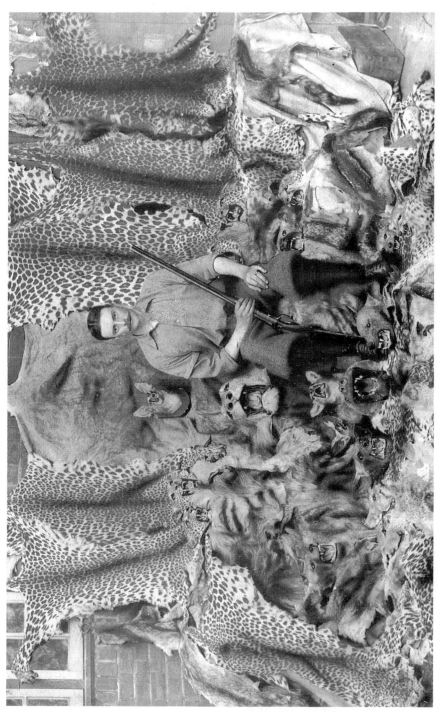

Plate 6.   Col. Charles Peel surrounded by a selection of his trophies, taken about 1920. The Peel Collection is now in Exeter City Museum (photo: Exeter City Museum).

can be succinctly expressed employing the broad style that Edmund Leach used to describe hunting psychology (1977). We see that the action can be boiled down to a set of opposed pairs, and that the inference to be drawn from these opposed pairs is that ritual hunting establishes the correct relationship between mankind and the natural world which the trophy on the wall makes manifest (Figure 4.1). Sporting silverware and collections of regimental trophies work in very much the same way, and are intended to give the same kinds of messages. I am reminded of a *Punch* cartoon which showed foxes in evening dress sitting at ease around the ancestral mahogany, surrounded by mounted human heads and hands on the walls.

Souvenirs usually arrive as part of what curators call 'personalia' or 'memorabilia', and sometimes the personality to which they are attached was sufficiently interesting or notorious to throw a kind of glamour-by-association over the pieces. Laurence Binyon, formerly an Assistant Keeper at the British Museum and best known as the

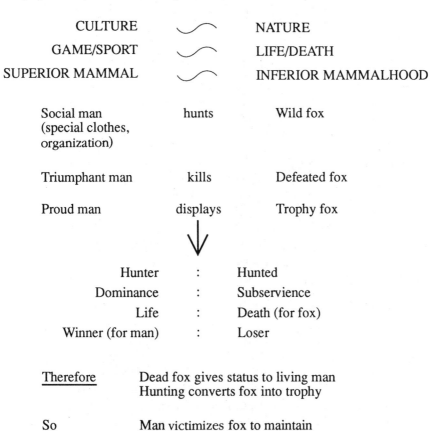

Figure 4.1 Analysis of the significance of animal trophies (drawing upon Leach 1977)

author of the lines which begin 'In Flanders fields the poppies grow', wrote a playlet in which he imagines an altercation between two exhibits, the bust of a Roman Emperor and the mummy of an Egyptian Queen (quoted in Holmes 1953: 3). Each claims precedence on the grounds of past importance and present popularity. The lady makes good her claims in one devastating couplet:

I lived in scandal and I died in sin;
That's what the world is interested in!

Generally, however, the personalities are not particularly distinguished, and unless the objects have acquired the kind of interest which accrues to survival through the passage of years and increasing rarity, like the Leicester powder compact made for Boots Ltd. in the 1930s, they are experienced as boring and embarrassing. Such objects will not be displayed unless they can be hooked on to an historical exhibition in which their personal connections can be mentioned.

And yet we know, in our hearts if not in our minds, that souvenirs are moving and significant to each of us as individuals, otherwise we would not keep them. What, then, is the nature of these pieces? Souvenirs are intrinsic parts of a past experience, but because they, like the human actors in the experience, possess the survival power of materiality not shared by words, actions, sights or the other elements of experience, they alone have the power to carry the past into the present. Souvenirs are samples of events which can be remembered, but not relived. Their tone is intimate and bittersweet, with roots in nostalgic longing for a past which is seen as better and fuller than the difficult present. The spiral is backwards and inwards as the original experience becomes increasingly distant, and contact with it can only be satisfied by building up a myth of contact and presence. Souvenirs discredit the present by vaunting the past, but it is an intensely individual past – no-one is interested in other people's souvenirs. Souvenirs speak of events that are not repeatable but are reportable; they serve to authenticate the narrative in which the actor talks about the event. As a part of this they help to reduce a large and complex experience, like the Somme or the Western Desert, to a smaller and simpler scale of which one human can make some sense. They make public events private, and move history into the personal sphere, giving each person a purchase on what would otherwise be impersonal and bewildering experiences (Stewart 1984: 132–50). Souvenirs, then, are lost youth, lost friends, lost past happiness; they are the tears of things.

They are also something else, and the phrase just used, 'can make sense', was chosen deliberately. Souvenirs are intensely romantic in every way, and especially in the ways in which that idea is now often applied. The romantic view holds that everything, and especially everybody, has a place in the true organic wholeness which embraces human relationships, in the traditional continuity of past into present, in the landscape and the changing seasons. It asks us to believe that life is not fractured, confused and rootless but, on the contrary, suffused with grace and significance. It is no coincidence that in Europe generally, and especially in England, the romantic movement came to birth at the moment in the late eighteenth century when religion had begun to lose its hold over the thinking classes and when the new factories were manifesting the shape of things to come. It was this dislocation between things as they are and things as they ought to be which aroused the characteristically romantic emotions of alienation and despair. In terms of a concept, and nowhere more than in its mystical and metaphysical side, romanticism is about as convincing as a leaking sieve, but it unquestionably has a powerful hold over our deepest hopes and feelings; it shows life as we would wish it to be.

It is in these hopes and feelings that the souvenirs belong. They are an important part of our attempt to make sense of our personal histories, happy or unhappy, to create an essential personal and social self centred in its own unique life story, and to impose this vision on an alien world. They relate to the construction of a romantically integrated personal self, in which the objects are subordinated into a secondary role, and it is this which makes them, all too frequently, so depressing to curate and to display.

Objects of Desire: Fetishistic Collecting

An appropriate place to begin the discussion of the collecting mode presented under this title is the collection assembled by Sigmund Freud, firstly in his study and consulting room at 19 Berggasse in Vienna, and then, after 1938, in his house at Mansfield Gardens, London (see Plate 7). Freud's collection numbered some 1,900 pieces of Roman, Greek, Assyrian, Egyptian and Chinese antiquities, and the objects crowded the desk and cabinets in the two rooms where he principally worked. The collection, while still in Vienna, was described by Edmund Engelman in this way:

> antiquities filled every available spot in the room. I was overwhelmed by the masses of figurines which overflowed every surface. To the left of the door was a large bookcase covered with tall ancient statuettes. In the corner at the end of the wall facing these statuettes, was Freud's chair, almost hidden by the head of the couch . . . To the left and right of the door were glass show-cases filled with hundreds of antiquities. These were set up in several rows; every bit of cabinet space was filled . . . I was amazed by the unbelievable number of art objects.
> (Engelman 1976: 137–8)

Helga Jobst thought that Freud's office took on a museum-like appearance, and Peter Gay makes the point that: 'The first and overpowering impression that Freud's habitat makes on the visitor is the profusion of things . . . The sculptures have their assigned shelves and their glass cases, but they intrusively invade surfaces intended for other purposes: bookshelves, tops of cabinets, writing tables, even Freud's much used desk. The whole is an embarrassment of objects' (Gay 1976: 17). People who knew Freud well, like Ernest Jones (1955: 393), describe how he was in the habit of bringing new pieces to the dining room table, how before beginning work each day he would say 'Good morning' to a favourite Chinese figurine, how he would fondle a piece during the consultation with a patient (Spector 1975), and how he constantly rearranged the pieces in his rooms. Freud

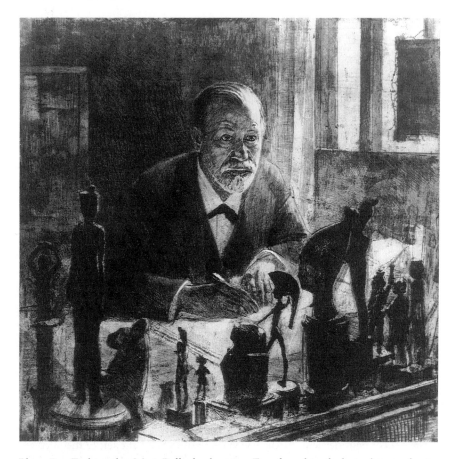

Plate 7.   Etching by Max Pollack showing Freud at his desk in his study, in
Vienna, 1914 (photo: Freud Museum, London).

himself has left us scant record of how he viewed the collection which clearly
meant so much to him, but there is one brief comment on collecting activity: 'The
core of paranoia is the detachment of the libido from objects. A reverse course is
taken by the collector who directs his surplus libido onto an inanimate object: a
love of things' (Freud 1908, quoted in Gamwell 1988). To this thought of Freud's
we shall return.

Freud is among the better documented members of a very large group of collectors
whose accumulations may be found in every large museum and many substantial
private houses in this country and who, as a type, run back into the Renaissance.
These accumulations include 'serious' collections, sometimes in the fine art and
antiquities fields, like those of Arundel (Ashmolean Museum 1986) or Townley
(Cook 1977) of classical marbles, and sometimes more mixed, like those of Joseph
Mayer (Gibson and Wright 1988) in Liverpool or the Tradescants and Sir Hans

Sloane (Brooks 1954), all of which stand at the beginnings of some of our most important national collections. Much of the material in all of these collections has always been valued for its perceived intrinsic, and therefore financial, quality, and has been taken correspondingly seriously by the museums which hold it. The famous collections, of course, represent merely the tip of the iceberg. Throughout the later seventeenth and eighteenth centuries and onwards to our own day, we hear of many collections both of art and of rarities, curiosities and *objets de virtue*, which did not survive the death of their owners.

This kind of collecting, especially when it concentrated upon curiosities and rarities, was the butt of much parody as the Enlightenment gathered momentum. Sir Charles Hanbury Williams, a friend of Sir Hans Sloane, wrote:

The stone whereby Goliath died,
Which cures the headache, well applied.
A whetstone, worn exceeding small,
Time used to whet his scythe withal.
The pigeon stuff'd, which Noah sent
To tell him when the water went.
A ring I've got of Samson's hair,
The same which Delilah did wear,
St Dunstan's tongs, which story shows
Did pinch the devil by the nose.
The very shaft, as you may see
Which Cupid shot at Anthony.

(Brooks 1954: 193)

The ponderous fun continues through the nineteenth century in places like the cartoons of *Punch*, where the slightly touched and essentially absurd collector can be mocked for his naive oblivion to all but his obsessions. This view of humour suggests two important things. Firstly, it shows, as humour can, a significant human trait which everybody shares (although some to a greater degree than others), and which like all such traits is double-edged, usually harmless but with some capacity for harm. Secondly, the official character of the humour suggests a wide tolerance of this kind of aberrant behaviour, of peculiarity kept within acceptable limits, which is a part of that broad charity towards eccentricity that is one of the more likeable characteristics of the English-speaking world.

Paralleling this socially-elevated collecting taste is the collecting mania which has gathered momentum across society through the course of this century, and now achieves the dimensions of a major social force. It has been calculated that one in every three Americans now collects something, and the proportion is unlikely to be very different for the United Kingdom and other parts of Europe. The range of collectables, to use the unlovely word which this activity has spawned, is endless. Most of it is twentieth-century material, much of it still in contemporary manufacture, which often does not fall within the regard of the traditional antiques collector, and which often, though by no means always, is relatively inexpensive, at least to begin with.

This kind of collecting has created its own world of clubs, large collectors' fairs, car boot sales and advertising material. It helps to support the hugely successful *Antiques Roadshow* which appears regularly at prime time on Sundays on BBC1, and which has now developed an associated magazine, *The Antiques Roadshow Collection*, described as 'compiled by experts, this 15-part magazine series will build into a unique reference book showing you how to identify things and estimate their value' (*Radio Times*, 5–11 January 1991, Midlands Edition: 17). It has proved a popular field for local radio. Jeff Owen's show, put on by BBC Radio Nottingham, 'has become a cornucopia of collectors. "We've had beer pump clips, Test Card music and stamp-hinges and are still on the look out for more" says Owen' (*Radio Times*, 1–7 December 1990, Midlands Edition: 70).

Among the specialist magazines devoted to this kind of collecting is *Miller's Magazine* (see Plate 8) founded in July 1991 by the firm who already publish *Miller's Antiques Price Guide* (founded 1979), *Miller's Collectables Price Guide*, and *Miller's Collectors Cars Price Guide*. *Miller's Magazine* has links with the *Antiques Road Show*, and tries to bridge the gap between those interested in 'antiques' and those who look for 'collectables', a distinction which revolves partly around the age of the piece, and partly around its perceived intrinsic merits, and is, in practice, difficult to pin down. Figure 4.2 gives an analysis of the contents of the first issue of the magazine, and this suggests that ceramics and furniture, traditional collectors' items, are still very popular, but that toys, bottles and boxes, and costume are the focus of growing attention.

Category	No. of pages	% of whole
General (Editorial, Competition, etc.)	10.75	13.1
Sale News	2.0	2.44
Ceramics	9.75	11.89
Furniture	20.5	25.00
Clocks, barometers, cameras	4.0	4.88
Silver	2.0	2.44
Musical boxes	2.0	2.44
Toys (inc. dolls and bears)	5.25	6.40
Costume (inc. embroidery and lace)	4.0	4.88
Treen	2.0	2.44
Cars	1.75	2.13
Garden furniture	2.0	2.44
Hearth equipment (fenders, fire dogs, etc.)	2.0	2.44
Lamp shades, etc.	2.0	2.44
Glass (decorative pieces and glasses)	2.0	2.44
Books	0.5	0.61
Metal Objects	1.0	1.22
Jewellery	2.0	2.44
Cigarette packs	2.0	2.44
Small boxes, marbles, ivories	1.5	1.83
Bottles and boxes	3.0	3.66
Total	82.0	100.00

Figure 4.2 Analysis of contents of first issue (1991) of *Miller's Magazine*

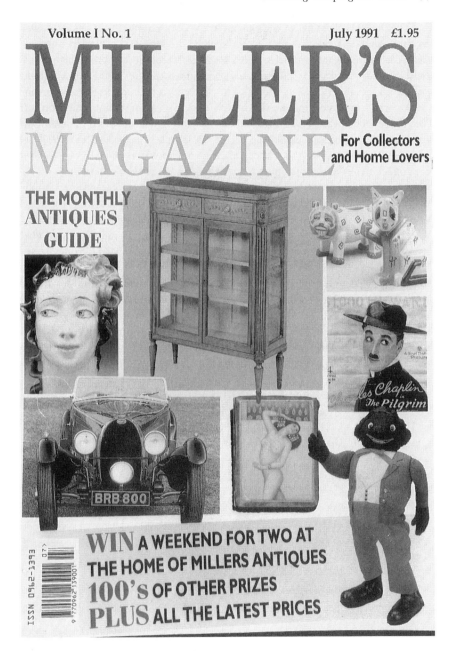

Plate 8.   Front cover of first issue of *Miller's Magazine for Collectors and Home Lovers* (photo: University of Leicester).

This kind of collecting, so widespread in the community that it clearly answers to a fundamental need, is beginning to be given the serious attention by museums which its social significance demands. In 1989 Stevenage Museum (Figure 4.3) held an exhibition called *Collectamania*, which featured the 'weird and wonderful collections of fifteen local residents'. The collections included cameras, souvenir bookmarks, wargames and model buses (Purkis, personal communication). In May–June 1990 Walsall Museum, under the able guidance of Peter Jenkinson, mounted a new kind of exhibition called *The People's Show* (Mullen 1991) (see Plate 9). Material for display was recruited by a flyer which said: 'We are looking for collections by Walsall people for a new exhibition at Walsall Museum and Art Gallery called *The People's Show*. If you collect anything as an interest or a hobby, or simply as decoration in your home, we would like to hear from you.' The range of material offered was characteristically wide and deep. It included collections of egg cups, pottery frogs, pin-on badges, Madonna posters and similar items, football shirts worn by famous players, ties, and international travel sick bags from aircraft.

Those who offered their collections for display were contacted and interviewed in their homes, with their collections, using a standard questionnaire as a frame-work for the discussion (Harbidge, personal communication). The questions were intended to enable the collectors to think about their own collections in some depth, and it appeared that this was something which most of them had not pre-viously attempted. The questions hoped to discover what was collected, when it was acquired and how, where it was kept, and why the collectors carried out their activity at all, in order to discover something about the nature of collecting and of being a collector. The results have not yet been fully absorbed, but some interesting perspectives are already emerging.

The collections are usually organized and stored according to a clear rationale, which relates in part to resources, but in part to individual ideas about what goes with what, which would not necessarily be those which would occur to museum workers: relationship to events in the owner's life seems to be a favourite ordering principle, showing how this kind of deliberate collecting overlaps with the souvenir mode already discussed. The way in which people came gradually to associate their collection with their personal identity is also interesting. The Frog Collector's identity came from friends, who decided to add to the collection, and the Scarf Collector was prompted by the idea of the exhibition itself to consider herself a collector. The Greetings Card Collector said: 'It was only when I got them out (after six years) and realised how many there were I thought gosh! you know, I didn't realise I'd started to collect this lot, and then I thought I am a collector now, I'll just carry on.'

What links the 'gentleman collectors' like Sloane and Freud with their humbler cousins of the cigarette cards and printed tee-shirts is partly the obsessive nature of the act of collection, and partly the lack of an intellectual rationale by which the material and its acquisition was informed. This last point needs elaboration since it would probably have been hotly disputed by some of the collectors themselves, particularly the earlier gentlemen who had inherited the Renaissance world-view of the collection as cosmos in miniature. It is true that the art collections could be

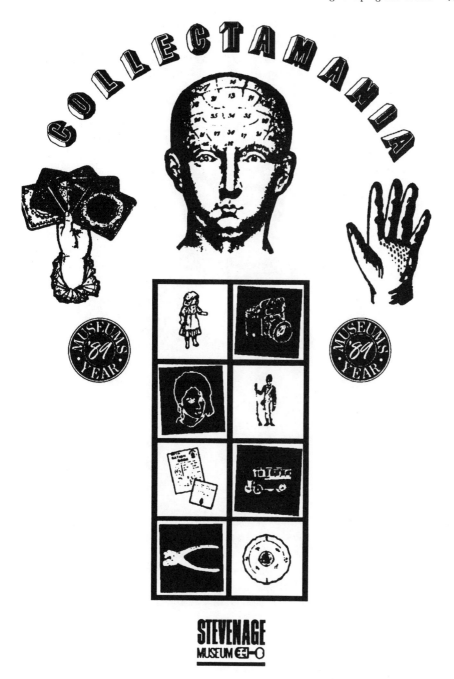

Figure 4.3 Advertisement for *Collectamania* exhibition, Stevenage Museum.
(Reproduced with the permission of Stevenage Museum)

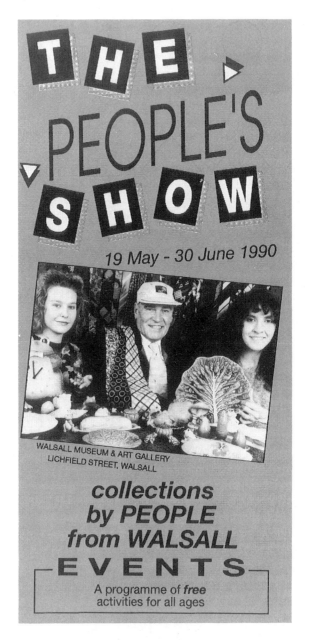

Plate 9.   Poster advertising *The People's Show* at Walsall Museum and Art Gallery, 1990 (photo: University of Leicester).

justified by reference to what we would call aesthetic quality, that the curiosities and rarities were held to demonstrate the hierarchies of the world, and that cigarette cards and so on exist in recognized sets which the collector aims to complete. But it is also true that the sets have no rhyme or reason outside the covers of the album, and that the pictures and *objets d'art* were acquired through a passionate desire to possess such objects of connoisseurship. The comic verse already quoted shows how far into decay the Renaissance tradition had come by the 1740s; and yet curiosity collections continued to be made and are still to this day. It is difficult to draw any useful conceptual distinction between Queen Elizabeth I's riding boots which figure in the Tradescant Collection, and Pélé's football shirt which is the pride of the collection of George Nicholls of Walsall. It seems that the personality of the collector, in a very particular sense, is the mainspring of this kind of collecting activity and runs beneath much collection-forming which is ostensibly presented in a more intellectual, dignified and objective light.

Art, in its uncanny way, can make manifest a collector's personality, as the portrait of Joseph Mayer painted about 1840 by William Daniels shows. Mayer sits in his study at 20 Clarence Terrace, Liverpool. He is seated in a throne-like chair in the Gothic taste, gazing reflectively at the Wedgwood urn he holds in his hand, while light falls on Greek and Etruscan antiquities set out on the table and touches marbles and paintings further back in the room. The collection is not organized, merely arranged by its owner in what seemed to be its best advantage; and indeed it seems to have grown up around him as an extension of his physical person in the sense we have already discussed. This notion touches the heart of the matter. This kind of collection is made by people whose imaginations identify with the objects which they desire. Powerful emotions are aroused by the objects which the objects seem to return, stimulating a need to gather more and more of the same kind. The urge is to samples, and as many as possible, rather than to examples – a notion we shall return to when we consider systematic collection. The whole process is a deployment of the possessive self, a strategy of desire, and this is part of the reason why this mode of collecting is described as fetishistic.

This is in many ways an unfortunate or even unpleasant term, but it is now so embedded in the literature that to avoid it would create more problems than it solves, so it will be used here on the understanding that nothing inherently pejorative is intended. A random dip into fairly recent writings in the related fields of literary and linguistic theory, material culture and museum studies begins to show us how the word is used. Terry Eagleton in his *Literary Theory: An Introduction*, published in 1983, discussed the nature of society in early industrial Britain. He says: 'In England, a crassly Philistine Utilitarianism was rapidly becoming the dominant ideology of the industrial middle class, fetishing fact, reducing human relations to market exchanges, and dismissing art as unprofitable ornamentation' (Eagleton 1983: 19). Two pages on, he continues: 'Art was extricated from the material practices, social relations and ideological meanings in which it is always caught up, and raised to the status of a solitary fetish' (1983: 21). Daniel Miller, in his 1987 discussion of material culture and modern mass consumption, speaks of how: 'An approach to modern society which focuses on the material object always invites the risk of appearing fetishistic, that is of ignoring or masking actual social relations through its concern with the object per se' (Miller 1987: 3). In the first of the Leicester University Museum Studies International Conference series, Peter Gathercole gave a paper entitled 'The fetishism of artefacts' where he explored the implications of the display of the Enigma Coding machine (Gathercole, 1989).

'Fetish' and fetishism have recently come into museum studies from the broader field of cultural investigation. Psychologists, of course, need the two words to describe a particular form of sexual orientation. Freud (1977) described the fetish as part of the body separated from the whole, or an object substituted for a bodily part, which then, like underwear, becomes the focus of sexual gratification in its own right. This, presumably, is linked to his remark (see p. 74) about the collector who directs his surplus libido on to an inanimate object. (Freud's more general psychological theories are not relevant to this discussion – see Eysenck 1991). The terms seem to have first been popularized by Richard von Kraft-Ebbing (1894), though it had earlier been used by Binet (1887) who himself picked it up from his readings of Rousseau, Darwin and contemporary anthropologists. Ellen makes the point that, psychologically speaking, fetishism is generally considered to be highly gender-specific and culture-bound, being rare in women, and although not restricted to European-based societies, not well documented elsewhere (Ellen 1988: 218). This may throw some interesting light on the fact that collecting, in the sense used here, is also essentially a European phenomenon, and has in the past been largely limited to men, although now is shared roughly between the sexes, perhaps another link in the network of cross-gender culture characteristic of post-modern times. It is, needless to say, this specifically sexual gloss, and of potentially aberrant sexuality at that, which has given a useful word an uncomfortable feel, but without pushing the argument too far, the notion does help to give us an understanding of the fierce energy which can be directed towards collection-making.

The anthropological literature, both that drawn upon by the early psychologists and of later writers, uses the word rather differently. The standard reference works trace the word back to the Portuguese *feiticos*, meaning 'a charm', which was used in the fifteenth century to describe contemporary Christian relics, rosaries and holy medals. When they arrived on the African coast later in the same century, the Portuguese naturally applied the word to the local wooden figures, stones and so on which were regarded as the residence of spirits, and W. Bosman in his *Description of Guinea* of 1705 uses the word in this connection. It is worth noting in passing that no racial or colour prejudice was involved: the devout Portuguese used the same word indiscriminately for religious objects regardless of origin, in the same way that contemporary descriptions of African settlements use an ordinary tone equally appropriate to the description of European towns. More to the purpose here, *feitico* also means 'made by man' and carries the idea of something 'artful' or 'magically active'. It was from this web of connections that the anthropologists appropriated the word and used it to describe material objects which were worshipped for their magical powers, believed to be inherent rather than deriving from an indwelling god or spirit. This uncovers more of the nature of fetishic collections and collection-making. Such collections are often very private, or rather, sometimes the owner suffers a degree of tension between his urge for privacy and his desire to exhibit his private universe to others. Mayer makes this point well: originally his material was in a series of private homes open only to close friends, but as it grew in size and fame Mayer was moved to open his own museum, originally called the Egyptian Museum, at 8 Colquitt Street, Liverpool (Gibson and Wright 1988).

We can take the analysis a stage further by reminding ourselves of the implications of that fact that the fetish concept was taken over not only by the anthropologists and psychologists, but also by the political scientists. In a passage of *Das Capital* famed for its obscurity, Marx says:

> It is a definite social relation between men, that assumes, in their eyes, that fantastic form of a relation between things. In order, therefore, to find an analogy, we must have recourse to the mist-enveloped regions of the religious world. In that world the productions of the human brain appear as independent being endowed with life, and entering into relation both with one another and the human race. So it is the world of commodities with the products of men's hands. This I call the Fetishism which attaches itself to the products of labour, so soon as they are produced as commodities, and which is therefore inseparable from the production of commodities.
>
> (Marx 1906: 203)

This seems to mean that through the operation of the capitalist system, the commodities which people produce come to have a life of their own, irrespective of their makers, the circumstances of their manufacture, or the personal relationships which all this involves. These commodities-endowed-with-life then operate in an independent fashion, detached from direct social relationships, and capable themselves of being the partner in a relationship with humans, an operation which Marx saw as a distortion of the proper relation between men and goods, an aberrant evil typical of mass production society.

Leaving on one side the specific argument about the extent to which Marx was right in his analysis of modern capitalist society and of the artefacts which are part and parcel of it (but see Miller 1987), his extended notion of the nature of fetishes gives us an important clue to the nature of the collections which we are considering, and the kind of response which it is possible to make to them in a museum (or anywhere else). These collections are detached from any context, they are removed from the sphere of actual social relationships with all the tensions, efforts of understanding and acts of persuasion which these imply. This detachment is, indeed, a very substantial part of the attraction for their collectors, who use them to create a private universe, but its sterility gives to the material that peculiarly lifeless quality which all curators recognize with a sinking heart. The detachment of fetish collections explains why they have so seldom been put on display: unless the collection contains objects deemed to be of intrinsic merit, usually in the art fields, or of historic interest, usually in relation to the early history of the museum, the collection languishes from decade to decade undisturbed.

The fetishistic nature lies in the relationship between the objects and their collector, in which the collection plays the crucial role in defining the personality of the collector, who maintains a possessive but worshipful attitude towards his objects. Such collections and their collectors are at the opposite pole to the souvenirs discussed earlier. Here the subject is subordinated to the objects, and it is to the objects that the burden of creating a romantic wholeness is transferred.

Although souvenirs and fetishistic collections stand at opposite ends of the romantic pole in terms of the ways in which their human subject relates to them, as is so often true, there is a point where opposite ends meet. Both are part of an attempt to create a satisfactory private universe, and both do this by trying to lift objects away from the web of social relationships, to deny process and to freeze time. In museums, therefore, they are perceived as dissociated and static, floating in a kind of purposeless limbo. Very different is the way in which we appreciate what I shall call the systematic collections.

Systematic Collecting

Historically, this kind of collecting can be traced back at least into the Renaissance, but it comes into its own in what we perceive as its classic phase as part of the scientific revolution of the late seventeenth century with the work of the pioneers of the Royal Society, and their successors during the eighteenth and nineteenth centuries, and because this discussion is concerned with intentions and implications rather than with historical analysis, we shall concentrate upon the characteristics of this classic mode. It is interesting to see how the word 'classic' comes to mind as the natural term for this collecting mode, as if it were the benchmark against which other kinds of collecting can be judged. For well over two centuries systematic collecting, both inside and outside museums, has in all its different manifestations in the various disciplines been accorded an intellectual primacy, which seems to derive from its apparent capacity to demonstrate understanding rather than feeling, and so to extend our control of the world.

The development of systematic collecting is an intrinsic part of the development of the natural sciences. 'Systematics' is a term drawn from biology, botany and geology where it means the practice of taxonomy, the ability to compare and contrast collected specimens in order to distinguish the fine detail which divides one species from another, and so carry out identifications. All work in the natural sciences, and in related human fields like agriculture and pest control, depends finally on our ability to tell one kind of life from another and to place any example in its correct place in the web of the natural world: here rests the significance of the massive taxonomical collections held by the Natural History Museum and other museums, by means of which the natural world is mapped out and classified into its nest-of-boxes system of phyla, genera and species, made manifest by exhibitions like that in the University Natural History Museum, Cambridge.

However, the serpent of knowledge is not absent from this natural Eden. As with all material objects, the perceived understanding which natural history specimens embody cannot be detached from the object itself, but only discussed with reference to it in concrete terms; in semiotic language, as we have seen, this would be expressed by saying that in the natural history specimen (as in all objects), signified and signifier combine. Similarly, the relationship of the scientist to the natural world is not a simple one. Specimens are selected for collections on the strength of their supposed 'typicality' or their 'departure from the norm' so that they may act as referents, a process which is clearly circular and self-supporting. It is justified scientifically on the grounds that, put crudely, it seems to work – that the notions of typicality and norm do square with 'objective' or 'natural' reality in the sense that decisions made on this basis do not normally backfire. However, as we have seen (p. 5–6), collected specimens have become artefacts in that the act of selection turns them into man-made products, and once they have entered our world they become part of the relationships which we construct for them and which, like all our social constructs, we are more prone to admire than criticize. This becomes painfully obvious when some new start of perception disrupts the careful web of relationships and involves realignment in the systems, as is happening at present with new ideas about how species evolve and how this relates to the idea of 'norms'.

The nature of systematic activity may be unravelled a little further by remembering that the concept of 'natural kind' is essentially no different to the categories that we apply to people, for both conceptualize groups of related objects as things, and this 'thingyness' involves the acceptance that the categories have some kind of objective existence of their own, the acceptance of the fiction that, for example, 'cousinhood' or 'buttercupness' exist as external realities. There is, in fact, a distinct human tendency to imagine classification systems in terms of human relationships, and a glance at any textbook will show how the (European) human family paradigm underlies our ideas about the relationship of animal groups or, say, known languages. But the matter goes further than this. As Ellen has pointed out (1988: 221), even entire classifications acquire a false objectiveness through our insistence on a model of two-dimensional multi-levelled hierarchies, and by turning abstractions into things we compound the illusion that categories exist independently of other categories.

These same principles of systematic classification have been brought to bear on human history objects, using the phrase in its ordinary sense, and this was done first, in wholly deliberate style, by Pitt Rivers and the collections which he created. Pitt Rivers believed two fundamental principles: first, that material culture reveals humankind's essential nature and development; and second, that the progress of artefactual development, and so of human nature, follows broadly Darwinian principles, so that types developed one from another according to a process of selection which modified their forms. The addition to this of diffusionist ideas about the spread of artefacts across the globe meant that the whole structure could be knitted together into a kind of three-dimensional lattice-work in which there might be a place for everything.

Pitt Rivers presented his views in three lectures on 'Primitive Warfare' at the United Service Institute in 1867, 1868 and 1869, and offered a general statement of them in *The Evolution of Culture* published in 1875. As far as possible, the material in his own collections, and in the Pitt Rivers Museum, was arranged to demonstrate these principles, but this fell short of Pitt Rivers' ideal museum which would take the form of a rotunda building arranged in concentric circles which would show the major human phases of artefactual evolution, with the innermost circle for the Palaeolithic, the next for the Neolithic, and so on (see Plate 10). The rotunda would also be divided into wedges, so that 'separate angles of the circle might be appropriated to geographical areas' and allied civilizations would 'occupy adjacent angles within the same concentric ring' (Chapman 1986: 41, quoting Pitt Rivers; see also Chapman 1991). So would the conceptual lattice-work be made museum flesh.

The detail of Pitt Rivers' views about material culture has now been discredited, but this does not touch the fundamental idea which informed those views, and which has been immensely influential in most areas of work in the material culture of human history. In spite of all kinds of recent developments in dating, scientific characterization and interpretation, typology, archaeology's equivalent to taxonomy, remains crucial to our efforts to understand the past. The same is true of the ordering of material like chairs, trade tools and fire engines into groups and sequences. More fundamentally, the idea of classification and sequence now has so powerful a hold over our intellectual imaginations that we gear a great deal of effort towards

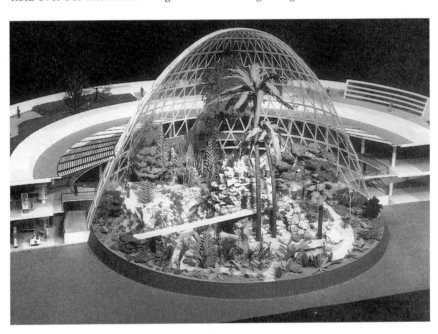

Plate 10.   'The Anthropological Rotunda' – the 1960s proposal for a new Pitt Rivers Museum in Oxford which would carry out the spirit of Pitt River's own hopes. This scheme was never built (photo: Pitt Rivers Museum, Oxford).

the notion of material lattice-works of perceived meaning. Archaeological excavations are organized in order to fill out blank areas in the 'pattern of the past', anthropological expeditions are planned to do the same for the present, and historical material is deliberately assembled in a significant relationship in order to create period rooms, like those at York Castle Museum. Even in Fine Art, that most anarchic of the museum disciplines, pictures are displayed in organized schools and periods. The key words here are 'organized', 'planned' and 'assembled', for they embody the key assumptions in the action of systematic collection across the disciplines, and it is to these that we must now turn.

Systematic collection depends upon principles of organization, which are perceived to have an external reality beyond the specific material under consideration, and are held to derive from general principles deduced from the broad mass of kindred material through the operation of observation and reason; these general principles form part of our ideas about the nature of the physical world and the nature of ourselves. Systematic collecting, therefore, works not by the accumulation of samples, as fetishistic collecting does, but by the selection of examples intended to stand for all the others of their kind and to complete a set, to 'fill in a gap in the collections' as the phrase so often upon curators' lips has it. The emphasis is upon classification, in which specimens (a revealing word) are extracted from their context and put into relationships created by seriality. This is achieved by defining set limits which apparently arise from the material. Collecting is usually a positive intellectual act designed to demonstrate a point. The physical arrangement of the finds sets out in detail the creation of serial relationships, and the manipulation implicit in all this is intended to convince or to impose, to create a second and revealing context, and to encourage a cast of mind.

From this emerges a fundamental difference between the systematic collections and the other two modes discussed earlier. Systematics draw a viewer into their frame. They presuppose a two-way relationship between the collection, which has something public (not private) to say, and the audience, who may have something to learn or to disagree with. This is one of the two reasons why curators generally give the lion's share of their blessings, and of their exhibition space, to this kind of collection. The second reason is implicit in the nature of this kind of collecting. It is conceived as display; it requires organized space in which to demonstrate its serial relationships. If museum galleries and glass show-cases had not existed, it would have been necessary to invent them; but, of course, museums as the public institutions which we know, and serial collecting, more or less grew up together, uniting to demonstrate the laying-out of material knowledge.

Hegel's concept of 'objectification' as developed by Miller may help us here. Hegel overcame the ancient dualism which separates subject and object, or humankind and the whole external world, and which must result in either the subordination of the object to a romantic vision of the essential self, as with souvenirs, or the subordination of the subject to romanticized objects, as with fetish collections: both are static, sterile, and take us nowhere. 'Objectification' is meant to describe the dual process by means of which a subject externalizes itself in a creative act of differentiation, and in return reappropriates this externalization through an act (of) sublation' (Miller 1987: 28). Put rather crudely, this means that the human person as subject creates from within himself an entity of whatever kind – including material artefacts – which assumes an external existence as an object, but then takes back this creation to use it as part of the next burst of creative activity. In this way, the gulf between subject and object is healed and neither is elevated at the other's expense. The essence of the link is relationship; that relationship is always in process, and process is always bringing about change.

This helps us to understand the nature of systematic collections in all the museum disciplines. They are formed by the imposition of ideas of classification and seriality on the external world, but the world itself has, one way or another, given rise to these ideas. However, this is a process without beginning or end. No-one starts to form or to display a collection without inheriting past process, and each collection or display in place contributes its mite to the dynamics of change. The whole continuous reconstruction is part of the concrete appreciation of the world, with all its awkwardness and dislocation, and each actor in the story can be involved in the struggle.

This discussion has tried to develop ideas about the nature of collections as a particular area of social experience. It has suggested that ideas current in the broad field of cultural theory may help us, and they have turned out to show us three common collecting modes: two at either pole, frozen and static, and the third engaging itself to bridge the gap. It must be stressed, of course, that many individual collectors and collections show elements of more than one mode, either at the same time or reflecting successive phases of activity and material which was a souvenir for one person will be an object of desire for another, and may finally become part of a systematic museum display.

All the material now in museums has arrived there as a result of the collecting activity described in Chapter 3, structured in one or another (or a combination) of the modes described in this chapter. We have seen that collections are the extended selves of their collectors, and with life goes the hope of immortality. Collections, being material, can outlive us, but through them we too can be turned into enduring things. The arena where this translation takes place is the established museum, but here, characteristically, the individual motives which construct the world of the collection are played down, and in their place we are presented with the public and social side of knowledge. It is to museums and their role in the development of this knowledge that we must now turn.

5 Museums: the Intellectual Rationale

And so you have in small compass a model of the universe made private.
(Francis Bacon, quoted in Impey and MacGregor 1985: 1)

The people's museum should be much more than a house of specimens in glass cases. It should be a house full of ideas, arranged with the strictest attention to system.
(George Brown Goode, Director of United States National Museum, 1891)

The main purpose of ethnological collections should be the dissemination of the fact that civilization is not something absolute, but that it is relative, and that our ideas and conceptions are true only so far as our civilization allows.
(Franz Boas, quoted in Stocking 1974: 61)

Introduction

The museums we see around us, in Europe and throughout the globe, did not spring ready-made from the earth like men from dragons' teeth, but have a long and complex history behind them which shapes what they are today. Museums and their collections have always been public institutions, not necessarily in the sense that they have always been open to the public, although the history of access is an important part of the whole, but in the sense that they embody and shape public perceptions of what is valuable and important at each period of their existence. Museums and their collections are part of the history and philosophy of knowledge in both the humanities and the sciences, and this history and philosophy is in part also created by them. Much of this creation is an explicit, self-conscious activity, 'public' in sense just described, and publicly endorsed as confirming prestige upon its practitioners. The process of collecting possesses its dark twin, its inward and private side as we have seen, but here we are concerned with a world working in the sunlight of presentable motives and intellectual and aesthetic rationales. This chapter will pick out the main museological themes as they have succeeded each other chronologically, and try to show the links between them, and to suggest how the ideas which they express, and the buildings with which they are connected, survive to influence contemporary museums, and to form part of the mental furniture of us all.

A framework for understanding the genesis and history of museums has been set out in Figure 5.1. It is clear that institutionalized collecting in various modes – as 'hoards', grave goods and accumulations of all kinds – is an activity with its communal and psychic roots deep in the prehistory of European society, and can be traced in detail through the centuries of later prehistory in the Iron and Bronze

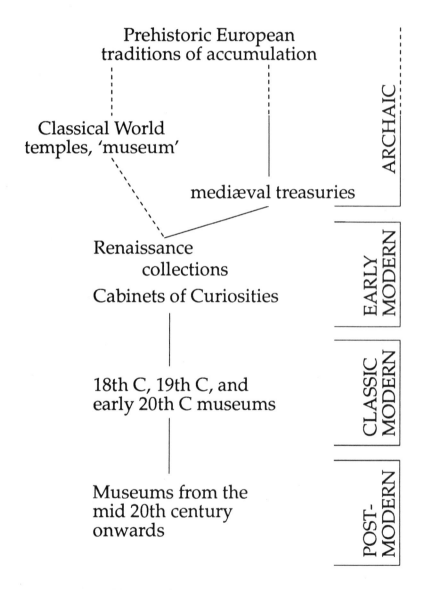

Figure 5.1 Genesis and history of museums

Ages back at least to the Neolithic communities of around 3000 bc with their hoards of stone and flint axes (Bradley 1990; Pearce 1983). By the later Iron Age this, in some places, is taking the form of accumulation connected with temple sites, of which an important manifestation is the quantity of bronze material collected as dedications in the Greek temples and treasuries of the sixth century BC (Snodgrass 1980). The notion of temples, and then Christian churches, as repositories was taken for granted throughout the classical world, and when this world succumbed to the northern barbarians around AD 400 they added to it ancient ideas of hoarding and depositing treasure, so generating a constellation of treasure houses across Europe, some belonging to churches and religious houses, and others, in a quasi-religious way, to royal and princely families. All of this, though of very great interest in its own right, stands as the archaic prologue to the origins of museums as they are understood in this book, but it contributed powerful ideas about objects as treasure, objects as relics connecting those alive with the mighty dead, objects as dedications, and accumulation as a way of manipulating social surplus, all of which have shaped our thinking about the nature of museums.

This was the immediate inheritance of the Renaissance princes and their associates, first of Italy and then of Europe north of the Alps, who inaugurated the collection-holding mechanisms of the new age which can be crudely lumped together under the term 'museum', and which form the starting point for this analysis. By the beginning of the eighteenth century the overarching modernist models developed in the preceding three centuries had modulated into what can be called the classical period of modern intellectual activity and institution-creation which lasted, with some internal adjustments, until the early to mid twentieth century. Thereafter, contemporary museums, like the world of which they are a part, have been endeavouring to come to terms with the growing momentum of post-modern ideas. One point needs heavy stressing. Collecting inside and outside museums is a very human activity and such activities do not reflect intellectual movements in a direct fashion. Modes of collection, which belong in spirit with early phases of the history of collecting, continue to be the mainspring of some collecting activity up to and including the present day. These are not merely occasional fossils; they are living traditions flourishing fruitfully alongside newer approaches, and the world of museums and collections would be the poorer without them.

Curiosity: Princes and Cabinets

The early origins of museums and the 'cabinet of curiosities' idea has aroused a surprising amount of interest in recent years, and it is to this body of literature that the enquirer is directed for historical detail about the collecting activities of the Medici (Hooper-Greenhill 1992 and references there), the other Italian princes, prelates and businessmen from roughly 1450 to 1700 (Pomian 1990), and their equivalents in Northern Europe (Impey and MacGregor 1985). Other writers have considered the collecting activities of the English kings and lords (Wilks 1989), and men of the middling sort like the Tradescants (MacGregor 1983),

Ashmole (Hunter 1983), Sloane (Brooks 1954), Thoresby (Brears 1989) and the men of the Royal Society.

What can be said straight away is that by about 1650 or a little sooner, collecting had become the widespread mania which remains its characteristic up to the present day, a fact which reflects both the Renaissance stress on the importance of the individual, and the development of contemporary early capitalism with which it went hand in hand. It is no accident, either, that the museum as an institution gathers momentum in a rising curve which corresponds to the declining curve of the intellectual and institutional power of religion to provide adequate narratives, and their physical depositories: museums rose steadily through to the early nineteenth century as churches declined. A steady state was reached through the later part of the nineteenth century, and then the churches declined again. We are not, therefore, surprised to realize that the principles which formed this early modern collecting rest in the boundary land between theology and what a later age will call science.

A number of typical words accompanied this new collecting strategy. The curious man, according to Antoine Furetière's *Dictionnaire Universale* published posthumously in 1690, was one who

> wishes to know and learn everything. When those who have a thirst for learning and desire to look at the treasures of art and nature are described as having an *Inquiring Mind (curieux)* it is meant as a compliment. He who has travelled throughout Europe, and has perused every fine and rare book has an *Inquiring Mind (est un curieux)*. Fine experiments and discoveries are the work of a *keen (curieux)* Chemist. He who has gathered together the very rarest, most beautiful and most extraordinary works of art and nature is an ENTHUSIAST *(un curieux)*. There are book, medal, print, paintings, flower, shell, antiquities and natural objects *enthusiasts (curieux)*.
>
> The rarities which are collected or remarked by the *enthusiast (curieux)* are also described as *curiosities (curieux)*. This book is a *curiosity (curieux)*, that is, rare, or contains many singular things, unknown to many. This secret is *curious (curieux)*. This experiment, this comment is *curious (curieux)*. This man's museum is most *curious (curieux)*, full of *curiosities (choses curieuses)*.
>
> (Quoted in Pomian 1990: 55)

As we can see, the material in which he (it was usually he) was interested in became 'curiosities', and the assemblage a 'cabinet of curiosities' in English, or *Wunderkammer*, 'Wonder-Room' in German. Paralleling the curious man was the *amateur*, usually intended to reflect a love of the fine arts rather than objects used for study (Pomian 1990: 54), and in German, what he possessed was a *Kunstkammer* (although these contained more than what we would call 'fine art'). 'Studio', 'repository', 'depository' and 'theatre' were all also used at different times and places to describe the spaces in which the art and the curiosities were housed, and so were the two words which alone have survived to the present day, *galleria* and *musaeum*. 'Gallery' is a relatively simple word which refers to the long, narrow room, originally more-or-less a corridor, then fashionable throughout the courts of Europe which could be used as a meeting ground and social space, and which was ideally suited for the display of pictures. *Musaeum* has a more complex history and etymology.

Originally *musaeum* had two definitions, both very familiar: in general a place consecrated to the nine muses, goddesses of poetry, music and the liberal arts; and in particular the name given to a learned institution in late Classical Alexandria, the exact nature of which is obscure and which may or may not have been linked with the great Library of legendary fame (but see Canfora 1990). Neither of these source meanings seem to have had anything specifically to do with the collecting or housing of material and, in fact, until well on into the eighteenth century, the word 'museum' could mean not only a physical institution holding collections, but also the principle behind an organizing cast of mind. As Findlen has put it: 'in its crystallization as a category which incorporated and ultimately unified a variety of – from our own perspective – seemingly disparate activities, the museum was indeed a central organizing principle for cultural activity by the late sixteenth century. It was a conceptual system through which collectors interpreted and explored the world they inhabited' (Findlen 1989: 61).

The word 'museum' seems to have triumphed eventually over all the possible terms partly through the cachet supplied by its classical past, but chiefly because (again as a result of this classical dimension) it carried liberal, humanist and conceptual possibilities through which the world surrounding man and his place in it might be understood. The idea of the museum was a fitting metaphor for the mentality of the age, and its translation into collecting strategies could demonstrate the humanist project and offer a means to fulfil the social demands of prestige and display.

The nature of this mentality and its collecting strategies can best be demonstrated by contemporary views. As we have already seen, art collections right from the beginning had something of a specialized vocabulary of their own, and matched this with a special outlook: pictures have always tended to be different. The set of guidelines drawn up by Gabriel Kaltemarcht in 1587 for the founding of an art collection, addressed to Christian I of Saxony, which seeks to reconcile art and iconoclastic Lutheran dogma and to identify important artists, shows us how art collecting was regarded (Gutfleisch and Menzhausen 1989). The *Kunstkammer* would have other material beside pictures and sculptures, but:

> The best adornment and treasure of a prince and sovereign includes not only and above all orthodox religion, faithful subjects and sufficient money, but also his possession of magnificent munitions and military equipment, of a glorious library and book collection, of artful sculptures and paintings. In this way he earns immortal praise both from friend and foe, from the learned and the ignorant, from artists and art lovers.
>
> (Gutfleisch and Menzhausen 1989: 20)

Princely picture collections were meant to celebrate the power and wisdom of the prince, and to dazzle courtiers and visitors with a tangible show of his splendour. In the seventeenth century the Emperor Rudolf II's collection formed an iconographic programme which showed the Emperor as the centre of a harmonious microcosm, and the Antiquarium of Albert V of Bavaria featured portraits of the ancient great whose virtues the prince claimed as his inheritance (Duncan and Wallach 1980: 455). To this end, the pictures were arranged in suitable groups, sometimes made to cover an entire wall to give a tapestry-like effect, and often cut down or enlarged to fit in.

Appreciation of art was inextricably bound up with appreciation of the antique and hence, right from the mid fifteenth century, with an interest in discovering and collecting classical marbles. Important collections were assembled at the Vatican and in Florence, among other places (Haskel and Penny 1981), where they were seen by men like Thomas Howard, Earl of Arundel who was inspired to form his own collection, now largely in the Ashmolean (Haynes 1975). Arundel was one of a group of English art collectors in the early decades of the seventeenth century which included Henry, Prince of Wales, his brother Charles I, and the Earls of Somerset, Worcester and Southampton, as well as many others (Wilks 1989). They stand at the head of the English tradition of connoisseurship and taste.

The kind of material which the collections of curiosities held is shown by John Evelyn's description, written in 1645, of the Ruzzini Collection in Venice, which is worth quoting at some length:

> On *Michaelmas* day I went with my *Lord Mowbray* (eldest son to the *Earle of Arundell* & a most worthy Person) to see the Collection of a Noble *Venetian* Signor *Rugini*: he has a stately Palace, richly furnish'd, with statues, heads of the *Roman Empp*, which are all plac'd in an ample roome: In the next was a Cabinet of *Medals* both *Latine & Greeke*, with divers curious shells, & two faire *Pearles* in 2 of them: but above all, he abounded in things petrified, Walnuts, Eggs, in which the *Yealk* rattl'd, a Peare, a piece of beefe, with the bones in it; an whole hedg-hog, a plaice on a Wooden Trencher turned into Stone, & very perfect: Charcoale, a morsel of *Cork*, yet retaining its levitie, Sponges, Gutts & a piece of Taffity: Part rolld up, with innumerable more; In another Cabinet, sustained by 12 pillars of oriental *Achat*, & raild about with Chrystal, he shew'd us severall noble Intaglias, of *Achat*, especially a *Tiberius's* head, & a Woman in a Bath with her dog: Some rare *Cornelians*, *Onixes*, *Chrystals* &c in one of which was a drop of Water not Congeal'd but plainly moving up & down as it was [shaken]: but above all was a *Diamond* which had growing in it a very faire *Rubie*; then he shew'd us divers pieces of *Amber* wherein were several *Insects* intomb'd, in particular one cut like an heart, that contain'd [in] it a *Salamander*, without the least defect; & many curious pieces of Mosaic: The fabrique of this Cabinet was very ingenious thick set with *Achats*, *Turcoies*, and other precious stones, in the midst of which a *dog* in stone scratching his Eare, very rarely cut, & Antique, & comparable to the greatest Curiositie I had ever seene of that kind, for the accuratenesse of the work: The next chamber had a Bedstead all inlayd with *Achats*, *Chrystals*, *Cornelians*, *Lazuli* &c, esteemed worth 16000 Crounes.

(Quoted in Pomian 1990: 71)

This was a famous collection but its range of material, historical, artistic and natural, is very characteristic and so is the enthusiasm with which Evelyn viewed the assemblage.

Collections like this were usually organized according to what were (and in many ways still are) regarded as fundamental distinctions, and these formed the basis upon which the catalogues, which most collections possessed, were arranged. Schultz (1990) has described four key texts – of which that by Quiccheberg appeared in 1565 and may be described as the earliest museological tract – which set out the correct system of museum classification as it was seen from the mid sixteenth to the early eighteenth century. Quiccheberg identified five main classes of collection which relate to the whole universe: paintings and sacred objects; objects made of inorganic material; organic materials representing the three realms of earth, water and air; artefacts; and material glorifying the founder. It is astonishing how closely this mirrors both the kinds of material and its basic groupings still usual in museums (fine art, applied art, natural history, historical material) and the hierarchy of prestige which the different main groups still enjoy.

In the introduction to his catalogue, published in 1656, John Tradescant (see Plate 11) makes a simpler distinction between *natural* and *artificial* (man-made) material:

> Now for the *materialls* themselves I reduce them into two sorts; one *Naturall*, of which some are more familiarly known and named amongst us, as divers sorts of Birds, foure-footed Beasts and Fishes, to whom I have given usual *English* names. Others are lesse familiar, and as yet unfitted with apt *English* termes, as the shell-Creatures, Insects, Mineralls, Outlandish-Fruits, And the like, which are part of the *Materia Medica*; (Encroachers upon that faculty, may try how they can crack such shells). The other sort is *Artificialls*, as Utensills, Householdstuffe, Habits, Instruments of Warre used by several Nations, rare curiosities of Art, etc. These are also expressed in *English* (saving the Coynes, which would vary but little if Translated) for the ready satisfying whomsoever may desire a view thereof.
>
> (Tradescant 1656: a2–a3)

These curious collections were conceived as making manifest the existing harmonies of the universe, as acting as microcosms of universal nature, the assembling and contemplating of which was at once an act of discovery and definition and a mystical exercise. The collecting mind behind the collections saw the world as an elaborate series of divinely-ordained relationships, in the ordering of which, however, man might sometimes play an active part and hence the interest in alchemy, esoteric wisdom and the philosopher's stone which is a characteristic thread in the weave. The whole project was expressed in 1594 by the Englishman, Francis Bacon:

> First, the collecting of a most perfect and general library, wherein whosoever the wit of man hath heretofore committed to books of worth . . . may be contributory to your wisdom. Next, a spacious, wonderful garden, wherein whatsoever plant the sun of divers climate, or the earth out of diverse moulds, either wild

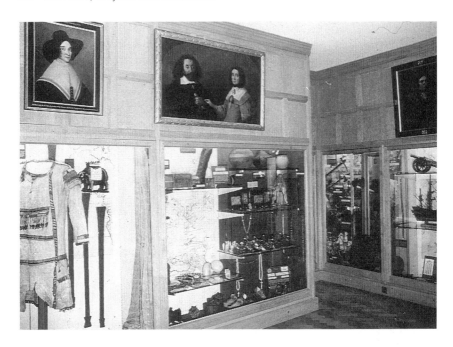

Plate 11.   The Tradescant Room at the Ashmolean Museum, Oxford, displaying material from the Tradescant Collection (photo: Ashmolean Museum).

or by the culture of man brought forth, may be . . . set and cherished: this garden to be built about with rooms to stable in all rare beasts and to cage in all rare birds; with two lakes adjoining, the one of fresh water the other of salt, for like variety of fishes. And so you have in small compass a model of the universal nature made private. The third, a goodly huge cabinet wherein whatsoever the hand of man by exquisite art or engine has made rare in stuff, form or motion; whatsoever singularity, chance, and the shuffle of things hath produced; what-soever Nature has wrought in things that want life and may be kept; shall be sorted and included. The fourth such a still house, so furnished with mills, instruments, furnaces and vessels as may be a palace fit for a philosopher's stone.

(Quoted in Impey and MacGregor 1985: 1)

Surviving illustrations give us some idea of how these collections were organized and displayed. The engraved frontispiece of Olaus Worm's catalogue of his collection, *Musei Wormiani Historia*, published in Leiden in 1655 is now known to be a fairly faithful depiction of Worm's museum (or at least the major room of it) (Schepelern 1990) (see Plate 12). The back wall seems to have measured about 3m. in breadth and 3.3 m. in height, and the two side windows suggest a room of some depth, possibly a corridor. The objects are placed upon open shelving or are hung from the walls and ceiling, where large fish and birds swing with a kayak. Like is often grouped with like: there are sections for horned shells and horns, clothing,

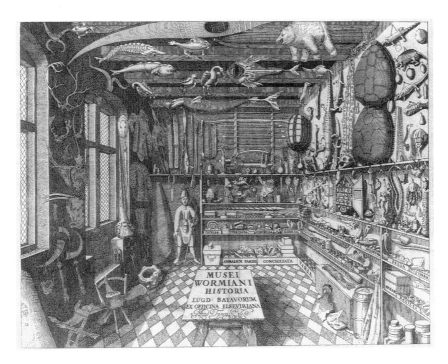

Plate 12.   Engraved frontispiece, *Musei Wormiani Historia*, Leiden 1655 (photo: British Library).

edged weapons and arrows. An L-shaped bank of shelving, four shelves deep, has its lowest three shelves divided into named sections with titles like LIGNA (woods), ANIMALIUM PARTES (animal parts) and CONCHILIATA (shells). The general feel is not unlike what we know of broadly contemporary apothecaries' shops, which represented the commercial end of the same intellectual spectrum. It seems clear that the collection was arranged partly in response to the size of the pieces (just like any modern store) and partly in an effort to create the distinction between *artificialia* and *naturalia* and to classify the *naturalia* into groups based upon their apparently obvious physical characteristics. The artefacts (then as now) proved more difficult to sort. Scattered illustrations suggest that most of the cabinets looked much like this, and presumably the Tradescant and surviving Ashmole collections were laid out in similar fashion when the Ashmolean Museum opened, as the first freely accessible museum, in Oxford in 1683.

The Ashmolean was originally housed in a rectangular building, good but of relatively modest consequence, with its three floors intended for the museum, lectures and a laboratory (see Plate 13). This seems to be the custom-built version of the straightforward room within an existing building, equipped with various shelves and storage cabinets, which is quite frequently depicted in the art of the sixteenth and seventeenth centuries. A powerful image in the designing of buildings to

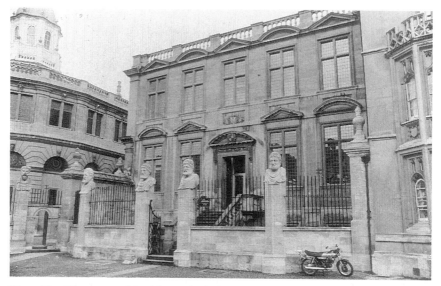

Plate 13. The original building which housed the Ashmolean Museum, Broad
Street, Oxford (photo: author).

house collections, especially collections of art, was the domed rotunda with its reference to classical temples, and to museums in their other sense as homes of the
Muses. The frontispiece for the catalogue of Michele Mercati's collection, produced in
1580, shows a rectangular room housing the material opening through an arcade
on to an elaborate courtyard with a small domed and open colonnaded building
containing a statue (Fabionski 1990: 122).

   These early museum collections have set their indelible stamp upon the way in
which we see the world and so on the place of all subsequent museums in that
vision. They manifested the link between the physical reality of the world and its
metaphysical being, contending that the one could only be understood in the light
of the other, and they clothed this in the compelling pomp of classical iconography,
glorified by art. The mystical relationship between things and ideas, and the nature
of ideas, could be expressed by the classification of the physical world, primarily
into artificial things and natural things, and then into smaller groupings. These
groupings were the music of the spheres in the compass of a single room, tran-
scendent reality made visible. We are in a neo-Platonist world seen through Christian
stained glass, and as the eighteenth century unwinds, the coloured lights will drop
away and the vision of understanding clarify. It had become possible to see the
world in a properly curated grain of sand.

Classification and Public Statement

As the eighteenth century unfolded a museological path, clear and broad, opened
up before the gaze of collectors and museums, encyclopaedic, classificatory, uni-

versal and organized, which drew upon the collecting rationale of the past two centuries but gradually added to it an increasing depth of scientific knowledge, of which the collections were themselves a part. In 1727 C. F. Neikelius produced his *Museographia*, published in Leipzig and Breslau (Schulz 1990). Man, he writes, can only acquire knowledge of the physical world through libraries and curiosity collections. Museums are to help man understand himself and his world, both divine creations, and so should contain *naturalia* and *artificialia*, and books. He divides the natural creation of *naturalia* into three realms of *regno animali*, *regno vegetabili* and *regno minerali*, a triple distinction which yet shows its mark on our minds and language. To this is added *artificialia* ('art') which includes both fine art, which he stresses should be originals and by famous masters, and applied art of all kinds, adding that art is multiple and so more difficult to define.

Neikelius goes on to tell us that pictures must be stored in dry conditions and not in direct light since this can damage them, that a register of new acquisitions and a *general-catalogum* are indispensable, and that proper procedures, including clean hands, should be drawn up for access. All the material should be shelved in an order which reflects the classification, and at the entrance to the museum should sit terrible lions or tigers to symbolize the silence necessary for study.

Needless to say, events did not always match this admirable early effort at a collections management policy, but Neikelius's classificatory scheme remained at the heart of the museum enterprise. Institutionally the nature of the collections and of the museums underwent a sea change as what had been princely or private collections were, very gradually and with many backward glances, transferred into state or public museums of the kind whose presence still looms large in most capital cities. These museums inherited the universal or encyclopaedic idea of the world-in-microcosm from the earlier generation, as they had inherited the collections themselves, and many of them continued to amass material in both the artificial and the natural classes, but the broad distinctions which had opened up between natural history, 'art' meaning fine art and higher craftsmanship, and 'artificial' meaning all the remaining human artefacts, began to widen as the different fields took their distinctive paths as the eighteenth and nineteenth centuries progressed. Fine art remained the queen, particularly in France, Germany and Italy.

Gradually, many of the great royal art collections (although not that of the English sovereigns) were turned into public museums by royalty itself. The Viennese Royal Collection was moved out of the Stallburg to the Belvedere Palace in 1776; the Royal Collection in Düsseldorf and the Dresden Gallery were opened to the public in the middle of the century; and the Uffizi was donated to the state in 1743 by the last Medici princess. The Glyptothek in Munich was built as a public museum for the Bavarian royal collection by Ludwig of Bavaria about 1820, and even the Hermitage was opened to the public in 1853, although as Barzin shows, it kept much of its character as a princely reception room: 'The [Hermitage] museum was completely integrated with the palace, being used for evening receptions and after-theatre suppers . . . The Czar permitted the public but on conditions recalling those of the *Ancien Régime*. One visited the emperor, not the museum; full dress was *de rigueur* and visitors were announced' (Bazin 1967: 198). Plans had been in hand to create public access to the Royal Collection in the old Louvre Palace since 1747, although this was not achieved until 1792, in very different political circumstances. Duncan and Wallach (1980: 453) quote a pamphlet of 1747 of Lafont de Saint-Yenne which argues for a Louvre gallery which would be a monument to the King, a 'sanctuary' for art that would augment 'the glory of our nation', an inspiration to modern artists, and a wonder to foreigners.

These sentiments, although translated into the language of the 1790s, appear again directly in the letter of 17 October 1792 addressed to the painter David by Roland, Minister of the Interior:

> As I conceive of it, it should attract and impress foreigners. It should nourish a taste for the fine arts, please art lovers and serve as a school to artists. It should be open to everyone. This will be a national monument. There will not be a single individual who does not have the right to enjoy it. It will have such an influence on the mind, it will so elevate the soul, it will so excite the heart that it will be one of the most powerful ways of proclaiming the illustriousness of the French Republic.
>
> (Duncan and Wallach 1980: 454)

The points, although naturally made most clearly in France, have a broad application. The public art museum makes the nation a visible reality, and the visiting public are addressed as citizens who have a share in the nation. The museum displays spiritual wealth that is owned by the state and shared by all who belong to the state. The political abstraction is given symbolic form in the shape of tangible 'masterpieces', which exhibit humanity at its best and highest, so identifying the state with these spiritual values and sharing them with all comers. The museum is the place where, in exchange for his share in the state's spiritual holdings, the individual affirms his attachment to the state. This is why the creation of national museums was a matter of concern at the highest political levels, and why, from Napoleon to Göring, pictures are politics.

The new public art museums required a new philosophy and a new iconography which would draw upon the idea of classification inherited from the previous century, and link this with the applied intellectual rationale characteristic of the developing European middle class, who wanted to see a clear increase in knowledge and understanding for their efforts, and who preferred this knowledge to underpin their own position. The outcome was the idea of the history of art, in which pictures could be placed in chronological sequence, to show 'high' and 'lower' points. Collections of classical marbles and other similar antiquities, either already existing or as they arrived in the national collections from private hands, took their natural place in this arrangement, both as the touchstones of spiritual excellence and as the glorious past to which the splendid present was heir.

All this gave visitors something to learn, a positive possession, rather than just something to appreciate – a much less clear yield. It had the effect of creating historical depth for a generation whose habits of mind were only just accustoming themselves to the idea of the present as the product of the past, and inevitably this turned upon that simplest view of progression and change, the lives of great men and great artists. The contemporary bourgeoisie felt very comfortable with all these interlocking pedagogic, judgemental and spiritually affirmative ideas: a cast of mind which explains why, as the nineteenth century progressed, nationalism was translated into the civic pride which created museums in most cities and large towns, especially in Britain which was now receiving the lion's share of the wealth of the world.

The arrangement of the new galleries made this quite explicit. When the Royal Viennese collection was rehoused in the Belvedere in 1776, the pictures were divided into national schools and art historical periods. They were put into uniform frames and clearly labelled, another change necessary for public visitors. A walk through the galleries was a walk through art history, as the accompanying *Guide* written by Christian von Mechel made clear. The new museum, he wrote, was to be 'a repository where the history of art is made visible' (quoted in Bazin 1967: 159). The Düsseldorf collection had had a similar arrangement since 1756, and the Uffizi since 1770. The Louvre adopted it in 1810, and it has been the scheme usual in art museums ever since.

The museums and collections of *naturalia* took a rather different turn, chiefly perhaps because they could not claim the prestige now seen to reside in artistic masterpieces. The only national museum which was strongest, not in art and antiquities, but in natural history (and books) was the British Museum, founded in 1753. Here the principal rooms were a miscellany of stuffed giraffes, oriental idols, fossils, elephants and sponges, all within Montague House, built in the French taste in the 1690s: when Celia Fiennes went there she found the *trompe l'oeil* so convincing that she could hardly find her way out (Crook 1973: 61). Judging by contemporary accounts the organization of the material was rudimentary, and the significant work upon natural history material was being done elsewhere. Gradually, and it is important to remember, chiefly through work on what survived of the seventeenth-century collections and then on these amassed in the first half of the eighteenth century, the classification system of the natural world associated with Carl Linnaeus (although actually tentatively begun and then much added to by those before and after him), began to take shape within the organization and layout of collections. John Woodward's geological collection of about 9,400 specimens which survives in the Sedgewick Museum, Cambridge with its original storage cabinets (Price 1989) (see Plate 14), is typical of the collecting effort which was shaping the development of knowledge.

Systematic collecting and classifying of this kind was to gather momentum as a pursuit through the later eighteenth and nineteenth centuries, expressing itself, especially in Britain, in a network of societies, field clubs and journals, which gradually extended into all groups of flora and fauna, and left us the great bulk of the natural history collections which loom so large in our museums. The history of the Yorkshire Philosophical Society and its museum is broadly characteristic of many such. The Society was founded in 1823, and its published aims were 'to establish a library' for consultation by persons of various scientific pursuits, 'to elucidate the geology of Yorkshire' and to contribute 'specimens from every part of Yorkshire to

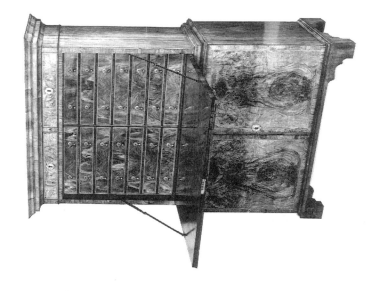

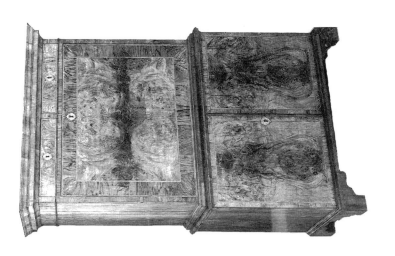

Plate 14.   Two surviving cabinets which held John Woodward's collection, probably commissioned in the 1690s or very early 1700s. Sedgwick Museum, Cambridge (photo: Sedgwick Museum).

a central Museum'. Pyrah has described how the collections accumulated as the century progressed (Pyrah 1988).

Throughout the eighteenth century, where the rest of the 'artificial curiosities' were concerned, that is with those artefacts which were not judged to be high art, the accent was more firmly on their curiosity value than on anything else: indeed, as the eighteenth century turned into the nineteenth, both 'artificial' and 'curious' began to take on the pejorative connotations which are still attached to them in the clothing and book trades. What we would call ethnographic material, like that which came back to Britain as a result of Cook's voyages (see Plate 15), was widely dispersed among private collectors. What we would call archaeological material was avidly collected by a wide circle in Britain, which included particularly clergymen and naval and army officers, who were gathering local Roman material and opening barrows from as early as the 1700s.

This kind of material, together with some natural history, some historical pieces from Britain and some objects of interest to the *virtuosi*, like quality craftsmanship and coins, were still being formed into collections of essentially a seventeenth-century type as the eighteenth and nineteenth centuries progressed. Sometimes, like that of Sir Richard Worsley of Appuldurcombe, the collection originated in an Italian Grand Tour, and achieved some classical material from Greece and Turkey. Sometimes it concentrated, like that of Thomas Bateman of Sheffield, on local antiquities; sometimes, like that of William Bullock during the early 1800s or of John Calvert in Leeds at about the same time, it was opened as a commercial attraction and taken on tour. There was a major market (Wainwright 1989 and references there) in all kinds of curiosities and antiquities, as well as in pictures and sculptures, and material constantly changed hands. Many of these collections are now dispersed, but separate or intact, they have served very frequently as 'feeds' for the national museums and for the developing provincial museums, most of whose major collections come eventually from this kind of eighteenth-, nineteenth- and early-twentieth-century source.

Artificial and antiquarian material was the last of the three great divisions to achieve an intellectual rationale of its own, but when it did begin to do so, around 1830, this, like art, took the form of historicism and, like natural history, of type classification, and like them both, the new rationale was worked out with the material already in the museum collections. The *locus* was Scandinavia, especially the Danish National Museum, itself the typical descendant of a royal collection, where, by 1836, Thomsen and Worsaae had displayed the archaeological material in terms of stone, bronze and iron and made the conceptual leap which turned a material classification into the chronological Three Age System. The System gradually gained ground, and by 1871 the newly-appointed Keeper of the newly-created Department of British and Medieval Antiquities at the British Museum had reorganized his displays along Three Age lines.

The mid-nineteenth-century intellectual revolution associated conspicuously with Charles Lyell, whose *Principles of Geology* (1830–33) established the idea of chronological stratigraphy, and Charles Darwin, whose ideas about evolution drew together classification and chronological depth in natural history to show how

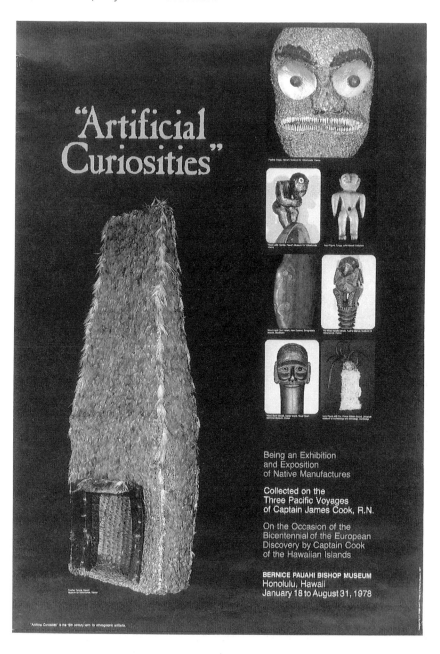

Plate 15.   Poster for exhibition *Artificial Curiosities* showing material collected by Captain James Cook on his Pacific voyages, held at Bernice Pauahi Bishop Museum, Honolulu, Hawaii, 1978 (photo: University of Leicester).

types changed, inspired Augustus Henry Pitt Rivers to form the first thoroughgoing theory of material culture interpretation, which offered a way of understanding the mass of archaeological and historical objects. As we have seen (pp. 85–86) he believed that, like animals and plants, artefact types developed one from another by a process of selection and diffusion which modified their forms according to natural laws. Artefact development sequences can, therefore, be built up to show progression from simple to complex, and this reflects a similar truth about social development. The theory did not displace, but built upon the Scandinavian Three Age approach.

Sufficient information survives to let us form some view of how museum rooms looked from the early nineteenth century. The watercolours made by George Scharf in the 1840s of the interiors of the old British Museum at Montague House, demolished to make way for Smirke's new building, give some idea of the casing which had been installed. His picture of the Entrance Hall shows a case nearly 10 feet high and perhaps the same in length, and with a breadth of about 3 feet, although the relationship of this installation to the fabric of the building is unclear. The case is glassed by a series of small (some forty-six visible) rectangular panes held in place by wooden beading (Crook 1973: 59).

From about 1850 to 1900 both table and wall cases were being produced by a range of firms, usually on four legs and measuring roughly four feet square. The bases were hard wood, usually Cuban or Honduran mahogany. The upper case frames were cast iron, and the glass used was the ordinary window glass of the day, drawn and hand polished. It is important to realize that this could not easily be made in sheets larger than about 3 feet square so most cases needed wooden cross bars, like an ordinary window. Equally, such glass does not have a plain surface and so up to 70 per cent of its surface would give some viewing distortion. All this meant that, in order to see objects clearly and in detail, they had to be taken out of their cases, and this had significant implications for access and museum visiting.

The technical progress largely associated with the First World War made possible the production of plate glass polished flat by electric motor, held in a case frame of strip metal – first mild steel and then various bronze alloys – drawn through dies to give angles and channels. By the 1920s Edmonds of Birmingham were equipping 90 per cent of their cases with plate glass: these are the famous Kensington cases which could be supplied with a variety of bases, and which, with various local imitations, were the mainstay of museum display until the technological changes of the 1960s (see Plate 16). Two points are particularly important about this case technology. Firstly, the development of plate glass is the technological aspect of the growing late-nineteenth-century need for clear and open, but secure and controlled public display, of which museums were a significant part. Secondly, although the basic case sizes were governed by the norms of the adult human body, the basic design module was cuboid. The ability of cases to stand in regimented rows contributed considerably to the solidity of the classificatory regimes: here, as always, mind and matter go together (see Plate 17).

As within, so without: museum architecture was designed to give clear and

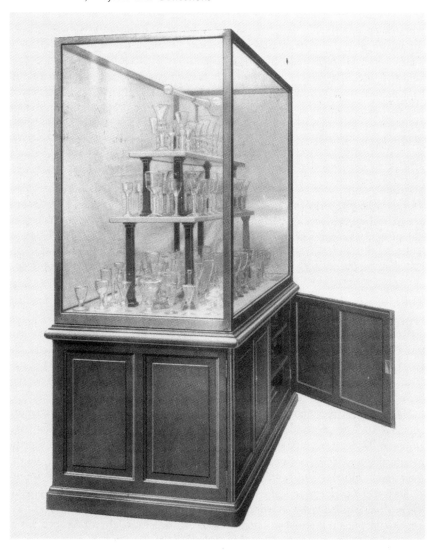

Plate 16.   Illustration from *Showcases and Display Equipment* published by A. Edwards and Co. Ltd, Birmingham, 1931. The caption reads: 'KENSINGTON TYPE CENTRE CASE. As supplied to Exeter Museum, with cupboard base. Case size 5ft. 7½in. long, 2ft. 6in. wide, 3ft. 9½in. high, on base 3ft. high. Interior of Case fitted with linen covered shelves, supported on mahogany runners. Interior of Cupboard fitted with runners for trays' (photo: University of Leicester).

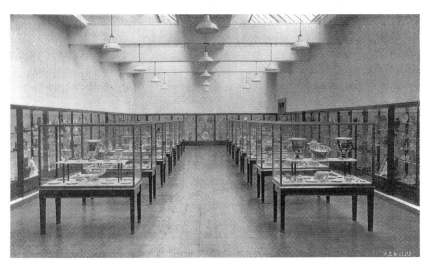

Plate 17. Illustration from *Showcases and Display Equipment* published by A. Edwards and Co. Ltd, Birmingham, 1938. The caption reads: 'Kensington Cases in bronze metal on hardwood bases and Wall Cases in Nigerian Walnut. Sheffield Museum Note – deeper cases at intervals give variety to display.' The nature of the cases and the display which they create demonstrates the laying-out of knowledge (photo: University of Leicester).

unmistakable public messages which matched, in both clarity and content, those being given by the displays. In 1800 there were fewer than a dozen public museums, and not all of these were in buildings of substance. By 1850 there were nearly sixty; by 1887 at least 240; and by 1928 over 500 and most of these were in buildings intended to impress. The notions of museums as temple habitations of the Muses, as glorious embodiments of the moral excellence of the state, and as monuments which created history by showing the present as heir to the past, especially the Greek and Roman past, came naturally together in the taste for grand buildings in the Neo-Classical and Greek-Revival styles. In Britain alone the number of classical-style museums, art galleries and libraries must run into hundreds. Even a selective roll call is sonorous: the Smirkes' British Museum was built between 1827 and 1857; Barry's Manchester City Art Gallery with its unfluted Ionic columns by 1823; Cockerell's Ashmolean at Oxford with its fusion of Greek, Roman and Renaissance forms by 1845; Playfair's Doric Royal Scottish Academy and Ionic Scottish National Gallery in the Athens of the North by 1857; and last but in no way least, we have Hibbert's *beaux arts* classicism in the Harris Free Library, Museum and Art Gallery in Preston, completed in 1893 (see Plate 18).

The classicists did not have it all their own way, for by the 1850s Ruskin was on the side of the angels, and the neo-Gothic invitation to a profusion of naturalistically carved but symbolically significant animals and plants seemed like Darwinism translated into stone. This gave us Woodward's Oxford Museum

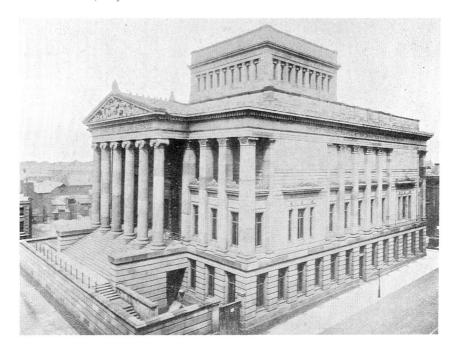

Plate 18.   The Harris Free Public Library and Museum, Preston, as it was in the early part of this century (photo: Harris Museum and Art Gallery, Preston).

begun in 1855 where each column is cut from a different British stone and the carvings of fruit and flowers are arranged in natural sequence and labelled; Gilbert Scott's museums at Lewes (1862) and Dundee (1873); Venetian Gothic at Exeter (1869) and Bristol (1872); and, above all, Alfred Waterhouse's Natural History Museum at South Kensington (1881) where the terracotta animals included, at Professor Huxley's suggestion, a statue of Adam on the apex of the central gable to represent 'Man: the greatest beast of all' (see Plate 19).

Duncan and Wallach (1980: 448–51) make the interesting point that museums are ceremonial architecture, inheriting the earlier display functions of temples, treasuries and crypts where war trophies, similar to much eighteenth- and nineteenth-century museum material, were prominent, and offering a space within which secular ritual activity of a kind appropriate to the museum age can take place. The museum acts as a central gathering place where group solidarity is made apparent. The building, its iconography, its gallery layout and its sequence of collections together provide what Victor Turner (1977: 94–7) called a 'script' or 'doing code' to be performed by individuals, alone or in groups. The walk around the galleries has been paced out by those before us, and anticipated emotions are aroused by the deliberate rhythms of case and structure: we emerge tired (ritual is always demanding), sometimes exalted, always with a feeling of piety, of duty satisfactorily performed. These are religious emotions, which the late modern age, especially,

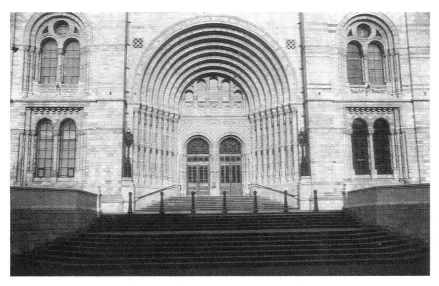

Plate 19.   Main entrance to Natural History Museum, South Kensington, taken in 1976 (photo: Department of Museum Studies, University of Leicester).

was at pains to foster. When, in 1768, Goethe visited the Dresden Gallery, its splendour and richness 'imparted a feeling of solemnity [which] resembled the sensation with which one attends a church' but was here 'set up only for the sacred purposes of art' (Duncan and Wallach 1980: 450).

This feeling for the sacred, translated into secular and national or civic terms, and linked with the conviction of progress towards superior understanding, both created museums and was created by them, and is a major characteristic of the age. It has given us a very large proportion of the collections which now make up museum holdings, and it has given us the physical museum presences which dominate our city centres and within which much museum activity still takes place.

Context and Community: the Twentieth-Century Museum

As the twentieth century gathered momentum the approach to knowledge and to collecting refined by the earlier generation came to seem inadequate, both intellectually and emotionally. Conceptually, the notion of type classifications had never gained the high ground in the human history fields, because although its capacity to order material into visible groupings was acknowledged, these groupings seemed to lack contact with the human communities from which the material had come, and real understanding remained elusive. Similarly, although the art history demonstrated upon gallery walls had its own persuasiveness, it seemed to miss the heart of the aesthetic experience. Even in the natural sciences, where systematic classification and its development remains crucial, other models, especially that which looked at the living whole as the sum of its different parts, began to exercise a powerful fascination. Emotionally, these doubts chimed in with the growing romantic attachment to local communities and cultures, all of which were steadily losing their characters as the later nineteenth and twentieth centuries progressed.

The upshot of this was a growing desire to appreciate material and understanding in terms of relationships which drew different threads together rather than which selected out like with like; to look, in a word, in terms of context rather than classification, to see the world in terms of separate articulating communities rather than of overarching systems. This was the more inspiring in that it provided opportunities for exciting research and field work. It was also – and this is an important point – admirably suited to a new kind of museum display which both demonstrated how the new thinking went, and reinforced it through the imaginative power of the exhibitions it could inspire.

The roots of the new contextual approach to understanding run well back into the nineteenth century. When the Natural History Museum opened at South Kensington in 1881 it was divided into five departments: Zoology, Entomology, Palaeontology, Mineralogy and Botany. The line of museological development which produced these divisions runs clearly back into the sixteenth century, and is so familiar to us that we are only now beginning not to take them for granted. But at the same time the first Director, Sir William Flower (1831–99), in planning his museum as a centre for conservation, research and education, introduced, apparently in the 1880s, instructional labels and illustrations, and the fabrication of the earliest dioramas and environmental tableaux. Putting stuffed and mounted animals together in dramatic poses in the same case (see Plate 20) was not a new idea; we know that in the early nineteenth century some of the natural history material in the Bullock Collection, as viewed by the paying customer, was displayed like this (Hancock 1980). But there the intention was to be sensational, while the aim of the Natural History Museum was to harness the particular qualities of museum display to show how Nature works.

And not just Nature: human communities also could be manifested in displayed habitat groups. As is so frequently the case, this idea seems to have occurred more-or-less independently to a number of people across the world either side of 1900. The Swede Artur Hazelius, romantically committed to the Pan-Scandinavian movement and inspired by a visit to the province of Dalarna and the destruction of traditional life which he saw there, began to collect folk material and information in 1872 (Kavanagh 1990: 16–19). He began to exhibit his collection in the following year, displaying the material in small scenes. At the *Universal Exhibition* in Paris in 1878 he built 'living pictures' or tableaux, like the 'Lapp Encampment', which utilized the popular technique of wax figures. Hazelius was the driving force behind both the Nordiska Museet (opened in 1907) and its popularity-orientated twin, Skansen (opened 1891), the first open-air museum where buildings collected from all over Sweden were re-erected to give a series of habitation groups – the contextualization of Sweden in miniature. Both the reconstructions and the 'living

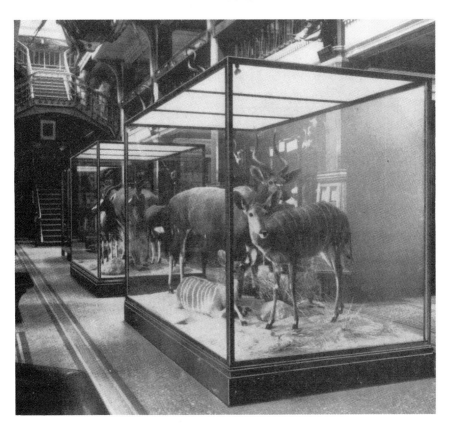

Plate 20.   Illustration from *Showcases and Display Equipment* published by A. Edwards and Co. Ltd, Birmingham, 1938, showing Stag Cases at Manchester University Museum. The caption to the illustration reads: 'Stag Cases, 10ft. 0in. long, 5ft. 0ins. wide, 6ft. 0ins. high, carried on 9ins. wood plinth. The top and each side are separately framed for easy erection on site. Top is glazed with obscured glass.' The photograph illustrates the less ambitious type of 'natural display' group (photo: University of Leicester).

pictures' have made their indelible mark on all subsequent museum activity in the human history field: Beamish and Jorvik are Hazelius's children.

Across the Atlantic Franz Boas was coming to much the same conclusions in relation to the material culture and community life of the North American Indian peoples. For Boas individual geographical terrain, historical sequence and language combined to create a series of specific and unique cultural situations which defied useful classification or prediction. For Boas, therefore, 'The main purpose of ethnological collections should be the dissemination of the fact that civilization is not something absolute, but that it is relative, and that our ideas and conceptions are true only so far as our civilization goes' (Stocking 1974: 61). The fullest realization of Boas's ideas was in the North West Coast Hall for which he was responsible at the American Museum of Natural History. The exhibit combined an introductory synoptic section showing material illustrating themes like house furnishing, dress and ornament, cases of archaeological material, independent cases each focusing on a particular social group, and two large cases containing life groups at either end. The approach included mannequins placed inside cases to show how costume was worn and tools used, and the life groups included a group of human figures at a reduced scale.

The appreciation of the more remote past was moving in a similar direction, and here the leaders (surprisingly) were the Greek and Roman Department at the British Museum. In 1908 the Museum opened the first exhibition of Greek and Roman daily life, an exhibit theme which has run on at the Museum to the present day. The reasons for the exhibition were set out explicitly:

> In this Exhibition an attempt has been made to bring together a number of miscellaneous antiquities which hitherto have been scattered through the Department, in such a method as illustrates the purpose for which they were intended, rather than their artistic quality or their place in the evolution of craft or design.
>
> Such a series falls naturally into groups which can be assorted according to the class of purpose they fulfil; and it has been found convenient to treat these groups as subjective to a general scheme, the illustration of the public and private life of the Greeks and Romans.
>
> (Quoted in Jenkins 1986: 67)

The decision to abandon the hitherto traditional art historical approach in favour of ideas about social function was an important innovation, and seen as such across Europe. *Deutsche Literaturzeitung* for 1 April 1911 said:

> In this exhibition the art-historical approach to Museum displays has been abandoned and the cultural and historical approach adopted in its place . . . The choice of objects has been made in such a way as not to make you feel the need for art-history. Here the opportunity has been taken to get to know Greek and Roman life in its context.
>
> (Quoted in Jenkins 1986: 67)

As Jenkins has put it, 'the exhibition stood aside from [the art historical] tradition by taking a synchronic instead of the usual diachronic approach, and by focusing not on the noble image projected by monumental Greek sculpture, but on the more mundane aspects of ancient culture' (1986: 68). The swing in ideas and sentiment speaks for itself. It was matched by the growing ability of excavation to yield information about ancient societies, and together the changes brought a new attitude to our view of the past manifested in subsequent archaeological exhibitions up and down the country.

The contextual approach stressed the unique value of each natural and human community and so undermined the judgemental certainties which an insistence on classification tends to develop. It sought to appreciate and understand each particular community within its own terms as a functioning whole – and the word is important because as 'functionalism', this view was capable of generating its own general explanations of man and culture (see Chapter 7). The special ability of exhibitions to demonstrate and confirm how the idea works in principle and practice is shown by the enormous development of exhibition and collecting policies with this kind of base. From the functional/contextual ideas of around 1900 come all subsequent museum concerns with ecology and the environment, and with the particularity of human communities. Inherent in such notions, from the very beginning, was a political dimension. Boas was forced to resign his post at the American Museum in 1905 because his relativist ideas were unacceptable to the Museum President Morris Jesup and Director Herman Bumpus, who wished to see 'a series [of displays] illustrating the advance of mankind from the most primitive form to the most complex forms of life' (Jacknis 1986: 107). Over the past two or three decades, community-based work with its roots in this tradition has been the focus of much museum activity, and to this we must now turn.

For the historians of twentieth-century popular culture the contextual idea carries crucial implications. It involves a translation of 'context' to 'community', and hence an involvement in the local community and its relationship to its material culture. Closely linked with this is the need to collect broadly contemporary material to be carried forward as historical evidence of our century into future centuries, undeniably one of the prime functions of a museum service. Community involvement is frequently linked with a social philosophy which places great importance on a museum turning outward to its people rather than inward to its collections and the exhibitions that arise from them. The argument is often posed in terms of a dichotomy between 'traditionalists' and 'innovators', or between 'carers' (broadly, traditional curators) and 'sharers' (who are anxious to attract bigger and different audiences to enjoy what is on offer). It is obvious that this is a false distinction; museums must clearly endeavour to do both if they are to fulfil their role.

Reference has already been made to the growing contemporary taste for accumulating 'collectables', and to the two museums, Stevenage and Walsall, which have invited members of the local community to use their museums as an arena in which they can show their own collections to each other (pp. 78–81). Both exhibitions were enormous successes by any and every standard; neither 'art' nor 'history' but something in between, they struck a spark between museum and community. Some of this kind of collected material is already in museums, although (at least until very recently) it has not usually been put on display. It is a fair guess that a substantial proportion of the great mass of material now in private hands will eventually find its way into a museum context of some kind, and will impart some of its own colour to the museums of the twenty-first century.

The need to collect twentieth-century material culture operates on a sliding scale, which has at one end traditional high culture embodied in works of fine and applied art, and at the other traditional historical domestic, rural and industrial material, collected with due regard to proper contextual recording. In between there is a huge mass of material which does not fit clearly into any category, like the 'collectables' just discussed, but which receives its significance from the ways in which it is regarded. Recording all this material for posterity is clearly an impossible task, and therefore fierce debate revolves around the nature and implications of the selection process.

Two major museums have recently given us an insight as to how they view their responsibilities here. The British Museum has mounted its *Collecting the Twentieth Century*, which brings together twentieth-century material collected by six departments, ranging from antiquities, prints and drawings to coins and medals and ethnography (Carey 1991). The *Introduction* to the accompanying publication tells us

> The broad spectrum embraced by the British Museum means that twentieth-century material is seen as part of an historical continuum in relation to the different cultures from which it has emerged. This deference to individual integrity does not, however, ignore the realities of the contemporary situation when identities no longer presuppose continuous cultures or traditions. Everywhere individuals and groups improvise local performances from (re)collected pasts, drawing on foreign media, symbols and languages.
>
> (Carey 1991: 9)

Carey makes the fair point that the museum collections themselves have played a significant part in providing the raw ideas for such (re) collections:

> The impact of the British Museum's collections on successive generations of writers, artists and designers is part of the dynamic of its relationship with the present, a dynamic which is sustained by its involvement with twentieth-century acquisitions. The accumulation of material thus continues unabated, since the museum is defined by its role as a reference and lending collection of infinite resource as well as by its public display galleries.
>
> (Carey 1991: 10)

Collecting, then, becomes less of an effort at *representation* and more a matter of individual and informed choice, which will in turn influence other individual choices: an interesting – and entirely legitimate, given all the problems inherent in representation and reality – approach to collecting, which is at once traditional and forward-looking.

In 1990 the Victoria and Albert mounted *Collecting for the Future: a Decade of Contemporary Acquisitions*, which attempted to explain how and why this national museum acquires examples of art, craft and design, who decides what to collect, and what criteria they use. It emerges that the museum collects on aesthetic, technical, historical and documentary criteria, with due recognition of the practical problems of collection management. The exhibition itself divided into a number of categories, which included 'Polemical Objects' (objects intended to make design points), 'Objects for the Collector' (up-market material, but an interesting link to the Walsall and Stevenage shows), 'The Design Process' (with working materials from designers' drawing boards), and 'Marketing', 'Objects for Decoration' and 'Daily Use' (where the paramount importance of objects to the user was stressed). Both the objects themselves and the way in which the exhibition was structured present a museum which is aware of all the issues and is grappling with the problems of making them make sense within its own terms.

Collecting broadly contemporary material involves, it is clear, a difficult range of intellectual and moral decisions which revolve around questions like 'cultural identity' (regional, national and civic), linked with notions of what constitutes 'community' and how this relates to the ways in which real people experience their real lives (King 1985–6; 1990). As Mayo puts it, drawing upon her experience in the Division of Political History at the Smithsonian: collecting contemporary historical artefacts requires a great 'leap of faith' (1984b: 8), because the political problems can never be solved to everybody's satisfaction and yet material must be selected and collected if the museum is to do its job. With this process many museums link the practice of oral history recording (Griffiths 1987) and 'people'-orientated display projects like those undertaken in Glasgow by Mark O'Neil at Springburn Museum. Exactly the same problems, of course, face museums wherever in the world they may be, and whether or not the collected material will remain in its country of origin.

The collecting debate is one aspect of a broader debate which preoccupies much of the late-twentieth-century museum world, and has to do with the role of collections in a fundamental sense and with the ways in which the material and the public responsibility should be balanced in the forming both of new collecting policies and management structures. Some voices have doubted the ability of material to encapsulate experience or tell a story, and therefore expect that 'the relative importance of massed collections will, in most museums, decline' (Davies 1985: 29) as museums turn their attention away from 'things' and towards themes, issues and people. This appears to be a failure, not in the potential interest of material culture, but in the imagination of the curator, but it does highlight how what is now sometimes perceived as undue object worship must be redressed by carefully-considered display and access policies, matched by a better division of work responsibilities so that collection management is not neglected, and coherent research programmes are pursued. This, in turn, is set within a political agenda which for a decade or more has (in Britain and to a certain extent elsewhere) been set by the radical right with its anti-intellectual commitment to market forces and popular choice taken in its lowest sense (Walsh 1992), although strangely enough the new right and the old radical left have not found a meeting of minds in their mutual dislike of cultural élitism.

Past and Present: Towards an Historiography of Museums

Part of the purpose of the preceding discussion has been to suggest that the history of museums, far from being a recreation for the museological dilettante, plays a vital role in our effort to understand how and why we are as we are. The discussion has started from the assumption that museums and their collections are part of the creation of the philosophy of knowledge, and of its history, in the humanities and the sciences (if, indeed, knowledge can be divided so tidily), and of the ways in which society at large is involved in this creation. We have inherited a complex structure, both theoretical and physical, which is essentially social in character and which has, therefore, done its share towards the construction of social character. The museological structure, paralleling modern structures of knowledge and sentiment in general, is now moving towards its sixth century, and carries with it, like a snail its shell (an inevitable comparison given the elaborate nature of much museum architecture), its stratified accumulation of collections and buildings, and the traditions, or mind-sets, which accompany them.

The social character, and the consequent bias, of museums and their collections needs to be stressed. Kuhn (1970), in his discussions of the way in which knowledge is generated, has given us two significant ideas: that all knowledge is a product of social interaction rather than of a dramatic process of discovery; and that in order to understand the social character of knowledge, we should look to the integrity of the historical context which produced it, a notion of context which, as we have seen, has dominated understanding within museums for the last half century or so. It is an instructive exercise to take any collection or group of associated museum objects and ask, not 'What are they?' and 'What can this tell us?', which are the usual museum questions, but rather, 'When and how was the collection formed?', 'Who formed it?' and 'Why did this person/these people choose to assemble these objects?' The answers to the first question tell us about what collecting procedures were considered intellectually appropriate at the time, and give insights into the nature of archaeological exploration, for example, or the contemporary killing of natural history specimens, or the attitudes of Europeans abroad to indigenous cultures. They reveal the ways in which, for much of the past in most disciplines, only 'fine' or 'complete' or 'typical' material was collected, and the rest discarded. The answers to the question 'Who formed it?' show which sex, social classes and kinds of corporate groups have been involved in broadly museum activities down the centuries, and the answers – mainly middle- and upper-class males and their characteristic social groupings in clubs and societies – come as no surprise.

These people did what they did because their activities seemed to them to reflect, in a satisfactory and prestigious way, the intellectual climate of their times, and so as we can see, helped to underwrite and stabilize the intellectual tradition to which they had committed an important part of themselves. In turn, our recognition of the nature of all this social activity enables us to understand better the various kinds of bias inherent in our collections. Museum people must come to terms with the ways in which the selection and collection, and the ordering and interpreting of evidence, are related to the problems and issues successively facing society, up to and including that of our own time, and to its history of values.

With this is intimately linked bias of a related kind, which makes it impossible for us ever to present an impartial account of anything, past or present, native or exotic. We can never, in the first place, assemble anything like the totality of things, but only a minute fraction of any past reality. Secondly, what we have is at a collected remove from its original context, and is therefore hopelessly coloured by contemporary attitudes. As Lowenthal has put it, 'evidence can never be checked against the past itself, only against other evidence' (1987: 13). Finally, as we have seen, all this lopsidedness is part and parcel of a web of interacting social knowledge, of which our actual collections and museums are a (very) physical expression.

We can therefore see that, down the centuries, museums have operated with a range of agendas, sometimes conflicting, but more often mutually supportive, and that contemporary museums have inherited the sum of these with which to construct their presents. One such agenda, that explored principally in this chapter, revolves around the overt or socially-applauded construction of knowledge as an institution. Another, closely linked with the first, revolves around the professional agendas of museum staff as these have gradually gathered momentum over the past 150 years, and it is to this that we must now turn.

6 *Making Museum Meanings*

The Collection has a character; it is made up of many separate collections and collection minds, and reflects the changing taste of different periods and individuals. It is, as a whole, an entity reflecting the community, curators, private collectors and other organizations who have contributed to its growth.

(*Art Gallery of Ontario Policy*)

Inventory is never a mental idea; to catalogue is not merely to ascertain . . . but also to appropriate.

(Barthes 1982: 222)

. . . for the roses
Had the look of flowers that are looked at.

(Eliot 1959: 20)

Introduction

As we have seen in the foregoing chapters, museums as institutions, and the collections which they hold, are one of the characteristic modern meta-narratives through which society, in its ideas about knowledge and reality, has been constituted since roughly the middle of the fifteenth century. The notion of exhibition is a significant part of this meta-narrative since the physical organization of pieces in relation to each other is an important way in which knowledge and understanding is generated. Curatorial theory and practice underpins this whole narrative structure, but is itself constituted by it.

This chapter and the next three are concerned with the ways in which curators make museum meanings from the material and the traditions which they inherit. The word 'curator' was used in this sentence only after a great deal of thought. It is, it goes without saying, true that all the kinds of museum staff members – most obviously designers and educationalists, but also attendants and volunteers as well – are involved in the business of presenting meanings in a museum. Equally, the idea of what constitutes curation is becoming increasingly difficult to define (see Murdoch 1992). Nevertheless, the traditional word 'curator' was finally chosen to express the conviction that in the museum, meanings arise from the direct interpretation of the collections, mixed with other interpretative traditions like design, and that of these the first, which is broadly the curatorial side of the matter, is indispensable. To put the thing at its simplest, no extended interpretations are possible until a piece has been identified, and identification, with all that this implies, is the curator's job, even if, as in some contemporary social history projects, the job consists of listening to what a participant has to say and writing labels accordingly.

This chapter will concentrate upon the curatorial process by looking first at what it has inherited, and then at how practices like classification and research and the management of collections affect meanings. It will conclude with a review of the nature of exhibition from a formal position, rather than from a view of content. The subsequent three chapters will pursue the argument by analysing how museum meanings are developed within the three main philosophical parameters which have emerged in material culture studies and which express the three main characteristics of objects: their functionalist existence as material goods, their semiotic or structuralist role as messages, and their historicity.

We begin by considering the curatorial inheritance of collection and academic field or discipline, of collection as museological heritage, and of curatorship as professional practice.

The Inheritance

Disciplined Collections

Collections embody two kinds of statements (and a third, as we shall see shortly). One of these revolves around the implicit, individual or psychic reasons why they were formed, and this we have explored in earlier chapters. The second contains explicit statements about how and why we understand the world and what values we attach to this understanding, and this we explored in the previous chapter. The most obvious thing about these explicit statements, and one which has shaped curatorial theory and practice down the centuries, gathering momentum and definition as the distinctions themselves have gathered strength, is the way in which they are divided between the main academic disciplines which serve in general as our means of structuring knowledge, and in particular as the traditional framework for the ordering of museum work. To put it another way, the curatorial meta-narrative is subdivided into a number of narrative strands, each of which has its own history and intellectual rationale, and between which there is not always complete harmony.

In museums the individual discipline strands are usually identified as Natural History, with Zoology, Botany and Geology as its component parts, Archaeology, Anthropology or Ethnography, Art divided into Fine and Applied, and History. This classification is almost always inadequate in real terms, and certain material, like Numismatics and Militaria or Arms and Armour, notoriously floats between the larger disciplines unless the collection is big enough to justify a separate specialist. Each discipline creates a particular mind-set within its adherents which gives shape to their thinking and feeling, and sets up bondings and loyalties. Each has established the parameters within which particular versions of the broad paradigms of research, classification, contextualization and criticism will take place. These museum divisions form part of the history and philosophy of the creation of Western knowledge, matching similar divisions within the education system and universities, and within the social structure of learned societies and gatherings, grant-giving foundations, publishing, and some aspects of the Civil Service. It is a theoretical framework which structures a surprisingly large slice of the practical world of work.

. . . and Undisciplined Collections

Museum collections embody an important part of the discipline-based intellectual inheritance by which we understand the world, and they transmit the aspirations of collectors from one generation to another, but they have a third, equally significant, characteristic which may be labelled their museological nature. Museum material does not come in bland pre-packaged form, like crates of baked beans arriving at a supermarket. Quite the contrary: the material comes in fits and starts. It comes in all kinds of relationships to the progress of human lives including bequests made after death, sometimes after the second death of a wife. It comes incomplete, imperfect, and with associated documentation and information itself immensely variable in quality and quantity. Once in a museum it will be subject to a series of vicissitudes, ranging from the rare catastrophe like the Second World War bombing of Dresden and Liverpool Museums, to the more familiar problems of inadequate storage and insufficient staff. All of these factors have a bearing on the kind of interpretation which the material can yield, and in turn help to produce priorities in the allocation of resources, including study. They are all part of the flux of chance and muddle, which determines successful survival and contextual association to a much greater extent than the sane man cares to dwell upon.

To describe this museological inheritance, it is helpful to borrow a term from archaeology, where it came into prominence as a result of the Frere Report (Frere 1975) and to call it the archive. The museum archive embraces the entire holdings of a museum service and includes both the material – the collections themselves – and also the entire associated record. The collections of most museums, depending upon their size and length of history, are likely to involve a wide range of material, even if theoretically this is concentrated in a narrow band of disciplines. The collections tend to relate to their disciplines in a patchy way, covering some aspects in great detail and others thinly or not at all. Some of the holdings will be only parts of earlier collections or finds, because the group was split between several museums. Associated with all this will be a considerable volume of written, printed, and pictorial record, including letters, manuscript note books, annotated maps, offprints from journals, watercolours, photographs and field notes, all in an enormous range of sizes and formats. Some of this material will have arrived with the original collection, and some will have accrued down the years as the collection has been worked upon in the museum in a range of ways. To this should be added old packaging, boxing and labelling which sometimes survives to give crucial links between objects and provenances. I was once able to identify some important Polynesian material because it became clear that the whole of an associated group had once had distinctive mid-Victorian octagonal stuck-on labels, now illegible, which some of the pieces still retained, while others showed characteristic eight-sided negative fade marks.

Problems of documentation and provenance also have a bearing on the wider issue of authentification and what constitutes an authentic collection or object. The first point is the relationship between 'authentic' and 'original'. Much museum material, particularly that on display, has undergone various kinds of improvement designed to turn a 'raw' specimen into a display piece: ceramic material is turned into a whole pot by the use of filler; preserved animal skins are stuffed, given glass eyes and posed; fossil skeletons are strung on wire, and pictures are cleaned and consolidated. Closely related to this is further conservation work which, although entirely necessary for the continued existence of the piece, nevertheless frequently involves irreversible changes within it, quite apart from vexed questions involved in the reconstituting or reshaping of objects (see Keene 1980). Visitors probably do not always appreciate the difference between the carefully presented museum specimen and the design studio's model, and curators are sometimes in the position of the New Guinea islander who told an anthropologist that this was his grandfather's axe, but his father had given it a new head and he had given it a new shaft. Important pieces are likely to have a lengthy history of conservation and display improvement, as a result of which their original form and content has become altered or obscured, and their claims to be 'the real thing' damaged. This is a part of our museological heritage which we have to live with, bearing in mind that the number of pieces involved in such problems are fairly small, although they may be perceived as important. It is always going to be an area where philosophical speculation about the meaning of objects and collections and practical museum problem-solving are inextricably intertwined.

All this museum material will have arrived in the museum by donation (including bequest), by loan, by purchase, by exchange, or through field collecting undertaken by the museum itself, and any of it may have arrived by any of these means. In fact, it is quite common for a large collection to arrive in several lots and by more than one of these acquisition routes. Associated with the material may be a range of constraints like an obligation to display in whole or in part, or a requirement to keep a personal collection together. Split gifts, special requirements and loan arrangements over the years all tend to separate collections up and to divide them from their archive, so that reassembling the whole data base becomes heartbreakingly difficult.

These difficulties are exacerbated by two further problems. Firstly, each collection archive embraces a range of material types – paper, film, organic and inorganic – which have different storage and conservation requirements and perhaps different security demands as well. Equally, parts of any given group will be in much greater demand by scholars, teachers and curators than other parts. Good storage management suggests that collections and archives are cross-cut so that, for example, all the metal is housed satisfactorily together, or much-used material is close at hand while unfashionable material may be less accessible. However, this means that in addition to the usual division between collection and record material, there is a further division between the various material groups in a collection, which can lead to further fragmentation and loss of association.

Secondly, there are problems which revolve around the formal documentation systems in use. Most museums are operating with a range of documentation systems which show both horizontal variety and stratigraphical depth. These usually begin chronologically with hand-written leather-bound ledgers, and progress, via between-the-wars and early post-war card indexes, to an assortment of computerized projects over the last few decades. Generally speaking, all of these are more-or-less incomplete, all are to incompatible formats, and all have to be consulted in order to harvest all the available information. In practice, the information yield depends to a very large extent on the curator's knowledge of the systems and of the collections themselves.

The museological inheritance, then, is all too human, and in its conflicts, confusions and absences, it plays its own part in limiting interpretation and defining the ways in which meaning can be created. We might say that, just as the intellectual qualities of collections and collecting are permeated by psychological and social motives, so the curatorial understanding of meaning in collections is coloured by inherited museological procedures and customs.

Professional Practice

Whether museum curators and their colleagues constitute a 'museum profession' or not is a subject of some debate, although the existence of a museum culture (or cultures) with its own tradition and mind-set cannot be doubted. As Kavanagh has shown us, one approach to estimating professionalism is to look at a range of characteristics, and on an assessment of these characteristics – skills based on theoretical knowledge, the provision of training and education, tests of competence for members, organization, adherence to a code of conduct, and altruistic service – the museum curator's professional nature is clear (Kavanagh 1991b: 42). Nevertheless, the profession is very fragmented between the various types of museum and the differing emphases of tasks performed within them, so that it has no unified history and its passage from the past to the present day has been strewn with what are now seen by many as missed opportunities, particularly in the area of education and in the establishment of national networks.

What is clear is that the *idea* of belonging to a profession, modified certainly by discipline loyalties, is important to many curators, however differently they may interpret it as individuals. As various modes of audit and assessment gain ground, this feeling is likely to grow rather than lessen. Codes of practice and codes of loyalty form an important part of the mind-set within which curators and museums operate.

Classification

All museum objects have names, frequently, as we shall see, more than one name reflecting their movement from one context to another, and those pieces that lack names exist in a kind of limbo. This proposition, however, can be turned round the other way: it is the function of the museum to provide objects and specimens with names through the interrelated process of classification and research, and to express this process in the formal procedures of documentation (here taken to mean the actual operation of an information system derived from classification and research) and collection management. The act of classification, which museum workers often call 'identification', is not as simple or transparent as it might at first sight appear.

A name is a medium for the communication of information although, as we have seen in Chapter 2, linguistic names are often a very clumsy way of conveying information about physical material and this is why museum people are driven to communicate with each other in terms like 'razor Type 3b' (for a Bronze Age piece of uncertain contemporary function) or 'with urn-shaped baluster stem with gadrooning' (for silver ware). These elaborate compound names are created in order to express fine shades of perceived difference between one object or specimen and another. The differences are structured as binary pairs, that is as pairings of yes : no answers given to possible questions. For Bronze Age metalwork, for example, the first question might be: does this object have a blade or not? For the razor, the answer would be 'yes'. The second question might be: is the blade of the right shape to fight with? Here the answer would be 'no'. Through the contrasting answers to simple questions like these, binary structuring can create classificatory sets capable of great elaboration as the questions become more complex. Figure 6.1 shows how beds are classified according to the yes/no answers given to three questions.

This is the fundamental principle of all classificatory systems and works both in ordinary life and across the museum disciplines to give us collection classificatory systems. In the life sciences it gives us the taxonomic system, based on the original insights of Linnaeus and now further developed in the fields of phenetics and cladistics (see Ross 1974; Eldredge and Cracroft 1980; Sokal and Sneath 1963) where the binary structures are organized in a hierarchical sequence in which the individual elements correspond to points in the structure. These taxonomic systems are often capable of expressing both synchronic relationships and diachronic or

head/foot board		canopy		single	
divan	-	divan	-	divan	+
double bed	+	double bed	-	double bed	-
single bed	+	single bed	-	single bed	+
fourposter	+	fourposter	+	fourposter	-

Figure 6.1 Beds: classification according to yes : no answers

sequential relationships through time. In archaeology, broadly the same approach gives us typological systems, which similarly encompass two-dimensional contemporaneity and the third dimension of time. In the fine and applied arts, and social history and anthropology, the same typological thinking and the same binary structure is at the base of all classificatory thought, although its nature is often obscured by the traditional historical scholarship upon which the answers to the questions in these disciplines depend. The recent heated controversy over true and false Rembrandts, for example, is being fought out through detailed historical research into provenances and ownerships and through judgements about lines and brush strokes, but the answers to the question 'True or False?' are structured in terms of the same yes : no pair. Social history has generated a number of classificatory systems, but their base, too, is the same.

The difficulties with the binary system are easier to state than to solve. The principal difficulty revolves around the framing of the questions that are asked. The questions have cultural content, that is, they express a particular stance derived from contemporary culture and past history, and they provoke a cultural answer which fits into the same pattern of relationships (even taking account of the fact that, especially in contemporary Western society, the local culture may inspire a deliberately anti-cultural response). This is, of course, why a biology curator and an archaeology curator may identify the same piece quite differently: to one, shells in a Bronze Age barrow are fossil *dentalium*, and to the other they are grave goods (Annable and Simpson 1964: 61). Further, a number of objects, of whatever type and whatever question system is being employed, always return ambiguous answers, and the system cannot show if this is because the piece is a genuine hybrid (and therefore potentially of great interest), or because the questions are inadequately framed, or because the classifier is not using the system correctly or bringing enough to it.

The nature of the classificatory sets which the binary questions produce can be further analysed by the methods of the taxonomical linguists (Berlin *et al.* 1973). Berlin makes the point that classification is based on similarity – like to like – organized by gradually increasing degrees of specificity. In Berlin's system the most general levels fill the top branches of the taxonomical tree, and the lower we go the more specific we become. The most general category is called the *unique beginner*, followed by the *intermediate level*, and then by the *generic level*. In daily life this *generic level* is the most socially and psychologically significant; it is the level at which we normally communicate with each other and at which we teach the link between things and names to children who, in baby-talk, are given words like 'birdie' (rated as a generic level word in ordinary speech) but not 'larkie' (a lower level word) (Wierzbicla 1985: 152). Below the generic level comes the *specific level* which embraces particular kinds of things from the generic level, and the *varietal level* which takes in particular types of things from the specific level. Berlin makes the interesting point that the words which represent the generic and higher levels are usually simple primary lexemes (i.e. one word), while the words for the two lower levels are usually secondary lexemes (i.e. the word glossed by a further descriptive word or words).

Figures 6.2–6.4 give three examples of how this taxonomic structure works, one

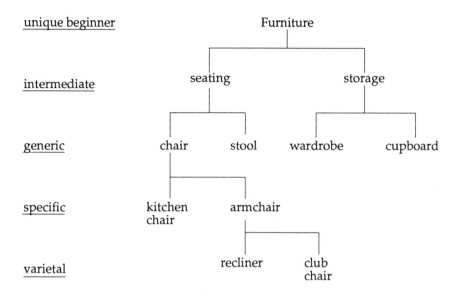

Figure 6.2 Furniture: taxonomic structure in daily speech

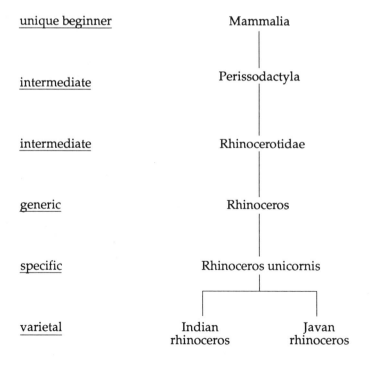

Figure 6.3 Natural history: Linnaean structure

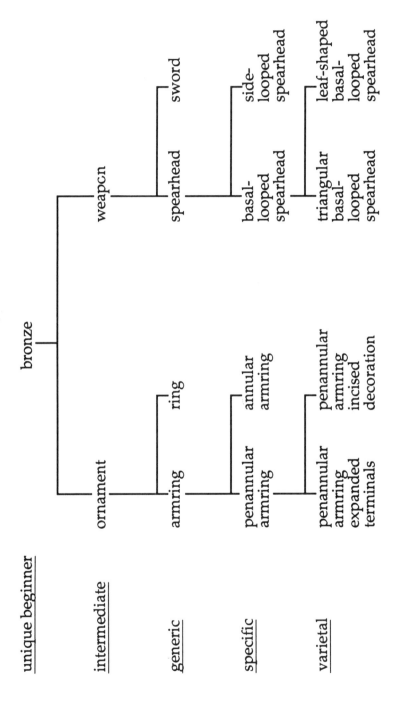

Figure 6.4 Bronze Age material: typological structure

drawn from furniture and representing a structure in use in daily speech, one drawn from the classic Linnaean taxonomy in use in the natural sciences, and one drawn from the kind of typological system used by archaeologists for a type of material culture, in this case Bronze Age metalwork. We can see here that the approach is more or less the same across the group and that the use of primary and secondary lexemes matches up, bearing out Berlin's analysis. However, there seems to be one important difference. In the Linnaean scheme, the distinctions between specimens at the sub-generic levels are produced by the same kind of yes : no questions which produced the distinctions at the higher level, that is by questions which relate to formal characteristics inherent in the material itself, while in the daily-use furniture structure, the questions which produce the higher two levels relate to a mixture of form and function and at the sub-generic level they relate to form ('armchair'), function ('recliner'), and location ('kitchen'). In the archaeological scheme there is an unclear and uneasy mixture of function and form within the questions asked, especially at the generic level, reflecting the fact that archaeologists usually have no direct way of knowing what function a piece was intended to perform and rely either on 'obvious' guesses – what we call a spearhead presumably *was* a spearhead – or on observations of form with which to create their categories.

On the face of it, this would suggest a fundamental difference between classifying in the natural and human fields, because in the human field the meaning behind the category is created as much by historical understanding of function and location – in a word, context – as it is by an understanding of form. Closer inspection suggests that this distinction is much less keen than might be supposed. The natural history collections of the past, upon which the Linnaean system and its developments depend, were formed through the workings of the human personal characteristics and intellectual preoccupations of the periods in which they were accumulated, as we have already seen. Natural history specimens carry with them their own histories of original selection and subsequent study and of placement within schemes, both on paper and in storage cabinets, and these create their own contexts which influence the meanings attributed to them.

We must now return to the point made at the beginning of this section – that objects inside museums usually have more than one name. This is because in the world of objects and specimens, several sets of classificatory systems are involved, and each piece occupies a place in several such: often these form a chronological sequence, but old names and sets do not drop out as the next is formed. We may distinguish three such sets: a production context (presumably unavailable to us for natural history specimens unless we take the Book of Genesis at face value); a daily life context (true for a large proportion of material); and a collection context (true, obviously, for all museum pieces). The collection context may be complex, including first collection by a private individual or an institution not a museum, and then collection by a museum, and this may involve two distinct or overlapping classificatory sets. There are two points of primary importance here. Firstly, the museum, as the holding institution at the end of the sequence, inherits all the previous nomenclature in which the specimen has been involved so far as this is known. All the names and sets will constitute entries in the documentation system, and all are likely to be used in one way or another. An exhibition label, for example, will probably draw on both daily life names and collection names. Secondly, the giving of the collection name, like the giving of all names, is a rite of passage which in this case marks the translation of the piece from the secular state of ordinary life to the sacred state of the established collection.

The production context set of names will include daily terms ('sugar bowl', 'saucer'), technical terms ('transfer-printed'), and terms somewhere between the two ('hand-painted'). It will also include trade names or descriptions which are purely social rather than technical and designed to flatter the potential purchaser ('Queen Charlotte's Ware'). The daily use context matches fairly closely the kind of thing given in the set for furniture in Figure 6.2, in that most native English-speakers in England would recognize and understand all the terms used there, although their understandings might not quite coincide. However, in normal conversation a sort of shorthand of this list is used, which relies chiefly on the generic level but draws on the specific or varietal levels as necessary. This, of course, applies as much to natural history specimens as it does to human history material. 'Dog' (primary lexeme), for example, would be the generic term most frequently employed, modified to 'large dog' (specific secondary lexeme describing form), 'next door's dog' (specific secondary lexeme describing location), 'sheep dog' (specific secondary lexeme describing function) or 'Cocker Spaniel' (varietal level secondary lexeme) as needed to clarify the message. In daily speech living things from the natural world, whether domestic or wild, are treated as if they are social beings, like people or artefacts, reflecting their integration into the normal social stucture.

The language of collection will absorb much of what has gone before, but will add to it in a number of illuminating ways. At the simplest and most private level of collection, the point at which everyday objects are taken out of circulation and put in a specially segregated place, the pieces acquire secondary descriptions of the 'Christening present', 'Granny's teapot', 'jug bought in Leicester market' type, the collecting processes associated with which we have explored in Chapters 3 and 4. At a more deliberately accumulative level the collector's language becomes more standardized and impersonal, moving very close to the museum language of the curator: this is equally true of the wealthy connoisseur who purchases Chinese ceramics, and the little girl with her fossil collection who struggles to identify her specimens 'properly'.

Once a piece has been formally accessioned into the collection of an established museum it has achieved, as it were, its collection apotheosis. It will now have two names which give it identity within two different (although sometimes inter-linked) museum systems. The first name is its unique accession name, which normally merely consists of a set of digits, sometimes with letters, in forms which have varied down the years. This name is a necessary identity in the processes of collection management, but a more particular name, with a different and larger kind of cultural content, is needed if the identified object is to be memorable and recognizable. This is because our memories, which are cultured, work through the interlinking association of image–name–object, while numbers only link with images and objects if they have come to take the place of a name, a process which our memories cannot manage for anything like the numbers of objects which museum collections involve. The cultural name the object is given derives from one or another, depending upon discipline, of the kind of collection context classificatory systems set out in Figures 6.3 and 6.4 for natural history and archaeology.

As we have seen with the Linnaean and archaeological classifications systems, these collection context systems share the same binary and hierarchical structure that the systems in other contexts have. What distinguishes the collection context systems is their intended impersonal and universal nature. They operate on the normative principle which suggests that typical assemblages of traits can be defined, and recognized as characteristic of particular individual specimens which then act as standards for their type. Individuals which do not conform, therefore, either run the risk of being disregarded or, alternatively, are the subject of special study. They are meant to overcome the communication gap brought by idiosyncratic identifications (of, for example, the informal collection kind) and to give specialists a common language, and this means that they must be comprehensive. Finally, they claim to be different, not in structure, but in kind, from systems in use outside the broad museum world, in that the classificatory system as a whole and the individual points upon it are together held to represent objective realities, or at least to be capable of defence in these terms, no matter how difficult this may sometimes be. In fact, of course, the truly impersonal and non-cultured is forever beyond our reach.

Most museum areas now possess terminology thesauri which set out lists of names and definitions for use in museum nomenclature and which have received various degrees of acceptance (e.g. for archaeology RCHME 1986; for costume ICOM 1982; for social history Stevens 1980 and SHIC 1983; general Orna 1983, Chenall 1978). Some of the largest established systems come from the social history area, and we will try to draw together the themes of this discussion by analysing one of these, the system in use in the Welsh Folk Museum which was established in the 1930s (Stevens 1980). Part of the Welsh Folk Museum system relating to Transport is set out in Figure 6.5. This shows that the classification uses a hierarchical system, in which there are two intermediate levels (air and land; slide cars and sleds, wheeled vehicles) before the daily speech generic level is reached with entries like 'coach' and 'farm cart'. However, sometimes the system lacks a clear distinction between the intermediate and the generic levels, which is most obvious in the section for sliding vehicles where the same words are used twice at the two different hierarchical levels.

This difficulty points to a fundamental characteristic of the system. It does not use a specialized curatorial or collection vocabulary of the kind employed in archaeology or the natural sciences; instead it draws its terms from the production and daily life nomenclature sets, and endeavours to organize these into a conceptual or 'objective' collection classificatory set through the use of the higher descriptive levels. As we have seen, in daily use structures (including those which relate to natural specimens like the dog), the questions which produce the structures usually involve a mixture of form, function and location, and this is why the

unique beginner	TRANSPORT
intermediate	LAND
intermediate	slide cars and sleds
generic	sledges
generic	slide cars
intermediate	wheeled vehicles
generic	ambulances
generic	bath chairs
generic	bicycles and tricycles
generic	coaches
varietal	coach horns
varietal	coach trunks
varietal	coach whips
specific	coaches, private
specific	stage coaches
generic	farm carts
specific	gambos
specific	horse carts
specific	Irish carts
specific	ox carts
specific	truckle carts

Figure 6.5 Part of Welsh Folk Museum classification system

Welsh Folk Museum terms are not intelligible within the terms of the system itself, but only with reference to other kinds of cultural and contextual information – a significant aspect, as we have seen, of all taxonomic classifications, but one which the social history systems make particularly clear.

We may sum up by saying that all objects and specimens operate simultaneously within several classificatory sets, including that which we recognise as museum-style nomenclature. All of these sets have characteristics in common: they all demonstrate a hierarchical structure, closely related to the way in which language works, of the kind that Berlin has demonstrated; and they are all built around perceptions which embrace not only formal matters of shape or intrinsic content, but also contextual matters to do with a broader knowledge and understanding of function, location and history. The various classificatory sets within which each piece operates are not clearly distinct, but overlap and intermingle, and in particular the museum collection classificatory systems frequently include both their own language and language from other sets, of production or daily use.

Research

The creation of knowledge and understanding from which the classification systems spring is, of course, the province of what is usually called research. It is this knowledge and understanding which frames the questions that create the binary structure upon which classification depends; and, equally, the current state of classification always exercises a major influence upon the nature of questions and knowledge (see, for example, in relation to natural history systematic collections Morgan 1986; *Biological Collections UK* 1987). The whole process generates meaning, and it rests on the assumption that taxonomic classification of this kind corresponds in some direct way to the real world.

The research approaches particularly relevant to museum material are those which arise from the specific nature of objects as lumps of the material world, a nature which, as we saw in Chapter 2, generates a need to understand their physical properties, their biographies in time and their locations in space. In the most immediate sense, the physical properties of objects are the result of a range of technological processes, all of which generate their own suite of investigatory techniques. The technology of object production, embracing the manufacturing processes which run from the selection of the raw materials through to their initial refinement, their combination in a huge range of ways to produce the embryonic object, and the equally enormous variety of finishing processes to create the final piece, has generated a range of scientific characterization techniques and a vast literature of its own (see, for example, Philips 1985). Indeed, until the last few decades, and always with the exception of high art objects, what passed for material culture studies have concentrated upon the making of objects virtually to the exclusion of all other aspects of their being, and these aspects of object study can indeed give considerable illumination provided they are linked with other conceptual considerations.

The most important, and most difficult, of these considerations is the vexed question of what constitutes form or style and how forms or styles can be distinguished one from another: crucial questions in the formation of any classificatory system (see Sackett 1985; Weissner 1985). The way in which we perceive the form of an object, taken to include both its basic 'shape' and any further work or ornament which it may carry, or the structure of a natural history specimen, governs the ways in which we understand its relationship to other pieces which are seen as 'identical', 'very like', 'like' or 'different' along a sliding scale which ends with 'completely dissimilar'. The trained eye automatically performs an act of classification on the material before it, creating sets, clusters and sequences on the strength of similarity and difference, great and small. This, the normal way of distinguishing one form from another, however refined by the addition of accurate measuring and other quantitative and qualitative techniques, is clearly subjective and runs the risk of becoming enmeshed in a kind of chicken-and-egg circularity of argument. The only way forward is by continual critical reappraisal of the evidence, influenced, as it will be, by the discovery of fresh specimens and by new ideas.

What is clear in the human history field (as art historians have always realized), is that change in form and style is part and parcel of the whole broad body of contemporary economic organization, thought and feeling, and can only be appreciated as part of the effort to understand the historical situation of which material culture itself was an important part. This is another way of saying that the study of form and decoration should be linked with the development of object biographies. This study will use the normal documentary techniques of the historian, which will produce information about the circumstances of the object's making, of its progressive owners and of its use up to its inclusion in a museum collection. It will also, particularly for archaeologists and sometimes social anthropologists, involve the techniques of location analysis designed to show up various kinds of patterning in the physical and human landscape (see Haggett 1965). All this is such familiar ground to museum workers that it needs no stressing, but the reason for the activity bears underlining: it is the understanding of the object's historical position, no matter to what extent this understanding is inferential, which gives meaning to the object, which gives it cultural content. It is from this cultural meaning that all scientific importance, all designated value and all pleasure flows.

Let us take one example, from the thousands possible, to illustrate the point. In his study of stylistic changes in silver candlesticks between 1680 and 1780, Sinclair (1987) was able to gather descriptive information about the shape and decoration of the pieces and historical information about their dates and makers. He was able to use this information to distinguish five groups of formal and decorative features, each of which characterized a period and, of course, defined the existence of that period in candlestick terms. From this he was able to construct a battleship curve graph (Figure 6.6) showing the popularity of different design motifs over time. These design motifs match the main art styles of the day as these have been recognized by art historians, so that 'there is a pattern existing at the national level, in silver, corresponding to some form of common "taste" held by people who bought silver' (Sinclair 1987: 50). Baroque art, for example, used the techniques of closure followed by expansion to achieve the illusion of distance, relief and triumph, and of this technique the contemporary urn-shaped baluster stem candlestick is a fine example. With this can be linked themes from contemporary political, social and economic history to give us a rounded appreciation of why candlesticks were as they were.

The creation of meaning in natural history specimens is probably different in emphasis rather than in kind. For plant specimens in an herbarium, techniques of comparison are crucial to the creation of classification, and here also an understanding of the *meaning* of the revealed similarities and differences can only be achieved through the reconstruction of past ecological contexts, which show both why plant species developed as they did and what relationship the species had one

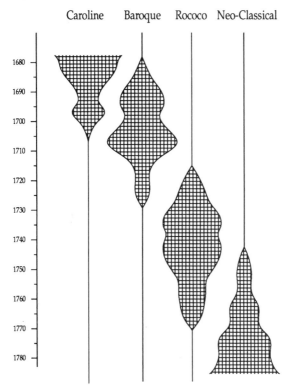

Scale ⊢—⊣ = 20% of sample

1660–1705	Caroline	Classical features; column stem, fluting, leaves, etc.
1685–1715	Baroque	Control of perspective; urn-shaped baluster stem gadrooning, palmettes
1712–1725	Queen Anne	Absence of decoration; facetted stems
1720–1765	Rococo	Naturalistic motifs; scrolls, scallop shells, leaves, animals
1755–1800	Neo-Classical	Classical features; column stems, cartouches, garlands, ram's heads, geometric decoration.

Figure 6.6 Stylistic change in silver candlesticks, 1660–1800 (after Sinclair 1987, fig. 5.4)

to another. Charts showing the incidence of pollen in ancient environments, for example, sometimes look like the battleship curve diagram used for the candlesticks, and are conveying similar information. When natural history becomes environmental history, human affairs, political, social and economic, are as much a part of its meaning as they are in the fine arts.

Historical research has a further museum dimension, and this is the study of what has happened to objects and specimens after they have been collected, a study quite separate from that designed to understand the processes of collection formation, or of that involved in discipline-based research just discussed, but with its own significance in the creation of knowledge and meaning. Collected objects have a second life, into which they carry the accumulated meanings of their original lives, but in which they are treated quite differently. While they are still in private hands they come and go from one owner to another like any other piece of valuable (or at least valued) moveable property, and sometimes drop out of sight and out of mind in obscure resting places. Even if they have been formally accessioned into a museum collection, their original associations may have become lost or confused. Reconstructing the pedigree of objects and tracing pieces back to their original provenances is, therefore, an important part of museum work. Kaeppler's identification of the material which survives from Captain James Cook's Pacific voyages, using the actual material and documents like the catalogue of the Leverian sale (1806) and Sarah Stone's sketch books (produced before 1786 and published in 1968), was a classic of this kind of work. The eighteenth-century Cook-voyage Pacific material culture held in many museums, and the identificatory work performed with it, together constitute a body of knowledge of great significance for our better understanding of early contact-period Polynesian cultures, and of how they were perceived by Europeans (Kaeppler 1979).

All this interlinked conceptual and information-gathering effort of classification and research through which meaning is generated has to be translated into practical museum effect, and so it is to the broad area of collection management policies and their implications that we must now turn.

The Implications of Collection Management Policies

As we have seen in the foregoing chapters, 'the collections' are an immensely complex body of material evidence, an archive which embraces not only the physical evidence of our human and natural past, but also of how this past has itself been interpreted as decade has succeeded decade, and layers of meaning have been generated through study and research. This accumulation of material and meaning must be translated into practical museum policies if it is to be kept from disintegration, and these are what we call collection management policies. Much has been written about the detail of collection management policies (e.g. Lord *et al.* 1989) and about the ideas which they embody in relation to contemporary collecting and acquisition, de-accessioning and disposal, storage and basic conservation, documentation and some aspects of collection use. The analysis of eighteen such policies, taken from museums with significant holdings of British archaeology (Pearce 1990: 85-6) shows the range of topics which, to a greater or lesser extent, individual policies take into consideration.

The superstructure of detailed collection management policies rests upon three fundamental points. Firstly, the policies describe a relationship among the existing museum and its collections, the museum authorities and staff, and the outside world. Secondly, the trajectory of this relationship is set by the sum of the previous relationships among these three parties, all of which have to be taken into account whatever decisions may be made in the future. Thirdly, the relationship between the three is in a constant state of interaction, and in particular the museum worker's relationship with the archive is a steady process of action and reaction in which existing and incoming collections, the management of museum policies and the exercise of judgement are woven together into the explicit actions which make up every working day. The last point is crucial and needs amplification. Collection management policies may be intended to regulate activities in the present and future, but they take their character from the accumulated archive and associated meaning of the past, that is, from all the museum and collecting characteristics already described, and particularly from the curatorial inheritance described in the first main section of this chapter; the daily curatorial decisions made by museum workers are framed in the light of the social traditions, including study and research, which they have inherited.

The implications of this come right down to the most basic levels of resource expenditure. Those pieces which have already responded well to basic classificatory information-gathering are likely to get the larger share of future research work, while other pieces about which, through chance or through early lack of interest (itself, of course, a product of the system), nothing much is known, will perforce remain neglected. These chosen pieces will also be those which are displayed, published and used to illustrate posters. Decisions about which pieces get conservation priority or a place in top-class storage are made in relation to their perceived value in the museological scheme of things, that is in terms of their intellectual meaning, their aesthetic quality, their potential for public interpretation and their political implications (if any).

Choices have to be made because care resources are always inadequate. They are made on the basis of current thinking, so, for example, herbaria up and down the country were neglected for a substantial period in the middle part of this century. The information which they contain is now seen to have an interesting bearing both on changing habitats and green issues, and on the broader history of science, but significant elements of this information are now irretrievably lost. The same is true of old archaeology collections and of considerable holdings of social history material. Policies about the organization of collections, in the most fundamental sense of what racking is bought and how it is used to house material, help in the construction of narratives about value and importance which pick up an existing story and carry the serial forward into the next episode. To pursue the metaphor, sometimes the significance of individual characters waxes or wanes, or the characters disappear altogether, but the story retains its thrust and coherence.

The same is true of the vexed questions of acquisition and (especially) disposal, its dark twin. Acquisitions are made as matters of curatorial judgement with all that this implies. Disposal (or de-accessioning as some quarters prefer to call it) violates the supposed sanctity of museum collections and forces the curator to be explicit about the conceptual reasons for retaining or shedding particular groups of material, generating corresponding unhappiness (see Besterman 1991; Borg 1991; Fleming 1991 for discussion of current views).

The accumulated decisions of all these kinds which make up the management of a collections policy serve to reinforce the conceptual system which created them. This is clearly true in acquisition and disposal, the product of which is likely to be (is intended to be) a collection 'truer' to itself than it was before. It is equally true in the operation of documentation. Documentation, in the sense used here, is the translation of gathered information, classification and research into a usable information record system. Once this record is set up, however, it plays its part in solidifying the whole system, whether in amber to our admiration or in concrete to our despair. The thrust of the decisions already embodied in the system will have a pervasive feedback effect upon all other decisions. The same is true of publications which, in museums, in addition to all the usual forms of publication, include exhibition catalogues and *catalogues raisonnées* as well as a large range of information leaflets and the like. Here again, what will be published in the future feeds upon what was published in the past, in terms both of content and of social access to the range of publication approaches and formats.

The thrust of this argument has been to suggest that collection policies and their operation are not the neutral or passive instruments of policy which has been decided elsewhere. They play a significant part in the interactive process through which museum meanings are constructed. They are part of a cycle which includes the nature and history of collections before and after they have entered a museum, and the inherited mind-set of the museum worker, itself in part created by the existence of collections amongst which he will work.

Meaningful Exhibition: Knowledge Displayed

The exhibition of collected material within a specific roofed space – a 'room' or a 'gallery' – is the characteristic or traditional (which here means much the same) form of museum exposition, so much so that 'museum', 'collection' and 'exhibition' are and always have been intertwined ideas and interdependent activities. The way in which exhibitions work is at the heart of the museum phenomenon, yet this aspect of display has generally been neglected. Attention and discussion has been lavished upon the *content* of exhibitions, upon what material is shown against what choice of background, but very little has been said about exhibition as *form* and of the formal characteristics of the type. It is this side of exhibitions that the discussion here will concentrate upon.

Museum exhibitions are events in their own right, a medium which embraces many media but in which the whole is richer than the sum of its parts. Each exhibition is a production, like a theatrical production, and like a play, it is a specific work of culture with game rules of its own. The seeming obviousness of these points – their apparent naturalness – should not blind us either to their importance or to their historical particularity as an aspect of traditional modern Western culture. Exhibitions make their statements through their own formal conventions, and these comprise firstly the enclosed space of the gallery. The gallery will have specific dimensions of length, width and ceiling height, and possibly of window positions and sizes if any natural light is permitted. It must have at least one doorway as entrance and exit point. Within this space are the three-dimensional installations which range in complexity from the hanging of modern pictures directly on to four white walls, to the complex display units required to house an exhibition like *Human Biology* at the Natural History Museum, London. Associated with these installations are the objects themselves, and a range of lights, plinths and two-dimensional graphics including labels.

The nature of museum exhibition, then, comprises an enclosed indoor space, divided into units by display casing which tends, the nature of a room being what it is, to cling to the four walls and to cut up the central space into various shapes. This casing transmits the objects and other display pieces through glass, and does so in vague relationship to the size and scope of the human body. A certain amount, sometimes a considerable amount, of influence can be brought to bear upon the viewer by choosing paint and fabric colour, and above all lighting, which maximize or minimize the impact of all these features, and direct the viewer's attention.

The way in which the installations are organized within the space, what we may call exhibition morphology, and the implications of this has been the subject of study at the Royal Ontario Museum (1976: 107–13) and the Bartlet School of Architecture and Planning, London University (Peponis and Hesdin 1982). Work in Ontario has shown that, since most people take the shortest route between two points, the floor plan of an exhibit has a crucial influence on how much of it most people will see. A fairly typical exhibition plan is shown in Figure 6.7, and the Ontario work demonstrates that most people will take the unshaded path and look at those cases marked A; a few will linger sufficiently to look at those marked B; and a very few will penetrate the shaded areas to those marked C. With this plot in mind, it is possible to create an exhibition plan which links information hierarchy and visitor flow.

The conclusions of Peponis and Hesdin are more fundamental, and show how the relationship between spaces in a gallery crucially affects the ways in which knowledge is generated, and the kind of knowledge that it is. Three relational properties can be isolated. The first concerns the relative separation of spaces between one display unit and another; this is defined as *depth*, and the aggregate of space separation shows that some exhibitions are deeper than others. The second concerns the provision of alternative ways of going from one space to another, that is the number of *rings* in the plan. The final property bears on the ease with which the viewer comprehends the structural planning of the gallery; this property is known as *entropy*, and the more entropic a gallery is, the less it is structured.

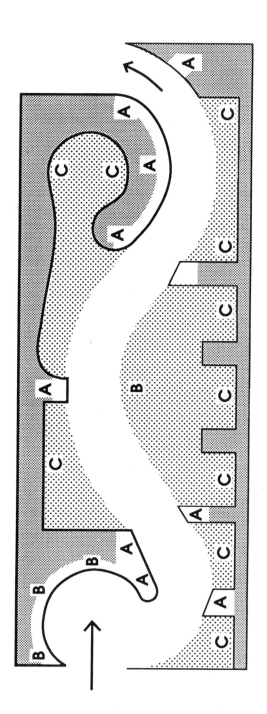

A   Constant flow

B   Crowd stoppage

C   Variable

Figure 6.7 Exhibitions: the organization of space in relation to visitor flow and information hierarchy (after ROM 1976: 107)

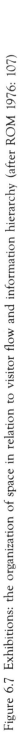

The social connotations of this morphological analysis are important, because the whole process crystallizes what many curators and visitors feel in an intuitive way when they walk round a gallery. To put it rather crudely, exhibitions with strong axial structures, shallow depth and a low ring factor present knowledge as if it were the map of well-known terrain where the relationship of each part to another, and all to the whole, is thoroughly understood; exhibitions whose plans show a high degree of entropy (or a weaker structure), considerable depth and a high ring factor show knowledge as a proposition which may stimulate further, or different, answering propositions. Peponis and Hesdin illustrate this by reference to two contrasting galleries in the Natural History Museum, London (Figure 6.8). The Bird Gallery, with its taxonomic base, belongs to the 'knowledge understood' class, while the Hall of Human Biology belongs in the 'knowledge proposition' class. These, and other potential ways of analysing the presentation of knowledge in exhibitions, serve to emphasize the underlying reality that galleries are a closely defined production, following their own clearly marked conventions, which form their own mode of showing and telling, with characteristic limitations and possibilities.

This brings us to the next important point about exhibitions, a point which is implicit in much of what has been said. Although museum exhibition from very roughly the later fifteenth century to the present day has its own internal history, it is itself an element of the modern ways of thought of which museums as a whole are a part. Exhibition, the belief that knowledge can be laid out as a demonstration in temporal, three-dimensional space and that this is morally desirable and promotes the development of fresh knowledge, is itself a meta-narrative of the modern world. It is an overarching image which transcends the individual topics upon which any particular exhibition might concentrate. Exhibition is a characteristic construction of the age, like the printed book, the framed picture, the secular musical or theatrical performance. It is the *opus* which demonstrates the work of collection and curation, and the creation of the lattice of reference and interrelationship, which requires controlled space for its exposition.

It is doubtful if the taxonomic relationships of animal and plant species, or the stratigraphic relationships of geological beds and the fossils within them, could be made intelligible, could really be said to exist at all as a meaningful concept, without the organized space and serried cases of the gallery which demonstrate the related specimens and make knowledge actual. The same is true of chronological sequences of historical material or typological sequences of artefacts. This kind of knowledge and its demonstration in exhibition are one and the same. Like the other constructs of the age, it takes for granted the notion of public exposition as an element in the idea of progress, but like the others, it can be fully understood only by those who have been trained to do so, who understand the conventions and feel at home in the performance.

The notions of 'actuality' and 'performance' bear closer investigation. The earlier discussions about the relationship of individual objects to their past (p. 24) and of collected material to this original context (p. 38), which drew on broadly Saussurian semiotic insights, showed that both objects and collections carry a two-

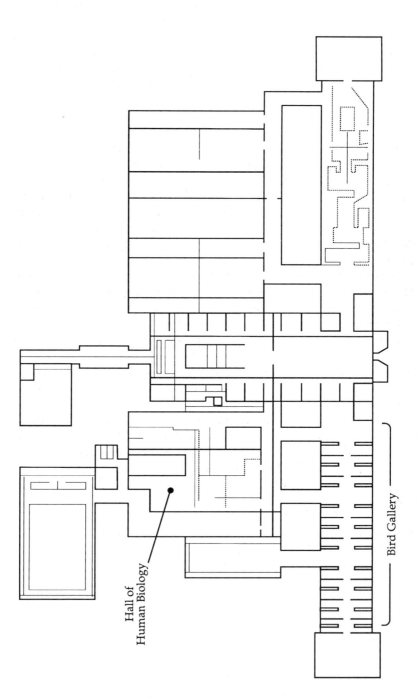

Figure 6.8 Plan of ground floor of Natural History Museum, London (after Peponis and Hesdin 1982)

fold nature which embraces a continuing real or metonymic relationship to their own time and place and a metaphorical relationship to their original context, which arises from the processes of selection and interpretation with which they have been involved. Material is transformed by the collecting process into a museum collection archive, and clearly it is transformed again as a further stage in the same sequence by the exhibition process. Figure 6.9 shows how this happens by adding the exhibition phase on to the original context and collection phases which have already been set out in Figure 3.2. It is obvious that the body of material which represents 'the past' (whether this past is of a human or a natural context) appears in a sequence in which the *parole* of the previous form becomes the *langue* of the next. In other words, the physical embodiment, the *signifier* and the concepts which it embodies, and the *signified* (that is, the operation of the *langue*) together constitute the *sign* (the *parole*) which then goes on to become the signifier of the next stage. The exhibition (and of course any succeeding exhibitions, and the publication and poster material which may accompany them) is the final element in this chain. It bears a metaphorical or symbolic relationship to all that preceded it, and this is implicit in the idea of performance, but it retains its integral link with past reality through its display of real material, and this is the essence of its actuality.

There is much more to this kind of analysis than a mere playing with terms and diagrams, no matter how irritating the semiotic games can sometimes be. The perpetual creation and re-creation of meaning by which existing signs and symbols go towards the making of new ones seems to be a fundamental part of the way in which we humans understand the world and come to terms with our place in it. It is the crucial act of imagination by which we make sense of our common pasts and presents and project these into the future, and museum exhibition is an important part of this process.

Meaning in exhibitions is made through a range of processes in which the medium and the way it gives its message are indistinguishable. Exhibitions make meaning through the conventions proper to them, the organization of enclosed space which carries displayed material. The kind of meaning which is generated, and the exhibition form which this meaning takes, is part and parcel of the overarching meta-narrative of knowledge and understanding which form the basis of the modern world. Within this, exhibitions are tied to past realities by the material which they show, but as works of interpretation, they bear only a metaphorical relationship to this reality. Like all metaphor, this interpretation is a narrative, an inscription, a mediation between one thing and another, in which the curatorial work of selection and description and the design work of presentation play the crucial creative role. Exhibitions are works of imagination operating within an understood tradition of knowledge and interpretation, and contributing their share towards both the maintenance and the development of this tradition.

This chapter has explored the position of the curator, and of his characteristic activities in the classification, research and exhibition fields, in the construction of knowledge and the making of meaning in museums. This has underlined the inextricable nature of theory and practice, structure and content, method and outcome. It suggests that the kinds of meanings which are going to be generated are implicit in

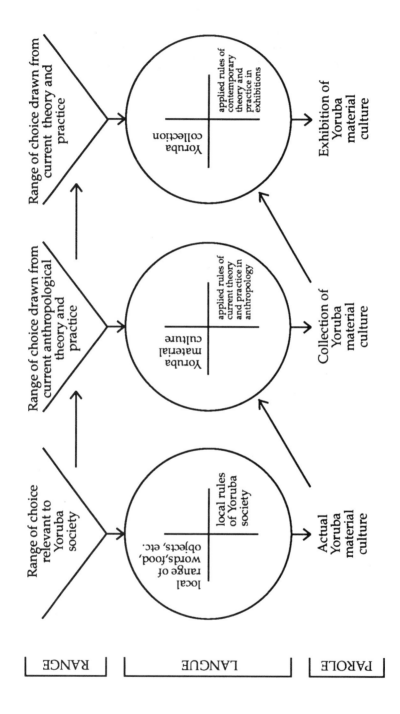

Figure 6.9 Semiotic analysis of exhibition

the ways in which recognized fields of study and collection management operate. These contribute their share to the broader ways of thought through which meaning is made, but these broader ways themselves also provide frameworks within which the meaning of museum material is generated. It is to these ways of thinking about the material word, and their implications, that we must now turn.

7   Meaning as Function

According to the materialist conception, the determining factor in history is, in the final instance, the production and reproduction of the immediate essentials of life. This, again, is of a twofold character. On the one side the production of the means of existence, of articles of food and clothing, dwellings, and of the tools necessary for that production; on the other side, the production of human beings themselves, the propagation of the species.

(Engels 1940: Preface)

When a gallery lecturer ignores the sheen on the Virgin Mary's robe for the Church's use of religious art in the Counter-Reformation, the new art history is casting its shadow.

(Rees and Borzello 1986: 2)

Red Clays and White
From about 1720 white clays began to be imported from Devonshire and were used with the local clays. This made new sorts of ware and decoration possible. John Astbury (1688–1743) is believed to have introduced the white clay, and to have pioneered its use, as applied decoration on teapots, and mixed with red clay to make figures.

(Label, Decorative Arts Gallery, 1992, New Walk Museum, Leicester)

Introduction

The objects, the accumulated collections and museum material, whose nature, history and curation we have traced in the preceding chapters both generate and are illuminated by overarching interpretative philosophies. These philosophies fall into three broad types, each of which links up with the principal characteristics of objects discussed in Chapter 2. We saw there, in the section entitled 'Subject and Object: Mind and Matter', that a basic trend in European thought has been to treat objects as the passive recipients or expressions of thought and action. This eventually gave rise to the functionalist view of material culture, where objects, in common with other social forms, are given an essentially materialistic or utilitarian role. In the second on 'The Social Life of Objects' we saw, among other things, that objects act, like language, as the communication systems through which society is constituted: their ability to do this can be analysed using the approaches of semiotics and structuralism. In the section entitled 'The Real Thing' we saw that objects have a unique relationship to their historic contexts, and this gives them a particular role in the interpretation of the past.

One way or another, one or more of these interpretative approaches is involved in every effort to generate meaning with museum material. This is true for the study of museum material and for the publications which come from that study. It is also true for museum exhibitions, where the underlying rationale of the exhibition draws explicitly and implicitly on one or more of the interpretative stances. A moment's reflection shows that this is true across the museum disciplines, and does not only relate to human history material in the broad sense. Natural history material, as we have seen (p. 30), bears a semiotic relationship to the natural world, and acts as its own kind of communication system. It also draws its authenticity from its real relationship to its own historical or original context. Similarly, it is frequently treated from a functionalist stance, and this in two ways: partly because nature is seen as an element within human culture, and partly (and more significantly) because nature viewed as an ecological system provided the basic metaphor which stands at the root of the modern functionalist idea. It is to the nature of this idea that we must now turn.

Objects in Use

As we saw in Chapter 6, the reaction against Pitt Rivers' view of material culture as a Darwinian origin of types and survival of the best-suited generated an interest which turned away from objects as such, and concentrated upon the study of the whole social context of an individual community. The practitioners of what was to be called 'functionalism' were almost all anthropologists working generally on non-European communities, and included Emile Durkheim in France, whose *Règles de la Methode Sociologique* appeared as early as 1895, Boas in North America (see Jacknis 1986), and Radcliffe-Brown (1922) and Malinowski (1922) in England.

These functionalist anthropologists were not all of the same breed, as Leach points out (1982: 28). For Malinowski the approach served as a way of 'understanding' what he observed and seeing how it 'made sense' within its whole social context, but the point of this was to advance the understanding of the nature of man, whom social institutions existed to serve – not the nature of society. As Leach says, 'Malinowski viewed the integration of society from the inside, rather than the outside; as the consequence of individual self interest rather than social necessity' (1982: 28).

Radcliffe-Brown, on the other hand, saw anthropology as a 'generalizing science', 'a comparative sociology' which was intended to produce universally valid 'laws' about human society through a comparative process. He saw the problem from the outside and perceived a range of social types, each of which finds expression in a characteristic system of belief and practice. It follows that the establishment of a taxonomy of social types should be possible, classified according to their kinds of internal structures. As we shall see, Radcliffe-Brown's cross-cultural approach, with its predictive and determinist implications, was to prove more influential, especially in the 1960s and 1970s, than Malinowski's individualist sympathies. The idea of a 'functionalist school' with internal coherence of thought and method must be rejected, following Radcliffe-Brown himself who bluntly declared 'the Functional School does not really exist; it is a myth' (1952: 188). Nevertheless, 'functionalism' remains a useful, indeed necessary, word to describe several strands of thought which share a common basis.

This basis rests in the general proposition that the principal aim of a society is to continue to exist. It follows that all its institutions, including its technology and material culture, embody a series of adaptations to the environment, both physical and social, which enable it to survive. Accordingly we can look at these interrelated parts and explain one component by showing how it works in relation to all the others, and hence the concern with communities as a whole. The analogy between society and living organisms is as old as the functional stance, reflecting the power of biology in the scientific philosophy of the day, and thus we read analogies between social elements and the way in which the stomach plays its part in keeping the whole animal alive: the stomach is necessary to the whole, but by itself it lacks any meaning. The corollary to this organic model often seems to be the detached observer gazing into the glass-sided ants' nest, but the theory stresses the essential materiality or utility of social practice, seeing social elements fitting together in ways that make sense in survival terms, and doing this by adaptations which make equilibrium achievable.

There is a further point which is of particular interest to us. Functionalist thought may stress materiality in the broad sense, but it has shown little interest in material goods as such. The functionalist writers were not concerned to develop a theory of material culture interpretation, and the general impression given by their work is that artefacts, though essential to social operation, are merely passive reflections of needs, not active constituents of social practice. Objects are seen as the outcome of thoughts, feelings and decisions which have been taken elsewhere, and of which they are deemed to be a simple mirror image. They are, as it were, the hyphen between technology and environment. When the New Archaeologists of the 1960s began to develop a broad archaeological systematic functionalism (see below), material culture was given an enhanced role, but the notion of a direct one-to-one relationship was retained. One by-product of this view of objects was the relatively low esteem in which museums and their collections were held in the early and middle parts of the twentieth century, a view which has only recently begun to change.

In functionalist terms then, the aim of a society is to perpetuate itself by good adjustment internally through the mutual support of its component parts, and externally through its stable relationships with its environment, including other societies with which it is in contact. Within this framework, three types of adjustment are necessary in order to create stability and survival. The first involves sensitive adaptation to the physical environment – ecological adaptation; the second concerns the internal arrangement of social components, broadly cultural institutions, so that they complement each other; and the third revolves around the process by which each individual finds a 'useful' place in his or her society.

Whatever considered functionalist theory may suggest, there is in functionalist writing a distinct tendency to give the first of these types priority, and to understand culture as the outcome of adaptation to the environment through a process in which technology is the adaptive medium of mechanism, and material culture the outcome. This presumes, as it were, a clear slate in which the human group has to make a living from the ecological conditions in which it finds itself, and does so by creating the best possible kit from the available resources in order to exploit the available food and shelter. From this basis, social institutions naturally shape themselves to give communal and individual life patterns.

This theoretical sequence of environment–survival strategy–material culture–social institution lies at the heart of the great majority of exhibitions mounted in the human history field, in which a simple relationship between environment and social strategies is taken for granted, and considerable effort is characteristically devoted to demonstrating exactly how the artefacts are made in terms of their raw material and technology, the organization of production and how they are used.

A typical exhibition based on this interpretative stance would be that showing Inuit life and the role of the Inuit kayak (see Plate 21). The exhibition would explain that kayaks are a response to the need to hunt sea mammals, especially seal, in the Arctic seas: these animals are, with caribou, the main food source. They are constructed from material native to the environment and exploitable within a stone tool technology, chiefly sea mammal hide, sinew and bone or ivory, and driftwood. The lack of metal is an advantage because the organic materials will not rust, and the binding and lashing techniques produce a craft which is light, lacks sharp edges which would cut into the skin cover, and has a certain amount of flexibility. The display would demonstrate that the slender shape is well adapted to the Arctic sea, but within the broad design, finely congruent variations are possible.

The Greenland kayaks are the longest and most slender, we would be told, because this works best in the local conditions of sea and ice. The kayaks of the Central Arctic archipelago, which must operate in relatively narrow sea channels through which the pack-ice flows, tend to be rather heavier and broader. The kayaks of the Bering Sea and the Alaska coast are broader in the beam and blunter in the bow to suit the strong ocean seas. All these craft are designed to carry a single seal-hunter who is equipped with harpoon gear which makes it possible to kill at a distance and so avoid the possible upset caused by a relatively large animal in its death throes close by, which can be quickly fatal to a man in such cold water. The labels would tell us that experience has shown that this is the best hunting method, and it has helped to create the social institution of the solitary hunter who, in a society where many things are held in common, possesses his hunting equipment in individual ownership.

This very simple example shows some of the drawbacks of this characteristic approach. It is possible to live in the Arctic both as our Inuit hunter and as an American airman on a base equipped with nuclear warheads, and the functionalist

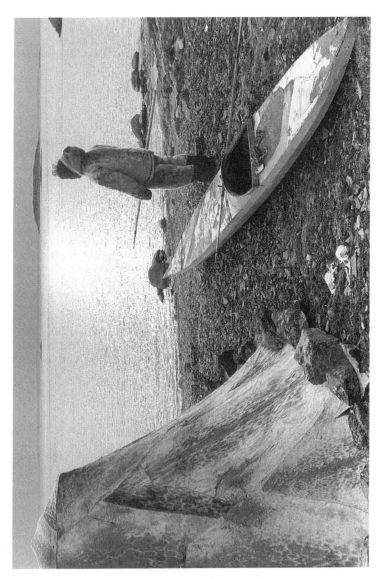

Plate 21.   Inuit looking out to sea, standing beside skin tent with kayak on the ground, Pelly Bay, North West Territories, Canada, in 1961. This photograph was used to demonstrate the functional role of the kayak in the exhibition on Inuit culture held at Exeter City Museum in 1975, and in the transfer of the exhibition to Anchorage, Alaska, in 1976 (photo: D. Wilkinson, Information Canada Photoleque).

line of argument gives us no help in deciding why one or the other (or both) has come about. In this simple form, it cannot explain why Inuit society itself has changed, because it rests on the assumption that stable equilibrium is the natural state of things. This means that all change has to be initiated by external events which impinge upon the social structure and upset its system of finely attuned adaptions. Hill, for example, wrote: 'no system can change itself; change can only be instigated by outside sources. If a system is in equilibrium, it will remain so unless imputs (or lack of outputs) from outside the system disturb the equilibrium' (1977: 6). This has meant a concentration on the social imput of 'outside' or independent variables, especially long-distance trade, like that which brought guns and alcohol to the Arctic communities, war, environmental change, and population growth. However, the last two certainly, and sometimes the first two also, are quite as much the result of internal social adaptation having unforeseen consequences as they are of external impact.

Decoration and Distinction

Before we examine these difficulties more closely, let us turn to a second example drawn from a complex society, which brings the second two types of adjustment, institutional and individual, into sharper functionalist focus, and do this in terms of the kind of object which can be said to exist only in a collection context, as souvenir or fetish, or as part of a museum's holdings. On 20 March 1990 Christies held a sale in London of orders, decorations and campaign medals. Among the items sold was a rare George Medal and Bar, awarded to Able Seaman William Bevan, Royal Navy. Bevan won the original decoration on 22 December 1940 when he helped to defuse a bomb threatening the Electricity Power Station, Trafford Park, Manchester, and he won his second George Medal on 11 May 1941 by defusing a bomb jammed in the girders of the roof of the London Palladium Theatre. It is clear that during these years the country's institutions were all adapted to the purpose of keeping Britain on a successful war footing, and that these institutions included both the traditional ones like law and order, and new ones like conscription of human beings, increased production through control mechanisms like compulsory shift work, and rationing. All these arrangements worked together to bring about the country's survival and ultimate victory, in that very specialized interaction with neighbours we describe as 'war'. The individual was integrated into the system through the personal determination, socially endorsed, to 'do my bit'. In Bevan's case this meant service in the Royal Navy, itself a major adaptive strategy for an island state and so one attracting prestige and recognition (both highly valued) for its sailors.

Bevan's first award was in connection with the maintenance of the Manchester power supply, a utility vital to the war effort. His human need to prove himself brave and resourceful had been harnessed into a social role which made him willing to risk his life to save a power station. His second award recognized his effort to save the London Palladium, at which Flanagan and Allen appeared with the Crazy

Gang throughout the war. London in general, and theatres like the Palladium in particular, were crucial to morale during the war, and here a belief in the English sense of humour, shared by all English men and women but incomprehensible to inferior foreigners, played a very special part. Bars to George Medals are very rare, and we may wonder if Bevan received his chiefly because he was involved in so morale-boosting an incident.

The decoration itself, like all others of its kind, is equally an institution with a social role, to encourage and endorse bravery and self-sacrifice in the interests of the community. The metal and ribbon is useless of itself, but the object represents a ritual of great social significance. A decoration achieves a quasi-religious quality, which is underlined when it takes a cross-shape, as many of the most highly regarded British decorations do, and the frequently dead or injured recipient is more-or-less explicitly identified with Christ. The individual is persuaded to value these awards very highly, and so the supposed moral qualities of religious feeling, courage, manhood and humour are turned into functioning institutions of the community with a role in its survival. We may add, also, that the right to choose who receives an award is one of the ways in which the country's establishment maintains its own role in the system.

We should not forget that nearly fifty years after the first award, Bevan's George Medal was sold at Christies where it (and his two service medals) fetched £2,640, a modest figure by London saleroom standards, but still a substantial outlay for many collectors. The great auction houses are a functioning part of Britain's economy, so much so that it is probably for their benefit that the United Kingdom has so far failed to ratify the UNESCO *Convention on the means of prohibiting and preventing the illicit import, export and transfer of ownership of cultural property* (1970). Where sales of fine art are concerned, it is clear that aesthetic qualities are harnessed to a classic functionalist role, paralleling those given to the moral qualities we have just discussed. The functionalist ethic can even help to determine how aesthetic judgements operate because steady prices, changes in fashion and the emergence of new groups, and the expertise of art historians all have a 'useful' role, not only from a cynical point of view, but also because the very notion of aesthetic value has a part in the maintenance of social equilibrium. At the 20 March 1990 sale, the auctioneer's role successfully adapted to these purposes both the collector's urge to acquire, and the present nostalgia for the forties, underlined by the use on the front of the sale catalogue of the famous photograph from the Blitz, showing the dome of St Paul's Cathedral rising serene above the skeletons of burnt-out houses and the smoke of the bombs. A museum display of the George Medal and Bar would probably carry a label giving the details of the award, and the meat of the functionalist analysis given here would be immediately apparent to the visitor.

A number of analytical processes have been devised as ways of demonstrating the functional role of social components, showing both the directly explicit strategies of social survival which the Inuit kayaks embody and the socially strategic symbolic role of the medal. In his discussion of the Yorkshire Early Bronze Age and its patterns of land, settlement and society, Pierpoint analysed the artefacts and other features associated with Early Bronze Age burials by defining qualitative categories associated with the material and plotting these as factor analysis graphs (Pierpoint 1981). So, for example, his Figure 4.4 (Figure 7.1) gives the factor score plots for the differentiation in the quality of Beaker pottery placed in graves. The quality of vessels, defined as relating to large size and 'good' decoration, increases from bottom left to top right, with the finest vessels being placed with males. Throughout, the factor analysis distinguished very clearly between men and women, and the graphs showed that male burials had more and finer artefacts, and greater care and labour in burial treatment.

A similar analysis can be carried out upon more recent material culture, for example school uniforms. In Figure 7.2 factor 1 is headgear, scored from 1 to 4 as no special headgear; berets/caps; elaborate hats like velour hats, panamas and boaters; and Eton top hats. Factor 2 is clothing on the upper body, scored as no uniform clothing; coloured wool pullover; special school blazer; and elaborate school jackets. The application of these factors to a range of children drawn from across the school scene and related to gender would show that boys and girls are treated without gender difference in the material culture plotted in the lower left hand and centre part of the graph, but in the upper right hand area boys appear alone. The inference is that the most elaborate and expensive uniforms are reserved for young males, upon whose education society as a whole is presumably willing to lavish a privileged level of support.

These two examples show how this kind of artefact analysis can help to demonstrate the role the objects are playing in the maintenance of social function. Pierpoint says of the Yorkshire Early Bronze Age that this society showed very marked distinctions in terms of land, artefacts and social groups within which male authority is apparent, and within it fine artefacts and elaborate burials would have acted as useful levers for maintaining these differences. Much the same could be said for the school clothes. Work of this kind is one of the typical ways in which meaning is generated from material in museum collections.

Objects in Systems

Functional analysis as described so far clearly has its illuminations to offer about the things we make, but equally clearly, its very loose application of general principles renders it rather naive. This had become apparent in North American and Britain by the 1960s and there generated a kind of neo-functionalism which was intended to create a firmer theoretical structure that could answer some of the weaknesses of the older version, particularly its inability to cope with the fact of social change. This was achieved by looking both to a fundamental functionalist principle, its notion of society as a functioning system, and developing this by drawing upon the then newly emerging systems theory: it is interesting to notice how the artefact disciplines, especially anthropology and archaeology, always reflect the climate of their times, so that mid-twentieth-century systems theory replaces early-twentieth-century post-Darwin ecology.

According to the functionalist view expressed in the language of systems theory,

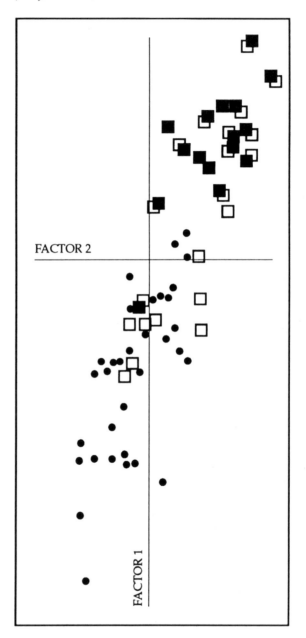

Figure 7.1 Factor score plots of Beaker pottery: differentiation in the quality of the vessels. Open square: tall beaker (over 19 cm. high); solid square: beaker with high quality decoration; small circle: small and/or poorly decorated beaker. The quality of the vessels increases from bottom left to top right, with the finest vessels being placed with males (after Pierpoint 1981, fig. 4.4)

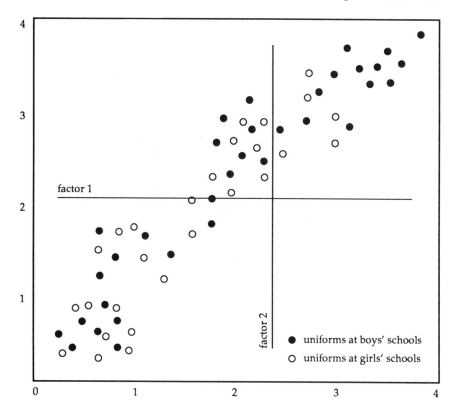

Figure 7.2 Factor score plot for differentiation in school uniform

societies reach an equilibrium called homeostasis, and this happy state is vital because a society can only continue to exist if it is well-adjusted, externally and internally. The social importance of maintaining an equilibrium with the environment is stressed here, and as Renfrew wrote in 1972, 'the whole purpose of utilizing the systems approach is to emphasize man–environment inter-relations, while at the same time admitting that many fundamental changes in man's environment are produced by man himself' (1972: 19–20). The literature here is very large, but David Clarke's (1968) early analysis of how a past society can be viewed as system is still influential and helpful. He envisaged a social system bounded by its natural environment within which four (admittedly arbitrary but certainly arguable) subsystems can be seen to be operating (Figure 7.3) (together with a fifth, the psychological, which is centrally encased by the other subsystems). Clarke summarizes the content of each subsystem as (1968: 102–3):

> *Social subsystem.* The hierarchical network of inferred personal relationships, including kinship and rank status.
> *Religious subsystem.* The structure of mutually adjusted beliefs relating to the supernatural, as expressed in a body of doctrine and a sequence of rituals,

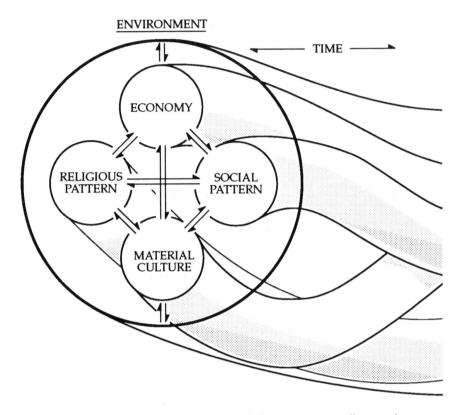

Figure 7.3 Schematic model drawn up by Clarke to suggest oscillating subsystems in the networks of a sociocultural system in dynamic equilibrium with its environment (after Clarke 1968, fig. 14)

which together interpret the environment to the society in terms of its own percepts.

Economic subsystem. The integrated strategy of component subsistence methods and extraction processes which feed and equip the society.

Material culture subsystem. The pattern constellations of artefacts which outline the behaviour patterns of the system as a whole and embody that system's technology.

All these are in a constant state of subtle oscillation, adapting to each other and to the environment as the checks and balances created by social practice vibrate across the whole. Clarke's system gave a specific place to material culture, and this represents a departure from traditional functionalism. Nevertheless, for Clarke and most of his colleagues, 'the syntax of [material culture] subsystem essentially reflects the moving equilibria between all subsystems and that it is only in the light of the coupling within [this] subsystem, between the subsystems, and within the environing system that the essential factors in this . . . vector may be defined' (1968: 119). Material culture may be 'the information subsystem of patterned constellations of artefacts which outline the behaviour patterns of a socio-cultural system and embody that system's technology' (p. 120), but we notice in the use of 'reflect' and 'embody' that artefacts are still passive recipients rather than active ingredients. In spite of this, many writers on material culture, especially archaeologists, have seen the application of systems theory as a good way of helping the mute stones to speak.

Functioning Display

Let us, by way of illustration, take an exhibition brief (prepared by the author) for an exhibition intended to show what society was like in Somerset during the late Roman and post-Roman period, roughly AD 300–600. The material to be worked upon, and ultimately displayed, included pottery, the debris associated with manufacture, burial materials including skeletons and grave goods, Early Christian carved stones and the evidence for church sites, and material from settlements. What was known about the area in the late Roman period could be expressed in the form of a distribution map (Figure 7.4). It is important to remember that this map, and all others like it, is showing (and only showing) material culture which in terms of functionalist thinking is deemed to reflect the social code idiosyncratic to this particular society. The artefacts (in the broader sense) are plotted within an image of their geographical environment, which we know has been produced by a complex intermingling of previous natural and human factors. These artefact categories have been determined on the basis of what things seem to be 'the same' and to have been performing 'the same role'. It is clear that functionalist ideas are written into the substance of this geophysically based analysis in a number of profound ways.

The map prompts the suggestion that more, and more varied, activity was happening in the eastern part of the region than in the western part during the period, and in particular, that finds which seem to belong together, like towns, villas, temples, roads and industrial sites, are concentrated in the east, suggesting that a market economy operated in this area, while a simpler economic form, perhaps (given the lack of any visible central sites) person-to-person exchange, was used in the west. This observation can be linked with the fact that the western area is largely relatively high, grassy moorland suitable for grazing, while in the east the principal finds are concentrated on some of the best arable lowland in the whole region, avoiding the large areas of marshland in the Somerset Levels.

A functionalist exhibition model begins to emerge in which the east is dominated by the land-holding and business classes, supported by productive mixed farming which has generated sufficient wealth to enable the exploitation of the local mineral resources on an industrial scale, so making possible comfortable country houses, viable towns and relatively elaborate sacred sites. The social bonds here seem likely to be those of master and man. In the west the artefacts show us very little indeed, and we can only suppose a thin population supported by flocks and herds, with little in the way of surplus or its visible products. The presumption

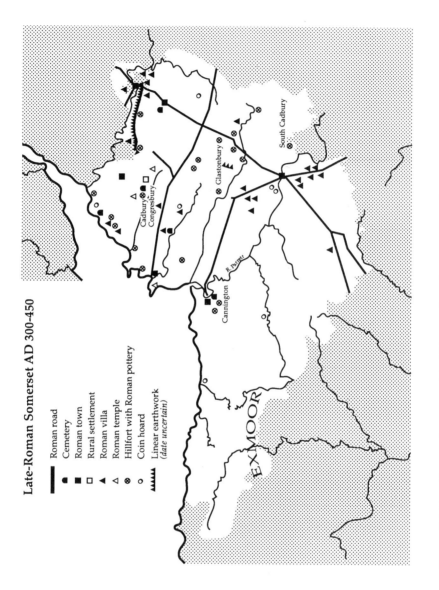

Figure 7.4 Late Roman Somerset AD 300–450 (based in part on Rahtz 1982, fig. 10.1)

here is that blood kinship is an important regulator of social relationships. This can be expressed through a deliberately simple systems analysis model, based on Clarke's scheme (1968: 104, Figure 13). Figures 7.5 and 7.6 show us the dynamic equilibrium between the subsystem networks of these two sociocultural systems and their environments. It is worth pointing out that, while most of what we know suggests that this model, although limited, is broadly correct for the eastern area, it may be grossly unjust to the quality of social life in the west.

The language already used to pursue this line of argument demonstrates one of the characteristics of functionalist thinking. We noted earlier that the artefact categories are created largely by intuition, and that their relationships can then be discussed in terms of economic types, like market economy or person-to-person reciprocal exchanges. This brings out the way in which later functionalist theory works, tacitly or explicitly, by defining a series of society types to one of which all actual societies have belonged, each presumed to have a typical cluster of institutions

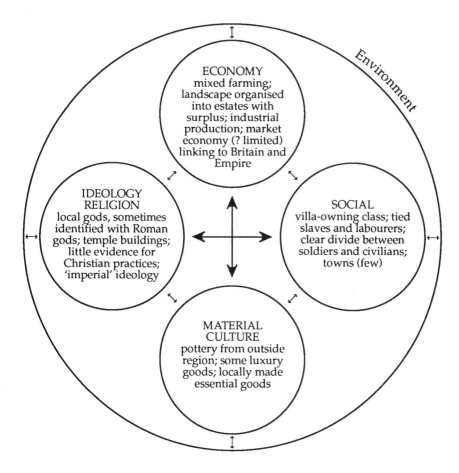

Figure 7.5 Simple systems analysis for late Roman east Somerset

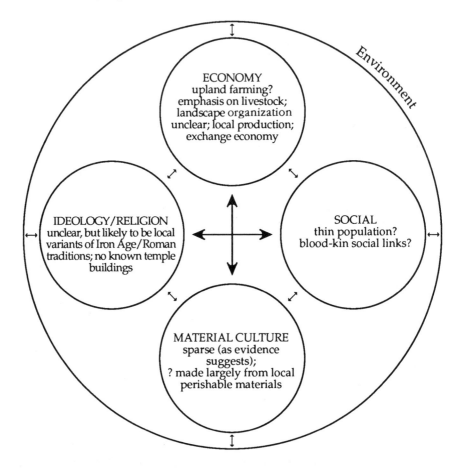

Figure 7.6 Simple systems analysis for late Roman west Somerset

linked with appropriate technology and artefact production. The types have usually been identified in broad terms, as hunter/gatherer bands, peasant communities, chiefdoms or aristocracies, palace/temple states, complex states, and modern industrial states, each with its characteristic cluster of attributes, and they have been distinguished on the basis of material culture and written record. This generalizing tendency creates a certain determinism in which societies take inevitable forms and work out predetermined destinies. Accordingly, late Roman east Somerset would be characterized as belonging to a complex state, while contemporary west Somerset looks more like a peasant community. The exhibition based on this reasoning would consequently group the objects into corresponding patterns and relationships, backing these up by the map, by labels, and by scenic photographs.

This paves the way for a discussion of how functionalist thinking copes with the problem of understanding social change, including of course change in the material culture range. As we have already seen, the older-style functionalism as employed chiefly by anthropologists tended to treat the social systems studied as existing only in a 'frozen now', a synchronic moment in which there was no past or future. The intellectual vigour achieved by coupling functionalist theory to systems analysis has made it possible to modify this inability to cope with the fact of change. Flannery, for example, produced a systems model for the development of complex societies in which he identified a self-regulating mechanism within the social system which serves 'to keep all the variables in the sub-systems within appropriate goal ranges – ranges which maintain homeostasis and do not threaten the survival of the system' (1972: 409). This means that growth or surpluses within the system can be harnessed to a forward spiral of development in which the social system gradually changes, usually by becoming more complex, but succeeds in retaining its essential balance. We should add that a characteristic of this process is the production of more, and more various, material culture, and the ways in which this comes about can be identified as interacting sequences across the subsystems. The same happens, but in a downward spiral towards breakdown, when social pathologies occur and the organic unity is breached as a result of maladaptation. This process, too, can be expressed in a general model.

Figure 7.7 shows the distribution throughout our area of finds in the succeeding post-Roman period from roughly AD 450–600. This suggests that the eastern material culture characteristic of the earlier phase has now disappeared, while slightly more material evidence is now available for the west. Moreover, the difference between the two areas has shrunk considerably, with a range of broadly similar Christian sites appearing across the region, accompanied by hill-top occupation, some of it inside ancient fortifications, and stone memorials inscribed in Latin with people's names. The inscriptions, the defended hill tops, and the churches and graveyards combine to suggest that we are now looking at a society built around chiefs or aristocrats who commanded the distribution of goods. The systems analysis might now look like the model set out in Figure 7.8, and this would be the basis of the post-Roman part of the exhibition.

As we have seen, questions about how and why society in the region moved from that shown in Figure 7.4 to that in Figure 7.7 are answered in functionalist terms by reference to general models of social collapse and transformation which are deemed to be applicable in specific cases because the individual cases can themselves be fitted into one of the types defined by attribute cluster. Renfrew has developed a model intended to show how the collapse of the Maya civilization in Central America and that of the Myceneans in Greece each resulted in the ensuing Dark Age, and Rahtz (1982) has shown how the post-Roman period in Somerset conforms to the general pattern (Figure 7.9). So the gap between the two functioning systems is bridged by the identification of malfunctions across the subsystems and their multiplier effect across the whole system: for the Roman Empire and Roman Britain, this would involve an analysis of the growth of an unproductive civil service and army, rural unrest, inflation, pressure from a growing barbarian population beyond the frontiers, and similar factors. Thinking of this kind is implicit in the structure and content of the exhibition, it is at the heart of the exploration of the past which it offers.

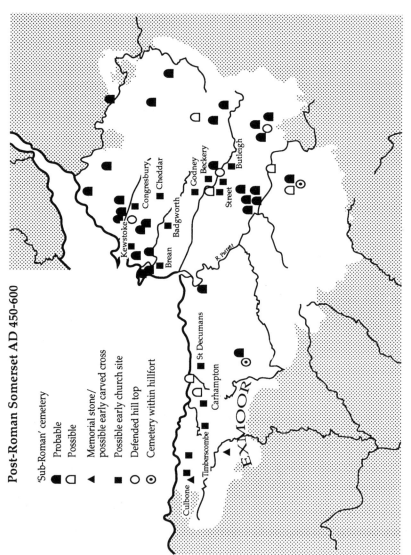

Figure 7.7 Post-Roman Somerset AD 450–600 (based in part on Rahtz 1982, fig. 10.4)

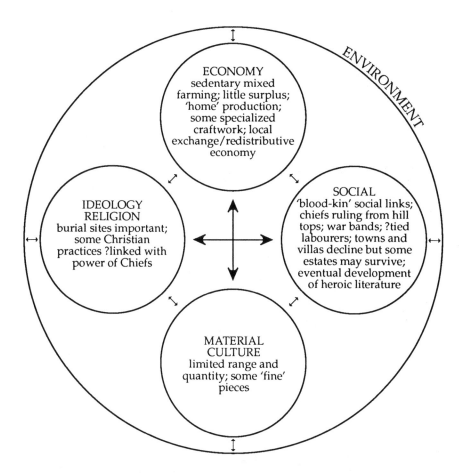

Figure 7.8 Simple systems analysis for post-Roman Somerset

Some Implications

We must now stand back and try to assess what functionalist theory offers towards an understanding of objects and the way in which they are interpreted. We have seen that in its more sophisticated systems form, it can offer a way of analysing, and so of better understanding, how societies and their characteristic artefact ranges change. Generally, our available data is rather thin and we cannot, therefore, generate the elaborate systems models that a modern business economist, for example, would employ to analyse the effect of changes in taxation; but if we had this information, our forecasting and observing of change would be as detailed as theirs. It is, in part, to fill this information gap that recourse has to be made to the generalizing principles which identify social types, and so make the task of understanding and prediction easier.

DARK AGE SOCIETIES (MYCENAE, MAYA, ETC.)	PARALLELS IN DARK AGE WESTERN BRITAIN
Collapse of central administration organisation:	
- decline in central places	decline of Roman towns
- fragmentation of military organisation	withdrawal or disintegration of Roman military units
- survival of small, independent political units	possible survival of civitas nuclei
- abandonment of palaces, storage	not applicable
- eclipse of temples as major centres	destruction or devolution of Roman temples and Roman Christian churches
- survival as local shrines	survival of Roman shrines and building of new ones
- loss of literacy, secular and religious	decline in epigraphy, etc.
- end of public buildings and works	decline in Roman works in 5th century or earlier
Collapse of traditional elite class:	
- end of rich burials	not applicable
- end of rich residencies	decline of Roman villas and wealthy town houses
- their re-use for different purposes	villa 'squatters' and industrial use
- end of luxury goods (except as survival)	end of Roman luxuries (some objects survive into post-Roman period)
Collapse of centralised economy	
- end of large scale trade, distribution/exchange	end of Roman external and internal trade
- end of coinage	end of coinage c.400–410
- survival of pieces	coins re-used in Dark Age and Anglo-Saxon contexts
- end of craft/specialist activity	end of pottery manufacture, building, etc.
- end of specialised/organised agriculture	decline in organised villa economy
- new local homesteads	not yet found
Collapse of settlement and population	
- settlement abandoned	widespread in 5th century
- shift to dispersed pattern	not yet shown
- choice of defensible locations, the 'flight to the hills'	re-occupied hillforts

Aftermath development of romantic Dark Age myth
- attempt by new power groups to legitimise themselves by genealogies linking to former state or relating to deeds by which invaders achieve power by arms

  Dark Age genealogies with Roman names - later also by Anglo-Saxons with battle myths

- tendency for earlier chroniclers to personalise historical explanation; individual deeds, battles, invasions; decline attributed to external hostile powers

  Gildas, Hist. Brit., Arthur, etc.; later Bede and Anglo-Saxon Chronicle; ultimately Geoffrey Monmouth

- confusion between old Golden Age and new Heroic Age
- paucity of archaeological evidence after collapse

  Dark Age? Romanitas and glorification of deeds against English sparse evidence for Dark Ages

- tendency among historians to accept as evidence traditional narratives first set down in writing centuries after collapse

  old-style Dark Age 'history'

- slow development of Dark Age archaeology, hampered by above and by focus on larger and more obvious central place sites of the vanished state

  old-style 'alien' Roman archaeology

Aftermath transition to 'lower/earlier' socio-political organisation:
- new segmentary societies analogous to those of centuries or millennia before; fission of realm to smaller units

  'Celtic re-emergence' ?=Iron Age systems

- boundaries of earlier polities
- ?peripheral survival of organised communities retaining features of collapsed state

  not yet shown; possible hillfort territoria survival or re-emergence ? Carlisle

- survival of religious elements as folk cults or beliefs
- peasant craft imitating former specialists
- local population movement

  sub-Roman religion in shrines of 5th - 7th centuries hand made pottery, etc.
  not yet demonstrated but likely in view of abandonment of Roman sites

- language change?
- regeneration of chiefdom or state, influenced by earlier remains

  Latin/Celtic/English
  'British Kings' of Dumnonia etc. - later by Anglo Saxons

Figure 7.9 Model for the collapse of civilization: general trends and the end of Roman Britain (after Rahtz 1982, fig. 10.8)

The notion of general principles brings before us all the difficulties such notions always bring, because many societies manifestly fit into any such scheme only with great difficulty. The value placed upon such thinking really depends upon whether our eyes are attuned to looking at the wall or looking at the differences between the individual bricks, and we will all do both, depending on our need at the time. A more fundamental objection (but one not exclusive to functionalist) is the problems of the empirical observer. Functionalist empiricists like Malinowski were prepared to trust their senses and to believe that they were recording objective facts. Nobody now is likely to believe any such thing, but it is still true that even latter-day systems functionalism does not allow much scope for the student to identify his own engagement.

Much the same holds true for the role of the individual within each society, in either his own eyes or those of the observer. The thrust of the argument is towards community adaptation which leads to the creation of systems, but this allots a passive or automatic role to each individual which we know, as a matter of history and personal experience, does not explore the individual's social participation adequately, or his individual intentions and creativity. Men and women are not like some insects among whom the specific social roles of individuals are brought about by a predetermined programme of differential feeding (or only the completely disillusioned would contend so), and any theory which hopes to be persuasive must integrate the individual's hopes and fears into its account. Functionalist theory in its systems theory forms and in its generalizing and predictive modes can *describe how* a society operates without reference to its individual components, but it finds it difficult to *explain why* things are as they are. The causes of social character, the reasons why this particular thing was made or done and not that, lies in part in the aggregate of personal histories, and within this aggregate some personalities are more influential than others; it is this which contributes to each life much of its tone and colour, which helps to give the Inuit their Inuit-ness and to make England English.

An equally telling criticism revolves around the inadequacy of function and utility as explanations of social form or of actual events which take place within this formal framework. Ideas about function and usefulness are themselves a product of culture, not the other way round, and all social activities, from the making of a boat to the dropping of rubbish, take place within, and arise from, the cultural framework. These activities are not just the result of some imperative adaptive expediency, but are the sum of a cultural matrix within which expediency plays only a part, albeit an important part. This explains why many social forms have recognized significance without possessing any obvious social utility: most English people cannot bear the thought of eating horse meat, a practice which is commonplace across the Channel. This argument links up with the point already made about the inability of functionalist theory to explain the reasons for social choices, but deepens it by suggesting that the nature of these choices transcends the utilitarian intention.

A final point must be underlined. We have already noted that functionalist theory tends to assume that not only can all material culture be explained by the application of utilitarian ideas, but that it is the passive reflection, directly or indirectly, of man's activities. But as Hodder says, 'there is more to culture than functions and activities. Behind functioning and doing there is a structure and a content which has to be partly understood in its own terms, with its own logic and coherence' (1982a: 4). Material culture is part of this structure and content, and its social life shapes as well as reflects our activities, severally and collectively. It is to our understanding of the structuring role of objects that we must now turn.

8 Meaning as Structure

The bowl of the (sacred native north American Indian) pipe is a sacrificial vessel that itself is a miniature cosmos.

(Paper 1987: 301)

The structure of kinship relationships is just one possible way of looking at patterns which also crop up in the spatial arrangements of buildings, in areas of economics, and in the cosmology which links the land of the living to the land of the ancestral dead.

(Leach 1982: 208)

With rue my heart is laden
For golden friends I had,
For many a rose-lipped maiden
And many a light-foot lad.

By brooks too broad for leaping,
The light foot boys are laid;
The rose-lipt girls are sleeping
In fields where roses fade.

(A. E. Houseman, *A Shropshire Lad*, LIV)

Introduction: It's Like Treating Bee Orchids as if They Could Sting

If the above sentence can be taken as offering a fair idea of the flavour of a good deal of structuralist analysis then it is obvious that we have moved into a world in which common sense ceases to be any kind of a reliable guide. This objection, which is one of the fundamental reasons why structuralist analysis has aroused such bitter passions in some quarters, can easily be countered: 'common sense' is a poor guide to reality since, for example, it will always suggest to us that the world is flat, and it makes these mistakes because to describe something as 'only common sense' is one of our favourite ways of elevating our own particular mind-set to the status of 'natural truth'. There are a number of serious objections, or at least limitations, to be levelled at structuralism, and we shall look at these in due course, but its superficial oddity is not one of them.

Semiotics, semiology and structuralism (the three words are generally used to describe much the same body of thought) have acquired a massive literature, charting a complex history of orthodoxy, heresy and backsliding. This can be followed in a number of books, of which that by Terence Hughes (1977) is one of the best (and see also Jackson 1991). We have already employed some of the fundamental elements in structuralist thinking to tease out the relationship of objects to their historical context (p. 24), of collected material to the original material from which it was selected (p. 41), and of exhibitions to the collected museum holdings (p. 141). The intention here is to see how this kind of thinking works in relationship to objects, in the broader sense of understanding and display. The examples selected to illustrate points have been deliberately chosen from the relatively small amount of published structuralist literature dealing specifically with material culture and museum interpretation, and structuralist theory itself has been drawn upon very selectively in ways which, of necessity, involve over-simplification. What happened to structuralist thought, and the implications for museums, will be the theme of Chapter 11; here we are looking at structuralist analysis as one positive way of making meaning with objects.

As a starting point, we may take ideas and relationships as they are set out in Figure 1.2. This diagram gives us the genesis of semiotic or structuralist theory, and at the same time acts as a simple plot of many of the main intellectual preoccupations of nineteenth- and twentieth-century Europe. Like its predecessors, the structuralist edifice is based upon the conviction that all members of the species *Homo sapiens* are the same, that just as any pair of healthy adults chosen at random across space and time could produce healthy children, so all humans share a common mind which works in the same way, experiences the same problems, and approaches their solution in ways which, after a certain effort of understanding, are mutually intelligible. At a fundamental level, the preoccupations of a traditional Inuit, an Indian farmer, or the inhabitant of a Birmingham council flat are the same: all are anxious to be both part of a group and a recognized individual, and all suffer from tensions and anxieties which mar their content. All three belong to communities which use a range of organizing and communicating systems to describe and (in some ways) solve these problems, and so it should be possible to distinguish the common skeleton from the changing flesh and discern the underlying structuring principles which are at work.

The two key words in the argument are 'anxiety' and 'information'. On the one hand are all the anxieties and conflicts which our psyches generate, and which operate both in our relationship with other members of our community, and in our relationship with ourselves. This is the hunting ground of classic psychological studies by Freud, Jung and their successors, whose insights and perceptions, whatever view we may take of them (see Eysenck 1991), have altered the way in which we look at ourselves for good. On the other hand are the information and communication systems which humans invent in order to resolve or ratify these conflicts, so that organized social life, without which individual people cannot survive, becomes a realistic possibility. How humans 'invent' these systems is a further point to which we shall return. The most important information systems are language, the division and use of space, kinship, food, myth (and related spoken or written works like traditional songs and stories), material culture, and ritual in the broadest sense which usually draws on one or more of these. As a matter of history, it was the nature of language as communication which first attracted attention, and so it is upon linguistic theory that analyses of the other communication systems have drawn, although in many ways the analysis of material culture has followed its own subsequent development.

The Language of Clothes

Let us begin to get a purchase on how structuralist ideas may work with objects by starting with the relatively (but perhaps deceptively) simple example of clothes as they were understood and used by the broad English middle class during the 1950s. We have already employed Saussure's recognition that language operates at two distinct levels: that of *langue*, which represents both the whole content or vocabulary of the language and its rules of use or grammar, and that of *parole*, which represents an actual spoken sentence, intelligible only if it is a selection of the vocabulary organized according to recognized grammatical constructions. This model is now recognized to have a number of limitations when it is applied to language, and would probably be regarded by linguists as superseded by models like Chomsky's generative grammar (e.g. 1964; 166). However, the scheme provides a useful model for the formation of broad social structure in communication systems like food, space and objects and their modes of operation in actual social events, although subject to all the difficulties discussed later in this chapter.

This concept of the workings of the *langue* and the *parole*, although it has been much refined by later semioticians like Barthes (1977), is crucial to an understanding of semiotic and structuralist thought, and of the contribution which this can make to our understanding of ourselves, the only matter of any importance at the end of the day. It suggests that in the double-axis of vocabulary and rules, or content and form, we really do touch the deep structure of the human mind and so give ourselves an analytical approach which can reveal the mechanism of patterning through which we make sense of ourselves and our surroundings. In a very real sense, we are beginning to look at how our minds work.

Figure 8.1 shows how this works out with the object, 'trousers'. The *langue* of English society about 1960 contained the concept 'trousers', which issued in the word and the artefact. To these, within the *langue*, are applied the social rules of use, giving us, as an intelligible concrete event in *parole*, the sentence which might have run, 'He put on his shirt and trousers' and the equivalent object set, 'shirt, trousers, tie'. The important point is that both these *parole* events defined categories which ordinary, living people, through whom society actually operates, recognized as distinct: the *parole* of 'Lipstick, powder, eye-shadow' or in sentence form, 'She puts on her eye-shadow', communicated a message which was quite different to that of 'trousers', because according to the accepted rules of this society, trousers and eye-shadow were normally quite distinct.

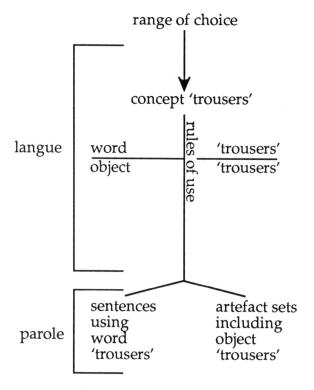

Figure 8.1 *Langue, parole* and trousers

This does not mean that objects are capable of 'speaking for themselves' to the observer, or at least not to the extent of giving out the whole of their message. Material culture is in structuralist terms only meaningful within its whole social context – we have to see who is doing what with what and with whom for significance to emerge, and the more we can do this, the fuller our appreciation of significance will be and the better it can be verified. This is not to undermine the claim for the equality of meaningfulness between material culture and other communication systems: language, for example, would be equally difficult to understand without context, that is, if we had no idea what object the sound 'bicycle' represented. It is, however, to say that structuralist analysis cannot begin without contemporary and historical studies designed to tell us as much as possible about the social content of the culture with which we are concerned.

Here we must pause to dwell a little on the problem of how humans 'invent' the content and rules of their systems, touched upon a moment ago, and why it is that the trousers of our example have the social value and significance which we have begun to explore. Put another way, we have to ask why Saussure's scheme can account for the formation of social structure, but not the creation of its content, specific as this is to each society in its own time and place. The easy answer is that this is a product of each society's unique history. This undoubtedly provides part of the solution, but to suggest that vocabulary (of all kinds) and rules of use simply derive from those of the generation before is clearly not a satisfactory solution because it leaves open the question of real origins and changes. The answer, it seems, must lie somewhere in that nexus of accumulated history, geographical circumstance and influential individual restlessness which makes each community what it is at each moment in time. Somewhere in here, too, lie the insights of the psychologists, and the two twentieth-century traditions of psychology and structuralism bear a brotherly relationship. Both depend upon a conviction of human sameness, and the psychologists would doubtless argue that their investigations into human personality have yielded some understanding of how and why certain social 'choices' about the content and rule system which operate in the *langue* have been made, and why these tend to reflect basic similarities across the human race. We have, therefore, to imagine a 'range of choice' which shadows the *langue* of any society and which includes all the possibilities which were actually excluded by society, individually and perhaps collectively, in the formation of its concrete nature.

Let us return to our trousers. We saw that the structuring process in the *langue* puts together separate bits of content in a meaningful way. The essence of this lies in its combination of items into message-bearing groups. A single word is meaningless by itself, and a moment's thought shows that if a single word is uttered we immediately and automatically fill in the rest of the *parole* which gives it meaning; in the same way a single item of clothing only makes sense in conjunction with others of its kind. A word group is normally called a sentence, and the object equivalent may be called a set. Clearly, the combination of objects (or any other content) into a set implies the exclusion of other objects, which will be formed into their own sets, and the decision as to what constitutes a 'proper set' is taken as part of the *langue*'s mysterious structuring process, the nature of which we have just glanced at.

How this can work with clothes is suggested in Figure 8.2, where six clothes sets are shown which individually and collectively do give clear and distinct social messages to a middle-aged English person, and are likely to seem to him or her to embody real social experience. The six sets fall 'naturally' into three vertical columns, where each set is both opposed to, and the equivalent of, each of the other two sets. These relationships are described as transformations, and each set is a transformation of all the others. There is also a horizontal distinction into two bands, with male garments at the top and female garments at the bottom, and here again the idea of transformation applies.

This notion of the relationship between message-bearing sets brings us to another of the key notions in structuralist thought, of which, again, we have already made use. All the objects in the left hand column are pieces of mid-fifties evening dress, and as such they bear an intrinsic or metonymic relationship to each other in which any one piece can stand for all the others; this fact is habitually exploited by advertisers and graphic artists who show us the merest sketch of a man in dress jacket and tie, knowing that we will take this for the whole ensemble

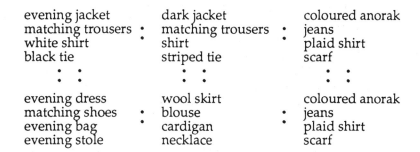

Figure 8.2 Sets of clothes

of man, woman and occasion which our imaginations will automatically supply. Our imaginations, faced with this sketch, are much less likely to supply an image of a man in the business suit or the gardening clothes which are listed in the central and right hand columns. This is because, while each constitutes a metonymic set of its own, the relationship between the sets is *metaphorical*, a word intended to express the nature of their opposite but equivalent relationships. We shall return again to the contrast between metonymy and metaphor, but the important point here is that again we seem to touch upon something fundamental about the way our minds work. The sets which emerge from the axes of content and order fall into grid patterns of contrasting categories, and this patterning, it appears, is the way in which we create the mental and social order which enables us to live our collective lives.

The clothing analysis can be taken several stages further. Study of the pattern shown by the sets suggests that it is possible to deduce from this *parole* some idea about the deep structure of the society which needed these clothes, that is, of the nature of its *langue*. We can see that a sharp distinction is made between formal leisure on the left of the figure, daily work in the centre and informal leisure on the right. We can perceive further underlying structural pairings such as those set out in Figure 8.3. All of these show some of the fundamental distinctions or categories by which this society organized itself. Looking back at Figure 8.2 we can see that what we have done is to reduce the specific expressions of difference into a series of binary pairs which seem to express fundamental distinctions and, as such, may be presumed to belong to the *langue* itself. This kind of analysis into fundamental binary pairs linked with their community-specific expressions is, particularly, a part of Lévi-Strauss's structuralist technique. The binary pairs involved are invariably the common stuff of basic human experience, and the same broad range crops up in most analyses, taking us back to the point made earlier about the link between this kind of thinking and classic psychology.

The analysis can progress by incorporating these underlying structural pairs and their specific social expressions into a diagram of the broad type much favoured by social anthropologists (Figure 8.4). This shows up a number of interesting patterns.

work	:	leisure
man	:	woman
black/dark	:	colours
clean	:	dirty
social	:	domestic
night	:	day
formal	:	informal
weekday	:	weekend

Figure 8.3 Binary pairs drawn from sets of clothes

Dark shades are associated with men on clean, formal and social occasions, while women wear colours at these times, but men can adopt women's colours on informal, domestic and rather grubbier occasions, like working in the garden. Equally, the most formal occasions show the greatest contrast of dress forms between the sexes, while at informal, domestic and dirtier times women can cross-dress, although this is strictly prohibited to men. Daily work, in an office for example, occupies the middle ground throughout the system. We might conclude, from a study of one small part of the material culture of this society, that it took an ambivalent view of sexual distinctions, which ramifies throughout its activities.

It is clear that the kinds of relationships which structuralist study reveal are true not only for the real workings of clothes in our day-to-day lives, but also for the way in which clothes are interpreted in exhibitions. The plotted relationships presented in Figures 8.2 and 8.4 would express equally the patterned layout of material in many costume displays, in which it is usual to contrast male and female dress, evening and day dress, and so on. Naturally enough: the patterns of exhibition reflect the patterns of real life, and both are clearly operating in ways which structuralist analysis can reveal.

Extending the Metaphor

This deliberately extremely simple example of the structuralist analysis of mid-twentieth-century English clothes has, it is hoped, drawn out the principles upon which the system depends, and given some idea of the flavour of the approach, that all-important, if most elusive, aspect of any conceptual scheme. Another simple example may demonstrate the way in which metaphorical relationships are habitually

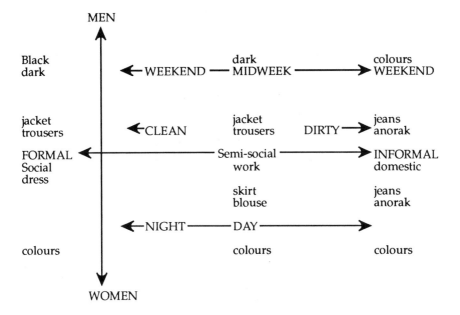

Figure 8.4 Structuralist plot of clothes

public	private
waking	sleeping
clean	dirty
outside	inside
eating	defecating
downstairs	upstairs
front	back
day	night
healthy	sick

Figure 8.5 Binary pairs drawn from terraced house

extended in order to bring essentially dissimilar things into an apparently significant relationship with each other. Let us take the typical English terraced house. Figure 8.5 shows how this might be analysed into binary pairs which give meaningful categories. We would be genuinely bothered if we entered what we thought was a sitting room, to find that an oven was standing in the place where we expected to see the television. What we have here are artefact sets creating spatial organization, just as the clothing sets were creating activity organization, although it will be obvious by now that, for structuralism, social activity is in reality one continuous web. We note that museum interpretation, of all kinds and particularly in its exhibitions, reflects what structuralist analysis can make clear.

There is a sense in which we could describe kitchens and bedrooms as transformations of each other, bearing to each other a metaphorical relationship. The kind of metaphorical thinking in which a society extends an image to parallel but separate areas of life has often been noticed, and may reveal more about the structure in the *langue*. Hodder (1982b: 115), following Hugh-Jones, has published two diagrams which show the internal arrangement of Pirá-paraná longhouse and and the model of the house as body (Figure 8.6). This, among other things, shows us that in this part of the world women and faeces are equated with each other: we cannot fail to find this a revealing correspondence and it could only have been made manifest by this sort of analysis. A very similar plot, but lacking this sexual discrimination, can be made for our English terrace and our bodies (Figure 8.7), and to the objection that, with our 'sensible' minds, we do not usually think of our homes like this, a structuralist would reply that it is precisely to help reveal hidden transformations that this thinking is intended.

The argument which shows how these transformations, or extended metaphors, come about is rather tortuous, and is best approached by using a diagram which draws on that published by Leach in 1976 (Figure 8.8). Let us follow this through, taking as our guide an ordinary brown glazed pottery teapot of the kind which can be bought in any crockery or hardware shop. At the head of the chart stands the communication event in which the message-entity, our teapot, conveys its immediate message – that it is a vessel for holding and pouring liquid, and that judging by the broad curve of the handle, designed to allow the freest possible passage of air, and by the steam hole in the lid, the liquid will be hot. All this would be clear to somebody who had never seen a teapot before. However, as a result of social choice, which an outsider could not know but which is part of the mesh of our society, the teapot is used for one specific type of drink and it is deemed to have a particular relationship to the lady of the house, who 'presides' over the pot, who knows good tea from bad, and whose responsibility for making and dispensing tea supports her particular position ('Shall I be mother?', 'Ask your mother if there's another cup in the pot'). The message-entity has acquired an enhanced message and stands now as a *signum*.

As we have already seen, individual objects, words and so on are not meaningful in isolation, but only as a member of a set. The teapot clearly belongs with its apparatus of tea cosy, stand, tea cups and saucers, milk jug and sugar bowl, and people drinking tea. Again as we have seen, the members of this set form a metonymy because their relationship is real and intrinsic. But let us consider the use of a teapot in the recent series of television advertisements for PG Tips Tea, which feature chimpanzees. The advertisements draw upon the sentimental capital which has accrued from the fact that chimpanzee tea parties have been a popular feature of many zoos for a long time and are part of our nostalgia for childhood;

A HOUSE

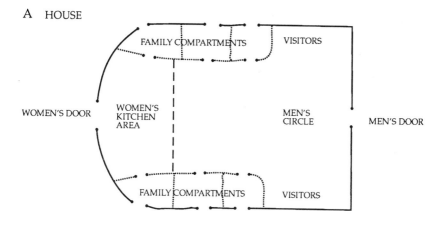

B HOUSE AS BODY

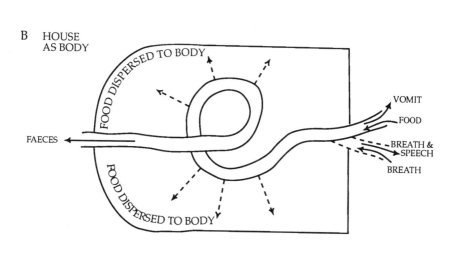

Figure 8.6 Internal arrangement of Pirà-paranà longhouse (A), and model of the house as a body (B) (after Hodder 1982b, fig. 29)

also, we enjoy the spectacle of these near-human animals behaving 'like' us (however unfortunate this may be from an animal rights point of view). But this is essentially a confidence trick. There is no intrinsic relationship between our enjoyment of tea, or the quality of any particular tea, and a species of the great apes. The magician turned ad-man is trying to palm off on us much the same trick as he did when he poured water from a gourd to make the rain come, as Frazer showed long ago (Frazer 1957: 63–5). In the chimpanzee scenario the teapot has been plucked from its 'true' context and is made to work in a symbolic way in a new context, and this second context bears a metaphorical relationship to the first.

We have already used this line of thought to show how collected material, both

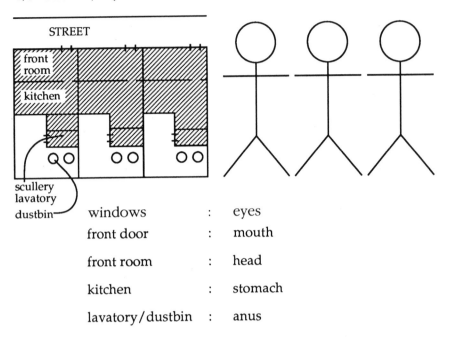

windows	:	eyes
front door	:	mouth
front room	:	head
kitchen	:	stomach
lavatory/dustbin	:	anus

Figure 8.7 Terraced house as body

of human and natural history, bears a metaphorical relationship to the world from which it came, but made the point, which must be stressed again here, that collections *also* have an intrinsic or metonymic relationship to their contexts, a peculiarity of physical objects. This is not true of the relationship between human tea parties and the chimps' party, and it is equally not true of the great mass of religious or ritual activity which endeavours to impose a structure on the world by treating metaphorical relationships as if they were real.

It is clear, from the chimpanzee tea party, or for example from rituals designed to promote fertility, that the underlying operational principle is the belief that the human and the extra-human, or the cultural and the natural worlds, including 'natural' morality, are not essentially distinct, and so actions performed in the human world have a parallel influence upon events in the other world, provided they are 'properly' carried out. This belief is at the heart of all religious ritual and of much of our otherwise inexplicable social action; also, as we have seen, it is drawn upon by modern advertising in its own way. The belief is, of course, quite unfounded: the jumping of masked men does *not* make the corn grow, and chimpanzees in business suits are a fundamental absurdity. The whole Western rational and scientific tradition has (painfully) succeeded in showing that there is no logical connection in all these symbolic links. But, apparently, we habitually and instinctively behave as if there were, and this is why the objects which give them expression can sometimes arouse some of our deepest feelings. We feel that what they say is true, in spite of the fact that both rational thought and accumulated

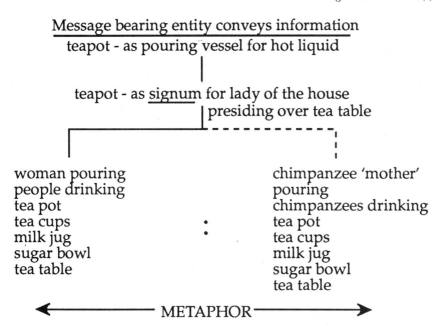

Figure 8.8 Semiotic analysis of tea drinking

empirical experience shows that it is not. Analysis can demonstrate a profound difference between the two, for one works in the human world and the other does not; but common human practice ignores this difference, and treats the whole cosmos as its social environment, to be organized accordingly.

This is why the elaborate structuralist plots produced by anthropologists show the whole of social practice as a seamless web, for this is how it is experienced by the people concerned. Those produced by Miller (1985, Figure 51) and Pearce (1987a and 1989b) were intended to show how artefacts take their place as a distinct category within the social system. Miller's work (Figure 8.9) shows the association between pottery types and other social variables in an Indian village, and enables us to 'read' that *karela* (cooking pots) are symbolic of, or metaphorically equivalent to, pollution, black colour, low caste and wheat, while *divali* (water pots) are equivalent to divinity, red colour, Brahmin and water. Pearce's analysis of the traditional Central Inuit (Figure 8.10), following a paper of McGhee's (1977), unites (among other things) the mythology of Sedna the Sea Woman, the alternation between summer and winter and the main festival which marks their division, and the main food animals of seal and caribou into a plot which embraces equipment made of sea mammal ivory and bone (in the lower half of the chart) and caribou antler (in the upper half). It is important to notice that this account of the Central Inuit started with their material culture held in museum collections, and that only work on this museum material could have revealed large parts of the structuralist plot.

In the sum, we can say that the structuralist concept gives us a theory of com-

POT	STATUS	GENDER	COLOUR	CASTE	CONNOTATION	CONTENT	EXCHANGE	HEAT	RIGHTS
Kalash, Dhupana, Diwali matka, Akhartij gagra, Mamatla	Divine		Red painted	Brahman					Contractual
Goli, Matka, Gagra, Chukiya, Batloi	Ritual	Male		High castes	Auspicious	Water	Jajman system, Embedded exchange	Cold	Proprietorial
Brahman dohni, Patya, Wariya, Kunda			Red and Buff						
Neutral Pots	Human			Middle castes		Milk			
Bhartiya, Karela, Dohni, Kareli, Dhatri		Female	Black	Low castes	Inauspicious	Wheat	Market system, Monetary economy		Non-contractual Non-proprietorial
Charya dohni, Jhawaliya dohni						Sorghum, Pulse		Hot	
Harawla	Polluted			Untouchables					

Figure 8.9 Association between pottery and major social variables in an Indian village (after Miller 1985, fig. 51)

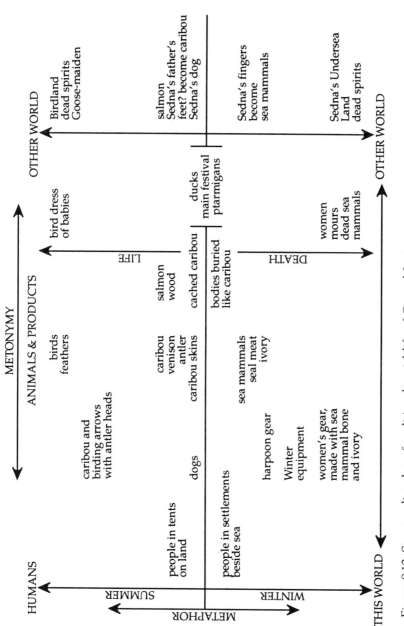

Figure 8.10 Structuralist plot of traditional social life of Central Inuit

munication which enables us to distinguish the two crucial axes of vocabulary/ content and grammar/rules of use. These are seen to be fundamental deep structures within the human psyche, and they enable us to organize our world by the creation of sets or categories through which significance is created. The sets are either internally the same (metonymic) or externally 'like' (metaphorical), and the characteristic human confusion between 'same' and 'like' enables the construction of a single system to embrace both the whole human and the external natural world into a habitable structure. Objects are a fundamental element in this process, because their social life enables them to play a crucial part in the creation of tangible social structures, without which real life cannot be lived. The study of material culture from this angle is therefore an important part of the way in which the meanings of objects can be understood, and correspondingly much of this meaning must be arrived at through the study of material now held in museum collections, as was done with the Inuit material.

Appreciation of this kind of meaning is a fundamental element in the organization of museum exhibitions which, especially in the human history field, commonly embody a structure of similarities and contrasts which expresses the structural nature of life. Binary pairs like life : death, hard : soft, young : old, urban : country, work : leisure provide the axes around which the display is created. From the throng of examples, let us choose that mounted by Somerset County Museum Service in the medieval abbey barn at Glastonbury (Stevens and Brown 1978) (see Plate 22). Stevens and Brown tell us that, 'We aimed at a display which would teach about people, and after much thought and discussion the idea emerged of illustrating the life of a particular farm labourer "from the cradle to the grave", using objects and illustrations from the museum's collections' (p. 24). The farm labourer chosen was John Hodges, and 'details from the records provided a series of stepping stones (birth, school, family life, work etc.) and objects were chosen to illustrate each of these. Thus, under the general heading of 'Birth' the objects include a willow cradle, Christening robes and feeding bottles' (p. 25). The display was organized around a series of sections with themes like Household Economy, Harvest, Birth, Workhouse and Death. The essential structure is clear, and from the pairings could be developed the kind of structuralist plot which has been drawn up for the Inuit and will in the following section be offered for one element within the life of a nineteenth-century southern English farm.

Some Problems

We must now try to come to a view of the advantages and disadvantages which structuralist and semiotic thought offers for the study of objects. Let us approach this by way of criticism of a final example, and this time we will start with two animals which have resulted from centuries of human genetic interference and are in that sense artefacts: a South Devon bull and cow. These generate the binary pairs set out in Figure 8.11. When we add to the animals the traditional cattle-processing

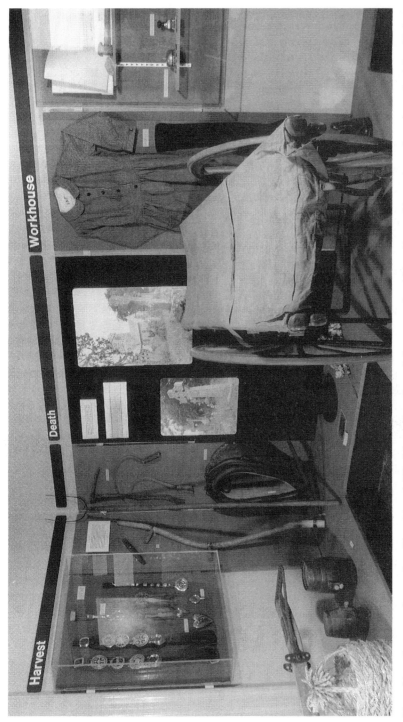

Plate 22. Sections devoted to 'Death' and 'Workhouse' in the exhibition at the Abbey Barn, Glastonbury, based on the life of John Hodges, 1978. Somerset County Museum Service (photo: Somerset County Museum Service).

bull	:	cow
male	:	female
dangerous	:	gentle
meat	:	milk
killing	:	milking
red	:	white
roast beef	:	cheese, butter
hot	:	cold

Figure 8.11 Binary pairs drawn from bull and cow

implements from a nineteenth-century southern English farm, and the farm spaces and humans which relate to them, we can add to this list (Figure 8.12). This binary list can then be expressed in the kind of plot with which we are familiar (Figure 8.13). It is, however, capable of a further extension which it is useful to add at this stage of criticism. In 1977 Leach published what he described as 'A View From the Bridge: A Fantasy of Mammoth Hunters' to demonstrate his contention that 'material objects . . . are representations of ideas' (p. 167). A treatment of our traditional dairy farm in Leach's style gives us something like Figure 8.14, and we have already used this kind of analysis to illuminate the nature of trophy material (p. 71).

This final example serves to bring home the kind of things which we can expect structuralist analysis to deliver. Simple commonsense, we have already suggested, must be ruthlessly abandoned, but this does not mean that the structuralist need succumb to complete absurdities. We may recall Bush's article, first published in 1956, entitled 'Mrs Bennet and the Dark Gods: The Truth about Jane Austen' which suggests, tongue firmly in cheek, that 'the occult structuring of *Pride and Prejudice* will establish Jane Austen's claim to be the first great exemplar of the

stock men	:	dairy maids
iron tools (pole axe, knives)	:	wooden tools (butter pats, butter moulds, churn)
slaughter yard	:	dairy

Figure 8.12 Binary pairs drawn from traditional English cattle processing

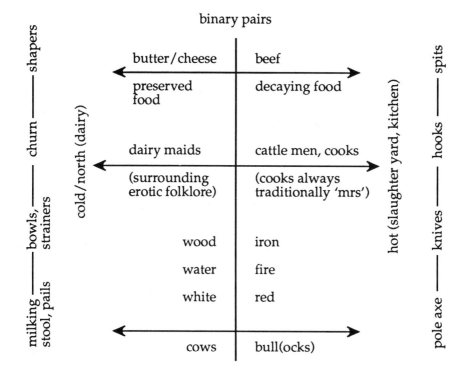

Figure 8.13 Structuralist plot of traditional dairy farm

modern mythic consciousness' (p. 1), a mock-serious contention which makes a neat point. What an analysis like Figure 8.14 does suggest is that all social patterns, from material culture and domesticated animals to food and moral or behavioural rules, are all transformations of each other.

The dairy plot brings home to us with unmistakable clarity (and is, therefore, one of the reasons why it was chosen) the incurably literary quality of structuralist analysis, though as we shall see, if it is a species of literary criticism, it is one of a peculiar kind. The analysis of our dairy farm could stand in, with not many alterations, for an analysis of *Tess of the d'Urbervilles*, and it would be hard to deny that Hardy's book was not somewhere in mind when the analysis was written. Similar echoes seem to linger in much of this kind of thinking. This is not, of itself, necessarily a very serious objection; the structuralist can reply that if we are looking at a novel of the period written by a man with first-hand knowledge of its subject, and at a study by a material culture student of the relevant tools and related historical material available in the Dorset County Museum and Record Office, then naturally the two analyses will be virtually the same, and there would be something very wrong if they were not. The same argument can be extended to cover the more general literary or mythical flavour which pervades much structuralist criticism, whenever this is applied to social systems rather than narratives: after all, we share

humans	⌐∿⌐	cattle
man	kills bullock, roasts beef in kitchen	dead bullock
woman	milks cow, processes milk in cold ▼	live cow
well fed humans	eat beef	cattle
hungry humans	exhausts beef ▼	cattle
OR hungry humans	store milk foods	cattle
fed humans	dole out milk foods ▼	cattle

INFERENCE

death : life

bull : cow

men : maids

decaying : long lasting

fire : cold

THEREFORE   By fire are male, dead creatures turned into decaying food, but by cold are live female creatures turned into stored food

SO   Society is sustained by a balance of sexual abstinence (maids, white, cold) and sexual activity (men, bulls, red, fire) which gives general fertility, new cattle and humans, and cows-in-milk

Figure 8.14 Analysis of traditional dairy farm (after Leach 1977)

a common human mind, so it is not surprising if all our characteristic modes of expression turn out to have similar content in structuralist terms.

This brings us to a more serious objection. Like literary criticism (or psychoanalysis or any work in the humanities), structuralist enquiry is not susceptible to check or proof. The choice of the data to be analysed, and the basic binary pairs which are abstracted from it, can be castigated as wholly subjective. This can operate on a number of levels. In the dairy farm analysis, the dairy workers have all been assumed to be unmarried women, but on any actual Dorset dairy farm of the period at any given moment this would probably not have been true. Even in *Tess* the girls in the dairy in the Valley of the Great Dairies are helped by Dairyman Dick Crick; no doubt special pleading could create for Dick, who is elderly, gentle and apparently asexual, a quasi-feminine persona, but this kind of detail remains a problem and we are left sometimes with the uneasy feeling that the analyst has muttered to himself, 'If it wasn't like that, it jolly well ought to have been.'

There remains the problem of subjectivity, even provided that the analysts have honestly demonstrated the dislocations or gaps in their material as a commentary to their plots. In 1982 Ernest Gellner wrote: 'The structuralists seem to be far too willing simply to trust their intuitions in this matter and to expect their readers to extend this trust to them . . . Has anyone ever put it to the test by locking diverse structuralists in insulated cubicles with the same text, and seeing whether they all emerge with the same binary opposites at the end?' (1982: 97–124). This was tried in a Museum Studies seminar in 1990, when two groups were given identical English late-nineteenth-century plates from willow pattern-decorated dinner services. The results were interesting. As Figures 8.15 and 8.16 show, the two groups did not produce exactly the same binary pairs, but each group produced roughly half of what might be described as the fuller analysis, together with a certain amount of overlap. Together, the sets would lead to a plot showing the daily focus on evening dinner and the weekly focus on Sunday lunch. Obviously, the groups were members of the same class course, had read the same articles, were (at least numerically) dominated by white English-speakers, and intended to become professional curators

willow-pattern plates	:	plain plates
elaborate service	:	simple service
Sunday	:	weekday
roast joint	:	cold meat
formal	:	informal
wine	:	water

Figure 8.15 Binary pairs drawn from willow pattern plate – 1

willow-pattern plates	:	plain plates
elaborate service	:	simple service
elaborately laid table	:	informal service
dinner	:	breakfast/lunch
evening	:	daytime
hot meat	:	simple food
father carves	:	mother cooks
dining room	:	kitchen

Figure 8.16 Binary pairs drawn from willow pattern plate – 2

(and we may add, knew what kinds of things were expected of them, although this does not mean that they intended to provide them). This supports what we already know: that people's minds do tend to work in the same ways.

The argument is not really one of subjectivity as such, but rather one of consensus about what may constitute a norm. Most people who can remember the late fifties in England would probably agree that the clothing categories and pairings in our first example do fairly represent what social life was like and what norms it embraced. A typical snatch of conversation might have run, 'It was an evening dress event. We didn't wear evening dress, and some others didn't, but it was an evening dress event.' We are likely to agree with the speaker about the nature of the event, and in this way norms have reality. Clearly, all work in the social sciences must proceed by way of normative assumptions (as does that of the historians also, in spite of themselves), and this is perfectly possible, providing that practitioners never forget that they are taking a stand in the eternal conflict between individual and community, with all which this implies. Linked with this is an argument about the epistemological basis of 'hard' science, which is supposedly more secure and more objective than knowledge in the social sciences, but which, in fact, also depends for the creation of understanding upon theoretical extensions which reach beyond observable phenomena and which also involve the construction of analogical models (Wylie 1982).

This brings us to a further important point. Recent criticism (e.g. Jackson 1991) has tended to treat structuralist theory as if it were a 'hard' science in which advances in understanding follow chronologically as one set of concepts is shown to be inadequate and to require replacement by a fresh set. This may be true of logic and linguistics, as it is true generally of philosophy, which occupies a special space between the sciences and the humanities. But it is not true of the insights of structuralism (in spite of the early claims made by some structuralists) any more than it is true of art or writing. Work in science, although equally based in imaginative effort, is progressive and cumulative, and by and large old and now-seen-to-be-inadequate work becomes a fossil in the history of the subject. This is not true in the arts; Rembrandt was not a poorer painter than Monet because he happened to live earlier and to work in a different mode, and the way in which they both have altered our vision of the world remains authentic and will do so while their pictures survive. Art is, in a sense, competitive, in that its practitioners compete for our attention, and have to be judged by each one of us as best we can in a world with no certainties and in which all judgements are fluid. The structuralist insights of writers like Saussure, Lévi-Strauss, Leach and Barthes share in this nature, and they too offer a shift in our world vision.

Changing Structures

There remains another area where structuralism is vulnerable to criticism, and this is its inability to cope with change. Late 1950s England, which we described in our clothes analysis, was on the point of fundamental change, in which, among other things, trousers and eye shadow worn together by a woman would become socially acceptable. It is worth noting that change involves muddling up what had been clear-cut categories within the structure, and that this confusion frequently focuses upon areas like sexual conduct, religious observance, or use of time and space, which are the areas upon which our deepest feelings tend to be focused; but this does not mean that the structuralist system provides a way of understanding how or why changes take place. Structuralism is a way of describing what (apparently) is, but it cannot relate this snapshot in time to the different system which went before and the equally different system which will succeed.

The reason for this lies in structuralism's essentially ahistoric nature. Change certainly involves structural transformation, but within the structuralist analyses themselves there is no mechanism which can show how or why change is generated and then express it. The problem lies in the lack of a link between structure and process, which itself reflects structuralism's lack of interest in the active, restless individual who seeks for things to be different. Structuralism's only answer to this is to occupy the Olympian heights, from which all human life *does* look much the same, and to observe that from this distance both the deep structures at work and the binary pairs which they throw up are common to all human social manifestations, as they are to all individual human psyches. This may be true, but it takes us nowhere in our effort to understand why each society is like it is, and not like others.

Structuralism, then, is a rigid model and cannot succeed in expressing the interplay of developing meaning between signs and people. This limitation shows up particularly acutely in relation to societies within the developed world, for whom the inhabitant of the Birmingham council flat stood as typical at the beginning of this chapter. It is no accident that structuralist analyses are usually carried out in relation to (supposedly) stable, traditional societies, like rural India, 'Old England' or the Inuit, just as they work best with the more traditional kinds of fictional nar-rative. In part, this stems from the fact that the very rapid change which highly developed societies experience means that pinning them down and systematizing them in detail at a moment in time poses difficult research problems. But the problem is more fundamental than this. Change in such societies has become a way of life in itself, and the deliberate rejection of structural patterning, in social, family or individual life, has often become the only fixed attitude of mind. Structuralist theory has difficulty in coming to terms with societies which eschew fixed points, and has to fall back upon the suggestion that such rejection is more hoped for than real: that while everything changes, everything is also the same, a proposition which is less than satisfactory.

Valued Opinions

A further fundamental difficulty, because it is of general application, is the way in which structuralist theory *demystifies* objects. To put the same point in another way, it reduces objects to *form* rather than *content*, and concentrates attention upon the role which objects perform in their given social organization while denying that there is anything special about any of them outside this role. An (easily imag-ined) structuralist analysis of the Houseman verses at the head of this chapter might well draw out the metaphorical links between girls, roses and death, but would miss the sadness which the poem breathes. A similar analysis of Michelangelo's *Virgin and Child* would reduce it to the level of a child's drawing: both are the same in point of form and equally 'true' in terms of deep social struc-tures. Hoffman's (1977) careful analysis of the decoration of Athenian *askoi* reveals that this can be treated as a cluster of signs with a common iconic message on the theme of sacrifice. This is an interesting conclusion to draw, but it adds nothing to our understanding of whether and how individual vase paintings show 'quality'. It is not only 'high taste' or 'aesthetic judgement' which is at stake here. To return to our first example, the structuralist plot does not reveal to us that there is always something funny about trousers: the forked radish's decent drapery is the stuff of low comedy. Structuralist analysis robs us of our appreciation of tone and humour, as well as our recognition of beauty and design.

Similarly it takes away our individuality, since in its thinking, people become 'woman' or 'old man' – not actual people with all the quirks and personal failures and successes which make up a large part of our experience. This returns us to the problem of norms which we have already touched upon, but more is involved than the need to recognize social norms, without which, we might all agree, it is impossible to discuss any society. By concentrating upon forms rather than content in people and objects, life is stripped of moral quality as this is generally understood, because issues of individual choice between good and bad become, as we have seen with the dairy farm analysis, merely a matter of obeying rules that lie within the social pattern.

All this, of course, is the mainspring of the hatred which structuralist theory has attracted (and which post-structuralist theory then went on to attract). Loose sub-jective chatter which divided objects into 'quality pieces' and 'ordinary things' is, so to say, forced to recognize that all artefacts are *constructs*, and are therefore all available to the same kind of analysis rather than being sometimes reserved for special categories of appreciation. Meaning, it appears, is not a private experience and does not derive from the solitary individual subject; on the contrary, it comes from deep communal structural patternings, and far from being produced by indi-viduals, individuals are produced by it. Even further, this meaning is not 'natural': men and women may start with a common mentality which leads to a common set of fundamental binary pairs, but what they then go on to make of them is not 'naturally' right or wrong, but merely one human statement among many. Meaning in objects, and in everything else, becomes internal and contingent. 'Reality' is not reflected in the objects people make and use, but is a reflection of them.

The romantic prejudice which saw special objects as harbouring a vital essence, a spirit which must be approached in the prayer and fasting of a taste long-cultivated, is apparently unmasked as a bit of secret theology which turned collected things into objects of arcane worship for the critical élite, and in so doing, served to sanctify and support the élite's superior position. Structuralist thinking is seen to under-mine the great Western (and to some extent other) tradition of aesthetic scholar-ship and liberal humanism, of 'high culture' which has taken some two-and-a-half millenia to grow; this tradition now stands revealed as merely one historical phe-nomenon among many others of equal weight. It is no accident that the early structuralists developed their ideas in a Europe which the First World War had turned into Western civilization's common grave, or that their successors lived, largely, in a Paris demoralized by France's actions in the Second World War. This helps to explain why structural theory took the form it did, but does not blunt the sharpness of its criticism or provide an answer for its adversaries; once something has been thought, it cannot be unthought. It has a very particular importance for museums, a large part of whose perceived *raison d'être*, especially in the art fields, has been to enshrine traditional value judgements, expressed in the ways in which material is selected for acquisition and display, and for research.

Objects in Structures: Some Conclusions

Two final points have now become clear. In the first place, structural theory in practice is a *technique* of analysis. This, indeed, is one of the reasons for the many applications to specific cases which it generates: once the basic rules of the game have been learnt, these can be applied to the particular set of circumstances without great difficulty, but often with interesting results. In object interpretation, as in all the humanities generally, analytical techniques of this sort are rare, and so are all the more compelling. It is not, of course, quite as simple as this. A technique is a medium, and may therefore be relied upon to generate its own kind of message, to have its own effect upon the nature of the outcome, and structuralist technique makes this point particularly clearly. Nevertheless, its whole approach remains that of the application of external procedures as a means of understanding the nature of objects or interpretative displays.

In the second place, structuralism clearly shares its character as technique with the way in which functionalism works: in both there are clues which enable the whole plot to be unravelled. There are other correspondences between the two approaches. Both are ahistorical, treating societies as fixed synchronic units, and both show little interest in individuals. Both probably start from the premise that community survival is what life is about, and although they express this in very different ways, these ways are not incompatible. The implications of this appear in the simple systems analysis of the dairy farm given in Figure 8.17, which as a comparison with Figure 8.13 shows, tells the same story as the structuralist plot of the same material.

In one sense, functional ideas are more helpful, and more 'primary', because we must use iron tools rather than wooden ones to butcher cattle and hold the joints over the fire. In another sense, structuralist ideas take precedence, because they

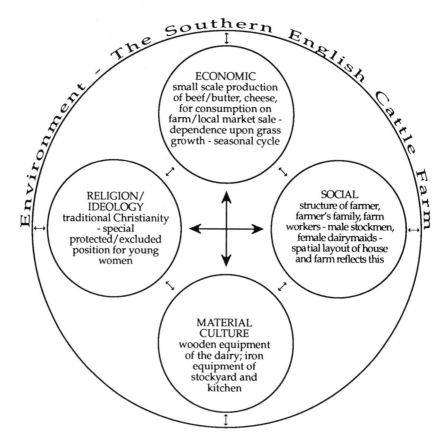

Figure 8.17 Functionalist analysis of southern English nineteenth-century dairy farm

can produce clusters like 'white, cold, maids' which help to explain why women's wedding dresses, once they were thought proper, were white and not red; functionalist ideas can only tell us that a specific dress form is necessary but not how and why society agrees what it shall be. This suggests that a combination of the two modes of thought is likely to be fruitful. But both also share some of the same limitations, particularly their difficulty in accounting for the flow of history. This often gives them a curiously passionless tone of bland content in which we creatures of flesh and blood, and pride and prejudice, do not recognize ourselves. Structuralism, like happiness, has no history, but life is far from happy and objects are a part of the strife and struggle which makes up our histories.

The most fundamental question in a book concerned with interpreting objects and museum holdings is to ask what the structuralist method can contribute here. The gains are considerable. The whole thrust of semiotics as a means of analysing communication, and the specific application of this to objects, serve to assert as theory what we know in daily practice: that material culture is one of our great communication systems, and that it works in its own right as a contribution to the way in which we form ourselves, rather than being, as the functionalists would have us believe, merely the means by which thoughts and feelings worked out elsewhere can be put into effect. Taking objects and their material properties, like the substances from which they are made, as the starting-point for semiotic analysis, demonstrates that social organization can be 'read off' from them as it can from other social texts: the whole of a community's life is implicit in one black bow tie.

Structuralist theory contributes to our general understanding of ourselves by the notion of *transformation*, and does so at a deep level of analysis. Objects, throughout the examples here, are shown to be not a reflection or a representation of society, but one way of seeing social relationships. Material culture is revealed as one among several kinds of human activity, all of which are transformations of each other and of the same deep patterning. The implications of this for museums, the principal material-culture holding institutions of the world, are profound.

9 Meaning in History

Some day I will go to Aarhus
To see his peat-brown head,
The mild pods of his eye-lids,
His pointed skin cap

(Heaney, S. 'The Tollund Man', 1990: 31)

Mr Kantwise skipped about the room with wonderful agility, unfastening the boxes, taking out the contents, while Joe the boots and James the waiter stood by assisting. They had never yet seen the glories of these [iron] tables and chairs . . . 'Its the real Louey Catorse' said Mr Kantwise . . . Then, one after another, he brought forth and screwed up the chairs, stools and sundry screens, and within a quarter of an hour he had put up the whole set complete.

(Trollope 1985: 59–60)

'Look,' he would say, 'at the museum of the future. The Russians are already stocking their museums, not with sculptures or ceramics, nor with copies in fibreglass or plaster, but with these constructions of light. Everything can be everywhere, our culture can be, is, world wide . . . with modern technology, mere possession of the relics of the past is of little importance.'

(Byatt 1990: 386)

Introduction: Objects in the Production of History

The relationship of our museum material to the ways in which we view the past and produce our narratives of what happened in the past, is both one of the most important and one of the most difficult questions which museum collections pose. In this chapter we are not asking how historical study gives meaning to material, a question addressed in Chapter 6, and nor are we asking how a particular body of thought can give its own kind of meaning to objects, as we did in the two preceding chapters, although we shall give some thought to the nature of traditional historical writing. Essentially, we are asking how our possession of objects from the human past influences or informs the way in which we understand that past. The time-scale is a very long one, extending back to the beginnings of human beings as a species, running through the long period of prehistory for which we have only material culture from which to draw conclusions, extending through the much briefer period for which we have material and written evidence, and coming up as recently as midnight yesterday.

In relation to the production of historical narrative in general, objects have had a chequered history. A number of studies have begun to show how in the decades either side of 1780 the development of an emotional interest in the objects from the past, especially the medieval past, led to an interest in that past as a whole and to the effort to write its history. It is interesting to remember that a similar interest in the standing monuments of (very broadly) prehistory, which had been a characteristic of the late seventeenth and earlier eighteenth century among men like John Aubrey and William Stukeley, had not led directly to an effort to write the narrative of the past: the world had to wait until the medieval past (loosely conceived) could be seen through Romantic eyes, a vision which Sir Walter Scott, and some of his predecessors and contemporaries, brought the world to share. The part which objects played in the creation of this vision needs careful consideration.

Scott's own emotional relationship with objects came to clothe itself in the idea and the reality of Abbotsford and of the artefacts which were an integral part of it. Scott had been collecting well before he came to build Abbotsford. As early as 1791, Jeffrey, the future Lord Advocate of Scotland, called upon Scott and found him 'in a small den on the sixth floor of his father's house in George Square (Edinburgh) surrounded with dingy books'. Jeffrey adds,

> I may add here the description of that early den, with which I am favoured by a lady of Scott's family: 'Walter had soon begun to collect out-of-way things of all sorts. He had more books than shelves; a small painted cabinet, with Scotch and Roman coins in it, and so on. A claymore and a Lochaber axe, given to him by old Invernahyle, mounted guard on a little print of Prince Charlie; and Broughton's Saucer was hooked up against the wall below it.'
>
> (Lockhart 1900: 151–2)

The saucer was part of a cup-and-saucer which had been used by Murray of Broughton, the Prince's secretary during the 'Forty-Five, and had been saved by Scott when his father broke the cup. Alexander Stewart of Invernahyle had been out in the 'Forty-Five and, so he told the young Scott, in the 'Fifteen also, and his stories were the basis of parts of *Waverley* and *Rob Roy*. The collection of arms and armour eventually assembled at Abbotsford is of considerable importance in its own right (Norman 1963). It is clear that for Scott, Abbotsford and the collection there were not merely an appropriate setting for a man whose fame waxed hugely in his own lifetime. There was an essential relationship between the man and his home; his imagination and Abbotsford were one.

As early as 1808 a reviewer of *Marmion* had noted that Scott's genius, 'seconded by the omnipotence of fashion has brought chivalry again into temporary favour; but he ought to know that this is a taste too evidently unnatural to be long prevalent in the modern world. Fine ladies and gentlemen now talk, indeed, of donjons, keeps, tabards, scutcheons, tressures, caps of maintenance, portcullises, wimples and we know not what besides' (Wainwright 1989: 149). In fact, the reviewer stood at one of those few moments in which prevailing sentiment undergoes a

deep and genuine change and his 'unnatural and temporary taste' was to alter pro-
foundly and lastingly all that came after, creating, among other things, new ideas
about what history is. Bann (1988) has drawn attention to a paper by Riegl (1982)
in which Riegl discusses the 'meaning' of monuments in relation to three separate
criteria: their 'art-value', their 'historical value' and their 'age value', and the argument
applies equally to both architectural fragments of the kind Riegl discusses and
moveable objets like tabards and wimples. 'Art value' gives an aesthetic mark out
of ten, while 'historical value' relates the object to a particular and recorded
sequence of historical events. 'Age value' is different. It is a perceptible property
obvious to all, and not dependent upon cultural understanding of history or art:
we can all see (or think we can see) if something is old. As the later eighteenth and
earlier nineteenth centuries progressed, the 'age value' of objects witnessed by the
visible signs of age and decay became a part of the way in which the seeing eye
attributed quality and importance to the artefacts which passed before it.

This antiquarian sensibility became a way in which the past, especially the relatively distant past, was revalued and re-presented, so that in Bann's phrase, a novel
'view of the past' was created which 'contributed powerfully to the dominant myth
of Romantic historiography – that the past should be "resurrected" ' (Bann 1988:
45). The researchers and writers of antiquarian tastes gave to historic objects a
value in which the sheer fact of their age had an impelling emotional significance,
an ability to give colour and drama to the past that was not drained from the
object by historical narrative, but to which such narrative added force and feeling.
Here lies the impulse behind works like Thora and Charles Stothard's *Monumental
Effigies*, a truly monumental survey of medieval funerary sculpture, which carefully
analysed the finer points of the individual pieces, but harnessed this detail to a
broader idea which their allegorical frontispiece, 'The Monumental Effigies rescued
from Time', makes clear: the aim is the resurrection – almost the resurrection of
the body – of the past.

This idea lies at the heart of the early kind of historical reconstructions created
by some of the early-nineteenth-century collectors. Sir John Soane had his tongue
in his cheek when he created his 'Monk's Parlour' at his museum in Lincoln's Inn
Fields in 1824, but the Gothic antiquarianism of the display may have been taken
more seriously by some of his visitors. Alexandre Lenoir was wholly in earnest
when he created his Musée de Monuments Francais which first opened in Paris in
1795, and which contained tombs, monuments and other works of fine and
applied art arranged together in period rooms, each one spanning a century. His
line was taken up by Alexandre du Sommerand who opened his Musée de Cluny
in Paris in 1832. Here, in the town house of the Abbots of Cluny, he organized his
historical materials so that they might 'aim to represent, through a fullness of texture
and an absolute degree of integration, the reality of the lived life of the earlier periods'
(Bann 1988: 53–6).

The central position of objects in the re-creation of the past was undermined as
the nineteenth century progressed. Most historians writing in English have written
within a broad cultural tradition which attempts to produce convincing accounts
of the past, usually parts of the past specifically limited in time and space, by inves-

tigating and assessing primary written sources, by drawing on secondary material already in print, and by bringing all this together into a more-or-less continuous narrative through the historian's individual qualities of imagination, sympathy and writing power. Historians sometimes concentrate on one very limited period of the past, and when this happens it gives their work more of the feel of social anthropological or sociological investigation, but generally the effort to describe and explain the chain of events, the how and why one move followed another, is of the essence, even though in reality 'explain' usually means 'describe in greater detail'. The primary sources which contribute to this narrative of interlocking events are themselves almost always written narratives of one kind or another (including administrative records) because historians work from the assumption that the most important and significant evidence about the past is preserved in this mode.

When archaeologists attempt to write as prehistorians in the strict sense and to produce narratives of aspects of our early history, rather than as social anthropologists dealing with societies that happen to be far in the past (although the distinction, needless to say, is very blurred in practice) they are faced with the need to extract a chain of cause and effect from the material evidence alone. However carefully this is camouflaged today, it is clear that it can only be done by falling back on Gordon Childe's ideas about the clustering of material types to form a 'culture', which can then be observed developing, shrinking and interacting with other cultural elements to produce process and change. Archaeologists have over the past years devoted much effort to the attempt to dismember Childe's idea of materially-defined culture as an historical or social reality, so it is not surprising that the historians of later periods, who by upbringing and tradition see themselves principally as concerned with written evidence, usually turn away with relief from any effort to integrate objects into their reconstructed narratives. At the heart of this is a feeling that, since objects are seen as merely the brute outcome of thoughts, feelings and actions, without any active role of their own, it is the historian's job and pleasure to concentrate attention upon the significant movements of mind, heart and hand, and to look for their effect not among the passive and soon-discarded material creation, but upon other hearts and minds. The result of this is a curious kind of double vision which impairs much historical writing and exhibition and is passed on to the viewer and reader.

Briggs' book *Victorian Things* (1990) makes this point very clearly. This formed (predictably) the last in a trilogy of which the first two were *Victorian People* (1972) and *Victorian Cities* (1968). Briggs tells us that his research 'has led me *not only* from library to library, *but* from museum to museum and from shop to shop', and that he set out 'both to deal with the kinds of questions professional historians ask and to place in historical perspective for general readers shelves of specialized books on such subjects as pottery, furniture, textiles and photography *which are not usually studied by professional historians*' (1990: 12, my italics). This whets the curator's appetite, but after an introductory chapter which takes account of some recent study of material culture, what Briggs actually gives us is a detailed sequence of descriptions of objects, treated as if they were pictures on the walls of the building in which life was taking place. Where they are integrated into action, this takes the form of biographical information about their inventors, manufacturers and users, not about their role in the creation of cause and effect.

The same limitation shows up throughout Thompson's *The Making of the English Working Class* (1968). Chapter 10, which is entitled 'Standards and Experiences', starts with a section labelled 'Goods'. This begins: 'The controversy as to living standards during the Industrial Revolution has perhaps been of most value when it has passed from the somewhat unreal pursuit of the wage rates of hypothetical average workers and directed attention to articles of consumption: food, clothing and homes' (Thompson 1968: 347). The following discussion concentrates upon the importance of the potato and the levels of meat and beer consumption. The section on 'Homes' concentrates on jerry-building and sanitary conditions. The goods and the homes themselves (clothes are not discussed here at all) are some-how by-passed; we know that they must be there for how else would the people who are the subject of the study have lived, but they are taken for granted while interest concentrates upon 'levels of consumption' and returns of health and longevity. The *relationship* between the uneven flow of material goods and the processes of trade and health is broadly ignored. Arguably the most important consequence of the British Industrial Revolution was the enormous production of artefacts which it made possible, and this sentence can, equally arguably, be reversed: the enormous production of artefacts is what the Industrial Revolution was. Artefacts are capitalism just as much as capitalism means artefacts. Material goods have a life of their own which has a profound effect upon our lives, their creators though we be, but any feeling of this is lost in Thompson's concentration on documents and records as the means of decoding the past.

These ideas about the role objects play in the production of history, developed as they have been over the last two centuries or so, have played their part in forming the notions which underlie the various modes in which museum material is treated, particularly the manner in which museum objects are put on exhibition. However, as we have seen, academic history has been characterized by a lack of interest in material culture and a corresponding lack of a theory about the place objects hold in the production of historical narrative. Accordingly, it comes as no surprise that the production of history in the museum has taken its own, rather different, forms. In the following pages we shall distinguish four principal museum modes: material as relics; material as art and treasure; the past as illustrated narrative, and the past as re-creation, and from these we shall draw out their conceptual implications. We shall be interested, not in discussing the various obvious pitfalls which surround the framing of museum history displays, like whether or not the Museum of London mock-up Mesolithic shelter was too small, or exactly how Colonial Williamsburg distorted the record by failing to show black slaves, but endeavour to get below representational patterns or particular interests to concentrate on the museums aesthetic, the codes of presentation through which meaning is created. At the centre of all the museum's presentational modes lies the dual reality, discussed in detail in Chapter 2, of the objects as 'the real thing from the real past' and as perpetually redefined meaning in concrete form.

Relics of the Past

'Relic' is the word commonly used to describe collected material which has come down to us from the past both in academic circles (see Lowental 1985: 238–324) and in everyday speech, where museum pieces are ordinarily described as relics, with or without the addition of further adjectives. The use of the word is instructive. 'Relic' means 'something left behind' or 'left over', like the widow whose active life is past and whose passive period now begins. It implies the idea of lifeless debris, of the dead shell of purposeful energy which has moved elsewhere, the remains (another distinctive word much in use) of past activity. But to an earlier age 'relic' meant the living dead at work amongst us, a voice from a past not left behind but entering into present life.

This kind of material has a number of significant characteristics. The English crown jewels are kept in the Jewel House at the Tower of London and together they form one of the most frequently visited displays in the entire world (Mears 1986). The pieces are very eye-catching, and the gem stones in them known to be worth very large sums of money. These things contribute to their power of attraction, but by themselves would not draw such crowds. At the heart of their power is the living history which they seem to embody. Visitors are told that the four large drop pearls in the Imperial State Crown belonged to Mary, Queen of Scots, and then to Elizabeth I (two of the very few historical characters that everybody has heard of), and that the Black Prince's Ruby in the same crown was owned by Edward the Black Prince and worn by Henry V at the Battle of Agincourt (Mears 1986). They know that these things were worn by Elizabeth II at her coronation in 1953 and will be worn by Prince Charles when his time (presumably) comes.

The value attached to such objects seems to be a universal human sentiment. Malinowski observed:

> When, after six years' absence in the South Seas and Australia, I returned to Europe and did my first bit of sight-seeing at Edinburgh Castle, I was shown the Crown Jewels. The keeper told many stories of how they were worn by this and that king or queen on such and such an occasion . . . I had the feeling that something similar had been told to me . . . And then arose before me the vision of a native village on coral soil . . . and naked men and one of them showing me thin red strings and big worn out objects, clumsy to sight and greasy to touch. With reverence he also would name them and tell their story . . . Both heirlooms and *vaygu'a* are cherished because of the historical sentiment which surrounds them. However ugly, useless, and – according to current standards – valueless an object may be, if it has figured in historical scenes and passed through the hands of historic persons, and is therefore an unfailing vehicle of important sentimental associations, it cannot but be precious to us.
>
> (1922: 88–9)

Pieces of this kind act essentially as community souvenirs, that is as souvenirs which are part, not of one individual's brief life, but of the long life of a society. They take the souvenir role of acting as a tangible means by which past history can

be selectively rearranged so that continuity is stressed while dislocation and fragmentation is denied, and a romantic wholeness and significance is achieved. We
can see that the idea of 'living history' is rather beside the point. The undoubted
historicity of objects like these is lifted out of history into mythology, where they
remain in frozen timelessness. If, for some reason, the English Crown Jewels were
unavailable for Charles's coronation (and this kind of thing has happened a number of
times in the course of the history of the English coronation), this would be a matter of
regret but not real effect, in that the ceremony would take place as planned and its
authenticity would not be impaired. This is not simply because contemporary England is a 'sophisticated' society over which 'magical objects' have a limited hold; it
is always true that when pressing 'reality', the brute facts of history in action, break
through, the myth has to bend and accommodate. We shrug our shoulders and say
'It can't be helped', and the theatrical illusion is revealed.

Collections relating to illustrious individuals work in much the same way, and
their kinship with the medieval relic of actual (or believed to be actual) human
remains is very apparent. What gives the naval displays on board HMS *Victory* particular power is the special reverence paid to the actual timbers where Nelson
received his fatal wound, and in Germany the translation in 1991 of the remains of
Frederick the Great from his previous resting place in southern Germany to Berlin
is indistinguishable from the normal activities of medieval Europe. As Geary has
put it in relation to medieval relics,

> The value attached to the special corpses that would be venerated as relics
> required the communal acceptance of three interrelated beliefs: first, that an
> individual had been, during his life and more important after his death, a special
> friend of God, that is, a saint; second, that the remains of such a saint were to
> be prized and treated in a special way; and third, and for our purposes most
> important, that the particular corpse or portion thereof was indeed the remains
> of that particular saint.
>
> (Geary 1986: 175)

This translated into secular terms in which something like perhaps personal cha-
risma, an interesting modern use of an essentially religious term illustrating the
demand for modern sainthood, takes the place of 'God' is a fair expression of the
value attributed to such remains. They are the immediate sources of supernatural
power for good or ill, and close contact with or possession of them is a means of
participating in that power (Geary 1986: 176).

The actual body need not now be present. Its place can be taken by objects
which were close and familiar to the person in life, especially if these can be
arranged in displays which re-create a study or living room or bedroom. The
Thomas Hardy Collection in Dorset County Museum Service is a good example
of a very common museum phenomenon (see Plate 23). The Hardy Collection is
housed partly in the store and partly in the Victorian Gallery of the museum. A series
of cases down the wall to the right of the entrance house Hardy material, and
those on the opposite side have material relating to other Dorset worthies like
William Barnes. The centrepiece is the reconstruction of Hardy's study at Max

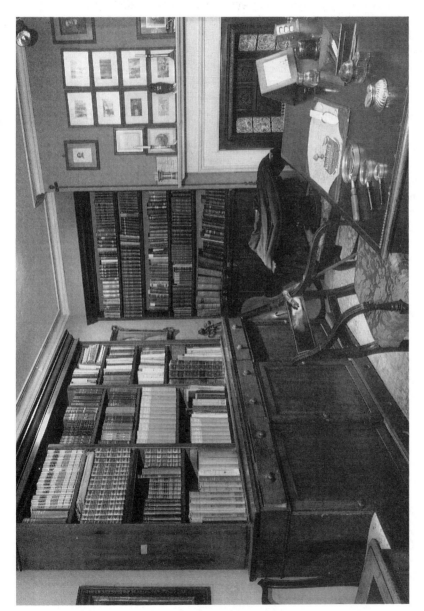

Plate 23. Reconstruction of Thomas Hardy's study at Max Gate, Dorset, in the Dorset County Museum (photo: Trustees of the Thomas Hardy Memorial Collection in the Dorset County Museum, Dorchester, Dorset).

Gate, his house during the final part of his life, and this occupies a kind of large alcove at the back of the gallery, shielded from immediate view by stage blocks and a screen (Figure 9.1). The collection contains a wide range of literary and personal material which came to the museum in part from a bequest made in 1937 by Hardy's second wife Florence (the Thomas Hardy Memorial Collection) and in part from other related sources. It is clear both that material was relatively widely distributed during the lifetime of Thomas and Florence to those who valued tangible memorials of the novelist, and that there was a degree of pressure on such people to contribute back what they had when the formal collection was established in the County Museum.

It is also obvious that the material is far from showing Hardy through a clear glass. In her will, Florence instructed her trustees to include in the bequest to the museum 'the more important manuscripts and those articles which were most closely associated with my husband or may be regarded as characteristic of him and his work' (Museum Acquisitions 1941). Hardy himself had begun to select from his material when writing his autobiography with Florence, and they seem to have destroyed material which did not match the image they wished to create. After his death Florence again burnt 'all the fabric of Hardy's private file which he never wished to be revealed' (Sullivan 1976: 33). The same motives appear in her arrangements for Hardy's funeral at Westminster Abbey (Orel 1976).

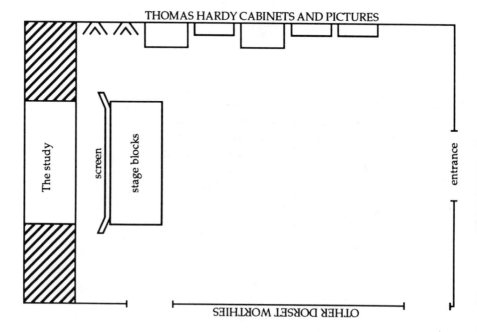

Figure 9.1 Plan of Victorian Gallery, Dorset County Museum, Dorchester, showing position of Thomas Hardy Collection displays (based on information from Sarah Harbidge).

Evidently at work here is the conscious desire to manifest 'the great novelist as national hero' through the sanctification of objects and the erection of a shrine. The effort has been successful, and the shrine attracts many pilgrims who are gaining merit from their tour of 'Hardy's Wessex'. The life of the writer has been reified through the objects associated with it, and these have been lifted out of the historical process and into a mythology which helps to support feelings about 'greatness' and 'Englishness', objectified ideas which are gazed at, not experienced.

Objects as relics established in display reliquaries are not limited to national souvenirs or the creation of individual mythical heroes. The same forces are at work in the American museum displays which celebrate New England pioneers or those who opened up the West. The strength of the myth is most forcefully demonstrated when it is attacked. The 1991 exhibition *The West as America: Reinterpreting Images of the Frontier* at the National Museum of American Art, Washington, contained over 160 paintings, sculptures and engravings of the way American artists between 1820 and 1920 portrayed the nation's expansion across the Prairies and to the Pacific. The leader label at the entrance to the exhibition said:

> Images from Christopher Columbus to Kit Carson show the discovery and settlement of the West as a heroic undertaking. A more recent approach argues that these images are carefully staged fiction, constructed from both supposition and fact. Their role was to justify the hardship and conflict of nation-building. Western scenes extolled progress, but rarely noted damaging social and environmental change. Looking beneath the surface of these images gives us a better understanding of why national problems created during the West-ward expansion still affect us today.

The exhibition featured the painting *Defending the Stockade* by Charles Schreyvogel, making it clear that this famous scene was actually painted some decades after the kind of historical events which it celebrates had taken place, and that Schreyvogel's art has more contemporary cultural resonance to events happening in Eastern America around 1900, when white Anglo-Saxon Protestant Americans were attempting to hold the line against a new flood of immigrants from Southern and Eastern Europe. The entrance label continues: 'The paintings reveal far more about the urban culture in which they were made and showed. For it was according to the culture's attitudes – about race, class and history – that artists such as Schreyvogel and Remington created the place we know as the "Old West".

Another famous Western artist, Frederic Remington, whose classic *Fight for the Waterhole* included in the exhibition, features a desert scene showing five cowboys grimly defending their precious water against encircling Indians, made his racist views unmistakably clear: 'You can't glorify a Jew – coin-lovin' puds – nasty humans,' Remington wrote to a publisher friend. 'I've got some Winchesters and when the massacreing begins which you speak of, I can get my share of 'em and what's more I will.' He went on to attack 'Jews, injuns, Chinamen, Italians, Huns, the rubbish of the earth I hate' (quoted in Walker 1991). When he was sent to Chicago by *Harper's Weekly* to cover a strike, he made his political views equally clear, describing the strikers as: 'a malodorous crowd of anarchistic foreign trash . . . vicious wretches with no blood circulating above the ears . . . will follow readily any demagogue with revolutionary tendencies (quoted in Walker 1991). The exhibition label for *Fight for the Waterhole* said, justly in the light of Remington's views, that the painting is a metaphor for 'the plight of an embattled capitalist elite in an era of strikes, violence and widespread immigration . . . Does it borrow its imagery – a group of outnumbered whites desperately defending against the 'strike' of a racial enemy – from the urban world where Remington lived?'

The approach of the exhibition attracted much vituperation. Senator Ted Stevens of Alaska may be taken as a typical example when he said, 'when the gallery administrators next apply for government funds they will be in for a battle,' and that, 'Why should people come to your institution and see a history that is so perverted? I don't think the Smithsonian has any business, or has ever had any business, developing a political agenda.' The exhibition has been linked with the whole radical agenda: 'Ever since the 1960s, the one-time campus radicals of the Baby Boom generation have sought repeatedly and noisily to rewrite the rules of American society in ways large and small', ran a furious denunciation of the exhibition in the *Washington Post*:

> On the campuses they seized by force in the 1960s and 1970s they have moved from early demands as students for such things as black studies programmes to efforts as tenured professors to reshape not only the core curriculum of American higher education but its value system as well . . . aging radicals now as teachers and curators increasingly in charge of the nation's cultural patrimony.
>
> (Quoted in Walker 1991)

Clearly, we step upon holy ground at our peril. Myths, whether as community souvenirs, or folk heroes, or national characters are the object-stories which give culture its sense of meaning, which justify culturally-determined behaviour among a community and towards outsiders. As Edward Hawes put it, drawing interestingly on the ideas of Jung,

> These myths are one key support for the identity of a culture. Just as the identity of an individual gives a raison d'etre, so does that of a culture. The myths give people in that culture a sense of themselves, who they are, why they are here, where they are going, where they could or should go. Just as the identity of an individual has a conscious dimension in the Ego, and an unconscious dimension in the Self, the identity of a culture also has conscious and unconscious dimensions.
>
> (Hawes 1985)

Art and Treasure

Exhibitions of this character have something in common with the mythology of relics, but can be described rather more briefly. Exhibitions of the art of the past, usually of paintings, drawings and sculpture, share an underlying aesthetic. The displays of Greek sculpture at the British Museum, of pictures at the Tate or the Walker Art Gallery or at the large number of temporary or permanent art exhibitions up and down the country (or, indeed, across the world) all display the same mode, and where some gallant recent attempts have been made to modify the traditional stance, these usually involve an effort to bring the pictures and sculptures into their social context, producing the kind of illustrated narrative which will be discussed in the next section.

Traditionally, the art objects are displayed in splendid remoteness from the daily round, icons of a spiritual life which is celebrated and exalted in all its elevation. The viewer classically sees this as 'like being in church' even though some of the pictures may actually show intimate scenes of ordinary life. The ideological difficulties, it goes almost without saying, which arise from the appeal to a 'high culture' created by a very limited and very special number of human societies, and usually created for an élite within those societies, are largely ignored within the art gallery, where the spiritual treasure is its own justification.

Such spiritual treasure, let us not forget, is generally worth large sums in the market-place and, in terms at least of the way in which it is usually displayed, it has considerable kinship with that very familiar kind of exhibition entitled *The Treasures of the Museum*. Such exhibitions usually have a fine art and an applied art content. The advertising leaflet produced by Lancashire County Museums (1990) is entitled *Treasures from Lancashire Museums*. One side shows an eighteenth-century picture featuring three gentlemen in a study largely furnished with statuary of the noble, nude and antique persuasion. The other side gives brief accounts of fourteen museums in the county, stressing collections like the Japanese netsukes at Blackpool and the Gillows furniture at Lancaster. The title is reproduced here, and it is matched by a second large caption which runs *A Wealth of Fine Collections*. The same note was struck by the British Museum exhibition of 1977 entitled *Wealth of the Roman World AD 300–700* which presented a dazzling display of gold and silver objects, many of them masterpieces of craftsmanship.

The collection as treasure has a long history which reaches through the churches and courts of medieval Europe to the Classical world beyond and, indeed, the prehistoric world before that. Museums have inherited this collecting mode and in the modern world have largely taken the place of the earlier depositories. Exhibitions of this kind, therefore, hold a deep-rooted place in our culture, and are correspondingly familiar to our sensibilities. We know that we are expected to gaze in awe and admiration at the wealth offered to view, which rests detached from time and place but re-constituted as objectified value.

Illustrated Narrative: Material Witnesses

In commemoration of the 400th anniversary of the destruction of the Spanish Armada, in 1988 the National Maritime Museum mounted an important exhibition entitled *Armada 1588–1988* (see Plate 24) which, like *The West as America*, caused considerable uproar in the press because it did not endorse the trumpet-

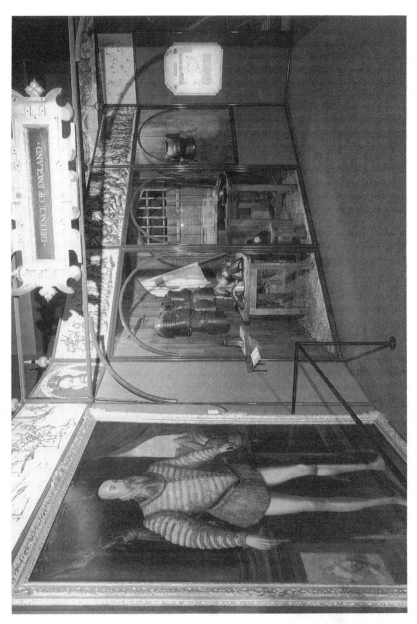

Plate 24.   View of the *Armada 1588–1988* exhibition at the National Maritime Museum, Greenwich, London, 1988, showing the section on the defence of England (photo: National Maritime Museum).

and-Drake's-drum view of the event still prevalent in the English popular mind. Our present concern, however, is with the way in which the objects in that exhibition were presented. The official publicity leaflet told us that,

> The finest available artefacts of the period will be deployed within an exhibition design which draws out the great visual appeal of this complex story. There will be paintings, sculpture, engravings, maps, charts, manuscripts, books, pamphlets, tapestries, jewellery, armour, guns and other artefacts of many kinds. A central attraction will be a large collection of material retrieved from the wrecks of Armada ships off the coasts of Scotland and Ireland. In total, there will be approximately 550 exhibits.
>
> (*Armada 1588–1988* 1988)

The exhibition was arranged in sixteen units. These explored the political background, featuring portraits of Elizabeth I and Philip II; the rival armies and the rival fleets, featuring a quarter-sized model of a Spanish ship at sea; aspects of life on board, where most of the artefacts were concentrated and where the siege gun cast in 1556 showing the arms of Spain and the words *Philipus Rex*, recovered from the wreck of *La Trinidad Valencera*, was especially highlighted; and an account of the sea battle and its aftermath.

This exhibition shared characteristics with very many other history exhibitions, including those put together with access to much less detailed scholarship and technical resource than *Armada* enjoyed. The storyline, the historical narrative, rests in the labels, graphics and original pictures, all of which we are accustomed to interpret by eye, and which are organized according to the codes of the academic historical narrative already described. Next, and intended to flesh out the visual material, come re-creations, like the diorama of the Armada battle and the model of the Spanish ship. This puts some 'action' into the show. Finally, standing silently in their places like old dogs waiting to be noticed, come the canon and the smaller objects, the plates, knives and leather bottles. The potential excitement of their real relationship to the actual events of the time is not caught. They are neither interesting nor instructive; instead they are merely mildly illustrative. They can serve, should anybody want such a thing, as a kind of authentification that what is said is true, but obviously nobody much does because this part of their character is largely ignored. This painfully familiar artefactual deadness arises from a failure to integrate the material world and the world of thought and action, and yet this integration is how we all live our lives.

Shanks and Tilley (1987a: 75), in relation to the narrative display of London's history at the Museum of London, make the further point that the narrative on offer, and its supporting objects, represents *information*, that is, narrative which is the result of a prolonged process of selection and discussion from which interpretation-as-information is distilled, and in the process of which other potential meanings are suppressed and objects which embody a potential play of difference are limited in meaning in order to fit in with the chosen story. They express this as the set of opposed pairs given in Figure 9.2. The objects are immediate and real before us, and so they confirm the meaning of the exhibition, but also they only

spatial	:	temporal
closed, completed	:	open, unfinished
past	:	history
eternity	:	history
reified	:	relational
repetition	:	particularity
identity	:	difference
presence	:	absence
homogeneous	:	heterogeneous
coercive	:	explorative
passive	:	active
monologic	:	dialogic
forgetting	:	remembrance
conservation	:	redemption

Figure 9.2 Opposed pairs showing nature of historical exhibition (after Shanks and Tilley 1987: 68–97)

represent the past, which is in truth not here and present, but past and distant. The past was the real substance, available to us now only as the trace the object leaves in its passage through time, like smoke trails which mark where once the aircraft was. The past (the signified) is what objects incarnate, but what it signifies is our idea of past as it seems now, in our present, a past tied down in the narrative of the exhibition. So in exhibitions of this kind we have a double problem: objects subordinated to the narrative presented primarily in terms of classic written historiography; and objects shorn of their potential multiplicity of meanings so that they can be integrated – as supporting cast – into that chosen narrative.

These difficulties show up particularly starkly in prehistoric displays, especially those of the usual kind which begin somewhere around the Lower Paleolithic and progress, period by period, to the 'Eve of Roman Britain'. Here the context and meaning of objects, arrived at strictly by the study of material culture, is transmitted into an historical narrative like that which would have been constructed if documents had been available, and the objects then arranged in relation to it and subordinated accordingly. The objects only come into their own when history is presented in technological terms and then they are detached from their social matrix, leaving the viewer not with any feeling for the past itself, but only with the past in terms of the present – 'Look, they had axes even in the Bronze Age.' The past becomes a sequence of meaningless detached moments, a string of empty instants, themselves turned into commodities which can be sampled whenever a viewer chooses to spend some time.

The Resurrection of the Body

In Britain today it is possible, with some gaps, to visit a series of slices of the past running backwards into prehistory. The Ironbridge Gorge Trust and the North of England Open Air Museum at Beamish give us the nineteenth and later eighteenth centuries; the Kirkgate displays at York Castle Museum give us that familiar period known as 'yesteryear'; the Middle Ages are curiously largely absent, but West Stow in Suffolk gives us the Anglo-Saxons, Jorvik the Vikings, The Lunt the Romans and Butser the Iron Age. We may add to this list also the stream of historical recreations which come from the BBC. The line between reconstructions of this kind, involving a large range of artefacts and installations, and the 'conserved' or 'preserved' monuments of the past, like the castles and abbeys in the care of English Heritage, is a fine one, and the two kinds of sites share a similar range of ethical and other problems (see Pearce 1990: 170–80). Here we shall take the intention of simulation, of the re-creation of the past within a closed environment where disbelief should be suspended, as the key distinguishing characteristic of the displays we are discussing. All of these exhibitions operate on a range of scales and with varying qualities of loving detail and commitment to serious research into the nature of the past, but the prime intention of them all is to provide an experience of what it was like to live in the past.

Such exhibitions, inside museum walls and in the open air, have their linear ancestors in the reconstructions which were the purpose of Lenoir's Musée de Monuments Français and du Sommerand's Musée de Cluny, and owe a great deal to the Scandinavian folk life movement. They share a number of obvious difficulties with such earlier manifestations of their type. The air of artificiality is unmistakable. The layout is contrived and is far more 'typical' than real life ever is. The displays are at once too clean and too grubby in an all-too-contemporary way. The arranger's hand shows at every corner; the visible ropes and pullies remind us inexorably that we are in a stage set.

In many such events the objects have been gathered together from a variety of times and places, and bear no integral relationship to each other beyond a vague one of 'period' and 'region'. The Beamish publicity leaflet tells us that 'Buildings from all parts of the region have been brought together, re-built and furnished as they were around the turn of the century' (Beamish 1991). The first outdoor museum in the United States was that created by Henry Ford at Greenfield village, Dearborn, Michigan, which featured:

a traditional New England green with church, town hall, courthouse, post office, and general store; the Scotch Settlement schoolhouse Ford attended as a boy; the Plymouth, Michigan, carding mill to which Ford's father took wool; Noah Webster's house; William Holmes McGuffey's Pennsylvania log-cabin birthplace; a 500-ton stone Cotswold Cottage; and the Sir John Bennet jewellery shop from Cheapside, London, with its clock graced by statues of Gog and Magog.

(Alexander 1979: 92–3)

Such *bricolage* now has its own place in the history of taste and sentiment. All of these displays can be criticized in a number of ways, and it is sad but inevitable that these generally involve that kind of puritanical academic comment which the public, for whom these exhibitions are prepared, most dislikes. The exhibitions, however honourable their intentions may (or may not) be, offer only an ersatz mix of shallow nostalgia and visible spectacle, a product to be consumed like any other. The moral dilemma implicit in this dislocation shows up particularly acutely in displays like the Second World War Blitz Experience and the First World War Trench Experience, mounted at the Imperial War Museum, which tend to claim an authenticity of sound, smell and experience to a degree which is both absurd and dishonest, but glossed by claims that the public like it. Heritage, for better or worse, has little to do with history. Heritage is about feeling good in the present, while history is the laborious struggle to come to terms with a past which was serious then and is serious now. The manipulation of history into a good day out is certainly popular and may be superficially harmless, but leaves us with the difficult question of whether 'popular' has to be the same as 'acceptable', to which only a confirmed cynic could give an unequivocal 'yes'.

The re-creation of history, the resurrection of the body of the past, has, however, been a recurrent preoccupation of European man ever since the Renaissance, itself a 're-birth', a second coming of the Classical past (Lowenthal 1985: 75, 84–7). For a time, as we have seen, in the nineteenth century, such resurrection was believed to be within our grasp, provided only that an adequate quality and quantity of material could be arranged with the benefit of sufficiently ample scholarship. But now we have lost our faith in such simple certainties, and recognize that what we thought was re-creation is only simulation. The artefacts do not re-create but are reassembled, the original authors are absent, and the voyeuristic viewers (Sontag 1979: 23–4) take their places in the queue.

Conclusion

The four museum modes of producing meaning from the past which we have discussed here can each be reduced to the operation of a single verb: relic displays ask us to believe; the past narrated asks us to learn; art and treasure on view ask us to admire; and the reconstructed past asks us to understand. All four modes have more in common than they have in difference. Always, it can be argued, we are looking at artefacts which have been objectified in the bad sense, lifted out of the flow of experience, actual and potential, and packaged in a way which creates a particular relationship with us. The real time from which the objects came no longer exists, and lumps of time have been lifted out to be offered as commodities, as available activities. We are offered not experience of the past, but a sequence of timeless myths abstracted from the past.

For the past is essentially unknowable, forever lost to us, and in museum displays its material traces are reconstructed into images of time past which have meaning only for the present, in which their genuinely intrinsic relationships to the past are used to authenticate a present purpose. That present purpose, it can also be argued, usually has the ideological motive of maintaining the status quo, of showing how smoothly the processes of the past led to the present day, of suppressing dislocation, fragmentation and false starts, and of reinforcing local value systems, of conservation rather than an opening to change and redemption.

The classic response to this pessimism is the flight into humanism, which thinks no man (or woman) alien, and which believes that the play of imaginative sympathy has a legitimate place in the art of creating the narrative of the past. The basis for this is the conviction that, across time and space, people are essentially the same and can therefore achieve an understanding of each other, and its touchstone is the real object in all its individual humanity, the thumb prints on prehistoric pottery, the veil which a woman wore at her wedding. The immediacy of this emotional link across the centuries is seldom brought out in display (no doubt because we fight shy of committing ourselves in labels to so raw an appeal to feeling), but it is the common stuff of most gallery talks and demonstrations. We must allow that the makers of the artefact *are* absent, and that the humanist sympathy which tries to call them up is only another form of rhetoric which makes the present of this past our present. Sympathy, however sensitive and well-read in the information which narrative history offers, cannot actually bridge the gap between past and present. But it can create an enlargement of the human spirit in the present which changes individuals and contributes to social change. It is the nature of the individual's response to objects and its consequences to which we must turn in the next chapter.

10   Objects in Action

How does it happen that the table leg
Has this curve in one age, that in another?
Or that the carved figures of men
Differ more than the men themselves?
Conception rules the art.
How then can one man speak to another?

(Sisson 1974: 173)

. . . a hat can transform your mood.

(Walsall collector, quoted in Mullen 1991)

The bored tourists . . . may believe that elderly nineteenth century gentlemen
. . . placed these exhibits here out of a virtuous desire to educate and amuse
the bourgeois and the radical taxpayers, and to celebrate the magnificent march
of progress. But no: Saint-Martin-des-Champs had been conceived first as a priory
and only later as a revolutionary museum and compendium of arcane knowledge.
Those planes, those self-propelled machines . . . were carrying on a dialogue
whose script still escaped me.

(Eco 1990: 8)

Introduction: Objects in Action

This chapter and the next are intended to explore how, in lived reality, the individual experiences objects, inside and outside museums. In this chapter we shall see how individuals and objects work in a dynamic relationship to each other which creates meaning and change. This relates to the social life of objects, to which attention was drawn in Chapter 2. In the next chapter we shall look at the oppressive side of museums and objects in relation to individual freedom of action and potential for change, and this will lead us into questions about the nature of the individual and the social values which the museum represents.

The elucidations of meaning in objects is, as we have seen, an important part of the curator's task, and this is done from a range of standpoints. But these stances share one major limitation: they do not help us to understand better the relationship between objects and each of us as individuals, or the ways in which objects can change their meaning as different people start to see them differently. Yet we know that life is never static, but in a continuous flux of change and process in which the contexts described by analysis are always in a state of becoming, and for which such analysis can always only offer us a series of Box Brownie snaps. And equally we know that societies do not and cannot act of themselves, however much social theory seems sometimes to suppose they can; only individuals can have feelings, make decisions and take actions which carry social life forward through change.

It is therefore, the business of this chapter to bring the individual back to his rightful place in the frame, since only through him can any social experience actually take place, in a museum gallery or elsewhere. This is another way of saying that we shall try to come to terms with that mysterious process through time which (turning *langue* into *parole* and *parole* into *langue*) makes meaning and creates changes as it goes along. As a part of this we hope to show that although the meanings of objects are constituted by past human experience, and in this sense objects are as passive as the traditional view holds, their embodiment of meaning has an active role in relation to the experiencing individuals. Objects are therefore actors in the story, not just the reflection of action, and themselves have a role in creating that change which we call the process of history.

Here, then, we might say that we are considering not the history of objects, but how objects make history. We might put that another way, and say that we are concerned with some important aspects of communication, of how people communicate with objects and with each other. We shall draw on ideas which are set under the broad phenomenological label, referring to the work of philosophers like Hegel and Husserl and literary critics like Wolfgang Iser, whose approach to the written text marches very well with a similar approach to museum objects. We shall then endeavour to put the argument within the broad historical stream by considering the ideas of the French *Annales* historians, and especially those of Fernand Braudel.

In our discussion of the nature of collecting (Chapter 4), we have already seen how Hegel's concept of 'objectification' supposes a dual relationship of process between subject and object, and for Hegel, 'object' means the whole of the world outside the subject, including not only material culture, but everything which may be called social practice. 'Process' is an important idea which plays a major part in all phenomenological theory. Objectification means the double process in which the subject, the individual, externalizes himself by creating an entity of whatever kind – including material culture – which then assumes an external existence as an object; but then re-appropriates this externalization through an act of sublation which takes back the creation to use it as a part of the next burst of creative activity. In this way subject and object are brought together, and neither is given priority. The essence of the link is relationship; that relationship is always in process, and process is always bringing about the change which we see as history in the making.

The word 'phenomenology' was contributed by Husserl, who linked it with the famous slogan 'Back to things themselves', as a reaction to the over-abstraction of much nineteenth-century philosophy, and in an effort to get back to the concrete which seemed necessary and responsible in the shattered world of post-1918 (1964). Husserl started from the position that, in spite of what common sense may tell us, we cannot be sure that objects in the world exist independently of ourselves, and that they can therefore only be regarded as creations of our consciousness: all we can be sure of is what we ourselves are conscious of, and these things Husserl called 'phenomena'. But phenomena are not random individual psychological happenings. They have a common content: pillar boxes are hollow and red to us all (or to all with 'normal' eye sight), and milk bottles straight from the 'fridge are cold. This 'shared understanding' is a way of describing the whole sweep of the past which has created society and the meaning of objects in it – we agree that pillar boxes are hollow and red because historically we have developed a letter-collecting Post Office, and associate red with the sovereign to whom it belongs. Accordingly, to his idea of phenomena, Husserl added that of 'essence', which means that we share a general consensus about the nature of the phenomena which all our consciousness creates. Being and meaning are therefore always bound up with each other; there can be no object without a subject.

There are difficulties with this line of thought which we shall pursue at the end of this chapter and in the next. Meanwhile, let us concentrate upon its positive side. Once the abstractions of the language have been penetrated, we see that it opens up a way of showing how people and the material world interact, and how the basis of this interaction can be intelligible to us all, sharing as we do the understanding of the essence of things because we share the past from which this social meaning has arisen. The continued interaction of people and things within this agreed framework carries social life forward and creates change. It remains to develop more detailed appreciations of exactly how this interactive process can be understood, and to this behavioural and reception theory contribute.

A Behaviourist Perspective: Objecting by Design

A behaviourist approach towards a better understanding of how people and objects interact has been cultivated over the last decades by American students of material culture, especially those inside and outside museums who are interested in the artefacts and folk life generally of nineteenth- and early-twentieth-century Americans (Schlereth 1982: 57–63; Jones 1975). The behaviourist approach offers one way of establishing a relationship between the cognitive processes of the individual and the social structure which we see manifested in actual life, and of putting this relationship within a temporal progression. As Jones put it, this kind of study endeavours, 'through personal observation or by means of records composed by others . . . to understand better and appreciate more fully what people make and do and how they think', and he seeks 'to discover a way to account for the nature of an object' in order 'to understand more fully human behaviour' (Jones 1975: vii).

The behaviourist approach in the United States has encouraged a development called 'performance theory', advocated especially by researchers like Del Upton and Thomas Adler who argue that the human process involved in conceiving, making, using, adapting, liking or loathing, and disposing of objects are intrinsic elements in individual experience and such experience as a whole is what the material culture student should try to understand. Adler, following Edmund Husserl, summarized the behavioural/phenomenological position in relation to objects (specifically North American folk life objects) in a way which is worth quoting at length:

> We are beginning to get a pretty good idea of the distribution of folk houses on the land, and we can all mostly agree how baskets were made, how bread was baked, and how quilts are put together. We are now in need of some perspectives that can help us to elicit and to generalize about the traditional meanings that underlie and are embedded in traditional artifacts. The hardest core of meanings to get at may be those that arise directly from the phenomenal stream, from the actual experiences a person has with an object.
>
> The study of such experiences necessarily involves the taking of an internalized view. In conducting a phenomenological investigation an analyst sets aside the referential knowledge he already has and momentarily divests himself of his memories of an object, recognizing crucial distinctions to be made between direct experiential knowledge, the memories of experience, and referred knowledge to others. Whether or not historical and personal know-ledge can actually be set aside is a moot point; phenomenologists make the attempt, because experiences are by their very nature things of the here-and-now. All we have, experientially speaking, is the present, and each moment of our experience is filled, in part, by material presence that is loci of denotational and connotational meaning. If we can create an appropriate language in which to speak of the ways we all experience artifacts, we may be able to commence an unambiguous discussion of the significance of objects, as well as of their dis-tribution and construction.

> (Adler 1985)

It should be noted, however, that Adler views each experience as a 'one-off, here and now' event, rather than taking on board the idea that it is the sequence of experiences which shows us how objects and people interact.

Some important individual studies which take this theoretical perspective have revolved around the study of gravestones (see Deetz and Dethlefsen 1982). Ludwig's (1966) research into the symbolism, forms and rituals of funerary art in Massachusetts and Connecticut reveals a story which differs from the conventional view of New England piety, based upon written sources. Verbal evidence suggests an early iconophobic, non-mystical Puritan piety which declined dramatically around 1700. But the material evidence – the gravestones – analysed by Ludwig suggested three quite contrary conclusions. Firstly, they suggested that religious sentiment flourished in New England well into the nineteenth century; secondly that the American Puritans created much figural as well as religious art, whatever the official written view may say; and finally that this art deserves serious attention as an aesthetic tradition in its own right. Here, within a relatively limited area, but a relatively extended time-scale of some three centuries, we can see a process of regular inter-action between people, and one important type of object which is generating its own momentum and, moreover, creating a history which parallels that of the written sources.

Let us try to demonstrate the process of this interaction in more explicit and concrete terms, using a deliberately simple scheme to represent the behavioural framework within which social action takes place. Within this we shall set a fashion-conscious woman in her late teens as the acting individual, and the clothes of the late 1980s as the acting objects (Figure 10.1). The framework sets out the main parameters within which action happens, giving us the environment both physical and social, the individual, and the psychological or cognitive processes of perception and learning which form a continuous cycle and link the whole together. The physical environment is straightforward enough, and for our example will be southern urban England with the normal English climate. The social environment is broken down into three groups, all fairly standard in social science: primary groups like family, peer groups comprising people of the same age and background who may or may not be friends, and reference groups who for our woman are likely to be members of the youth culture scene. The individual, the woman herself, is pre-sumed to have a personality, sets of attitudes, beliefs and values, and motives, all of which derive from her nature and nurture.

The Punk style of dressing (and incidentally, it is interesting that it had to look back to the subculture diction of seventeenth-century England where 'punk' meant 'ruffian' or even 'goblin', to find itself a name) had caught the attention of the public by 1976. It has been described as

> a classic case of avant-garde shock tactics. An assault on all received notions of taste, it is significant in being almost the only one of the post-war youth/culture/music movements fully to have integrated women. The style alluded to sado-masochism, porn, sleaze and tawdry glamour and inscribed itself by means of shaven or partially shaven heads and a sort of anti-make-up (reddened eyes, black lips, make-up painted in streaks across the face or in a pattern) on the sur-face of the body. Punks created an alienated space between self and appear-ance by means of these attacks on their own bodies; this was truly fit wear for the urban dispossessed, constructed out of the refuse of the material world; rusty razor blades, tin cans, safety pins, dustbin bags and even used tampons.
> (Wilson and Taylor 1989: 196)

The style was, unsurprisingly, actually worn only by a few, but by the late 1980s it had modified the mainstream of young fashion. Bright lipstick and heavy black eye make-up, 'ugly' short hair, shaved necks, sometimes spiky hair stiffened with gel, together with black leather, short black skirts and black tights became the normal metropolitan uniform for young women in the late 1980s. These fashions and the life style, for both men and women, that went with them were encouraged by the new style magazines of the eighties like *The Face*, *i-D* and *Blitz*. As Wilson and Taylor say,

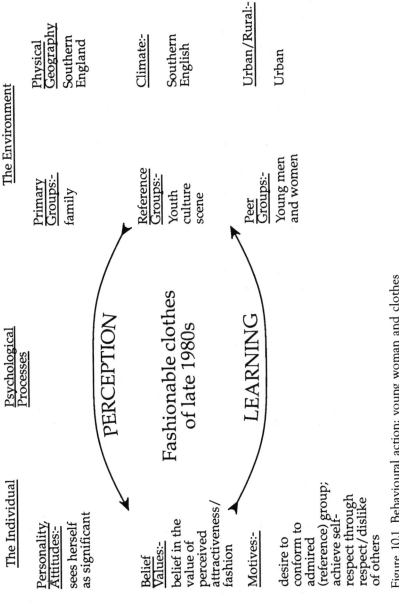

Figure 10.1 Behavioural action: young woman and clothes

The newly glamorous, male style setter of the eighties became as familiar in magazines and advertisements as his female counterpart, with his hair, short at the back, long at the front, sleekly gelled, his looks mean and tough, yet simultaneously blankly narcissistic. This new man is the empty object of anyone's desire, his sexuality ambiguous. It is unclear whether this beauty is destined for men or for women.

(1989: 204)

We can see what is happening in terms of the behavioural model. There is a large range of clothes available for wear, but our teenage woman learns in relation to her own personality and motives, that the pressure of her peer group, and of the reference groups which they admire, will lead her to buy and wear the fashionable black clothes and the look that goes with it, in opposition probably to some primary groups and rejected reference groups (e.g. parents). Once she has done this, however, she is herself perceived differently by all the groups to which she relates. This perception may for some take the form of greater acceptance and admiration, but it may suggest to others that the black clothes are now old hat, and that the time has come to turn into, say, a Laura Ashley milkmaid. So the cycle of learning and perception is matched by a cycle of old and new clothes, and the two interact at the level of actual individuals to produce the particular kind of social change which we call fashion, and all that this implies.

This kind of phenomenological experience transposes easily to museum exhibitions. Indeed, many exhibitions depend for their impact on the tacit reliance that, when we look at them, we will experience both a re-run of what the individuals and the various groups were feeling when the material on show was new, and a similar experience in relation to our own present when we realize the relevance of what we are seeing to our own behavioural responses. The thematic costume exhibitions promoted by Leicestershire Museum Service make this point very clearly. Exhibitions like that called *Working Women: The True Stories* mounted by Walsall Museum in 1991 work in the same way. This exhibition stated:

Half of the population are women, most of whom work! Much of the work has gone unacknowledged. This exhibition asks why . . . It focuses on the lives of local working women from the Victorian age to the present day . . . From factory floor to kitchen sink, from boardroom to fire station, it tackles issues which women have faced in the past and still face today.

(Exhibition Information Pack, Walsall Museum 1991)

Its impact arises from the way in which the images on show fit into our rhythms of understanding and response, perception and learning.

One difficulty revolves around the problem of getting to the bottom of why people make the choices they do. As Bronner puts it: 'The folk artist may not be able to recognize such inferences or he may acquiesce to the researcher's interpretation. Thus, the behavioural approach presents serious fieldwork problems, not only because an extraordinary amount of observation is required but because rationales for behaviour often are the most difficult information to elicit' (Bronner

1979: 160). This is, however, an essentially methodological problem, and not one where the difficulties of methodology need undermine the theoretical structures. For Bronner, the way round this is by what he calls 'praxis perspective' which attempts to 'consider the philosophical underpinnings of a researcher's concern for objects in a cognitive-behavioral way'; praxis may be defined as 'customary ways of doing, making and using things shaped by a dialectic between self and society, individual and environment, reality and artificiality. Praxis thus incorporates emphases on behaviors, processes, and thoughts that generate objects and culture, but adds an important consideration of the dynamic and complex relations between thought and action, conduct and communication, motivation and meaning' (Bronner 1983). This, I take it, is an expansive way of describing those elements which are here used to create the framework of the behaviourist analysis, although we do well to remember that we can never escape the subjective nature of analysis work.

Perception and Reception: The Common Viewer

The cluster of perception and reception theories offers us a way of understanding better what happens when a person views an object, or to put it another way, gives us a conceptual basis from which to explore what is actually happening within the behaviouralist plot set out in Figure 10.1. The ideas we shall discuss here are applicable, of course, to the viewing of an object in a sitting room or a shop window, but they are particularly applicable to museum objects because, like the literary theory from which they are in large part drawn, they embrace an element of active intention on the part of the viewer: one does not read even the most casual page, and nor does one visit a museum exhibition, without a flicker of intention (at least, as an adult).

I have chosen as the display objects against which to run this concept two soup tureens made by the Chelsea factory about 1755 and on show in the Fitzwilliam Museum, Cambridge. The tureens are in the forms of a crouching rabbit (see Plate 25) and a settled hen. They are of porcelain, moulded in a naturalistic style a little heightened, coloured with soft, bright shades. Their overall effect is of pleasure in charming things, saved from pretty-prettiness by the innate restraint of their period. Such objects are not to everyone's taste, and more particularly, judging by the student groups who have seen slides of the tureens, they are not to the taste of people now in their twenties and early thirties – an interesting point which underlines the way in which all objects are polysemantic and open to a range of interpretations.

At the heart of this theory stands the idea that the meanings of an object lie both in the object itself, with all the historical and structuralist/functionalist ways in which this meaning is constituted, and equally in the process which the viewer carries out in relation to the object. Iser, who created this approach to reception theory in relation to literary texts (1974), draws on the work of the Tavistock School, and in particular that of R. D. Laing, who has described the kind of interaction which his study of the structure of communication suggests. In assessing

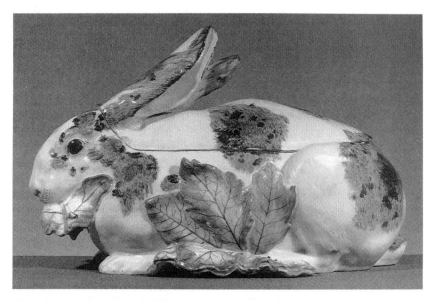

Plate 25.   Tureen and cover in the shape of a rabbit, porcelain, Chelsea, *c.* 1755, Fitzwilliam Museum (photo: Fitzwilliam Museum, University of Cambridge).

interpersonal relationships Laing says: 'I may not actually be able to see myself as others see me, but I am constantly supposing them to be seeing me in particular ways, and I am constantly acting in the light of the actual or supposed attitudes, opinions, needs, and so on the other has in respect of me'. (Iser 1980: 106).

It is clear that the view others have of me is not 'pure' perception, but the result of interpretation. We have some experience of each other, but no idea how others experience us. Laing continues this line of thought when he says: 'I cannot experience your experience. You cannot experience my experience. We are both invisible men. All men are invisible to one another. Experience is man's invisibility to man.' It is this invisibility, however, that forms the basis of interpersonal relations – a basis which Laing calls 'no-thing': 'That which is really "between" cannot be named by any things that come between. The between is itself no-thing.' In all our relationships, however, we work as if this 'no-thing' was a reality, basing our activities upon it. Action, then, is dependent upon the creation by us of material to fill the cultural gap in experience, and so interaction results from our basic need for interpretation, and we cannot do this without using our existing personalities. So 'dyadic interaction is not given by nature but arises out of an interpretative activity, which will contain a view of others and, unavoidably, an image of ourselves' (Iser 1980: 108).

It seems that this kind of creative interaction is what happens when we look at objects. Iser (1974) following Ingarden (1973) called this process *Konkretisation*, 'realization', which means the bringing to light of the story or experience inherent in the object. From this it follows that our soup tureens have, like all objects, two poles, which following Iser, we may call the artistic and the aesthetic. The artistic relates to the object as made by the manufacturers who produced what their society wanted, while the aesthetic describes the realization accomplished by the viewer at the show-case. It is clear that the meaning of a tureen cannot be completely identical either with the artistic object or with aesthetic realization of the object, but must lie somewhere between the two. The tureen only takes a meaning when a viewer realizes it, and this realization is to a large degree the result of the individual viewer's history and personality; but this realization is acted upon by the various themes which belong to object – here, the animal moulding of the vessel, the bright colours, the idea of the dinner service of which it was a part and of the dinner parties where it appeared. So it is the *convergence* of object and viewer which brings the meaningful object into existence, and this convergence can never be exactly pinpointed, but must always be *virtual* (Iser's word, 1974: 274). It is not identical either with the object itself, or with the individual personality of the viewer, but rests somewhere between the two.

It is this *virtuality* which gives rise to the dynamic nature of objects. As we stand in front of the show-case, we make use of the various perspectives which the tureens offer to us: these might include an appreciation of their charm, speculation about how much they are worth, or contempt for the useless prettiness of the *haute bourgeoisie*. Our creative urges are set in motion, our imagination is engaged, and the dynamic process of interpretation and reinterpretation begins, which extends far beyond the mere perception that the things are vessels for holding liquid. The object activates our own faculties, and the product of this creative activity is the virtual dimension of the object, which endows it with present reality. The message or meaning which the object offers is always incomplete and we all fill the gaps in our own ways, thereby excluding other possibilities: as the viewer looks he makes his own story about, for example, how people felt about the objects when they were using them.

In this act, the dynamics of viewing are revealed. The object is inexhaustible, but it is this inexhaustibility which forces the viewer to his decisions. The viewing process is selective, and the potential object is richer than any of its realizations. When the same person sees the same tureen ten years later it may appear in a new light which seems to him more 'correct', richer, and more perceptive, so that object is transformed into experience. In one sense, it is reflecting the developing personality of the viewer and so acting as a kind of mirror; but at the same time the effect of the object is to modify or change the viewer, so that he is a slightly different person from the one he was before. So we have the apparently paradoxical situation in which the viewer is forced to reveal aspects of himself in order to experience a reality which is different from his own, because it is only by leaving behind the familiar world of his own experience that he can take part in the excitement which objects offer; and many of us would feel that this lies at the heart of the museum experience.

The viewer's process may be taken a stage further. He will endeavour to bring all his imaginative impressions together into the kind of consistency for which we are always searching, since it seems that the creation of satisfactorily complete sets, which have a parallel or metaphorical relationship to other perceived sets, is the way in which our minds work to provide distinctions and explanations. We group together the impressions which the tureens give us, encourage them to react, and then project on to them the consistency which our hearts desire. The resulting interpretation arises not from the objects as such; it arises from the meeting between the objects and the mind of the viewer. The interpretation, therefore, is not the true meaning of the object, it is an individual's construction of its meaning, and so, strictly, an illusion created so that it fits into our individual imaginative world. But even in that world there are awkward ideas which do not contribute to the consistency which we seek, so as Gombrich has said: 'Illusion wears off once the expectation is stepped up; we take it for granted and we want more' (1962: 54). So the viewer has constantly to modify the illusion which he is creating, and he perpetually organizes and reorganizes the data he is given.

This brings us to the final notion to be considered here. The object as it survives has a fixed form and a definite factual history, without which it could not exist and we could not begin to understand it; but if viewing and interpreting it were to consist only of uninhibited speculation, uninterrupted by any 'realistic' constraints, the result would be a series of purely individual sequences with little relationship to each other, and meaningful only in terms of the individual personality, no matter how bizarre, idiosyncratic or simply ill-informed this may be.

If the viewer cannot conjure up the kind of consistency just mentioned, which may be described as an act of interpretation, with all the claims to validity which this implies, he will lose interest in the object. But if his interpretation departs too far from contemporary norms, his community will lose interest in him, at least as far as this subject is concerned. This can certainly happen, but more usually it does not and the reason seems to rest in the relationship between object and viewer. The object provokes certain reactions and expectations which we project back on to it in such a way that the polysemantic possibilities are greatly reduced in order to be in keeping with the expectations that have been aroused. To paraphrase Iser, the polysemantic nature of the object and the interpretation-making of the viewer are opposed factors. If the interpretation-making were limited, the polysemantic nature would vanish, but if the polysemantic nature were all-powerful, the interpretation would be destroyed (Iser 1974).

Much the same point may be made by saying that the object only exists if it is 'made meaningful' through somebody reacting with it; but at the same time that somebody only exists as a social being, as he is in the process of interaction (as of course, he is most of the time). The balance is held by the object itself, with its tangible and factual content. About the nature of these, there is a consensus within each individual's community, and so the act of interpretation will bear a relationship to this consensus. Herein lies the dialectical structure of viewing. The need to decipher gives us the chance both to bring out what is in the object and what is in ourselves; it is a dynamic, complex movement which unfolds as time passes, and in the act of interpretative imagination we give form to ourselves.

Structuration

We have now discussed the way in which people seem to behave in the face of phenomena like clothes in a shop window or porcelain on display, and suggested that this kind of analysis can give some ideas about how people and objects interreact to produce change. But this individual activity needs to be brought into a relationship with the broad social structure of which it is a part and to which it contributes. To put the matter very crudely, we need to find a way of uniting the behavioural process which is happening in Figure 10.1 with the functionalist/ structuralist analysis of the same social scene. How can people locked into social patterns behave in ways which make change come about?

The best response to this problem lies in the work of Anthony Giddens, who has developed the theory of structuration (e.g. 1984). This is now generally accepted as a very important development because it shows a way of breaking down the dualisms between pattern and actor, between static structure and dynamic process, and so between a deterministic view of society – which says that people are inevitably programmed to do what their social structure requires them to do, and a voluntarist view – which would try to argue that people are free to make the choices which bring change. Giddens' work is very important, but also dauntingly elaborate and wide-ranging (Bryant and Jary 1990). This discussion does not pretend to do more than bring out some of the salient features which relate particularly to the argument of this chapter.

Two important points must be made at the start. Firstly, all descriptions of social life, whether they are cast in the form of a traditional historical narrative or functionalist and structuralist plots, depend upon the creation of norms, the reduction of very many detailed individual lives to a small number of general observations. We have to do this in order to be able to do anything, but we recognize that it leaves out a very great deal, and to a certain extent distorts reality. Secondly, and relating to this, the mind-set of any given individual is very similar to, but not exactly the same as, the social description offered in a structural analysis. We might, to give a simple example, say that a material cultural norm of our society is that middle-aged women wear hats to weddings, and this is sufficiently true to be generally recognized as a social truth; but many an individual woman will turn up at a wedding bareheaded and then give a range of reasons why she made this choice (couldn't find anything suitable; thought it was going to rain; doesn't like hats anyway) which strike everybody as more-or-less satisfactory.

To get at an understanding of change in material culture (and other) practices therefore, it seems that we would need to have a very fine mesh capable of catching small individual shifts which, in the aggregate, make up social change – sometimes enormous social change. Because each individual's mind-set is like but not identical with the structure of the society to which he belongs, his social practices arise from that structure but they also transform it: people generate and negotiate their own changes in the social climate in ways which better fit their own emotional and economic needs, sometimes very slowly, in only tiny ways and not very successfully, sometimes rapidly and radically.

Action, in other words, has a dialectical relationship to social structure, and of this social structure objects are a meaningful constituent. Action begins in structure, happens through structure and ends in structure, but its realization in the actual world can result in a transformation of structure, for structure is both the medium and the outcome of lived life. Transformations of this kind are likely to happen when contradictions show up in the structure, as they invariably do in any structure, no matter how traditional it may be (witness the way it is always possible to answer one traditional proverb with another of quite contradictory meaning). Contradictions result in competing beliefs and evaluations which bring conflicts of interests between individuals and groups, and so produce choices, struggles and change, which help to resolve one set of contradictions but contribute towards the formation of the next.

This is what is happening within our small-scale example. The contradictions inherent in the position of a modern woman force her to respond to the objects – clothes – around her, and to make choices between them. The choice arises from the local structure, and acts as a piece of social practice within that structure, but will have resulted in a tiny shift of the patterning which will then form part of the structure for the next shift. The aggregate of such individual moves is what we see as social change.

Objects In the Long Range

There is an obvious need for all these interlinked approaches to the interaction of material culture, individuals and change in society to be knitted together into a broad idea about the nature of history as a long-term process. Such an idea is offered by Fernand Braudel and the French school of *Annales* historians, whose ideas have been attracting attention among British historians and archaeologists (e.g. Hodder 1987b; Bintliff 1991). In answering questions like 'Why did this event occur?', historians like Braudel think in terms of identifying all the relevant factors, 'total history'. Braudel (1972) identified three scales in the historical process (although recognizing these to be merely arbitrary divisions in the continuum): long-term factors which include structures of long duration; structural history showing collective social trends in the medium-term embracing forces, *conjonctures*, which mould human life; and the history of events in the short term which includes narrative of individual life and choice (see Figure 10.2). An important idea in this analysis is that of *mentalités*, mind-sets which embrace persistent cultural features like ideologies and world views.

The whole undertaking is often called 'structural history' (not to be confused with structuralism or structuration as such), and it offers the brilliant possibility of reconciling the general and the particular, the single event and the age-old trend, the individual and the society. It offers a way of bringing the behaviouralist and receptionist ideas into the broad historical sweep without denying their capacity to help us to understand how individuals work to bring change or the part that objects play in this. It is in many ways a restatement of Giddens' structuration, but

HISTORY OF EVENTS	SHORT TERM-EVENEMENTS
	Narrative, Political History; Events; Individuals.

STRUCTURAL HISTORY	MEDIUM TERM-CONJONCTURES
	Social, Economic History; Economic, Agrarian, Demographic Cycles; History of eras, regions, societies; Worldviews, ideologies, (*Mentalités*).

LONG TERM-STRUCTURES OF THE 'LONGUE DUREE'

Geohistory: 'enabling and constraining'; History of civilizations, peoples; Stable technologies, world views (*Mentalités*).

Figure 10.2 Braudel's scales in the historical process (after Bintliff 1991, fig. 1.2)

from the point of view of an historian rather than a social scientist: Giddens' social structure within which the individual operates is Braudel's Long Term and Medium Term, and Giddens' individual is the process of negotiating change in Braudel's Short Term. What Braudel's theory especially contributes is a way of studying and interpreting the part which behavioural/reception theory takes for granted, and structuration describes rather vaguely as 'society as it has come to exist' the factors which have contributed to the social mind-set in terms of which every individual acts.

The theory has had its critics. Braudel's disciple Le Roy Ladurie draws attention to the danger of overemphasizing the logical necessity of structures and ignoring the play of choice:

> such victories at the frontiers of knowledge, won by the historians of the last half century, are irreversible; but they would be even more satisfactory if history really was entirely logical, intelligible and predictable from start to finish; if the event or chance happening really could be exorcized once and for all . . . The transition from one structure to another often remains . . . the most perplexing zone, where chance appears to play a large part.
>
> (Ladurie 1979: 113–14)

Bintliff draws attention to a second vital criticism: '[Braudel] chooses to see the fundamental structures of medium and long-term as geographic constraints and stimuli or the impersonal swings of population history and economic cycles. The world of *mentalités*, of collective ideologies, is little explored' (Bintliff 1991: 9). However, he goes on to make the pertinent point that this dissatisfaction with Braudel is: 'in itself a statement of ideology, an expression of world views that allow more scope to events and individuals in forming history than Braudel acknowledges' (Bintliff 1991: 10).

Brundel's successors have given a good deal of attention to the problem of *mentalités* and how they develop. Bintliff singles out Febvre's development as a particularly useful contribution. Febvre understood that 'ideas cannot be understood without relating them to their social milieu' (Burke 1973: ix) and that, in Bintliff's words:

> Human individuals are certainly free to act, and to good purpose in moulding their own and others' lives. Yet the random, chance effects of individual thought and action, individual psychology and emotion, are still constrained by the social and cultural context as well as by the physical context of the 'author of historical action'. Whatsoever is said or done, then, by individuals or during short-lived events, is of no wider importance unless it creates or reflects a significant trend at the group level and in the medium to long-term.
>
> (Bintliff 1991: 12)

Conclusion: Objects Make History

During the final section of this chapter, we shall offer firstly the concrete example of an object which can be seen to be operating in the ways which have been discussed in the previous sections. Then we shall draw attention to some problems which underlie the scope both of this chapter and, by implication, much of what has been said in the preceding chapters.

The chosen object is the Becket reliquary made in Limoges around 1200 AD and now in the Burrell Collection of Glasgow Museums and Art Galleries (see Plate 26). It takes the characteristic medieval form for such pieces of a casket, and is composed of copper alloy plates fastened on to a wooden core (not original). The metal plates are decorated with the *champlevé* coloured enamel work for which Limoges was famous, and depict Thomas Becket's martyrdom in 1170, and the personified soul of Thomas rising to Heaven supported by two angels.

The reliquary is now nearly 800 years old and was perhaps made originally for a Kentish church. It has been a valued possession for a number of owners during that long period. It is not made of particularly valuable materials, but it does embody the value which society, throughout almost all of this long period, has attached to the perceived excellence of design and craftsmanship achieved by the Limoges enamellers. It expresses in iconographic form the long-term Christian tradition that the good man goes to Heaven, which was and is part of the mind-set of Western Europeans, regardless of how each of us individually may feel. It relates (in a very literal sense – it was intended to carry his relics) to Archbishop Thomas

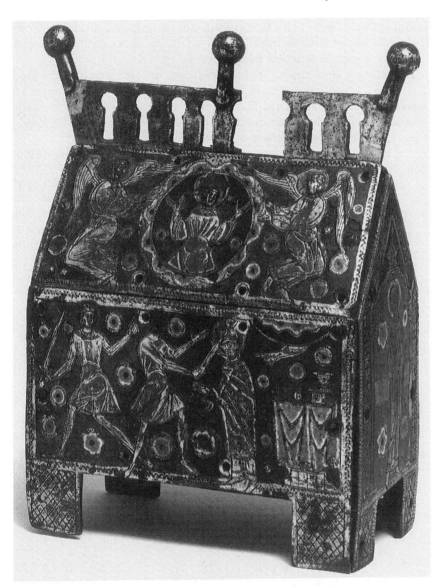

Plate 26. Reliquary châsse with decorative panels showing martyrdom of St Thomas Becket, made in Limoges, France c. 1200–1210. The Burrell Collection, Glasgow Museums and Art Galleries (photo: Glasgow Museums and Art Galleries).

Becket and to the story of his murder in 1170 in Canterbury Cathedral by Henry II's knights, one of those moments of crisis which sum up the conflicts of an age, both to contemporaries and to their successors.

The reliquary clearly embodies its share of Braudel's 'Structures of the Long Term'. It is a part of the history of Western civilization, of the geo-history of the region which has produced a specialized metal technology, of a Christian world view, and of a generally agreed idea of what constitutes 'art' and 'value'. Similarly, it participates in Braudel's 'Structural History of Medium Term'. It embodies the history of its era and region in terms of its design within a local tradition, of its method of production, and of the economic and social structure of thirteenth-century England and France, which meant that a Kentish church looked to Limoges to supply such a piece.

All objects, like all social practice, have their origins in the past, the past which we have just described in our Braudelian analysis of this piece, and this past must include Braudel's third process, the 'History of Events'. For the reliquary we have a very precise originating event, the murder of Becket on 29 December 1170, an event which has its own full fair share both of long-range issues and of immediate human folly, bloody-mindedness and confusion. The commissioning of the reliquary some thirty years after the event was the result of active intervention on the part of individuals, operating within a well-understood *mentalité* which was the result of forces in the long and medium term, but taking their own initiative to produce something new within that *mentalité* in response to a specific significant event.

The moment of the reliquary's commissioning and manufacture is the first moment in its history when it plays its part in the behavioural/reception process of interaction already described, and the long- and short-term reasons for the specific choices which brought it into being derive from Giddens' social structure within which the individual actors move. Henceforward, the reliquary will carry, as only objects can, the accumulated meaning of its past, drawn from all three of Braudel's levels, which gathers density as time goes by. The reliquary-as-accumulated-meaning then becomes an actor in its own right, stimulating behavioural/reception responses to it when it is encountered anew by individuals at various points in the flow of history. We know where the piece has been since about 1700, when it was in the possession of Thomas Batteley, Archdeacon of Canterbury (Alexander and Pinsky 1987: 225). It was an object of desire successively for Horace Walpole and Sir William Burrell, both of whom bought it for their collections. It will have paired off in a behavioural dance with at least some of those who viewed it in these collections, thereby enriching their experience of life, and it suggested itself for inclusion in the magnificent *Age of Chivalry* exhibition at the Royal Academy in 1987–8.

We could go on. The creation of the collections and exhibitions in which the reliquary has figured, beginning with those created by the unknown Kentish church who may have been its first owners, are themselves capable of analysis in Braudelian and behavioural terms. They act as carriers whose meaning is both all levels of our accumulated past and our provocative present, in a continuing spiral of interaction which contributes its mite to change.

The starting-point for the analysis presented in this chapter was Husserl's idea of two interacting forces which he called 'essence' and 'phenomena'. Very roughly, Husserl's 'essence' comprehends inherited social meaning, which both Giddens and Braudel have shown us ways of understanding, and his 'phenomena' are concrete social events, including objects, which embody meaning but which, as Hegel suggested, then in their turn trigger other meanings. How this triggering happens is analysed by behavioural and reception theory, and ideas about how we can understand the whole process have been developed by Giddens and Braudel.

In this analysis of the meaning of objects inside and outside museums, two fundamental difficulties remain, which are common to the broad scope of phenomenological and historical thought. Both have been described as aspects of the humanist or Romanic fallacy. In the first place, phenomenological ideas depend upon the existence of real human individuals who have real individual identities capable of having genuine experiences and of making real choices, even though they do all this within a constituted social structure. Secondly, there is an assumption that although the meanings of objects can influence people for change, those meanings are themselves 'real' and subject to addition and enrichment rather than possessing a fully polysemantic capacity for radical shifts. This is another way of saying that there is something 'real' for the individual to respond to, a point which Iser makes in his view of the dialectical structure of viewing and interpretation. The ideas discussed here depend upon the notion that social meaning, although not static, is stable in the sense that change is cumulative rather than disruptive and that underlying local changes, the forces in Braudel's 'Structures of the Long Term' have a staying-power that amount to a 'real' existence.

The apparent contradiction in these two positions – the acting individual and the steady progressive nature of change – is answered by a classic resort to checks and balances: change arises from the piecemeal interaction of individuals with their past which, like them, 'really' exists. Variations of this notion have been the traditional answer to ancient questions about the nature of human freedom and of our ability to respond to our environment, including the material which constitutes it, and makes it change. But does the meaningful constitution of men and matter rest upon a solid basis, or upon the shifting sand?

11 Problems of Power

There are nine and sixty ways of
constructing tribal lays,
And-every-single-one-of-them-is-right.
(Kipling R., 'In the Neolithic Age' 1990: 16. Rudyard Kipling's father was
Curator of the Bombay Museum)

Besides, Marxist-Leninism had never got to grips with the concept of the private
collection. Trotsky, around the time of the Third International, had made a few
off-hand comments on the subject. But no one had ever decided if the ownership of a work of art damned its owner in the eyes of the Proletariat. Was the
collector a class-enemy? If so, how?   (Chatwin 1988: 26)

Look! Out they come, from the bushes – the riff-raff. Children? Imps – elves –
demons. Holding what? Tin cans? Bedroom candlesticks? Old jars? My dear,
that's the cheval glass from the Rectory! And the mirror – that I lent her. My
mother's. Cracked. What's the notion? Anything that's bright enough to reflect,
presumably, ourselves? Ourselves! Ourselves!   (Woolf 1978: 133)

Introduction

Museums and the great bulk of the collections which form them are, as we have
seen, creations of the modern world which ran, roughly, from 1450 to 1950, but
museums, like us all, now live in what is frequently called the post-modern world
in which much has been changed. The previous chapters have analysed the ways in
which meaning is created within museums, their material and their exhibitions.
But now we must ask what underlies the creation of all these interlinked forms of
meaning, a question which is linked to the social operation of objects as value and
possession which, as we saw in Chapter 2, is one of their prime characteristics. It is
this question which post-modern criticism endeavours to answer, and with the
advantage of a certain hindsight we can see that it has done so in two ways, interlinked but separable, partly in their approaches and conclusions and partly historically
(see Figure 1.2). First in time comes the effort to expose the ubiquitous power
plans, the universal schemes of domination and subservience, inclusion and exclusion,
through which existing societies are supported. This kind of thinking is essentially

Marxist and from Marx's own writings in the mid nineteenth century has become, in the hands of a wide range of post-Marxist writers, a rich element in Western critical thought. Second comes what contemporary (largely) French thinkers of the broad post-structuralist school, and especially Michel Foucault, have made of this neo-Marxist and related tradition; in one sense their thinking is concerned to take the implications of the foregoing to their explicit conclusions, and within this, deconstruction, the demolition of the assumptions of the Western tradition, is a very significant activity.

In this chapter we shall first describe some of the salient features of the post-modern scene in contemporary Britain and draw out some of the characteristic radical thinking which is operating within it. We shall analyse a range of typical late-twentieth-century museum manifestations – collection valuation and the market, exhibitions, museum labels, posters and catalogues – in broad post-modern terms in order to show how their meaning has been created. Finally, we shall look at museums as they appear in the deconstructed cultural landscape, poised between a ghost town and a child's play pen.

Trends in the Post-Modern World

Post-war Britain, like most of Northern Europe and North America, demonstrates a society in which four-fifths of the population live in urban areas, and half of these in greater London. The great majority of these people have some kind of access to a family car, and virtually all have access to television, with its homogenization of culture, its advertising and its mass appeal (in spite of some valiant efforts by all the channels). This is matched by the experience, which many people now possess, of foreign countries, and by the development of a multi-cultural Britain out of the break-up of an imperial past. Throughout the 1950s and 1960s the emphasis on the nuclear family as a 'centre of consumption' developed, with a consequent impact upon the multinational trading companies and the High Street chain stores, including food supermarkets and patterns of shopping (Marwick 1990: 32–3). 'Home' as a consumption centre and a social centre came steadily to occupy a much more important place than it had done before the war, particularly to some blue-collar working men.

With this goes three other important traits. Firstly, in Britain as in the rest of Western Europe, the old upper or upper middle class has managed to retain a substantial share of economic and political power. Secondly, the idea of 'home as centre' must be balanced by the greater personal freedom (or social disruption: we can all take our choice) which has resulted from the eclipse of stable marriage. Thirdly, governmental social policy in Britain in the last fifty-odd years has seen violent swings from the socialist welfare state of the post-war period to its deliberate attack by the New Right in the 1980s. New Right policies stressed the ability of the entrepreneurial individual to make good and to make money in a capitalist land, and correspondingly attacked traditional intellectual values and standards and the professions who work within them, including museum professionals.

In Britain, and elsewhere, this has resulted in the development of the service side of the economy, including that revolving around 'leisure' and 'heritage', at the expense of traditional manufacturing industry. The workers who operate the service industries are encouraged to be flexible in their working arrangements. Many of them sell their skills primarily through the new information technology, which links up the globe but reduces time spans, distances the worker even further from the product, and helps to create the emotional rootlessness which is the character-istic state of the post-modern world. In the arts and design a sense of history has been deliberately abandoned in favour of a kind of eclectic pluralism which gives us a street-show of jokey pastiche, designed to avoid 'serious meaning' because, as Harvey has put it, 'The relatively stable aesthetic of (early twentieth century) Fordist modernism has given way to all the ferment, instability and fleeting qualities of a post-modernist aesthetic that celebrates difference, ephemerality, spectacle, fashion and the commodification of cultural forms' (Harvey 1989: 156).

Real-life political economy and philosophical speculation have gone hand in hand. Indeed, it should be stressed that post-modernism is not in any sense a coherent philosophical movement, but rather a condition, which Jameson has described as 'the cultural logic of late capitalism' (1984: 53–92). To do justice to these ideas in a few paragraphs is an impossible task, but this brief sketch will underpin the critiques of museums and museum products to which we shall come. One of the fundamental Marxist positions was that societies and their institutions only are as they are because this is beneficial to certain limited classes of society, who then arrange not only economic life to suit their own purposes, but also encourage religious, aesthetic, ethical and cultural systems – in a word, ideology – to permeate and underpin the social structure in ways which make for the mainte-nance of the status quo.

For Marx and his followers the benefiting section has, of course, been the great European middle class and all those who aspire to join it, and the basis of class oppression has been recognized in the workings of classic modern capitalism in which invested money yields a return through the labour of exploited wage-earners for whom work and product have become increasingly separate. The func-tionalist or structuralist plot of any social enterprise, seen through these glasses, ceases to be a morally colourless description and becomes an ethical landscape of glaring subservience and domination sustained by the ideology which the system embraces. Things, in other words, are not what they appear to be: 'all science would be superfluous if the outward appearance and the essence of things directly coincided' (Marx 1971: 817).

It is important to remember that, for most Marxists, their own enterprise has a moral purpose: once oppression has been revealed for what it is, fresh starts can be made and better worlds created. For Marx himself the idea of *praxis* was very important, emphasizing that 'human beings are neither to be treated as passive objects, nor as wholly free subjects' (Giddens 1979: 150–51). He wrote elsewhere: 'The chief defect of all existing materialism is that the thing, reality, sensuousness, is conceived only in the form of the *object or of contemplation*, but not as *sensuous human activity, practice*, not subjectively' (Marx and Engels 1970: 121). Individuals, that is, can understand their condition and bring about change, a position which obviously has much in common with the ideas discussed in the previous chapter. This is why all social structures are viewed as dialectical, dynamic processes – Marx's famous dialectical materialism – and can be reconstructed by engaged human beings. Whatever it may have usually turned out to be in political practice, Marxism as a system of thought has a strong positive and optimistic side, and as such carries the tone of the older modern world, even though its intention and its effect was to subvert that world.

Not so the thinking of Marx's successors, for whom the post-modernist European society just described is a contemporary reality. This thinking in the broadly post-structuralist writings of men like Baudrillard, Barthes, Derrida and Foucault (see Harland 1987: 167–83) is nihilistic in its denial of the possibility of meaning or reality, or at the least deeply pessimistic. Since the act of writing about non-meaning runs the risk of creating it, post-structuralist writing has a characteristically tinny tone, often deliberately making a labyrinth without clues and without centre, lit up only by verbal squibs and linguistic parodies. The fundamentals of this body of ideas have been described many times (e.g. Harland 1987) and here we shall concentrate upon those elements which bear particularly upon museums and their operations.

The draining away of meaning can be approached from two angles, although both are rooted in recent and contemporary society. The first, which is concerned with the nature of power, derives most obviously from Marx and his successors. The second draws on the linguistic and semiotic studies described earlier in this book. For Foucault, power and social relationships are much the same thing: without the operation of power there can be no society, because all relationships are dependent upon it. Power is, therefore, all-pervasive, running up and down society at all levels and linking the whole together. Power and knowledge are much the same thing, and they in their turn are linked to ideas like 'truth' and 'reason'. Power is exercised as an intentional strategy, but because it is everywhere, it is not linked, as Marx thought, with one particularly oppressing group. It cannot be clearly located in a distinct and manageable set of personal relationships, and consequently individuals, enmeshed in power relationships like flies in webs, have no hope of extricating themselves by normal historical processes, because these would simply set up more of the same.

In the modern state the operation of power is linked with a range of disciplinary and surveillance procedures which draw on knowledge in all its attributes, including the development of the necessary institutions and technologies. We see from this that not merely religion or moral codes but also scientific knowledge, the operation of human reason, and all value judgements are to be seen simply as strategies of power, as ways not of perceiving reality, but of creating social relationships. Viewed in this light, the traditions of the world, in art or science or anything else, are distinguishable one from another only in the sense that apples are different from pears and any partiality for one flavour or the other is merely idiosyncratic. Western humanism, or Marxism, are simply sets of confidence tricks with a face value in the power-broking game.

The semiotic argument arrives at much the same conclusion. In language as in all other forms of communication, including material culture and institutions like museums, the link between signifier and signified has been severed. To put it another way, there is no reason why the meanings which have traditionally been attached to anything should continue to be attached; meaning is what anybody cares to make it. Signifiers, objects and exhibitions among others, can trigger off a large range of meanings within the minds and feelings of those who experience them, and since the inherited signification of the past – roughly the consensus of meaning resulting from history – has been demoted, there is no way of judging between the validity of these experienced meanings. As Baudrillard has put it, 'today especially the real is no more than a struck pile of dead matter, dead bodies and dead language' (1980: 103). For Baudrillard there can be no reality, no meaning and no history, for what is history but a way of pretending that meaning exists?

It is clear that this denial of inherent meaning, and the value judgements which go with it, fit very well with the post-modern world of instant transglobal access, immediate experiences rather than experience, and the kind of superficial culture-swapping which television, tourism and much of the heritage industry has to offer. It is clear, also, that any effort to assert the validity of reason or experience can be gleefully countered by reference to the way in which all these forms of traditional knowledge are merely part of the play of power, a useful line for those now dominant in the world of late capitalism for whom such knowledge never had much appeal in the first place.

Museums in the Post-Modern Gaze: Objects of (Doubtful) Virtue

Let us then turn to museums, our own bit of praxis in a post-modern world turned strangely hostile. We may say that, where institutions like museums are concerned, the post-modern project involves admitting firstly that power play is implicit throughout the entire enterprise, past and present, and secondly, that this power operates through the social pattern.

A range of models have been used to describe the nature of social patterning. Chomsky describes his generative rules as an intricate system of rules by which patterns are formed, modified and elaborated (1964a: 58). Baudrillard speaks of the 'code', a typical word in this kind of discourse, and says that in the exchange of products, 'it is not only economic values, but the code, this fundamental code, that circulates and is reproduced' (1975: 54). For Foucault it is 'a group of rules that characterize discursive practice but these rules are not imposed from the outside on the elements they relate together; they are caught up in the very things that they connect (1972: 127). Bourdieu uses the word 'habitus', which he calls 'principles of the generation and structuring of practices and representations' (1977: 72). Gellner has called such a structure 'the norms of cognition' and, interestingly, relates the operation of these norms to an observation of Descartes, who said in a refreshingly homely metaphor, 'if the first button be wrongly done up, then so will all the others be; and the first button is concerned with how we know, how we authenticate truth claims, and not with what we know' (Gellner 1974: 28).

Museums are a part of the social code (or system, or rules, or habitus) of enlightened modernity, grounded in the belief in overarching narratives which tell of the reality of scientific reason, the value of past historical experience, and the conviction that there exist realities to know about, that people are capable of knowing about them, and that they are able to use this knowledge to create better social systems. The classic role of the museum in this is to hold the material evidence which witnesses to the truth of the reasoned assertions which have been made, to offer opportunities for further research work of the same kind which will help to push the narrative along and, perhaps even more significantly, to act as places where the code or habitus, in its physical form of the scientific and artistic (in the broadest sense) material objects of the past, can be laid out before the viewer in a tangible way. It is the concreteness of its participation in the code which gives the museum its particular place within that code, and the value which society has placed upon the concrete, visible demonstration is manifested, among other ways, by the impressive museum buildings which have been erected to house it.

Writers like Bourdieu (1977) argue that, since the premises within which this code is grounded are no more than nebulous and probably false presumptions for which any attempted demonstration is always circular and subjective, it follows that we should treat them as ideology rather than as 'knowledge', and look to discover the social mechanisms which they are intended to mask. This is not difficult. It is clear that such a corpus of premises must not only be produced, but invested with its own legitimacy and transmitted over time across the generations, if it is to help in the production of the legitimating code through which society continues to produce its socio-economic relations, continues, that is, to go on being itself. Museums are, quite specifically, charged by society with the job of keeping things for the benefit of future generations, though in this view the word 'benefit' is ironic. This long-term transmission in itself – and as we have seen, the great bulk of museum collections have been in place for some considerable time – contributes its own kind of legitimacy, human nature being what it is. Museums are an important part of the way society makes its history.

Legitimization of the 'habitus' is further advanced by the way in which museums, like the educational system, turn culture into institution (that great Victorian word) and so regulate access to the ownership of knowledge, and prescribe ways in which competence in its attainment can be achieved. This is seen to run across the museum operation, from the way in which reserve collections are only available to those with correct credentials, to the way in which objects are kept behind glass and must not be touched. It is also a fundamental part of the way in which curators and all museum workers operate and of the social role which they serve. We should not forget that the process of producing meaning through the creation of collections, publications and installations is not impersonal, but rests in the hearts and minds of flesh-and-blood museum staff, who carry out the 'work' of the museum in accordance with their professional mentality.

As Hooper-Greenhill (1989: 71) has put it, power relations in the museum are skewed to privilege the 'work' of the museum, and this is manifested in the division of space which creates public galleries where knowledge is offered for consumption, and private offices, workrooms and stores where knowledge is produced. The museum institution enables a particular type of pedagogic or curatorial action to take place. This is seen to be quite deliberate, albeit often unconscious, and involves the curator in a conspiracy to help keep in place both existing social patterning and his (relatively) respectable place within it – a selfish intention which flaws all professional activity. The purpose, in this view, of curatorship is to impose the code which the museum represents, that is, a set of values drawn from the social structure, upon the population at large.

Sets of values presuppose fixed value judgements, and these operate across the museum disciplines, but the inherent problems emerge particularly vividly when fine art is in question, for here aesthetic quality merges imperceptibly into moral quality: art, like love, is held to be ennobling. We can see that the work of the generations of art historians has given our ideas about taste and design a subtlety which has had a profound effect upon the way in which we view the world of objects, whether or not they would have crept into any art historian's canon. But here lies the essential point: the business (perhaps an all too appropriate word), traditionally at least, of the art historian and curator has been to discriminate, to judge the quality of one picture against another and of one artist against another, in order to establish a league championship in which there are winners and losers, in which Old Masters are 'high fine art' and products of celebrated clock-makers or silversmiths are 'high applied art', while some crafts, like basket weaving, have only ever the hope of fielding a minor counties side. The awkward charge of élitism looms clear, élitism directed equally against most of the objects which are around us, most producers of those objects, and most social groups either outside the magic circle of high civilization – Europe and parts of Asia – or within those areas but not of the cultivated classes. The social production of art, and of the art history which endorses it, is seen to underpin the status quo and to aggravate this crime by attempting to identify good taste with good moral temper.

At the heart of this, three evils are seen to lie. Firstly, the corpus of knowledge which the curator guards does not have any objective existence, but is merely a construction produced by dominant social groups in an effort to show that their interests are 'natural' and 'correct'. Secondly, it is necessary to conceal this truth by palming off curatorial knowledge as legitimate and authoritative. This is done partly by superficial but effective tricks which relate to the sombre splendour of the surroundings and the length of time which it has all been here. Partly it is done by mystifying the source of knowledge, by failing to admit that knowledge is a social construct, offering it rather as 'natural' or 'divine', as something which is discovered rather than produced. Since knowledge is social, and society is sustained by the authority which knowledge carries, the argument has a dishonest circularity which is, however, only made apparent to those permitted to join the curatorial charmed circle, and who have therefore a vested interest in its operation. Finally, if knowledge is held to be 'good' and 'natural', it follows that deviation from it is unnatural and punishable. Put another way, this means that the 'system manipulates a semantic repertoire which is directly concerned with the reproduction of power relations within a social formation' (Shelton 1990: 81). Since the knowledge on offer is particularistic and exclusive, it will conflict with other interests in the same social structure – whether of class, colour, sexuality, religion, gender, ethnicity or whatever – and so these must be diminished, unregistered, ignored and suppressed.

All this kind of curatorial action Bourdieu summed up as 'objectively, symbolic violence insofar as it is the imposition of a cultural arbitrary by an arbitrary power' (1977: 5). It is interesting to realize that, with their oppressive and mystifying behaviour within church- and temple-like buildings, curators are seen to reproduce what the modern men of the Enlightenment regarded as the worst features of priestcraft. Priests and what they have to offer are held in equally poor regard by the children of the godless post-modern world with its economic opportunism and rootless eclecticism, which, as we have seen, goes hand-in-hand with postmodernist thinking. This is also the world of late capitalism, and in a time of disintegrating values, a capitalist society has to find special ways of maintaining the value structure of goods, especially those goods for which the value has always been primarily cultural, in the simple sense of the word. Museums have always been, and are still, deeply implicated in the maintenance of the capitalist market system, itself a characteristic part of the code.

Museums and Late Capitalism: The Property of Various Gentlemen

Since museums hold material, they cannot avoid integration into the world of goods. Art galleries, in particular, have always been deeply embedded in the working of the capitalist mentality. The period of the traditional oil painting can be roughly set at between 1500 and 1900, and it created most of the characteristically modern European ways of seeing, and hence, our cultural assumptions, which are very different from those of the rest of the world. It affected what we mean by pictorial likeness and how we see landscape, women, food, important people, history and mythology. As Berger has shown, what is happening here is not just that art between 1500 and 1900 served the interest of the ruling classes dependent largely on the power of capital; rather, oil painting did to appearances what capital did to social relations, by reducing everything to the realm of objects in which everything was exchangeable because everything was commodity. Oil painting has the special ability to render the tangibility, the lustre and the solidity of fur, or silk, or marble which made it the ideal medium for a period which wished to celebrate the new dynamic power of money and what it could buy, and this broad thrust of the genre is not lessened by the fact that in the hands of a few great practitioners it could become something more – for the Rembrandts, the Vermeers and the Goyas were soon reabsorbed as the tradition closed in around them (Berger 1972: 83–109). The tradition can be seen on display any day in art galleries up and down the country, and these exhibitions do their share to endorse the commodity mind-set.

Contemporary criticism suggests that, although museums may wish to deny their implication in capitalist economic practices, they are in fact wholly integrated into them. This denial is based on the claim that museum collections are taken out of the sphere of commodities, that they are no longer available in the market-place but are now reserved in a place apart. Appadurai defines the commodity situation in the social life of a thing, that characteristic of things in a capitalist situation, as 'the situation in which its exchangeability (past, present or future) for some other thing is its social relevant feature' (Appadurai 1986: 13). The deliberate detachment of collections from commodity-hood and their elevation into sacred objects above and beyond the normal workings of the commodity market is one of the things which curators usually feel most strongly about, and is at the heart of impassioned debates about the sale of museum material. The closest analogy is, again, to ecclesiastical property which is similarly regarded as the white unicorn within the hedge, as the national storm raised by the proposal of Hereford Cathedral to sell the *Mappa Mundi* made clear. It also expresses itself in a characteristic curatorial unease at the need to place a market value on collections for insurance and similar purposes. However, to see commodity as a straightforward money exchange is to take too hopelessly narrow a view. As Bourdieu has put it: 'practice never ceases to conform to economic calculation even when it gives every appearance of disinterestedness by departing from the logic of interested calculation (in the narrow sense) and playing for stakes that are non-material and not easily quantified' (1977: 177).

Bourdieu shows in his *Outline of a Theory of Practice* (1977) how institutions, like museums, who are concerned with the authentification, conservation and transmission of accredited cultural objects, are able to build for themselves a practice of consecration which enables them to accumulate economic capital. Cultural agencies like museums must first disavow direct economic interest in order apparently to create for themselves a space different from that of the market-place, in which 'pure' quality judgement can be exercised. This pure curatorial judgement then works to create a corpus of approved pieces, of aesthetic importance in the arts, of significance in human history, of meaning in the natural sciences. This constructs what this kind of analysis calls a genealogy of sponsored works that help the institution to invest (an interesting word in a capitalist society) itself with a signature, an ability to bestow a seal of approval. Once this has been done, the museum provides an agency empowered to consecrate objects and convert quality value into economic value. Value accrues to an object according to the place it is given in the classificatory system made legitimate by the institutional signatory. It is easy to experience the effects of this at quite humble museum levels, in the disappointment of a coin enquirer, for example, who on being told that his coins are not very interesting and not worth anything, can be heard to mutter. 'They *say* they are no good!' This process gives the museums' own collections, as well as outside material, their own cash value, and plays an important role in the way in which museums are esteemed by the world at large, and in the way in which their league tables of rank are constructed.

This circularity of cause and effect in value construction operates across the museum world, partly in straight financial terms, and partly in the kind of respect which is accorded to accredited objects of knowledge even though they may not carry a high market value. But it operates at its clearest in the world of fine art. Here, the line between the legitimizing process in relation to particular schools of artists or particular painters, carried out by museums and particularly by the operation of the art market, is transparent. In March 1987 the Chairman of Yasuda Fire and Marine Insurance Company, Japan, bought Van Gogh's *Sunflowers* at Christies for £24.75 million. In 1990 the Dutch celebrated the centenary of Van Gogh's death with an energy that had more to do with keeping the market buoyant and encouraging tourism than it did with aesthetic appreciation (the opening of the celebrations was screened live on Japanese television) (Buck and Dodd 1991: 79, 108). When the Warhol collection was sold at Sotheby's New York in 1988, it included a range of objects from paintings to cookie jars, all of which were catalogued and displayed at previews as if they were accredited works of art. Leading collectors battled for the material and the 145 cookie jars fetched $113,000. Here we can see commodities being turned into art by the workings of the market (Buck and Dodd 1991: 61). It is clear from the attention which surrounds the big sales and the big exhibitions, that what is on offer is not art but life-style, a life-style that embraces gala nights, cachet, prestige, spectacle and glamour, in which the financial and credit schemes on offer by firms like Sotheby's help to spread opportunity, just as such schemes do in the real estate market, and prices are kept up.

Since so much hangs on authentification, museums and scholars are particularly vulnerable to authentification's dark angel, the practice of faking. The fakes now in museum collections have been produced over many years and in many particular circumstances. The most famous of them, like the Piltdown fake, occupy a position in popular journalism not dissimilar to that of the famous murder trials of the past, and are continually reassessed by scholars (see most recently Spencer 1990). Faking is a subversive activity intended to make illegitimate money out of human gullibility, to discredit scholars and undermine the world of expertise, and to falsify the record of the past, sometimes in the interests of specific individuals or groups. Fakers often have resentful, malicious, secretive personalities, with a cruel, hoaxing streak, which have their own psychological interest. Their work, however, has its own importance: 'Fakes, scorned or passed over in embarrassed silence by scholar, dealer and collector alike, are unjustly neglected; . . . they provide unrivalled evidence of the values and perceptions of those who made them, and of those for whom they were made' (Jones 1990: 11). Fakers need fakees or, to put it another way, successful fakes work because the perception of them by collectors, scholars and museums is set by the structure of expectations which underpins the activities of both parties. Fakes, with the originals which they mimic, are the right and left hand sides of the same system.

The interrelationship of cultural wealth and commodity in the capitalist system and the role of the museum as authenticating and projecting a clear hierarchy of value in which cultural qualities match cash is well demonstrated by the workings of two state-run schemes. On 20 April 1990 the Minister for the Arts, Richard Luce, announced that the government had accepted six paintings in lieu of inheritance tax. Four of these, from the estate of Mrs Eva Borthwick-Norton, satisfied tax of over £6.5 million and included paintings by Rubens, Gainsborough, Lucas de Heere and William Beechey. Here the quality and genuineness of the individual authentifications are guaranteed by the art gallery world, and their cash value is reckoned to be as good as money for legal purposes. The pictures become a form of state investment.

In 1987 Trevelyan and Davies published the details of the operation of the Victoria and Albert Museum Grant Fund, intended to help museums purchase new acquisitions, in 1985–6. One result of the hugely enhanced art market has been the inability of almost all of the world's museums to acquire 'major' new works, and the Purchase Grant Fund, with relatively modest sums at its disposal (£1,114,000 in 1986) cannot operate in the big league. However, the chart published by Trevelyan (Figure 11.1) gives an insight into the kind of interwoven value-and-cash judgements which are in play. It is clear that the fine and decorative arts take the biggest share, even though the Fund exists to assist the purchase of objects relating to the arts, literature and history by non-national museums, art galleries and record offices. Broadly historical material (archaeology, ethnography, numismatics) come next but some way behind, and the remaining miscellany trails after, with just £5,934 for regimental material. Here the self-authenticating quality-and-cost hierarchies of the code are clearly demonstrated.

It is no accident that modern museums began at more or less the same moment that modern capitalism began to get under way, or that both coincide with the beginning of the long eclipse of the Church as an institution and individual churches as repositories of cultural norms and objects of veneration. The hour brought forth the institution, an institution which, most appropriately, concentrated upon objects, physical specimens, wealth and treasure in an age which, increasingly as the Industrial Revolution gathered power, saw its social relations in these terms. More than this, it saw its command over knowledge in terms of the relationship between objects, as the operation of the natural physical world, as the mechanisms of technology, and as the tangible artistic achievements of the past; and to the institution which held and displayed the visible proofs of this mastery it accorded a prestigious place in the scheme of things, borne out by the deliberate magnificence of traditional museum buildings and the iconography with which they are embellished. Bound up with this prestige was an obligation to draw aside the skirts and, like the pure woman of the capitalist ascendancy whose face looks out to us from gallery walls, to provide the still moral centre and the authentification of knowledge and value without which the market system could not function.

Deconstructing the Museum Product

We can see, then, that museums are artificial constructions, occupying a carefully negotiated place in the scheme of things. Their ways of making meaning result in visible products which take the form firstly of collections and collection policies,

Number of applications and grant totals

Category	number of applications	Number of successful applications	Total in grants
Total Fund	636	491 (486)*	£1,077,319
Individual sections:			
'A' Fund	193	148 (139)	£750,319
'B' Fund	376	304 (292)	£122,560
'M' Fund	61	36 (51)	£44,023
'S' Fund	6	3 (4)	£160,000
Individual subjects:			
Ceramics	132	121 (98)	£112,041
Drawing and watercolours	101	71 (74)	£80,792
Manuscripts and documents	63	38 (51)	£134,023
Modern paintings	58	53 (48)	£111,399
Historical paintings	55	39 (35)	£195,942
Furniture and furnishings	46	34 (25)	£130,653
Metalwork	40	31 (26)	£84,125
Archaeology and ethnography	33	18 (15)	£25,276
Coins and medals	24	18 (23)	£25,079
Prints	22	22 (26)	£36,441
Textiles	13	13 (9)	£41,515
Printed books	9	8 (2)	£10,938
Modern sculpture	8	8 (15)	£10,525
Photographs	8	7 (5)	£57,625
Regimental	8	4 (-)	£5,934
Miscellaneous	7	3 (24)	£4,011
Buildings	5	2 (4)	£5,000
Historical sculpture	3	1 (4)	£6,000
Musical instruments	1	- (2)	-

Figures in brackets are for the preceding financial year

Figure 11.1 Grants under the Victoria and Albert Museum grant fund (after Trevelyan 1987, Table 2)

and then of exhibitions and similar expositions. These are interpretative acts intended to create value and significance, and are informed by ideological assumptions which invite analytical deconstruction. The following analysis of collection management policies picks up and underlines some of the points already made in the discussion of curatorship in Chapter 6. The analyses of individual exhibitions and related material enables us to look at detailed praxis in action and so highlight some specific ideological problems.

Collections and Collection Policies

It is clear that museum collections are a section of the ideological map (Geertz 1973), the reading of which should help us to understand the cultural or ideological assumptions which have gone into their creation. The first important point is the transforming power of collections as such. We have already traced the often anarchic or highly idiosyncratic reasons why material is taken into collections (Chapters 3 and 4) and this marks a definite stage in its transformation. But it is clear that the formal reception of material into a museum collection, institutional, impersonal and endowed with the classifying and authenticating power already described, is the rite which works the final transformation. Private collectors themselves often draw attention to this, for it is the main reason why they wish to found a museum themselves or bequeath their collection to an existing foundation. As Gombrich has pointed out in relation to fine art:

> When we write in our museums, 'Visitors are forbidden to touch the exhibits' – we are not only using a very necessary precaution for the preservation of works of art: we might argue with André Malraux that the museum turns images into art by establishing that new category, a new principle of classification that creates a different mental set. Take any object from a museum, say Riccio's *Box in the Shape of a Crab* from the Kress Collection. If I had it in my hand, or, better still, on my desk, I might well be tempted to play with it . . . On the desk, in short, this object would belong to the species crab, subspecies bronze crab. As I contemplate it in its glass case, my reaction is different. I think of certain trends in Renaissance realism which lead to Palissy and his *style rustique*. The object belongs to the species Renaissance bronzes, subspecies bronzes representing crabs.   (Grombrich 1962: 97–8)

The professional attitudes of curators and museum staff in general, the praxis created in each individual institution and broadly across the whole museum world as a result of custom and tradition, plays a crucial role here. Curators privilege certain sorts of material in relation to other sorts of material. 'Good stuff' is material considered to be rare or perhaps highly typical, of intrinsically high quality, in a relatively good state of repair, and relatively well documented so that we have the hope of 'finding out a lot about it'. 'Poor stuff' is not very interesting, commonplace in the wrong way, lacking much contextual information, and in an advanced state of disrepair. Poor stuff will be refused where possible, and if already in the collections may be considered for disposal. It will merit less study by curators and others, it will endure the poorest storage and have the least claims to conservation treatment. It will be the first material to become 'unavailable' during periods of financial or resource difficulty.

A similar kind of professional selection procedure happens when exhibitions are planned and material chosen for display. 'Good' collections are given gallery space and 'poor' collections are left in store, and particularly in the human history and natural science fields (but sometimes also in art), 'good' collections are usually those compiled and developed according to the systematic mode, which embody a clear intellectual rationale. In consequence the public is given a distorted idea of the nature of much material which museums hold, and this distortion is the result of a curatorial winnowing process which determines that material capable of production into clear meaning and knowledge of a 'scientific' kind gets the largest share of attention. The inconsistent, the incomplete, the awkward, the idiosyncratic –

these are left on their shelves, while attention concentrates upon those which can project social coherence, a sensible story.

The tale is self-perpetuating because that material which was considered of importance in the past is likely to have the right attributes in the present, and material newly come to interest, like contemporary culture, will be collected according to the same criteria. So the dance goes on, and in practical day-to-day decisions about which of equally vulnerable objects will be in the store with the dehumidifier and which will not, the inherited values, judgements and hierarchies of the capitalist world are maintained.

Exhibitions

Exhibitions represent the nature of the produced meaning and knowledge in very specific ways, which can be unravelled by asking questions like, 'What presumptions are made about why this display is worth looking at?' and 'What kinds of understanding is this display offering?' Some answers to these questions are given by looking at four exhibitions, two (as it happens) at the Royal Academy, London, one at Glenbow Museum, Calgary, Canada, and the fourth at the Royal Scottish Museum, Edinburgh.

The exhibition *The Spirit Sings* at Glenbow Museum in 1988 was intended to bring together the best examples of native Canadian material culture from the collections of the world. None of the paid curatorial team were native Canadians. The exhibition was sponsored by Shell Oil to whom the Alberta Government had recently leased large tracts of land claimed by the Lubicon Lake Cree people. The Lubicon gained considerable support for their efforts to have the exhibition boycotted, but nevertheless, it opened on time and ran its appointed course. It is clear that *The Spirit Sings* was open to the charge of simply reflecting White-Anglo-Saxon-Protestant and capitalist values, both in terms of the way in which it viewed the accumulated collections in museums around the world, and in terms of the way in which these can be displayed. The exhibition has been described as 'a typically traditional ethnological exhibition in which a museum of the dominant culture attempts to represent the heritage of a minority culture, largely in its absence' (McManus 1991: 203).

In coming to terms with the ideological nature of collections and of traditional display policies, museums are faced with a crisis of representation, centring upon what is collected, how it is shown and who decides, which concerns not only the representation of native peoples in countries which are now dominated by European-descended settlers, but also the exhibition of exotic cultures in general, of immigrants and of past indigenous generations. The significance of the issues which this raises in terms of multicultural societies, the representation of gender, the depiction of class and class exploitation, and the representation of war and of religion, cannot be denied and the difficulties are genuine and formidable. The central point is the need to recognize that our collections and our accustomed habits belong to a traditional mind-set which has been shaped by cultural bias.

The *Evolution* exhibition at the Royal Scottish Museum opened in 1975. *Evolution* occupies three floors unified by an open central well which contains a stylized and coiled-up phylogenetic tree of the vertebrates visible from all three galleries (see Plate 27). This, we are told, 'is not only spectacular, rising as it does through the whole height of the time sequence and suggesting by its sculptural quality the progressive expansion of vertebrate life through time, but it is essential in terms of the display since it reminds us that time is a continuum' (Waterston 1976: 10). The organizers tell us, 'Because of the obvious educative value of the modern theory of evolution, which has been claimed as the greatest unifying theory in natural science and which has influenced thought far beyond the confines of science, evolution was chosen as the introductory theme to the museum's displays of natural history and geology' (Waterston 1976: 10). The exhibition deals with two major themes. The first, 'The Story of Life', takes us through the earliest known cells to the development of early diverse phyla and so to the development of one of these phyla, the Chordata, which is then followed through in detail from fish to man. The second illustrates the 'mechanisms' which enable evolutionary change to take place. We are told that 'Particular attention has been given to showing the evidence related to the origin of each of the classes of vertebrates because of the particular interest which attaches to the evolutionary origins of major taxonomic groups' (Waterston 1976: 10).

Evolution is a classic exhibition on a classic theme, carried through with a relatively high level of resource. Its basic assumptions are easily unravelled. It starts from the view that knowledge is both theoretically knowable and actually known, at any rate to a worthwhile extent. It proceeds to the assumption that this knowledge can be demonstrated by good-quality three-dimensional display in which the chronological and spatial relationships of the selected biological material are made manifest. It underpins this activity by supposing that all this is good for us; that constructed knowledge of this kind is morally desirable in itself and that, very properly, it helps to create the kind of people who agree with the presumptions on offer.

Viewed in this light, *Evolution* and many exhibitions like it can be described in post-modern terms as simplistic endorsements of the prevailing capitalistic ideology, which approve and require an apparently effective understanding of the natural world in order to be able to exploit it in the interests of maintaining itself. Objections that evolutionary theory, broadly speaking, squares with the accumulated empirical evidence of scientific activity is met by echoing (and perhaps misusing) Karl Popper's assertion that facts do not prove a theory, because it is always possible that other theories could be devised to cover the facts: and theories are social constructs designed to fit not just 'known facts', but also specific human circumstances of time and place. Exhibitions of this kind, therefore, are tainted, not by what they say and how they say it as such, but because they keep some cards up their sleeves and fail to lay down the ground rules within which they are operating. As we shall suggest in the final chapter, curatorial honesty emerges as the best antidote to this kind of difficulty which, if left unanswered, opens the door to flat-earth theories and similar inanities.

The Age of Chivalry was a major exhibition held at the Royal Academy in 1987–8.

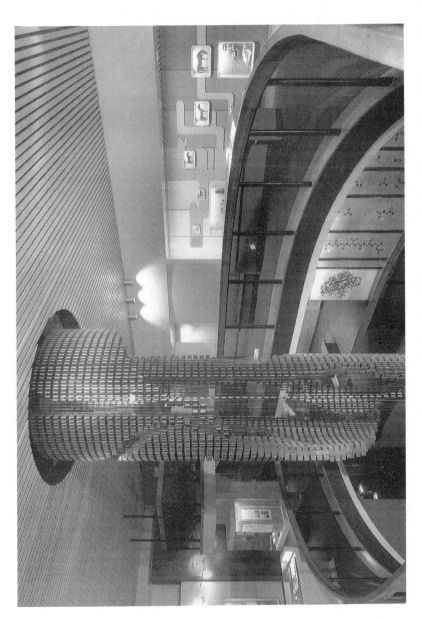

Plate 27.   Central feature of the exhibition *Evolution* at the then Royal Museum of Scotland (photo: Alastair Hunter Photography).

The exhibition comprised fourteen galleries, divided into two main groups, one of which provided historical context through the chronological sequence of the reigns of five Plantagenet kings, and the other thematic displays on society and art. The exhibition was not without its organizational difficulties, but it succeeded in bringing together a truly awe-inspiring display of Gothic works of art, and it is this content and the approach to it which concerns us here. The introduction to the accompanying booklet tells us: 'The Gothic style in England during the two centuries of Plantagenet rule developed its own distinct, national characteristics. This exhibition gathers together for the first time outstanding works of art which demonstrate the creativity and brilliant technical achievements of the English artists of the period' (Royal Academy 1987).

Several points are immediately clear. The nationalistic mood of the exhibition and the relationship of the quality of the works of art to 'Englishness' were made quite explicit; we were intended to draw comfort and support from this demonstration that Englishness as a possession in which we can take legitimate pride runs back as far as the thirteenth century. The outstanding aesthetic nature of the works on display, the creativity and technical brilliance which brought them to birth, were presented as facts, self-evident to every exhibition visitor. The virtue of aesthetic quality was similarly taken for granted as something which requires no defence or explication. The historical fact, that much of this kind of material was considered in poor taste for a considerable period in the late seventeenth and eighteenth centuries and returned to fashion through a 'revival', was forgotten in the interests of an ahistorical, monolithic assertion of value, which turns time and change into a commodity removed from historical process. In the light of all this, it is unsurprising that the exhibition attracted the sponsorship of one of the major capitalist organizations of the day, Lloyds Bank, whose association with past glories and present prestige was made clear in the cunning cover design of the *Background Material for Teachers* pack which translated the Bank's Black Horse logo into Plantagenet idiom.

This obvious ideological content, though important, is relatively superficial. Profounder implications lie beyond. The exhibition rested on the assumption that objects have a fixed meaning which comes from the accumulation of historical judgement that has gathered around them, producing unalterable states in which something is 'good' or 'not so good', judgements with which the viewer, when he has looked and learnt enough, will agree. It is enmeshed in a system of value judgements which, in the last analysis, appear to depend upon tissue-thin assertions of subjective opinion, and which, as we have seen, are tainted by historical relativity. Upon this foundation rests the further moral assertion that 'art and history are good', that a (carefully orchestrated) experience of the values of the past is in itself uplifting and enlarging. This assertion is at the heart of the museum aesthetic and is made plain in most contemporary authoritative statements about the purpose and value of museums.

The difficulties inherent in this ethic were focused by the exhibition, *Egon Schiele and His Contemporaries*, held at the Royal Academy in 1990. Schiele's pictures hover in the twilight zone between erotic art and pornography. Presumably we know that they are art because they are on show in the Royal Academy rather than resting on the top shelf at the newsagents, but the difficulty of making any distinction was brought home in the most practical way by the problems the Royal Academy experienced when it tried to find commercial sponsorship for the exhibition (Graham-Dixon 1990). This gut response of Barclays *et al.* is matched by the appropriately curious poses adopted by the art critics in their finally fruitless efforts to convince us that there is a categorical difference between art and pornography. The implications are of fundamental importance. As Graham-Dixon put it:

> Erotic art troubles the liberal mind because while taking to an extreme its ideas about the radical, exploratory nature of great art, it also punctures one of its fonder delusions. This is the received idea that the contemplation of great art is necessarily *good* for people. Major works of erotic art demonstrate, in a blatant and troubling way, that this is simply not true. They have what might be termed cultural significance – but they are hardly edifying or improving.
>
> (Graham-Dixon 1990)

The same might be said for many museum images of war, or for that matter in respect of that vein of sadism which runs back through much religious art, just as it does through some religious practice. They are all, in their way, legitimate visions of the human condition which, as perceived by Schiele, is one of essential loneliness and vulnerability. This is radicalism gone native to show us creations in which aesthetic power becomes 'power to shock', where we have no choice but to accept the message, and to conclude that these 'truths' are one side, but the underside, of modern capitalism making art its own image.

Posters

Posters are a very characteristic museum product upon which a good deal of resource is often spent. Sometimes they are widely distributed in popular venues like the London Underground, and sometimes they have a very limited circulation which may extend not much beyond the office walls of local curators and their friends. They are particularly significant in that, as direct advertising for exhibitions (and other events), they presumably present the image which museums think is the best one for them to project, in terms both of themselves and of their public. They are interesting also from the historic point of view, since they are frequently (with catalogues) the most important surviving record of an event upon which much effort was expended.

Six posters have been chosen for discussion from among the number which have been circulated in the museum world during the last few years. Three of these concern late prehistoric – principally Iron Age – Britain. The poster *Celtic Britain: Life and Death in the Iron Age 500 BC–AD 50* (see Plate 28) accompanied the circulating exhibition of the same name mounted by a range of museums in conjunction with the British Museum in 1989. It is pale yellow with dark green text, and features a full-colour illustration of, we are told, Celtic nobles about 200 BC. The picture shows an elaborately dressed man with shield and sword, looking

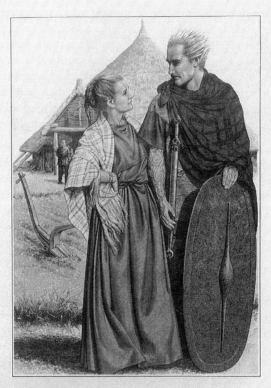

Plate 28.   Poster advertising the exhibition *Celtic Britain: Life and Death in the Iron Age 500 BC–AD 50* arranged jointly between the British Museum and other British museums in 1990 (photo: University of Leicester).

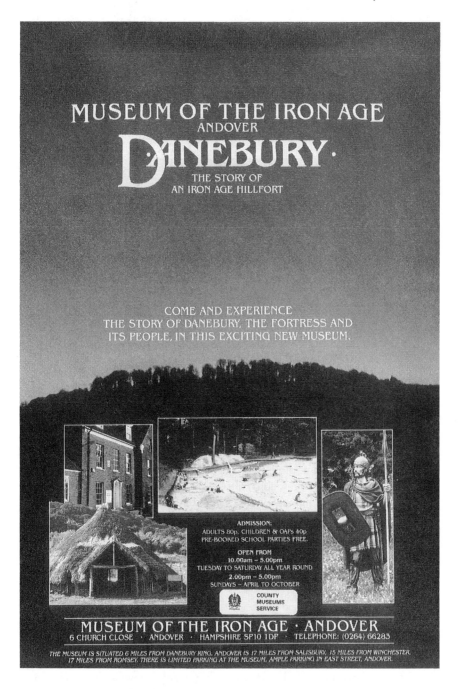

Plate 29.   Poster advertising the *Museum of the Iron Age: Danebury, the Story of an Iron Age Hill Fort*, Andover, Hampshire. Hampshire County Museum Service (photo: University of Leicester).

at a rather drably dressed woman, with behind them a round house with thatched roof and fore-porch and a plough. The poster for the Museum of the Iron Age at Danebury, Hampshire (see Plate 29), is intended to advertise the permanent display which relates to the excavations carried out at Danebury hill fort. The text, set against a dramatic sunset silhouette of the hill top, invites us to 'come and experience the story of the Danebury, the fortress and its people, in this exciting new museum'. The inset full-colour photographs feature another fully-armed Celtic warrior, a shot of a round hut (which in the case of both posters is drawn from the Butser reconstruction), a view of the Danebury excavation in progress, and a shot of the house where the exhibition is housed. The third poster advertises the *Warriors, Druids and Slaves* exhibition at the Museum of the North, Llanberis, Gwynedd, a branch of the National Museum of Wales (see Plate 30). It shows an elaborate late Bronze Age shield in poor condition, two sections of iron slave chains, and a Druid figure in sepia, cloaked, hooded and bearded, bare-kneed, holding a staff and equipped with a Middle Bronze Age axehead in his belt.

These posters are typical of most which try to stir up interest in the relatively remote past, a difficult task. They all promote the same three interlinked ways of seeing the past: firstly, that the past is essentially dramatic and mysterious, and therefore exciting; secondly, that the important people within it were all noble warriors and their ladies and priests; and finally, that the whole thing existed in a kind of limbo detached from the historical process (although the exhibitions themselves may not share this dislocation). The poster Celts are still presented as noble barbarians in a format which can be traced back to the classical world, and represents urban and modern fantasy, rather than prehistoric fact.

Two posters from the Museum of London operate in very similar ways. One advertises the temporary exhibition, *Treasures and Trinkets: Jewellery in London from pre-Roman Times* (1991) – a rather ambiguous title, which judging by the assemblage shown on the poster, means jewellery from pre-Roman times onwards (see Plate 31). This kind of display and accompanying poster makes unmistakably clear the 'treasure' motif in museum collecting and exhibition and runs the risk of creating a false public impression of the nature of museum collections and museum work. The second Museum of London poster is for the permanent exhibition, *Tudor London*, glossed: 'In the Museum of London's Tudor Gallery discover how Londoners lived under Henry VIII' (see Plate 32). The poster shows an anonymous portrait of Henry VIII, an English Elizabethan delft plate, and the Gresham weighing balance dated 1572, a very elaborate piece of metalwork in its own right. It is clear that the design of the poster merely continues to reinforce the stereotypes of the period in particularly glib and boring ways.

The final poster comes from the City Museum and Art Gallery, Stoke-on-Trent. It accompanied an exhibition (1989) of the early history of the museum service entitled *Useful and Beautiful: Museums in the Six Towns* (see Plate 33). The poster features two early black and white photographs showing the exterior and interior of the museum around 1900, and the cover of the 1890 museum guidebook entitled *Handbook and Catalogue of the Collection of Works of Art and Other Objects of Interest Exhibited at the Inauguration, with an Account of the*

Museum. This belongs in what may be called the commemorative poster tradition, and it presents the museum values of 1890 quite flatly, without any comment in text or design.

Labels and Catalogues

Labels and labelling have attracted a good deal of attention in their own right. McManus's (see 1991 and references there) work in the Science Museum and the Natural History Museum, London, shows that, contrary to museum folklore, most museum visitors do read, depend upon, and use exhibit texts, and that consequently these texts have an important place in museum communication. Indeed, very often 'the text must supply all the information needed to satisfy the interrogative framework' (McManus 1989: 183), and it appears to do so best when it comes closest to a conversational relationship between the label writer and the museum visitor. In the light of this the various studies about the readability of museum labels take on an enhanced significance, especially the classic study by Sorsby and Horne (1980) which suggested that label writers consistently overestimate the reading level of the general public in matters like vocabulary, especially technical vocabulary, and sentence construction, and that 'for the general museum visitor to be able to read a label, a reading level of no more than 15 years should be the aim' (1980: 158).

It also means that we should take the content of our labels, both apparent and less obvious, correspondingly seriously. Coxall's research into museum texts is primarily an exploration into how the use of language conveys meanings, and the way in which 'the writer's choice of language, and the final text, transmit both the official policy of a museum and the personal "world view" of that writer' (Coxall 1991: 85). Neither of these views is simple, and this also applies to the individual, as Roger Fowler cautions in his book *Linguistic Criticism*: 'It would be incorrect to think that each individual possesses one single, monolithic, world-view or ideology encompassing all aspects of his or her experience; rather, the ideational function provides a repertoire of perspectives relative to the numerous modes of discourse in which a speaker participates' (Fowler 1968: 149).

For museum policy, it is clear that local and national politics will be influential, particularly when these are tied to the operation of funding. Equally, the notion that language expresses 'the natural' or 'common sense' is inadequate in the light of the fact that it, like all our communication systems, is socially constructed. Accordingly, although writers may think that what they write is transparent common sense, they may well be implying meanings of which they are unaware and which will be revealed by critical linguistic analysis aimed at uncovering a text's hidden agenda. This criticism is particularly necessary where institutions like a museum are concerned, which, as we have shown, enjoy a privileged position of assumed innocence and objectivity.

Two examples will suffice to give an idea of the approach and its results. Coxall (1991: 89–90) took a label from the eighteenth-century section of the decorative arts Geffrye Museum, London, whose aim is to curate the history of English

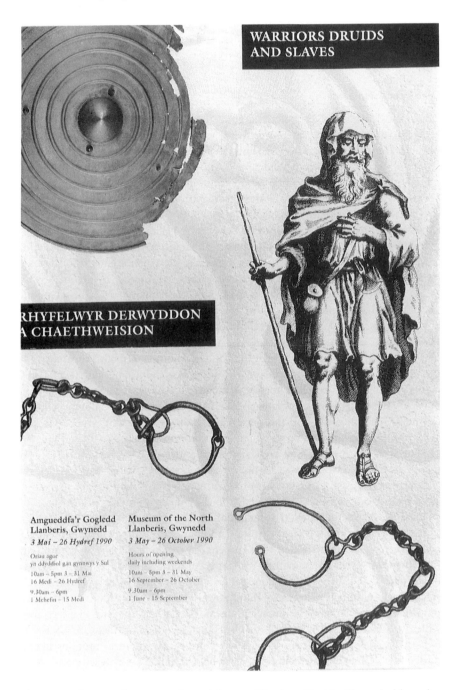

Plate 30. Poster advertising the exhibition *Warriors, Druids, Slaves* held at the Museum of the North, Llanberis, Gwynedd. National Museum of Wales (photo: University of Leicester).

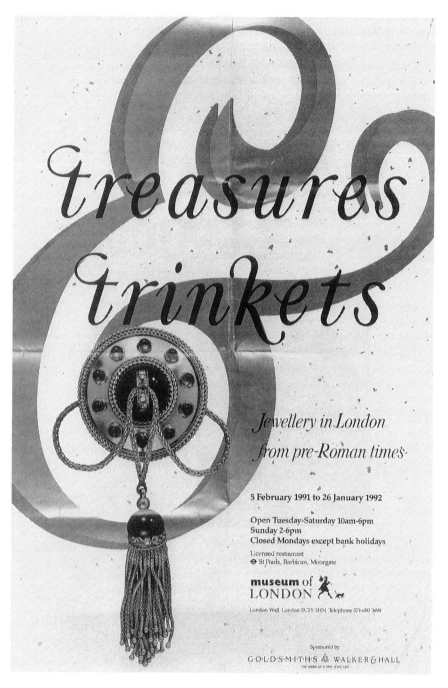

Plate 31. Poster advertising the exhibition *Treasures and Trinkets*, held at the Museum of London, 1992 (photo: University of Leicester; poster design: Sally Fentiman).

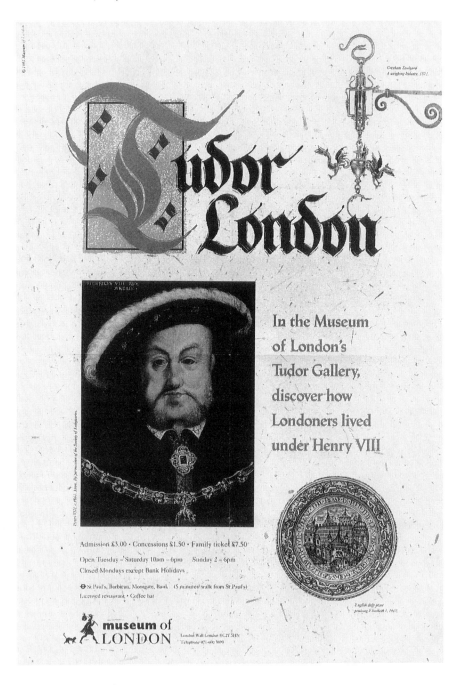

Plate 32.   Poster advertising the exhibition *Tudor London*, held at the Museum of London, 1991 (photo: University of Leicester; poster design: Sally Fentiman).

domestic interiors between 1600 and the present day: 'Expensive oil paintings could now be copied and mass produced in a variety of ways such as engraving or etching. These prints were cheap and widely available. By the late Georgian period it was fashionable to have an overall decorative scheme. Yellow silk damask was a popular fabric for curtains and chairs.' She points out that the adjectives 'expensive' and 'cheap' and 'available' are both evaluative and relative terms; that the terms 'fashionable' and 'popular' beg a series of questions about whose fashion and how 'popular'; and that in general the problem of whose history is on show is ignored so that in consequence only middle-class life is shown, while the rest of the population apparently had no domestic history at all.

The second example is taken from the catalogue accompanying the 1973–4 exhibition, *The Genius of China*, shown at the Royal Academy. The opening paragraph of the section entitled 'Introduction: The Scope of the Exhibition' runs:

> This is the first exhibition held outside China in which the greater part of her cultural history is illustrated wholly by documented material, mostly from controlled excavations. Particulars of provenance and associations are known in every case. The twelve sections begin with the paleolithic period, on which some important new evidence is available, and end in the fourteenth century AD, at a time when Europe, in the person of Marco Polo, first made direct contact with China. The masterpieces included in all the divisions of exhibits betoken the high achievement of Chinese artists and craftsmen, the anonymous spokesmen of an ancient, gifted and energetic people.   (Watson 1973: 10)

We notice the stress laid upon 'documented material' and 'controlled excavations' which can be seen as classic statements of the authoritarian stance taken by guardians of scholastic knowledge and professional practice (who take 'particulars' and authenticate both these 'provenances' and 'associations') and the whole idea of value inherent in such control. The exhibition ended at the point when 'Europe in the person of Marco Polo, first made direct contact', after which, presumably, China ceased to be China. The things on show are accredited 'masterpieces' because the writer tells us they are; they tell us that China, with its high-achieving artists and its gifted people, belongs within that select group of societies who have achieved 'high civilization' judged against the code of modern Western society. More could be said, but let us finally pick out the word 'ancient'. Alec Douglas-Home, fourteenth Earl of Home, said in reply to a jibe of Harold Wilson's, 'Presumably you are the fourteenth Mr Wilson,' but we know that it is not the same. All societies are 'ancient', but ancient lineage implies aristocratic background, old money, and refined sensibility, all qualities appropriate to 'high culture'.

'The Death of the Object' and Other Stories

We have seen how, in accordance with Marxist and post-Marxist ideas about the operation of ideology and power, museums can be seen as part and parcel of a particular system, that of historic and late capitalism, and to be fully implicated in the

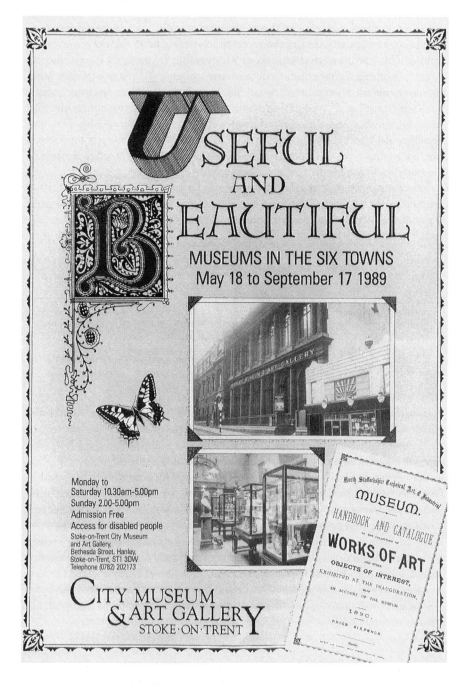

Plate 33.　Poster advertising the exhibition *Useful and Beautiful: Museums in the Six Towns*, 1989, held at City Museum and Art Gallery, Stoke-on-Trent (photo: University of Leicester).

construction of the cultural norms and value systems which support the capitalistic regime. This of itself is not necessarily pessimistic, because it allows for enlightenment and change. But post-structuralist theory in the hands of Foucault, Derrida, Lacan and others, regards ideas of value, enlightenment and knowledge as oppressive and power-laden, and sees the particular forms of absolute value created by the Western humanist tradition – scientific reason, scholarship based on evidence, and the institutions which support them – as merely the local versions implicit in Western capitalism. Philosophy, knowledge and scholarship all work by metaphors, like fiction does, and metaphors are essentially 'groundless', floating free in a world of interpretation unanchored in objective reality.

So we arrive at Barthes' famous 'death of the author' which, translated into artefact terms, means that since no values or interpretations can be objectively demonstrated, including those intended by the maker, all interpretations are equally subjective and equally valid. In 1968 Barthes wrote: 'literature (it would be better from now on to say *writing*), by refusing to assign a 'secret', an ultimate meaning to the text (and to the world as text), liberates what may be called an anti-theological activity, an activity that is truly revolutionary since to refuse to fix meaning is, in the end, to refuse God and his hypostases – reason, science, law' (1977: 147). The implications of this for museums are clear if the words 'object interpretation' are substituted for 'literature' and 'writing', and 'object' substituted for 'text'. This, taken to its conclusion, undermines the work of scholarship, curatorship and the whole humanistic project. It dismisses belief in the active participation of the individual in history and change as a fallacy, because the individual, deprived of a romantic capacity for any sort of self-integration through meaningful experience, becomes merely the site of passing thoughts and feelings which, like everything else, are groundless metaphors unrelatable to any kind of social reality.

Meaning is written on water and we are all free to construct our own kinds of reality. Museums are full of brightly-coloured, interestingly-shaped objects which, like children without judgemental let or hindrance, we can pile up into whatever forms we like; indeed, some manifestations of 'heritage' do seem to be like this. The original post-structuralists saw this as a liberating project which freed people from the dead hand of history, and this in spite of the obvious fact that for us all – but for some more than others – the dead hand of history still has a stranglehold on our daily lives and prospects. But we who work between the accumulated inheritance of the past and the public to whom we try to mediate it may see things rather differently, and so perhaps may those to whom this liberation is offered. The freedom of nothing is no freedom at all, and life with its culture drained of meaning is like a beautifully wrapped Christmas present which, once the gold paper and the red tissue have been stripped away, is found to contain only a dirty bit of paper covered with idiot scribble. It is therefore for curators and their kin to try to find not just emotional, but also conceptual justifications for our museum efforts, however flawed, and this will be the main topic of the final chapter.

12   Projects and Prospects

The next step forward must come, not from political agitation or premature experiments, but from thought. At present our sympathy and our judgement are liable to be on different sides, which is a painful and paralysing state of mind . . .   (J. Maynard Keynes in Harris 1955: 356)

Organizing the past in accordance with the needs of the present, that is what one could call the social function of history.

(Febvre, reprinted in Burke 1973)

Karl Popper has convinced me that neither in the sciences nor in the humanities must we aim at total solutions, but that we still have the right to go on asking and searching because we can learn from our mistakes. I believe that this also applies to our efforts at understanding other peoples, other civilizations, other ages.   (Gombrich 1991: 39)

The State of the Art

It is time to see where we have arrived and to suggest some departures. A number of interlinking themes have run through this book. The starting-point was the twofold notion that museums, objects and collections are all aspects of a single unity, which cannot be understood without an understanding of its integral and inseparable parts; and that the theory and practice of the museum as an institution, of collecting as here understood, and of objects in specific social practice, are a characteristic and essential element in that peculiarly European (and immensely important) cultural expression loosely called modernism.

Within this, material objects and specimens have emerged with two crucial characteristics. They are capable of organization into a large range of classificatory groupings – collections, taxonomies and typologies, historical analysis, and the exhibitions which descend from these – all of which constitute the metaphorical making of meaning, through behavioural interaction between material and person. But their materiality means that they always retain a concrete and intrinsic relationship to the original context from which they came, and to all subsequent contexts in which they have been placed. It is this capacity for reality which gives them, and so the museums which hold them, their ability to testify to the nature of past events, with all the moral weight which this has implied in a modern society which has needed material proofs of its knowledge and values, and in the capitalist system which has needed 'real' yardsticks against which to measure its world of goods.

The dual nature of objects as 'real things' and as 'constructed understanding' takes us to the heart of the matter. The long-term trend of European thought, increasingly cogently expressed from the late seventeenth century onwards, is to give a low value to the material world as such, and to regard it as the fit place for the exercise of human reason and enquiry through which real knowledge will be constituted. On this reading, objects in general are the passive result of social action, and museum collections enshrine the results of objective enquiry which has yielded real understanding; in other words, the metaphorically constructed understandings have been seen as superior to the concrete, contextual reality of the things. An important aspect of this is the tendency to regard language, the prime medium for classification and reason, as the faculty which creates social structure, although as we have seen there is not an exactly parallel relationship between language and the material world.

This line of thought taken to its conclusion carries the seed of the post-modern collapse of reason and value, because unless the external world of things possesses an intrinsic social reality, there is nothing much to stop the thinking enquirer constructing whatever knowledge he sees fit. The recognition of this lies behind not only the final attempts to deconstruct knowledge and its cultural expressions which characterize the writings of Barthes and Foucault, but also a more general willingness to come to terms with the subjective side of making meaning. Traditional conceptual thinking, however, also gives weight to the companion view which recognizes some intrinsic reality in the external world, and to this we shall return in a moment.

We can analyse the making of meanings in museums. The formation of a collection is an outward extension of the inward self, a private effort to shape the world and create romantic sense of a souvenir, fetishistic or systematic kind. The material held in museums, accumulated through these emotional and intellectual processes, is (more or less) selected for acquisition because it is seen as belonging in the 'durable object' class, and as embodying knowledge, understanding and value in a particular sense, a knowledge and value which is socially constructed and which museums play a large part in verifying and sustaining. We have traced the historical process through which some important aspects of this knowledge have been produced, and the role of museums in its creation, phase by phase, over the last five centuries or so. We can see that curatorial practice, in its professional traditions, its disciplinary traditions, its approach to classification and its use of resources, is emeshed within and underpins the construction of meaning. As a part of this, curatorial practice, in the framing of all interpretation and especially exhibitions, constantly draws upon one or other (or several at once) of the principal approaches to understanding – historical, functionalist or structuralist – which have emerged as later modernity has developed. However, as we have seen, the bias of traditional historiography towards the written or spoken, but in either case linguistic, narrative has relegated objects to a secondary place, with correspondingly depressing effects upon museum display. It is clear, also, that whatever view we may take of it, the thrust of the making of museum meanings is not socially transparent, but part and parcel of the operation and maintenance of power and control.

We can, therefore, say what museums are not. Museums are not 'natural' events, free from intrinsic questions and problems. Museums do not merely house material from the past and offer a set of ideas about it, and neither the chosen material nor the ideas on offer embody an inevitable or organic growth over the five centuries or so: things could have been different. Museums do not simply demonstrate what the past, including the natural past, was like or how people thought about it at the time. Museums should not be understood as places where knowledge lives, or where the progressive and cumulative efforts of museum workers steadily and necessarily add up to a clearer understanding of the human and the natural worlds.

Museums, in other words, are not privileged places. They, and the people who work in them, are part of social practice in a social world. Museums do not tell about things in the transparent sense; they are themselves complicated things, social constructs which lock into the complex sequences of action and interaction, and produce the cultural statements we see as acquisition and disposal, storage policies, exhibitions and posters. Museums are active creators of the natural and human past, including of course the very recent past, and their creations should be understood as product – not discovery.

In museums (as everywhere else), all understanding is historical and so context-based. This is true at all levels. It is true of the impulse which prompts us to put certain specific information in a label and to leave other information out. It is true of the ideas which will govern how we write the label text, and of detailed decisions about what size, colour and so on we will use for it. It is true of the concepts of communication which underpin this enterprise, and it is true of the philosophical forms which enable us to produce the matter (in every sense) to be communicated. It is true for the assumption that museum workers and visitors are all capable of understanding each other, and that there exists such a thing as the essential experiencing individual. It is these interlocking ideas – the nature of objects, collections and museums as social practice, the interrelationship of material and individuals within this practice, the ways in which meaning is generated within museums, and the relationship of all these critical approaches to historical context – which this book has tried to trace.

Objective Knowledge

We may now well feel that we have peeled all the skins away from the onion leaving only messy bits and tears, but – to pursue the metaphor – chopped onion is where many good meals begin. A clear-eyed view of the cultural position of museums and their contents by no means denies their sustaining role in social life. If we begin from the notion – as we must, for we have no feasible alternative – that we are social beings with individual and common pasts which play a crucial part in making us what we are, then we must look for ways in which that past, particularly its material embodiment, can be given legitimate meaning. The open abandonment of claims to special privilege on the part of museums does not involve an abandonment of ideas about the worth of what museums have to offer, nor does it destroy the meaning embodied in what they have to say, although it certainly puts it within a differently-conceived relationship between museums and the outside world. This brings us back to traditional conceptual thinking and to the way in which the idea of individually-constructed knowledge is balanced by the notion of social reality. How can we reconcile the claims of objective knowledge and value with those of social relativity and subjective instability? How can we as museum people recognize with our judgement the implications of critical analysis, while wishing to go on offering those created meanings about the past and its material which engage our deepest sympathies?

A number of writers are beginning to suggest ways in which this central dilemma of authority and anarchy can be resolved, or at least re-presented, and here we will concentrate upon the ideas of Karl Popper and R. G. Collingwood, especially those contained in Popper's *Objective Knowledge: An Evolutionary Approach* (1979). In the essay published here, entitled 'Epistemology without a knowing subject', Popper suggests that: 'We may distinguish the following three worlds or universes: first, the world of physical objects or physical states; secondly, the world of states of consciousness, or mental states, or perhaps behavioural dispositions to act; and thirdly, the world of *objective contents of thought*, especially of scientific and poetic thoughts, and works of art' (1979: 106, Popper's italics). This means, put rather crudely, that there is an external world of objective reality, and that there is also a world of experiencing and behaving human beings. Beside these, there is the 'third world' of critical arguments and 'the state of a discussion or the state of critical argument'. The third world contains journals, books and libraries and, Popper might have added, museum collections and exhibitions. Popper meets the argument that all these are essentially symbolic expressions of subjective mental states, and intended as a means of communication meant to induce subjective mental states in the audience or viewer, in three main ways.

Firstly, Popper draws a fundamental distinction between 'I know' which belongs in his second world, and 'knowledge' which belongs in his third. He argues that those ideas about knowledge which concentrate on the second world, or knowledge in the subjective sense, are irrelevant to our ideas about knowledge in the objective sense of knowledge without a knower. Secondly, he suggests that what is relevant for ideas about knowledge is the study of problems, hypotheses and theories, and of the role played by evidence. Thirdly, an objectivist view of knowledge which studies the third world can help to throw much light upon the second world of subjective consciousness; but the converse is not true. In addition to these three main theses, Popper offers three supporting theses:

The first of these is that the third world is a natural produce of the human animal, comparable to a spider's web.

The second supporting thesis (and an almost crucial thesis, I think) is that the third world is largely *autonomous*, even though we constantly act upon it and are acted upon by it: it is autonomous in spite of the fact that it is our product and that it has a strong feed-back effect upon us; that is to say, upon us *qua* inmates of the second and even of the first world.

The third supporting thesis is that it is through this interaction between ourselves and the third world that objective knowledge grows, and that there is a close analogy between the growth of knowledge and biological growth; that is, the evolution of plants and animals.

(1979: 112)

Popper pushes his argument forward by taking up the point about biological growth, and developing the example of the wasps' nest. Two categories of problem arise in the study of these structures: one group concerns the methods used by the animals, their behaviour and their act of production; the other concerns the structures themselves, their physical properties, their environment, their evaluation and their functions. All of these considerations, he says, can be applied to products of human activity, such as houses, tools, works of art, 'language' and 'science', all of which he refers to in a footnote as 'artefacts' (his quotation marks). Popper argues that the second category of problems, that concerning the products in themselves, is in almost every respect more important than those in the first category, the problems of production. Once produced, an artefact takes on an autonomous and objective reality which is independent of any knower: a book remains a book even if it is never read (p. 115). It is not the reader who 'turns spots on white paper into a book, or an instance of knowledge in the objective sense. Rather, it is something more abstract. It is its possibility or potentiality of being understood, its dispositional character of being understood or interpreted, or misunderstood or misinterpreted, which makes a thing a book. And this potentiality or disposition may exist without ever being actualized or realized' (1979: 116). Popper thus asserts that there is a kind of third world of books in themselves, theories in themselves, problems in themselves, problem situations in themselves, arguments in themselves, and so on. This is concerned not with dubious metaphysical or idealist essences, but with arguments, with theories true and false, with conjectures and refutations.

This is in some ways a restatement in up-to-date terms of the nature of historical, and so cultural, understanding developed in the 1930s and 1940s by Collingwood in England. For Collingwood, historical knowledge is not the 'passive' reception of facts – it is the discerning of the thought which is the inner side of the event (1946: 222). No certainty or security is envisaged here, and still less proof; the understanding of inwardness is experienced through continual debate and approximation. This does not mean, it is important to realize, that one person's experience of historical inwardness is as good as another's. Collingwood is at pains to show that 'we can be rigorous in our reconstruction of the past and we can devise criteria for judging between theories' (Hodder 1986, 94). The student must immerse himself in the contextual data: 'historical knowledge is the knowledge of what the mind has done in the past, and at the same time, it is the re-doing of this, the perpetration of past acts in the present' (Collingwood 1946: 218).

This is to say that all statements about the past involve making assumptions about its meaning, and this happens by asking questions of the assembled data (itself, of course, riddled by assumptions also). The basis of our ability to make assumptions about meaning at all depends upon a conviction that all humans across time and space are fundamentally the same, so that although each historical context is unique, it is explicable to us through our common humanity; although each event is unique, it has a universality which makes it accessible to us all. The quality of the assumption rests in its perceived internal coherence and its correspondence to the evidence, which is seen, though flawed by subjectivity, as possessing a genuinely independent existence in the real world. The perceivers are the community of those who have similarly spent time and effort in the struggle to create coherence and correspondence from the raw evidence. This may sound elitist, but in fact it has to do rather with struggle and self-awareness: for Collingwood 'we study history . . . in order to attain self-knowledge' (1946: 315).

This is to bring the experiencing individual, the common viewer whom we saw interreacting with fashionable clothes and Chelsea rabbits, into the centre of the action, and to assert the validity of the social content of the object with which he or she is interreacting. The notion of common humanity which all individuals share, and which therefore offers some possibility of mutual understanding, is best expressed not in high-flown terms, but in more basic ways. We all seem to share a lust of the eye, an interest in bright, shining things, which presumably has much to do with the way our optic nerves work and the way our minds understand what is seen. We share a pleasure in material intricacy, presumably because our hands are capable of achieving this kind of thing. A nicely plaited cord, it seems, is a nicely plaited cord the world over. At a more limited level we share a delight in the miniature, of large rendered in small, which perhaps has to do with the smallness of human young and the relatively long time which they remain small. As Gombrich has pointed out, the enjoyment of rhythmic movement is common to all normal humans, and on this foundation rests music, dance, poetry and decorative art (Gombrich 1979) and, we might add, part of the reason for creating social distinctions. It is from all these relatively humble things that social structures are elaborated, and the subtler creations of mind and art are brought into being.

These are shared dispositions which we can all understand in each other. They lead to a further thought of particular importance here. The shared dispositions are, at root, physical capacities, albeit complex ones, and have to do with our physical relationship to the material world. Notoriously, when language endeavours to describe fine shades of meaning or feeling, it does so through material references, so states of mind are described as hard, bitter, or playful, and language itself is called colourful. Material inference is fundamental to the way we construct ourselves as individuals and as societies. Museum workers should never allow the significance of this to be far from their minds, or underrate its implications for the creation of mutual understanding about how things are and how things change.

Objects, then, constitute social life and bring it into being. They carry the value which their society ascribes to them, and they help to create value. They, and the values and meanings which are ascribed to them and which they stimulate, are constantly changing as society changes. But while they are doing these things, they are also occupying Popper's third world, where they have their own concreteness and their own contextual solidity which the student can hope to begin to understand, and which understandings he can hope to communicate. Reliability of evidence and data is important here, and this includes attempting to get a purchase on how other people have looked at the object in question. Gombrich (1991: 58) gives the concrete example of Rembrandt's *Night Watch*, which is *not* a night watch, and so all comments which took their clue from this apocryphal title are not only obsolete but simply wrong, and anybody who now insisted on viewing the picture as if it were a night watch would be merely foolish. We may conclude, with Gombrich, that one interpretation is not as good or as bad as another.

This principle gives curators some solid footing, provided we accept that we are creating the past for the present and that all notions about good and bad interpretations are social facts, subject themselves to change. We work for here and now, not for then and always. Rembrandt's painting will not again be the *Night Watch*, but views about the importance of this fact may come and go. For curatorship, as for other areas, this is very close to the ideas which Kuhn has developed (e.g. 1970) about consensus and community in the creation of opinions, insights and knowledge. As we have already seen, his ideas suggest that there is a *research or professional community* made up of individuals who share a general interest and a network of communication, and a *speciality*, that is, a segment of the general community who are interested in a particular problem, say the nature and implications of the nineteenth-century collections of herbaria, viewed in all the ways discussed in this book. The speciality segment will come to a broadly-shared view of their subject which they will commend to the wider community, usually with some success. So is a consensus achieved, and the wider ripples of this can spread, the better for all concerned. But the terms of the consensus are not written on tablets of stone; they are part of the same dynamic process of perpetual change which makes up the relationship between subject and object, between people and the material world of museum collections.

Projects and Prospects

From all this, some significant thoughts seem to emerge. While the closed web of metaphorical relationships cannot carry an objective validity remotely approaching old modernist certainties, the interpretative process, with its historical and scientific curatorship and its efforts to evaluate ideas, can operate within Popper's third world, or Collingwood's 'coherence and correspondence', or Kuhn's consensus of the informed community, and can allow the energetic mind to fill with knowledge and judgements which offer understanding and inspiration, whether these are expressed as concrete collections, collection policies, exhibitions, books, or outreach projects of all kinds. All of these are, in one sense, metaphors for 'reality', but in another, they are available as some of the building blocks through which we may keep trying to come to terms with ourselves and our world. Metaphorical activity offers a capacity for reinterpretation amongst ideas which have become objective property.

It is apparent that the nature of the concrete interpretative act which emerges from the metaphorical effort is essentially that of a work of art, in the sense of a specific creative endeavour which is intended to have significance and which will be judged by those who view it. A work of art, whether expressed as a picture or an exhibition or any other communication event, addresses itself to a chosen set of human circumstances. It sets out to convey an intelligible, if complex, message by selecting from the muddle we call life and composing the selection into the best possible pattern to convey the artist's thoughts and feelings. The sum of this selecting and structuring process, which emerges as meaning, is clearly intensely subjective. But at a fundamental level artistic creation supposes that people share a common mind capable of grasping poetic truths about the human condition; if a communication effort departs so far from this norm that it makes no sense to a viewer prepared to bring a degree of sympathy to its understanding, it has failed, but if it strikes a chord of sympathy, then it has begun to achieve something. Such works are free-standing, and they themselves belong, once finished, to Popper's objective third world, where they are available to all comers. They will be judged according to the fruitful insights which they seem to offer the receptive mind about our human nature and the world in which we live.

The museum worker makes a selection from the materials to hand, both tangible and intangible, that form part of his social practice and which will include elements of Popper's objective knowledge. He orders these into museum narrative which will be judged by those who come to it. He is taking part in a rhetorical project of persuasion, but he does this as part of a participating community. This may well involve endeavouring to persuade others to share his belief that the cultural code represented by material is worth learning, for the sake of the insights and pleasures that its forms and styles can give, and for the bracing, self-reliant attitude which its views about evidence and understanding can foster. This is likely to involve a critically reflexive approach to museums and what they do, a struggle towards honesty in thought and expression which admits to problems and tries to strip the mystery away from solutions. It involves the effort to take on board a genuine dialogue between theories of meaning, data and museum practice; this means more work about the history and nature of museums and collections, more work upon the material from a range of standpoints, and more information about how people see museums and respond to them.

This may produce more exhibitions like *The West as America* (National Museum of American Art 1991) or *Still Life: Taxidermy Yesterday, Today and Tomorrow* (Manchester Museum 1992), an exhibition which aims to examine the social history of what was and still is one of the most characteristic museum media. It may involve projects like *The People's Show* at Walsall (1990) and its follow-up,

The People's Festival at museums across the Midlands, which explore the nature of the contemporary relationship with objects. It may involve 'open storage' (Rebora 1991), object-handling sessions, Identification Rooms equipped with accessible literature, comparative material and examination aids like lenses, and Resource Centres like the Archaeological Resource Centre at York. It should involve a rethinking of the ways in which 'historical' objects are presented so that the contribution of the material to the process of change is made more intelligible. Many more ideas are possible, and many more will emerge. They will be matched by developing professional practices as new skills join older ones. They all, in their different ways, draw on the notion of the experiencing individual who can respond to phenomena in ways which may be important to him, and which contribute to social change. In this, the curator is a responsible actor, taking part in an effort of negotiation and pleading.

The triple notion of objective knowledge, artistic endeavour and rhetorical curation sketches in a perspective within which the museum tradition, in the fullest sense, can be viewed. We who are part of this godless post-modern world must live with insecurities, uncertainties and uneasiness. But if we are to do anything at all inside or outside museums, we must start from what we have and what can be done with it, and these ideas are likely to be the more persuasive if they follow Collingwood's ideas of coherence and correspondence in relation to objective knowledge as Popper would define it. The tone of this effort will not now be that of the old childlike certainties, but rather the more painful adult perceptions of irony and self-doubt. The issues at stake are crucial, and curators can only ignore the problems at the price of dishonesty. If we pretend to be what we are not and to possess powers which we do not have we are practising magic, not curatorship, and dishonesty of this kind sins particularly against the central, traditional standards of curators and their kin. Equally, the anarchic and nihilistic post-modern position which denies our human ability to achieve any measure of coherence or satisfaction finds no echo in the ways in which our minds, or our societies, work. Perhaps if we are willing to live with more uncertainties than our predecessors, and to accept intentions rather than beliefs, we may see our way to behaviour patterns, negotiated rather than imposed, which allow a limited harmony and a provisional agreement. In the process curators have their part, as important mediators of social knowledge and value to society at large.

We ourselves – I who write these words and you who find yourself reading them – are actors in the story. It is our better understanding, as we live our lives, of the processes of making meaning which enables us, as museum workers and visitors, to analyse the nature of our relationship to the material which comes from the past, and to perceive how it affects us, for good or ill. So tension is generated, as it is precisely for these reasons that people collect objects, museums curate and display material, people visit galleries, and we all assemble our explaining stories from what we see, experience and remember. The past and present of the museum is part of the past, present and future of us all.

Appendix: Models for Object Study

Various efforts have been made to draw the processes involved in the study of an individual object into a single scheme which can be expressed in diagrammatic form to yield a model for object study. These, it must be stressed, have been intended by the different authors to act more as guides and *aides-mémoire* than as sets of rules; they are intended to stimulate enquiry, particularly student enquiry and, at the simplest level, to ensure that obvious matters relating to objects are not overlooked. Equally, and this too needs emphasis, they are not intended to lead the interpreter to any particular conclusion, or to suggest that there are any 'proper' conclusions or that only one, or one kind of, interpretation can be placed on any given object. What is true is that each of the models reflects the museum academic discipline in which its originator was bred and each, therefore, offers a slightly different perspective on the business of object interpretation.

Six substantial models for object study are known to me, and all of these have been published. Four (at least) of these – Fleming at Winterthur (Delaware), Prown at Yale, Elliott at New Brunswick, Pearce at Leicester – arose more-or-less directly from work carried out by their authors with university graduate seminars in museum studies. Experience in these seminars shows that each model can accept a good deal of modification to bring it into a better relationship with a particular object, and that the use of one model by no means necessarily precludes the use of another. No model for specimen study has yet been produced by the museum natural history community, a gap which needs redressing. Experience at Leicester shows that a modified version of Pearce's model works reasonably well as a scheme for drawing out the significance of such a specimen in the history and philosophy of science.

The original notion that the process of interpretation could be usefully tabulated into a scheme belongs to Panofsky, who produced his important *Studies in Iconography* in 1939 and included there a model of interpretation (1939: 15, Figure App. 1.1), which involves three stages in interpretation, each backed by statements about what the act of interpretation involves, what equipment is needed and what controlling principles are at work. The model sets out Panofsky's views about how the viewer can come to an understanding of the piece, not in a narrow formal sense, but in the broader (and much more interesting) sense of its intrinsic meaning and how this helps to constitute our symbolic values and hence our social life. Panofsky was careful to create in his structure a balance between the intuitive faculty, which he calls 'synthetic intuition', and the controls, if not finally of objective understanding, at least of broadly accepted consensus, expressed in his fourth column.

OBJECT OF INTERPRETATION	ACT OF INTERPRETATION
I - *Primary* or *natural* subject matter - (A) factual, (B) expressional -, constituting the world of artistic motifs.	*Pre-iconographical description* (and pseudo-formal analysis).
II - *Secondary* or *conventional* subject matter, constituting the world of *images, stories* and *allegories*	*Iconographical analysis* in the narrower sense of the word
III - *Intrinsic meaning* or *content*, constituting the world of *'symbolical'* values.	*Iconographical interpretation* in a deeper sense (*Iconographical synthesis*).

EQUIPMENT FOR INTERPRETATION	CONTROLLING PRINCIPLE OF INTERPRETATION	
Practical experience (familiarity with *objects* and *events*).	History of *style* (insight into the manner in which, under varying historical conditions, *objects* and *events* were expressed by *forms*).	
Knowledge of literary sources (familiarity with specific *themes* and *concepts*).	History of *types* (insight into the manner in which, under varying historical conditions, specific *themes* or *concepts* were expressed by *objects* and *events*).	HISTORY OF TRADITION
Synthetic *intuition* (familiarity with the *essential tendencies of the human mind*), conditioned by personal psychology and '*Weltanschaung*'.	History of *cultural symptoms* or *'symbols'* in general (insight into the manner in which, under varying historical conditions, *essential tendencies of the human mind* were expressed by specific *themes* and *concepts*).	

Figure App. 1.1 Model for object study by Panofsky (1939)

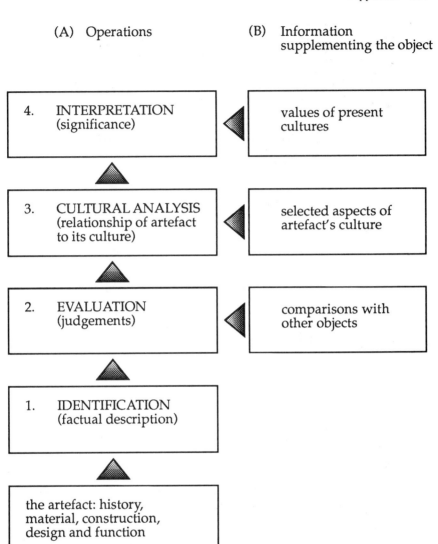

(A) Operations

(B) Information supplementing the object

4.	INTERPRETATION (significance)	values of present cultures
3.	CULTURAL ANALYSIS (relationship of artefact to its culture)	selected aspects of artefact's culture
2.	EVALUATION (judgements)	comparisons with other objects
1.	IDENTIFICATION (factual description)	

the artefact: history, material, construction, design and function

Figure App. 1.2 Model for object study by Fleming (1974)

DESCRIPTION
recording internal evidence of object itself -

    substantial analysis (physical description)
    content (representation, decoration)
    formal analysis (size, texture, shape, etc.)

DEDUCTION
interpreting interaction between object and perceiver

    sensory engagement (experience physically)
    intellectual engagement (appreciation of use, 'message')
    emotional response (subjective)

SPECULATION
forming hypotheses and questions leading from object to
external evidence for testing and resolution -

        sum up achievements so far

        creative imagining

        programme of research (as appropriate)

Figure App. 1.3 Model for object study based upon Prown (1982)

Question Categories

Analysis Procedure	Material	Construction	Function	Provenance	Value
Step 1 Observable Data (examination of the single artefact)					
Step 2 Comparative Data (comparisons made with similar artefacts)					
Step 3 Supplementary Data (other sources of information introduced)					
Step 4	Conclusions				

Figure App. 1.4 Model for object study by Elliott *et al.* (1985)

This interpretative process was developed primarily with pictures in mind, but the idea of objects constituting symbolic values is at the heart of all object and specimen interpretation, and the notion of balance between intuitive appreciation and knowledgeable understanding is at the heart of all interpretative activity.

E. McClung Fleming published his model for artefact study in 1974, writing from an applied arts perspective and in the context of the study of early American decorative arts and the discipline of American Studies (1974). His purpose was threefold: to urge that to know man we must study the things he has made; to press museum curators to think more systematically about the theoretical concepts upon which their material and its communication rest; and to provide a holistic framework that identifies the many possible approaches to the subject, so 'relating them to each other and thus suggesting the outlines of a programme of collaborative research for all who are engaged in the study of the artefact'.

Fleming drew upon the earlier work of Charles Montgomery and David Pye to develop a fivefold classification of the basic properties of every object (history, material, construction, design and function) and a set of four ascending operations (identification, evaluation, cultural analysis and interpretation) to be performed on each of these properties (Figure App. 1.2). In practice, once cultural analysis and interpretation have been reached, the separate assessment of the five basic properties becomes cumbersome and the various aspects of the object are best woven together into a single interpretative process. Fleming's distinction, in the supplementary information column, between the artefact in relationship to its own culture and in relationship to present cultures is a valuable one. A significant omission in this column is reference to the need to bring to the interpretative operation not only supplementary information about the object, but also a grip on the range of philosophical and technical ideas which inform the interpretation of material culture as whole.

Prown's paper, subtitled 'An Introduction to Material Culture Theory and Method' followed in 1982 (Prown 1982). Prown, too, worked from a background in the applied arts although, as his paper makes clear, he was well aware of theoretical developments in the fields of anthropology, sociology and linguistics. Prown's method of object analysis progresses through three stages and, as he says: 'To keep the distorting biases of the investigator's cultural perspective in check, these stages must be undertaken in sequence and kept as discrete as possible' (1982: 7). Prown did not himself express his method in tabular form, but it abstracts into such a form readily enough and a digest of his view is given in Figure App. 1.3. Like Panofsky, Prown balances the recording of evidence into the need to engage in speculation, 'creative imagining'.

The model published by Elliott (Elliott *et al.* 1985) represents the work of a graduate history seminary group, who took as their starting point the models of Fleming and Prown (Figure App. 1.4). Notions of Material, Construction, Function, Provenance and Value formed the core of the model. Here Provenance includes historical information and function, which were 'viewed as essential to determine the artefact's use and what implications, if any, were intended or unintended through that use (1985: 31). 'Value' was seen as the interpretative portion of the

1. Idea or invention

> Evolution of idea, discovery

2. Material from which it is made

> Analysis of materials

3. Making or manufacture

> Techniques and workers involved

4. Marketing

> Cost, wholesale and retail, home and abroad market

5. Art

> History of style and design

6. Use

> Function and application

Figure App. 1.5 Model for object study based upon Batchelor (1986)

model, and it was recognized that an artefact's value could be interpreted differ-ently by a range of observers. These five categories set out in the model diagram are backed up by a checklist of questions intended to help guide the examiner through the entire research process. The left-hand column creates three successive steps which serve to organize the way in which the assembled data is considered. The model is well organized, and experience has proved it to be a valuable approach to the structuring of information retrieval and interpretation.

Two models for object study appeared in Britain in 1986. Batchelor's model stemmed from his work in the Science Museum, London, and was intended to make the point that objects are capable of multifaceted interpretation. As he put it, 'We must not ignore the various and distinct significances an object can present, by giving trivial prominence to just one' (1986: 1). A digest of Batchelor's paper

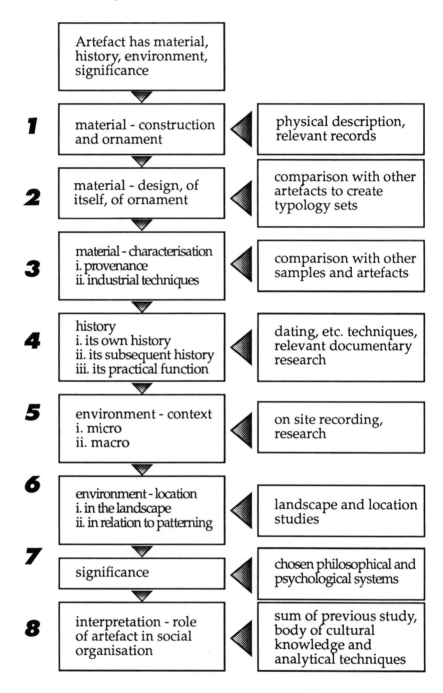

Figure App. 1.6 Model for object study by Pearce (1986a)

expressed in chart form is given in Figure App. 1.5. Pearce's model (1986) started from a discipline background in archaeology and anthropology (Figure App. 1.6). Like Fleming's, it begins with the premise that objects all have basic characteristics: a material body; a history; a place in the environment, and a cultural significance. The boxes numbered 1 to 6 express the various approaches to the gathering of the data about the object under study. At box 7 the student embarks upon an analysis of the object in the light of the data and within the framework of chosen philosophical systems (i.e. from a functionalist, structuralist, post-structuralist, etc. perspective). Box 8 represents the sum of this gathered into a final interpretation of the role of the object in social organization through time, and allows for an understanding that objects are capable of a very wide range of meanings.

Bibliography

Adler, T. 1985, 'Personal Experience and the Artifact: Musical Instruments, Tools and the Experience of Control' in Bronner 1985: 24–37.

Alexander, E. P. 1979, *Museums in Motion* American Association for State and Local History, Nashville, Tennessee.

Alexander, J. and Binski, P. (eds.) 1987, *The Age of Chivalry* Royal Academy of Arts, London.

Alsop, J. 1982, *The Rare Art Traditions: A History of Collecting and Its Linked Phenomena* Harper and Row, New York.

Ames, K. L. 1984, 'Material Culture as Nonverbal Communication: A Historical Case Study' in Mayo 1984: 25–47.

Ames, K. and Martinez, K. (eds.) 1992, *Material Culture of Gender/Gender of Material Culture* University of Michigan Research Press, Ann Arbor.

Annable, K. and Simpson, D. 1964, *Guide Catalogue of the Neolithic and Bronze Age Collections in Devizes Museum* Wiltshire Archaeological and Natural History Society, Devizes..

Appadurai, A. (ed.) 1986, *The Social Life of Things* Cambridge University Press.

Ardener, E. (ed.) 1971, *Social Anthropology and Language* Tavistock Press, London.

Aristides, N. 1988, 'Calm and Uncollected' *American Scholar* 57, 3: 327–336.

Armada 1588–1988, 1988, National Maritime Museum, London.

Arnold, D. 1985, *Ceramic Theory and Cultural Process* Cambridge University Press.

Ashmolean Museum 1986, *Patronage and Collecting in the Seventeenth Century: Earl of Arundel* Ashmolean Museum, Oxford.

Aston, M. and Burrow, I. (eds.) 1982, *The Archaeology of Somerset* Somerset County Council, Taunton.

Baekeland, F. 1988, 'Psychological Aspects of Art Collecting' *Psychiatry* 44: 45–59.

Bann, S. 1984, *The Clothing of Clio* Cambridge University Press.

Bann, S. 1988, ' "Views of the Past" – Reflections on the Treatment of Historical Objects and Museums of History (1750–1850)' in Fyfe and Law 1988: 39–64.

Barker, G. 1981, *Prehistoric Communities in Northern England* University of Sheffield.

Barnett, R., Klein, P. and Thomas, N. 1970, 'A New Gallery at Birmingham City Museum for the Pinto Collection of Treen' *Museums Journal* 70, 1: 24–8.

Barthes, R. 1977, *Image, Music, Text* Hill and Wang, New York.

Barthes, R. 1982, 'The Plates of the Encyclopedia' in *Selected Writings* Sontag, S. (ed.): 218–35, Fontana, London.

Batchelor, R. 1986, 'Not Looking at Kettles' *Museums Professionals Group News* 23: 1–3.

Baudrillard, J. 1968, *Le Système des Objets* Gallimard, Paris.

Baudrillard, J. 1975, *The Mirror of Production* Telos Press, St Louis.

Baudrillard, J. 1980, 'Forgetting Foucault' *Humanities in Society* 1980, 3: 1.

Bazin, G. 1967, *The Museum Age* trans. Jane van Nuis Cahill, Wang and Wang, New York.

Beamish, 1991, *Beamish '91: 21 Glorious Years* Beamish, Co. Durham.

Belk, R. 1988, 'Possessions and the Extended Self' *Journal of Consumer Research* 15: 139-68.

Belk, R. 1990, 'Possessions and a Sense of the Past' *Highways and Buyways*: 1-38, Association of Consumer Research, Provo, Utah.

Belk, R. and Wallendorf, M. 1992, 'Of Mice and Men: Gender Identity in Collecting' in Ames and Martinez 1992: 1-18.

Belk, R., Wallendorf, M., Sherry, J. 1989, 'The Sacred and the Profane in Consumer Behaviour: Theodicy on the Odyssey' *Journal of Consumer Research* 16: 1-38.

Belk, R., Wallendorf, M., Sherry, J., Holbrook, M. 1990, 'Collecting in a Consumer Culture' in *Highways and Buyways*: 3-95, Association for Consumer Research, Provo, Utah.

Belk, R., Wallendorf, M., Sherry, J., Holbrook, M., Roberts, S., 1988 'Collectors and Collecting' *Advances in Consumer Research* 1988, 15: 548-53.

Bellow, S. 1975, *Humbolt's Gift* Viking, New York.

Berger, J. 1972, *Ways of Seeing* BBC and Penguin Books, London.

Berlin, B., Breedlove, D. and Raven, P. 1973, 'General Principles of Classification and Nomenclature in Folk Biology' *American Anthropologist* 75: 214-42.

Besterman, T. 1991, 'The Ethics of Emasculation' *Museums Journal* September 1991: 25-8.

Binet, A. 1887, 'Le fétichisme dans l'amour' *Revue Philosophique* 24: 12-30.

Bintliff, J. (ed.) 1991, *The Annales School and Archaeology* Leicester University Press.

Biological Collections UK 1987, Report of the findings of the Museum Association Working Party on natural science collections in the United Kingdom, Museums Association, London.

Borg, A. 1991, 'Confronting Disposal' *Museums Journal* September 1991: 29-31.

Bosman, W. 1705, *Description of Guinea*, London.

Bourdieu, P. 1977, *Outline of a Theory of Practice* Cambridge University Press.

Bourdieu, P. 1984, *Distinction: A Social Critique of the Judgement of Taste* trans. R. Nice, Harvard University Press, Cambridge, Mass.

Bradley, R. 1990, *The Passage of Arms: An Archaeological Analysis of Prehistoric Hoards and Votive Deposits* Cambridge University Press.

Braudel, F. 1972, *The Mediterranean and the Mediterranean World in the Age of Philip II* trans. S. Reynolds, Collins, London.

Brears, P. 1989, 'Ralph Thoresby, a Museum Visitor in Stuart England' *Journal of History of Collections* 1, 2: 213-24.

Briggs, A. 1968, *Victorian Cities* Penguin Books, London.

Briggs, A. 1972, *Victorian People: A Reassessment of Persons and Themes 1851-67* University of Chicago Press, Chicago.

Briggs, A. 1990, *Victorian Things* Penguin Books, London.

Bronner, S. 1979, 'Concepts in the Study of Material Aspects of American Folk Culture' *Folklore Forum* 12: 133–72.

Bronner, S. 1983, 'Toward a Philosophy of Folk Objects: A Praxic Perspective' *Journal of American Culture* 6: 712–43.

Bronner, S. (ed.) 1985, *American Material Culture and Folklore: A Prologue and Dialogue* American Material Culture and Folklife Series, UMI Press, Ann Arbor.

Brooks, E. St. J. 1954, *Sir Hans Sloane* Blatchworth Press, London.

Browne, R. B. 1980, 'Introduction' in Browne (ed.) *Objects of Special Devotion: Fetishes and Fetishism in Popular Culture* Bowling Green University Popular Press, Bowling Green, Ohio.

Bryant, C. and Jary, D. (eds.) 1990, *Giddens' Theory of Structuration* Routledge, London.

Buck, L. and Dodd, P. 1991, *Relative Values, or What is Art Work?* BBC Books, London.

Burk, C. F. 1900, 'The Collecting Instinct' *Pedagogical Seminary* 7: 179–207.

Burke, P. (ed.) 1973, *A New Kind of History: From the Writings of Lucien Febvre* Routledge and Kegan Paul, London.

Bush, D. 1956, 'Mrs. Bennet and the Dark Gods: The Truth about Jane Austen' *The Sewanee Review* LXIV: 591–6.

Byatt, A. 1990, *Possession* Chatto and Windus, London.

Canfora, L. 1990, *The Vanished Library: A Wonder of the Ancient World* Helenistic Culture and Society Series, University of California Press, Berkeley.

Carey, F. 1991, *Collecting for the Twentieth Century* British Museum Press, London.

Carruthers, A. 1987, *Bias in Museums* Museum Professionals Group Transactions No. 22, 1987.

Chapman, W. 1986, 'Arranging Ethology: A. H. L. F. Pitt Rivers and the Typological Tradition' in Stocking 1986: 15–48.

Chapman, W. 1991, 'Like a Game of Dominoes: Augustus Pitt Rivers and the Typological Museum Idea' in Pearce 1991a: 135–76.

Chatwin, B. 1988, *Utz* Pan Books, London.

Chenall, R. G. 1978, *Nomenclature for Museum Cataloguing: A System for Classifying Man-Made Objects* Association for State and Local History, Nashville, Tennessee.

Chomsky, N. 1964a, 'Generative Rules' in Fodor and Katz 1964: 51–63.

Chomsky, N. 1964b, *Current Issues in Linguistic Theory* Mouton, The Hague.

Chomsky, N. 1966, *Topics in the Theory of Generative Grammar* Mouton, The Hague.

Clarke, D. 1968, *Analytical Archaeology* Methuen, London.

Clifford, J. 1988, *The Predicament of Culture: Twentieth-Century Ethnography, Literature and Art* Harvard University Press, Cambridge, Mass.

Clunas, G. 1991, *Superfluous Things: Material Culture and Social Status in Early Modern China* Polity Press, Cambridge.

Cole, H. 1884 (with Cole, A. and Cole, H.) *Fifty Years of Public Works* Vols. I and II, George Bell and Sons, London.

Collingwood, R. 1946, *The Idea of History* Oxford University Press.

Cook, B. 1977, 'The Townley Marbles in Westminster and Bloomsbury' *British Museum Yearbook* 2, 1977: 34–78.

Coxall, H. 1991, 'How Language Means: An Alternative View of Museums Text' in Kavanagh 1991 c: 83–99.

Crook, J. M. 1973, *The British Museum: A Case-Study in Architectural Politics* Pelican Books, London.

Csikszentmihalyi, M. and Rochberg-Halton, E. 1981, *The Meaning of Things: Domestic Symbols and the Self* Cambridge University Press.

D'Amico, R. 1984, 'Text and Context: Derrida and Foucault on Descartes' in Fekete 1984: 164–82.

Danet, B. and Katriel, T. 1989, 'No Two Alike: Play and Aesthetics in Collecting' *Play and Culture* 2: 253–77.

Daniel, G. 1950, *A Hundred Years of Archaeology* Duckworth, London.

Danneter, D. 1980, 'Rationality and Passion in Private Experience: Modern Consciousness and the Social World of Old-Car Collectors' *Social Problems* 27: 392–412.

Danneter, D. 1981, 'Neither Socialization nor Recruitment: the Advocational Careers of Old-Car Enthusiasts' *Social Forces* 60: 395–413.

Davies, G. (ed.) 1991, *Plaster and Marble: the Classical and Neo-Classical Portrait Bust, Journal of History of Collections* 3, 2 (whole volume).

Davies, S. 1985, 'Collecting and Recalling the Twentieth Century' *Museums Journal* 85, 1: 27–9.

Deetz, J. 1977, *In Small Things Forgotten* Doubleday Natural History Press, Garden City, New York.

Deetz, J. and Dethlefsen J. 1982, 'Death's Head, Cherub Urn and Willow' in Schlereth 1982: 195–205.

Donnington, R. 1963, *Wagner's 'Ring' and its Symbols* Faber, London.

Douglas, M. and Isherwood, B. 1979, *The World of Goods: Towards an Anthropology of Consumption* Allen Lane, London.

Duncan, C. and Wallach, A. 1980, 'The Universal Survey Museum' *Art History* 3, 4: 448–69.

Durkheim, E. 1895, *Règles de la Méthode Sociologique* Alcan, Paris.

Durost, W. 1932, *Children's Collecting Activity Related to Social Factors* Bureau of Publications, Teachers' College, Columbia University, New York.

Eagleton, T. 1983, *Literary Theory: An Introduction* Blackwell, Oxford.

Eco, U. 1990, *Foucault's Pendulum* Pan Books, London.

Eldredge, N. and Cracroft, J. 1980, *Phylogenetic Patterns and Evolutionary Process* Columbia University Press, New York.

Eliot, T. S. 1948, *Notes Towards the Definition of Culture* Faber and Faber, London.

Eliot, T. S. 1959, *Four Quartets (Burn Norton)* Faber and Faber, London.

Ellen, R. 1988, 'Fetishism' *Man* 23: 213–35.

Elliott, R. *et al.* 1985, 'Towards a Material History Methodology' *Material History Bulletin* 22, Fall: 31–40.

Ellis, L. 1985, 'On the Rudiments of Possessions and Property' *Social Science Infor-*

mation 24: 113–43.

Engels, F. 1940, *The Origin of the Family, Private Property and the State* Lawrence and Wishart, London.

Engleman, E. 1976, 'A Memoir' in *Bergasse 19: Sigmund Freud's Home and Offices, Vienna 1938. The Photographs of Edmund Engelman*: 131–43, Basic Books, New York.

Eysenck, H. 1991, *Decline and Fall of the Freudian Empire* Penguin Books, London.

Fabionski, M. 1990, 'Iconography of the Architecture of the Ideal *Musea* in the Fifteenth to Eighteenth Centuries' *Journal of History of Collections* 2, 2: 95–134.

Faris, E. G. 1972, *Nuba Personal Art* Duckworth, London.

Fekete, J. (ed.) 1984, *The Structural Allegory: Reconstructive Encounters with the New French Thought* Manchester University Press.

Fenton, J. 1983, *The Memory of War and Children in Exile, 1968–1984* Penguin Books, London.

Findlen, P. 1989, 'The Museum: its Classical Etymology and its Renaissance Genealogy' *Journal of History of Collections* 1: 59–78.

Flannery, K. V. 1972, 'The Cultural Evolution of Civilisations' *Annual Review of Ecology and Systematics* 3: 399–426.

Fleming, D. 1991, 'Changing the Disposals Culture' *Museums Journal* September 1991: 36–7.

Fleming, E. McC. 1974, 'Artefact study: a proposed model' *Winterthur Portfolio* 9: 153–61.

Fodor, J. and Katz, J. (eds.) 1964, *The Structure of Language: Readings in the Philosophy of Language* Prentice Hall, New York.

Foucault, M. 1972, *The Archaeology of Knowledge* Tavistock Press, London.

Fowler, R. 1968, *Linguistic Criticism* Opus Books, Oxford University Press.

Fraser, Sir J. 1957, *The Golden Bough* Vols. 1 and 2, Macmillan, London.

Frere, S. 1975, *Principles of Publication in Rescue Archaeology* (the Frere Report), Department of Environment, London.

Freud, S. 1977, *On Sexuality: Three Essays on the Theory of Sexuality and Other Works* Penguin Books, London.

Fromm, E. 1977, *The Anatomy of Human Destructiveness* Penguin Books, London.

Furby, L. 1978, 'Sharing: Decisions and Moral Judgements about Letting Others Use One's Possessions' *Psychological Reports* 43, 2: 595–609.

Fyfe, G. and Law, J. (eds.) 1988, *Picturing Power* Sociological Review Monograph 35, Routledge, London.

Gamwell, L. 1988, Personal Correspondence quoted in Belk *et al.* 1990, quoting Freud's comments as recorded by Otto Rank in Minutes of the *Vienna Psychoanalytic Society* 19 February 1908.

Gamwell, L. and Wells, R. (eds.) 1989, *Sigmund Freud and Art: His Personal Collection of Antiquities* State University of New York, Binghamton, New York.

Gathercole, P. 1989, 'The Fetishism of Artefacts' in Pearce 1989a: 73–81.

Gay, P. 1989, 'Introduction' in Gamwell and Wells 1989: 14–19.

Geary, P. 1986, 'Sacred Commodities: the Circulation of Medieval Relics' in Appadurai 1986: 169–91.

Geertz, C. 1973, *The Predicament of Culture* Basic Books, New York.

Gellner, E. 1974, *Legitimation of Belief* Cambridge University Press.

Gellner, E. 1982, 'What is Structuralism?' in Renfrew, C., Rowlands, M. and Segraves, B. (eds.) *Theory and Explanation in Archaeology* Academic Press, New York.

Gibson, M. and Wright, S. (eds.) 1988, *Joseph Meyer of Liverpool 1803–1886* Society of Antiquaries and National Museums and Galleries on Merseyside, London and Liverpool.

Giddens, A. 1979, *Central Problems in Social Theory: Action, Structure and Contradiction in Social Analysis* Macmillan, London.

Giddens, A. 1984, *The Constitution of Society* Polity Press, Cambridge.

Giddens, A. 1991, *Modernity and Self-Identity* Polity Press, Cambridge.

Goldberg, H. and Lewis, R. 1978, *Money Madness: The Psychology of Saving, Spending, Loving and Hating Money* New American Library, New York.

Gombrich, E. 1962, *Art and Illusion: A Study in the Psychology of Pictorial Representation* Phaidon Press, London.

Gombrich, E. 1984, *The Sense of Order: A Study in the Psychology of Decorative Art* Phaidon Press, London.

Gombrich, E. 1991, *Topics of Our Time* Phaidon Press, London.

Goode, G. B. 1891, 'The Museums of the Future' in *Annual Report of the Board of Regents of the Smithsonian Institution for the Year Ending June 30th 1889'* Government Printing Office, Washington, DC.

Gossman, E. 1975, *Frame Analysis* Penguin Books, London.

Goswamy, B. N. 1991, 'Another Past, Another Context: Exhibiting Indian Art Abroad' in Karp and Lavine 1991: 68–78.

Gould, R. A. and Schiffer, M. B. (eds.) 1981, *Modern Material Culture: the Archaeology of Us* Academic Press, New York.

Graham-Dixon, P. 1990, 'Telling a Naked Truth' *The Independent* Tuesday 27 November 1990, London.

Green, E. (ed.) 1984, *Ethics and Values in Archaeology* Macmillan Inc., New York.

Griffiths, G. 1987, 'Memory Lane: Museums and the Practice of Oral History' *Social History Curators Group J* 14: 26–8.

Grinsell, L. V. 1970, *The Archaeology of Exmoor* David and Charles, Newton Abbot.

Gutfleisch, B. and Menzhausen, J. 1989, 'How a Kunstkammer Should be Formed' *Journal of History of Collections* 1: 3–32.

Habermas, J. 1987, *The Philosophical Discourse of Modernity* trans. Lawrence, F. G., Polity Press, Cambridge.

Haggett, P. 1965, *Locational Analyses in Human Geography* Arnold, London.

Hall, S. and Gieben, B. (eds.) 1992, *Formations of Modernity* Polity Press, Cambridge, and Open University.

Hancock, E. 1980, 'One of those Dreadful Combats – a Surviving Display from William Bullock's London Museum, 1807–1818' *Museums Journal* 74, 4: 172–5.

Harland, R. 1987, *Superstructuralism* Methuen, London.

Harris, S. 1951, *John Maynard Keynes* Scribner, New York.

Harvey, D. 1989, *The Condition of Postmodernity* Blackwell, Oxford.

Haskel, F. and Penny, N. 1981, *The Most Beautiful Statues: The Taste for Antique Sculpture 1500–1900* Ashmolean Museum, Oxford.

Hawes, E. 1985, 'Artifacts, Myth and Identity in American History Museums' *International Committee for Museology Study Series* 10, 1985: 135–9.

Hawkes, T. 1977, *Structuralism and Semiotics* Methuen, London.

Haynes, P. 1975, *The Arundel Marbles* Ashmolean Museum, Oxford.

Heaney, S. 1990, *New Selected Poems 1966–1987* Faber and Faber, London.

Herrman, F. 1972, *The English as Collectors* Chatto and Windus, London.

Heseltine, A. 1990, 'Antique Amalgams' *Oxford Today* Hilary Issue, 2, 2: 34–8.

Hewison, R. 1987, *The Heritage Industry* Methuen, London.

Hill, J. N. (ed.) 1977, *The Explanation of Prehistoric Change* University of New Mexico Press, Albuquerque.

Hodder, I. (ed.) 1982a, *Symbolic and Structural Archaeology* Cambridge University Press.

Hodder, I. 1982b, *The Present Past* Batsford, London.

Hodder, I. 1982c, *Symbols in Action* Cambridge University Press.

Hodder, I. 1986, *Reading the Past* Cambridge University Press.

Hodder, I. (ed.), 1987a, *Archaeology as Long Term History* Cambridge University Press.

Hodder, I. 1987b, 'The Contribution of the Long Term' in Hodder 1987a: 1–8.

Hodder, I. (ed.) 1987c, *The Archaeology of Contextual Meanings* Cambridge University Press.

Hodder, I. (ed.) 1989, *The Meanings of Things* One World Archaeology, Unwin Hyman, London.

Hoffman, H. 1977, *Sexual and Asexual Pursuit: A Structuralist Approach to Greek Vase Painting* Royal Anthropological Institute Occasional Paper No. 34.

Holmes, M. 1953, *Personalia: Handbook for Museum Curators Part C, Section 8* Museums Association, London.

Hooper-Greenhill, E. 1989, 'The Museum in the Disciplinary Society' in Pearce 1989a: 61–72.

Hooper-Greenhill, E. 1992, *Museums and the Shaping of Knowledge* Routledge, London.

Hopkins, G. M. 1959, 'On the Origin of Beauty: a Platonic Dialogue' in House, H. and Storey, G. (eds.) *G. M. Hopkins: Journals and Papers* Oxford University Press.

Huizinga, J. 1955, *Homo Ludens* Beacon Press, Boston, Mass.

Humphrey, C. 1971, 'Some Ideas of Saussure Applied to Buryat Magical Drawings' in Ardener 1971: 21–37.

Humphrey, N. 1984, 'The Illusion of Beauty' in Humphrey, N. *Consciousness Regained*: 121–37, Oxford University Press.

Hunter, M. 1983, *Elias Ashmole and his World* Ashmolean Museum, Oxford.

Husserl, E. 1964, *The Idea of Phenomenology* Brill, The Hague.

ICOM, 1982, *International Committee for Museums and Collections of Costume*

ICOM.

Impey, O. and MacGregor, A. (eds.) 1985, *The Origins of Museums* Oxford University Press.

Ingarden, R. 1973, *The Literary Work of Art* Evanston, Illinois.

Isaac, G. 1971, 'Whither Archaeology', *Antiquity* 25: 123–9.

Iser, W. 1974, *The Implied Reader: Patterns of Communication in Prose Fiction from Bunyan to Beckett* trans C. Macksey and R. Macksey, John Hopkins Press, Baltimore.

Iser, W. 1980, 'Interaction Between Text and Reader' in Suleiman and Crossman 1980: 106–13.

Jacknis, I. 1986, 'Franz Boas and Exhibits: On the Limitations of the Museum Method of Anthropology' in Stocking 1986: 75–111.

Jackson, L. 1991, *The Poverty of Structuralism: Literature and Structuralist Theory* Longman, London.

James, M. R. 1953, *Ghost Stories of an Antiquary* Pan Books, London.

James, W. 1890, *The Principles of Psychology* Vol. I, Henry Holt, New York.

Jameson, F. 1991, *Postmodernism: or The Cultural Logic of Late Capitalism* Verso Books, London.

Jenkins, I. 1986, 'Greek and Roman Life at the BM' *Museums Journal* 82, 2: 67–9.

Johnson, S. and Beddow, T. 1986, *Collecting: The Passionate Pastime* Harper and Row, New York.

Jones, E. 1955, *The Life and Work of Sigmund Freud* Basic Books, New York.

Jones, M. 1990, *Fake? The Art of Deception* British Museum Publications, London.

Jones, M. O. 1975, *The Hand-Made Object and its Maker* University of California Press, Berkeley.

Kaeppler, A. 1979, 'Tracing and History of Hawaiian Cook Voyage Artefacts in the Museum of Mankind' *British Museum Yearbook* 3: 167–86.

Karp, I. and Lavine, D. (eds.) 1991, *Exhibiting Cultures: the Poetics and Politics of Museum Display* Smithsonian Institution Press, Washington.

Kavanagh, G. 1990, *History Curatorship* Leicester University Press.

Kavanagh, G. 1991a, *The Museums Profession: Internal and External Relations* Leicester University Press.

Kavanagh, G. 1991b, 'The Museums Profession and the Articulation of Professional Self-consciousness' in Kavanagh 1991a: 37–55.

Kavanagh, G. (ed.) 1991c, *Museum Languages: Objects and Texts* Leicester University Press.

Keene, S. (ed.) 1980, *Conservation, Archaeology and Museums* Occasional Papers Number 1, United Kingdom Institute for Conservation.

King, E. 1985-6, 'The Cream of the Dross: Collecting Glasgow's Present for the Future' *Social History Curators Group Journal* 13: 4–11.

King, E. 1990, 'Collecting for Cultural Identity' *Museums Journal* December 1990: 25–8.

Kingery, D. and Lubar, S. (eds.) 1992, *History from Things* Smithsonian Institution Press, Washington.

Kipling, R. 1990, *Gunga Din and Other Favorite Poems* Dover, New York.

Klein, M. 1977, 'The Importance of Symbol Formation in the Development of the

Ego' in *Love, Guilt and Reparation and Other Works 1921–1945*: 219–32, Dell Publishing, New York.

Kraft-Ebbing R. 1894, *Psychopathia Sexualis* trans C. Chaddock, F. A. Davis, Philadelphia.

Kristeva, J. 1980, *Desire in Language*, Chicago University Press.

Kuhn, T. 1970, *The Structure of Scientific Revolutions* 2nd edition, Chicago University Press.

Laclau, E. and Mouffe, C. 1987, 'Post-Marxism without Apologies' *New Left Review* 1987, 166: 79–106.

Ladurie Le, R. 1979, 'The "Event" and the "Long Term" in Social History: the Case of the Chouan Uprising' in *The Territory of the Historian*: 111–31, Ladurie Le Roy, Harvester Press, Brighton.

LaFontaine, J. S. 1972, *The Interpretation of Ritual* Tavistock Publications, London.

Leach, E. 1972, 'The Structure of Symbolism' in LaFontaine 1972: 239–75.

Leach, E. 1976, *Culture and Communication* Cambridge University Press.

Leach, E. 1977, 'A View from the Bridge' in Spriggs 1977: 170–73.

Leach, E. 1982, *Social Anthropology* Fontana, London.

Leone, M. 1982, 'Methods as Message: Interpreting the Past with the Public' *Museum News* 62, 1: 35–41.

Lively, P. 1979, *The Treasures of Time* William Heinemann, London.

Lockhart, J. 1900, *Memoires of Sir Walter Scott* Vols. I–III, English Classics Edition, London.

Lord, B., Lord, G. and Nicks, J. 1989, *The Cost of Collecting: Collection Management in UK Museums* Office of Arts and Libraries, HMSO, London.

Lowenthal, D. 1985, *The Past is a Foreign Country* Cambridge University Press.

Lowenthal, D. 1987, 'Bias: Making the Most of an Incurable Malady' in Carruthers 1987: 32–5.

Ludwig, A. 1966, *Graven Images, New England Stone Carving and its Symbols 1650–1815* Harvard University Press, Cambridge, Mass.

Lyons, J. 1977, *Semantics* Cambridge University Press.

MacGregor, A. (ed.) 1983, *Tradescant's Rarities* Oxford University Press.

Malinowski, B. 1922, *Argonauts of the Western Pacific* Routledge, London.

Marwick, A. 1990, *British Society Since 1945* Penguin Books, London.

Marx, K. 1971, *Capital: A Critique of the Political Economy* trans. S. Moore and E. Aveling, Progress Publishers, Moscow.

Marx, K. and Engels, F. 1970, *The German Ideology* Lawrence and Wishart, London.

Matarasso, P. (trans.) 1969, *The Quest of the Holy Grail* Penguin Books, London.

Mayo, E. (ed.) 1984a, *American Material Culture: The Shape of Things Around Us* Bowling Green University Popular Press, Bowling Green, Ohio.

Mayo, E. 1984b, 'Contemporary Collecting' *History News* 39, 2: 8–11.

McCarthy, E. 1984, 'Towards a Sociology of the Physical World: George Herbert Mead on Physical Objects' *Studies in Symbolic Interaction* 5: 105–21.

McClelland, D. 1951, *Personality* Holt, Reinhart and Winston, New York.

McGhee, R. 1977, 'Ivory for the Sea Woman: The Symbolic Attributes of a Prehistoric Technology' *Canadian Journal of Archaeology* 1: 141–9.

McManus, P. 1991, 'The Crisis in Representation in Museums: the Exhibition "The Spirit Sings", Glenbow Museum, Calgary, Canada' in Pearce 1991a: 202–6.

McManus, P. 1988, 'Its the Company you Keep . . . the Social Determination of Learning-related Behaviour in a Science Museum' *International Journal of Museum Management and Curatorship* 6: 263–70, 7: 37–44.

McManus, P. 1991, 'Making Sense of Exhibits' in Kavanagh 1991c: 33–46.

Mears, K. 1986, *The Crown Jewels* Department of the Environment, London.

Meltzer, D. J. 1981, 'Ideology and Material Culture' in Gould and Schiffer 1981: 113–25.

Merriman, N. 1991, *Beyond the Glass Case: the Past, the Heritage and the Public in Britain* Leicester University Press.

Miles, R. 1986, ' "Lessons in Human Biology": Testing a Theory of Exhibit Design' *International Journal of Museum Management and Curatorship* 5: 227–40.

Miller, D. 1985, *Artefacts as Categories* Cambridge University Press.

Miller, D. 1987, *Material Culture and Mass Consumption* Blackwell, Oxford.

Monte, C. F. 1977, *Beneath the Mask: An Introduction to Theories of Personality* Holt, Reinhart and Winston, London.

Moore, B. 1975, *The Great Victorian Collection* Paladin Books, London.

Morgan, J. (ed.) 1986, *A National Plan for Systematic Collections?* National Museum of Wales, Cardiff.

Moulin, R. 1987, *The French Art Market: A Sociological View* trans. A. Goldhammer, Rutgers University Press, New Brunswick.

Mullen, C. 1991, 'The People's Show' *Visual Sociology Review* 6, 1: 47–9.

Museum Acquisitions 1941, 'Extract from Probate of Will: Florence Emily Hardy' *Proceedings of Dorset Natural History and Archaeological Society* 62: 32–3.

Museums Association 1991, 'Code of Conduct for Museum Curators' in *Museums Yearbook*: 13–20, Museums Association, London.

Museum of Classical Archaeology, Cambridge 1986, *Catalogue of Casts*, Cambridge.

Murdoch, J. 1992, 'Defining Curation' *Museums Journal* March 1992, 18–19.

Mysteries of Diana: the Antiquities from Nemi at Nottingham Castle Museum 1983, Castle Museum, Nottingham.

Nash, O. 1972, *The Old Dog Barks Backward* Faber, London.

Norman, A. V. M. 1963, 'Arms and Armour at Abbotsford' *Apollo* 76: 525–9.

Olmsted, A. D. 1988, 'Morally Controversial Leisure: the Social World of Gun Curators' *Symbolic Interaction* II (2): 277–87, JAI Press.

Orel, H. 1976, *The Final Years of Thomas Hardy 1912–1928* Macmillan, London.

Orna, E. 1987, *Information Policies for Museums* Museum Documentation Association, Cambridge.

Panofsky, I. 1939, *Studies in Iconography* Reinhart and Winston, New York.

Paper, J. 1987, 'Cosmological Implications of the Pan-Indian Sacred Pipe Ritual' *Canadian Journal of Native Studies* 7, 2: 297–306.

Pearce, S. 1983, *Bronze Age Metalwork of South Western Britain* British Archaeological Reports 120, (i), (ii), Oxford.

Pearce, S. 1986a, 'Thinking About Things: Approaches to the Study of Artefacts' *Museums Journal* 82, 2: 198–201.

Pearce, S. 1986b, 'Objects as Signs and Symbols' *Museums Journal* 86, 3: 131–5.

Pearce, S. 1987a, 'Ivory, Antler, Feather and Wood: Material Culture and Cosmology of the Cumberland Sound Inuit, Baffin Island, Canada' *Canadian Journal of Native Study* 7, 2: 307–21.

Pearce, S. 1987b, 'Objects in Structures' *Museums Journal* 86, 4: 178–81.

Pearce, S. (ed.) 1989a, *Museum Studies in Material Culture* Leicester University Press.

Pearce, S. 1989b, 'Objects in Structures' in Pearce 1989a: 47–60.

Pearce, S. 1990a, *Archaeological Curatorship* Leicester University Press.

Pearce, S. (ed.) 1990b, *Objects of Knowledge* Vol. I, New Research in Museum Studies, Athlone Press, London.

Pearce, S. (ed.) 1991a, *Museum Economics and the Community* Vol. 2, New Research in Museum Studies, Athlone, London.

Pearce, S. 1991b, 'Collecting Reconsidered' in Kavanagh 1991c: 135–54.

Peckham, M. 1967, *Man's Rage for Chaos: Biology, Behaviour and the Arts* Schocken, New York.

Peponis, J. and Hesdin, J. 1982, 'The Lay-out of Theories in the Natural History Museum' *9H* 2, 3: 21–5.

Philips, P. (ed.) 1985, *The Archaeologist and the Laboratory* Council for British Archaeology Research Report 5, London.

Pierpoint, S. 1981, 'Land, Settlement and Society in the Yorkshire Bronze Age' in Barker 1981: 41–55.

Pocius, G. (ed.) 1991, *Living in a Material World: Canadian and American Approaches to Material Culture* Institute of Social and Economic Research, Memorial University, St John's, Newfoundland.

Pomian, K. 1990, *Collectors and Curiosities: Paris and Venice, 1500–1800* trans. Elizabeth Wiles-Portier, Polity Press, Cambridge.

Popper, K. 1979, *Objective Knowledge: An Evolutionary Approach* (revised edition), Oxford University Press.

Preeble, J. 1967, *Culloden* Penguin Books, London.

Prelinger, E. 1959, 'Extension and Structure of Self' *Journal of Psychology* 47: 13–23.

Price, D. 1989, 'John Woodward and a Surviving British Geological Collection of the early Eighteenth Century' *Journal of History of Collections* 1: 79–85.

Prown, J. 1982, 'Mind in Matter: an Introduction to Material Culture Theory and Method' *Winterthur Portfolio* 17, 1: 1–19.

Pyrah, B. 1988, *The History of the Yorkshire Museum and its Geological Collections* North Yorkshire County Council, York.

Radcliffe-Brown, A. R. 1922, *The Andaman Islanders* Cambridge University Press.

Rahtz, P. 1982, 'The Dark Ages' in Aston and Burrow 1982: 98–107.

RCHME 1986, *Thesaurus of Archaeological Terms* Royal Commission on the Historic Monuments of England, London.

Rebora, C. 1991, 'Curator's Closet' *Museum News* July/August 1991: 50–54.

Rees, A. and Borzello, F. (eds.) 1986, *The New Art History* Camden Press, London.

Renfrew, C. 1972, *Emergence of Civilisation: The Cyclades and the Aegean in the Third Millennium BC* Jonathon Cape, London.

Rheims, M. 1961, *Art on the Market: Thirty-Five Centuries of Collecting and Collectors from Midas to Paul Getty* trans. David Pryce-Jones, Weidenfeld and Nicolson, London.

Rheims, M. 1980, *The Glorious Obsession* trans. P. Evans, Souvenir Press, London.

Riegl, A. 1982, 'The Modern Cult of Monuments: Its Character and Its Origin' trans. K. Forster and D. Ghirardo, *Oppositions* 25, New York.

Rigby, D. and Rigby, E. 1949, *Lock, Stock and Barrel: The Story of Collecting* J. B. Lippincott, Philadelphia, PA.

Rochberg-Halton, E. 1984, 'Objects Relations, Role Models, and the Cultivation of the Self' *Environment and Behaviour* 16, 3: 335–68.

ROM 1976, *Communicating with the Museum Visitor: Guidelines for Planning* Royal Ontario Museum, Toronto, Canada.

Ross, H. 1974, *Biological Systematics* Addison Wesley, New York.

Royal Academy, 1987, *Age of Chivalry – Exhibition Booklet* Royal Academy of Arts, London.

Sackett, J. 1985, 'Style and Ethnicity in the Kalahari: a Reply to Wiessner' *American Antiquity* 50: 154–60.

Saisselin, R. G. 1984, *Bricobracomania: the Bourgeois and the Bibelot* Rutgers University Press, New Brunswick.

Sartre, J.-P. 1943, *Being and Nothingness: A Phenomenological Essay on Ontology* Philosophical Library, New York.

Saussure, F. de, 1974, *Course in General Linguistics* trans. Bashim Wade, Fontana, London.

Schepelern, H. D. 1990, 'The Museum Wormianum Reconstructed: A Note on the Illustration of 1655' *Journal of History of Collections* 2, 1: 81–6.

Schlereth, T. (ed.) 1982, *Material Culture Studies in America* American Association for State and Local History, Nashville, Tennessee.

Schultz, E. 1990, 'Notes on the History of Collecting and of Museums in the Light of Selected Literature of the Sixteenth to the Eighteenth Century' *Journal of History of Collections* 2, 2: 205–18.

Scott, Sir W. 1972, *Waverley; or, 'Tis Sixty Years Since* Penguin Books, London.

Shanks, M. and Tilley, C. 1987a, *Re-Constructing Archaeology* Cambridge University Press.

Shanks, M. and Tilley, C. 1987b, *Social Theory and Archaeology* Polity Press, Cambridge.

Shelton, 1990, 'In the Lair of the Monkey: Notes Towards a Post-Modernist Museography' in Pearce 1990b: 78–102.

SHIC, 1983, *Social History and Industrial Classification: A Subject Classification for Museum Collections* SHIC Working Party, Centre for English Cultural Tradition and Language, University of Sheffield.

Silverstone, R. 1981, *The Message of Television: Myth and Narrative in Contemporary Culture* Heinemann, London.

Simmel, G. 1978, *The Philosophy of Money* Routledge and Kegan Paul, London.

Sinclair, T. 1987, ' "All styles are good, save the tiresome kind". An Examination of the Pattern of Stylistic Changes Occurring among Silver Candlesticks of the

Eighteenth Century (1680–1780)' in Hodder 1987c: 39–54.

Sisson, C. 1974, 'What a Piece of Work is Man' in *In the Trojan Ditch*, Carcarnet Press, London.

Snodgrass, A. 1980, *Archaic Greece* Dent and Sons, London.

Sokal, R. R. and Sneath, P. 1963, *Principles of Numerical Taxonomy* Freeman, New York.

Sontag, S. 1979, *On Photography* Penguin Books, London.

Sorsby, B. and Horne, S. 1980, 'The Readability of Museum Labels' *Museums Journal* 80, 3: 157–9.

Spector, J. 1975, 'Dr Sigmund Freud, Art Collector' *Art News* 1975, April: 20–26.

Spencer, F. 1990, *Piltdown: A Scientific Forgery* Oxford University Press.

Spriggs, M. (ed.) 1977, *Archaeology and Anthropology: Areas of Mutual Interest* BAR Supplementary Series 19, British Archaeological Reports, Oxford.

Stevens, C. 1980, *Classification of Objects in the Welsh Folk Museum Collection* Welsh Folk Museum, Cardiff.

Stevens, P. and Brown, M. 1978, 'The Somerset Rural Life Museum' *Museums Journal* 78, 1: 24–5.

Stewart, S. 1984, *On Longing: Narratives of the Miniature, the Gigantic, the Souvenir, the Collection* Johns Hopkins Press, Baltimore.

Stocking, G. W. 1974, *The Shaping of American Anthropology 1883–1911* Macmillan Inc., New York.

Stocking, G. (ed.) 1986, *Objects and Others: Essays on Museums and Material Culture* History of Anthropology Vol. III, University of Wisconsin Press.

Stokes, A. 1978, *The Critical Writings of Adrian Stokes* Vol. III, Thames and Hudson, London.

Suleiman, S. and Crossman, I. (eds.) 1980, *The Reader in the Text* Princeton University Press, Princeton, New Jersey.

Sullivan, S. 1976, 'Friends and Critics 1840–1928' in Drabble, M. (ed.) *The Genius of Thomas Hardy*: 32–47, Weidenfeld and Nicholson, London.

Taborsky, E. 1983, 'The "Syntax" and the Museum' *Récherches Semiotiques/ Semiotic Enquiry* 3, 4: 363–74.

Thompson, E. P. 1968, *The Making of the English Working Class* Penguin Books, London.

Thompson, M. 1979, *Rubbish Theory: the Creation and Destruction of Value* Oxford University Press.

Tolkien, C. (ed.) 1960, *The Saga of King Heidrek the Wise* Thomas Nelson and Sons Ltd., London.

Tolkien, J. R. 1968, *The Lord of the Rings* Allen and Unwin, London.

Tomasson, K. and Buist, F. 1962, *Battles of the '45* British Battles Series, Batsford, London.

Tradescant, J. 1656, *Museum Tradescantianum: or A Collection of Rarities, Preserved at South-Lambeth near London* Grismond, London.

Trevelyan, V. and Davies, J. 1987, 'The V. and A. Grant Fund' *Museums Journal* 87, 3: 159–65.

Trollope, A. 1985, *Orley Farm* World's Classics, Oxford University Press.

Tuan, Y. 1988, *Dominance and Affection* Yale University Press, New Haven.

Turner, V. 1977, *The Ritual Process* Penguin Books, London.

Ucko, P. J. 1969, 'Penis Sheaths: a Comparative Study' *Procs. Royal Anthropological Institute* 2: 27–67.

Unruh, D. 1983, 'Death and Personal History: Strategies of Identity Preservation' *Social Problems* 30, 3: 340–51.

Veblen, T. 1899, *The Theory of the Leisure Class* Macmillan, New York.

von Holst, N. 1967, *Creators, Collectors and Connoisseurs: An Anatomy of Artistic Taste from Antiquity to the Present Day* G. P. Putnam, New York.

Wainwright, C. 1989, *The Romantic Interior: the British Collector at Home 1750–1850* Paul Mellon Centre for Studies in British Art, Yale University Press, New Haven.

Waldstein, C. 1889, *Catalogue of Casts* Museum of Classical Archaeology, Cambridge.

Walker, M. 1991, 'How the West was Won, or was it?' *Review Guardian* Thursday 13 June 1991.

Walsh, K. 1992, *The Representation of the Past: Museums and Heritage in the Post-Modern World* Routledge, London.

Waterston, C. D. 1976, ' "Evolution" and "Minerals" at the Royal Scottish Museum' *Museums Journal* 76, 1: 11–13.

Watson, W. 1973, *The Genius of China* Times Newspapers Ltd., London.

Watts, A. 1954, *Myth and Ritual in Christianity* Thames and Hudson, London.

Weissner, 1985, 'Style or Isochrestic Variation? A Reply to Sackett?' *American Antiquity* 50: 160–66.

Wernick, A. 1984, 'Structuralism and the Dislocation of the French Rationalist Project' in Fekete 1984: 130–49.

Whitley, M. T. 1929, 'Children's Interest in Collecting' *Journal of Educational Psychology* 20: 249–61.

Wierzbicla, A. 1985, *Lexicography and Conceptual Analysis* Karoma, Ann Arbor, Michigan.

Wilks, T. 1989, 'The Picture Collection of Robert Carr, Earl of Somerset (c. 1587–1645) Reconsidered' *Journal of History of Collections* 1, 2: 167–77.

Wilson, E. and Taylor, L. 1989, *Through the Looking Glass* BBC Books, London.

Winnicott, D. W. 1974, *Playing and Reality* Penguin Books, London.

Witty, P. 1931, 'Sex Differences: Collecting Interests' *Journal of Educational Psychology* 22: 221–8.

Woolf, V. 1978, *Between the Acts* Granada Publishing, London.

Wright, E. 1985, 'Modern psychoanalytic criticism' in *Modern Literary Theory* (eds.) Jepherson, A. and David, R.: 113–33, Batsford, London.

Wylie, M. A. 1982, 'Epistemological Issues Raised by a Structuralist Archaeology' in Hodder 1982a, 39–46.

Yamaguchi, M. 1991, 'The Poetics of Exhibition in Japanese Culture' in Karp and Lavine 1991: 57–67.

Index

accessioning:
  of objects 128–9
  see also collection management
accumulating 49, 56
  see also collecting process
acquisition policies 136
  see also collection management
activating stimulus 59, 60
Adler, Thomas 212–13
advertising 174–5
  posters 245–9, 250–2, 254
aesthetics 52–3
  and functional analysis 150
  and structuralist analysis 188–9
amateurs 92
American Museum of Natural History, Washington
    112, 113
Ames, K L 56
animal trophies 69–71
animation 41–3
Annales historians 211, 222–4
anthropological material 38–41
  see also museum collections
anthropology 145–6, 159, 171–2, 195
antiquarian collections 92, 94, 100, 103, 193–4
  see also museum collections
Antiques Roadshow 76
anxiety 167
Appadurai, A 236
archaeological material 8, 44, 49, 103, 135
  see also museum collections
archaeology 87, 124, 195
  New Archaeologists 146
architecture 67, 96–8, 107
archives see museum archives
Aristides, N 48
art collections 92–4, 99–100, 202–3, 208–9, 263
  classical sculpture 92, 94, 100, 103
  and power politics 100, 201–2, 234, 235–8
art history 100, 101, 109
artefacts 4–6
  see also objects
artificial objects 95, 97, 99, 103–5
Ashmole, Elias, 74, 92
Ashmolean Museum, Oxford 94, 96, 97–8, 107
auction houses 51, 149, 150, 237
authentification 121, 237
  fakes 237

Bacon, Francis 95–6
Baekeland, F 52
Bann, S 194
Barbie dolls 62–3
Bartlet School of Architecture and Planning,
    London University 137
Barthes, Roland 12, 26–7, 38, 168, 231, 255
Batchelor, R 271, 273
Bateman, Thomas 103
Baudrillard, J 49, 231, 232
beauty:
  concept of 52–3
  see also aesthetics
Becket reliquary 224–6
behavioural analysis 212–17
Being and Nothingness (Sartre) 56
Belk, Russell 9, 45, 49, 61–3, 65
Belvedere Palace, Vienna 99, 101
bequests see donated collections
Berger, J 235
Berlin, B 124
Bevan, William 149–50
binary classification 123–7, 171–2, 180, 205–6
  see also classification
Bintliff, J 223–4
Binyon, Laurence 71–2
Boas, Franz 8, 111–12, 113, 145
the body 56–9, 174, 175
  freaks 57, 59
Bourdieu, P 50, 52, 232, 233, 235, 236
  Outline of a Theory of Practice 236
Braudel, Fernand 211, 222–4, 226, 227
the breast 46
Briggs, Asa:
  Victorian Things 195–6
Bristol Museum 108
British Museum, London 101, 105, 107, 112,
    114, 203, 245–6, 248
Bronner, S 216–17
Bronze Age material 126–7, 150–1, 152
Browne, R B 45
Bullock, William 103, 110
Bumpus, Herman 113
burials 150–1, 152
Burrell Collection, Glasgow 224, 225
Bush, D 182–3

cabinets of curiosities 75–6, 90–8

Calvert, John 103
candlesticks 132, 133
Das Capital (Marx) 83
capitalism 83, 235–8, 242
Carey, F 114
Carnegie Museum, Melton Mowbray 59
cars 45
cases 105, 106, 107
  see also museum displays
catalogues:
  of exhibitions 253
  of objects 95, 96, 99
cattle 180, 182–4
Childe, Gordon 8, 195
china objects 185–6, 217–20
Chomsky, N 232
Christies 149, 150
churches 91
Clarke, David 153–4
classical sculpture 92, 94, 100, 103
  see also art collections
classification:
  binary 123–7, 171–2, 180, 205–6
  of museum collections 85, 87–8, 101, 103,
    105, 109–10, 119–20, 122–31
  of private collections 48, 50, 95, 99
  systematic collecting 84–8
  taxonomical linguistics 124–7
  taxonomy 84, 123–4, 125, 127
  terminology thesauri 129–31
  Three Age system 103, 105
  type classification 48, 50, 85, 87–8, 99, 109
  see also collection management
clothes 214–16
  language of 166–73
  school uniforms 151, 153
cognitive processes 38–9, 42
Cole, Henry 3–4
collectables 75–81, 114
collecting process 36–66, 90–1, 94–6
  completion of 54–5
  definitions 48–50
  and disposal 65–6
  to extend the self 55–63
  and gender 59–63, 64, 82
  hoarding 49
  as identity preservation 63–6
  prehistory 90–1
  private collections 7, 8, 48–66
  psychology of 45–55
  reasons for 36–47, 49–50
  romantic concepts of 69, 72–3
  see also objects and artefacts
collection disciplines *see* classification
collection management 9, 10, 118–43
  accessioning 128–9, 134
  acquisition policies 136
  displays 29, 87, 96–8, 105–17, 155–61, 192–209,
    245
  disposal policies 34–5, 136

documentation 121, 122, 136
  exhibition catalogues 253
  exhibitions 136–43, 141–5
  ideology of 241
  labels 249, 253
  museum archives 120–2, 135
  organization of objects 41, 78, 87, 96–8, 101
  professional practice 122
  provenance 121, 134, 269, 270
  research 124, 131–4
  resource expenditure 135–6
  storage 121–2
  see also classification
    museum collections
collection policies 134–6, 239–41
collections *see* museum collections
  private collections
Collingwood, R G 259, 260–1, 262, 264
commodities 83
  see also objects and artefacts
communication systems 167, 168, 177, 180, 211
  see also language
community involvement 78, 113
comparative sociology 145–6
competition:
  between collectors 51
consensus 185–6
conservation:
  of objects and artefacts 99, 121
conservation projects 69
contemporary collecting 75, 109–17
contest *see* competition
contextual displays 110–17
  see also museum displays
*Convention on the means of prohibiting . . . illicit
    import . . . cultural property* (UNESCO) 150
Cook, James 103, 104, 134
copies:
  of objects and artefacts 24
coronations 197–8
costumes *see* clothes
Coxall, H 249
craftmanship 33
creation myths 19–20
critical tradition 7–14
Crown Jewels (England) 197–8
Culloden, Battle of (1746) 24, 26, 27, 28, 30
cultural development:
  material culture 5–6, 8–9, 17–21, 85–6, 131,
    144–65, 169, 195
  and museums 2–4, 8
  national 201–2
cultural institutions 146–7
  see also sociology
curatorial process *see* collection management
  curators 87, 118–19, 234–5
curiosities 75–6, 90–8, 103
Czikszentmihalyi, M 56

dairy farming 180, 182–4, 190

Danet, B 51–2, 53, 54
Danish National Museum 103
Dark Ages 162–3
Darwinian theory 85, 103, 105
Davies, J 238
de-accessioning *see* disposal
death 59
decorations *see* medals
Deetz, James 5
departure from the norm:
    of objects 85
Descartes, Rene 12, 21, 232–3
Dictionnaire Universale (Furetière) 92
diffusionist theory 85
dioramas 110
    see also museum displays
displays *see* museum displays
disposal:
    of museum collections 34–5, 136
documentation 121, 122, 136
    see also collection management
donated collections 65–6, 121
    see also museum collections
Donnington, Robert 47
Dorset County Museum 198–201
Douglas, M 34
Dresden Gallery 99, 109
Duncan, C 108
Dundee Museum 108
durables 34–5
    see also objects
Durkheim, Emile:
    Règles de la Methode . . . 145
Durost, W 48, 49

Eagleton, Terry:
    Literary Theory . . . 81
ecological adaption 146, 147, 149, 153
    see also sociology
economic power 236–7
    see also power politics
economic subsystems 154–5, 157–8, 161, 190
    see also sociology
Edmonds of Birmingham 105
A Edwards and Co, Birmingham 106, 107, 111
Egyptian mummies *see* mummies
Egyptian Museum, Liverpool 83
elephant relics 65
Ellen, R 38–9, 41, 82, 85
Elliott, R 265, 270–1
Ellis, L 55
Engelman, Edmund 73
English Heritage 207
erotic art 244–5
essence:
    concept of 212, 227
ethnographic material 103, 104, 111–12
    see also museum collections
Evelyn, John 94–5
Evolution of Culture (Rivers) 86

Exeter City Museum 69–70, 108
exhibition catalogues 253
exhibition morphology 137, 139
exhibitions 136–43, 141–5, 147
    performance theory 139, 141–3, 212–13
    see also museum displays
experience:
    and stimulus 59, 60

factor analysis 150–1
fakes 237
family collections 63, 65
fashion 214–16
    see also clothes
feiticos 82
fetish objects 73–84, 149
    see also objects
fetishism 38–9, 41
Fiennes, Celia 101
Findlen, P 93
Fire Museum 61–2, 63
Fitzwilliam Museum, Cambridge 217, 218
Flannery, K 159
Fleming, E McCluny 265, 267
Flower, William 110
Ford, Henry 207–8
form 131–2
Foucault, Michel 229, 231, 232
Fowler, Roger:
    Linguistic Criticism 249
Frame Analysis (Gossman) 23–4
frames of reference 23–4
freaks 57, 59
Frere Report (1975) 120
Freud, Sigmund 59, 73–4, 82
Fromm, E 59
functional analysis 113
    and aesthetics 150
    and meaning 144–65
    and museum displays 155–61
    neo-functionalism 151, 153–5
    and social change 158–9
    systematic 146, 159
Furetière, Antoine:
    Dictionnaire Universale 92

galleries 92–3
    see also museums
garbage *see* rubbish
Gathercole, Peter 82
Gay, Peter 73
Geary, P 198
Geffrye Museum, London 249, 253
Gellner, Erneset 185, 232–3
gender:
    and collecting process 59–63, 64, 82
gender images 62–3, 64
geological collections 101, 102
    see also museum collections
George Medal 149–50

giants 57
Giddens, Anthony 221–3, 227
Glenbow Museum, Calgary 241
Glyptothek, Munich 99
von Goethe, Johann Wolfgang 109
gold 33
Goldberg, H 56
Gombrich, E 53–4, 220, 240, 261, 262
    The Sense of Order 23
Gossman, E:
    Frame Analysis 23–4
grave goods *see* treasures
graves *see* burials
gravestones 213–14
    see also monuments
Greenfield village, Dearborn, Michigan 207–8
gun collecting 61

habitat groups 110
    see also museum displays
Hampshire County Museum Service 247, 248
Hancock Museum, Newcastle 69
Hardy, Florence 200
Hardy, Thomas 198–201
Harland, R 231
Harris Free Library, Museum and Art Gallery,
    Preston 107, 108
Harvey, D 230
Hawes, Edward 202
Hazelius, Artur 110
Hegel, G W F 12, 69, 87–8, 211
heirlooms 63, 65
herbaria 135
Hereford Cathedral 236
heritage movement 11, 201–8, 230
Hermitage Museum, St Petersburg 99
Herrmann, Frank 7
Hill, J N 149
historical knowledge 260–1
historical past:
    meaning of 192–209
    narratives of 203–9
    object based 195–202
    reconstructions of 207–9, 245
historical process 222–4
hoarding 49
    see also collection process
hoards *see* treasures
Hodder, Ian 8, 174
Hoffman, H 188
homeostasis 153, 159
    see also sociology
Hooper-Greenhill, E 234
Horne, S 249
houses 173–7
Howard, Thomas *Earl of Arundel* 74, 94
Hughes, Terence 167
Humphrey, N 53, 59
human body *see* the body
humour 75

hunting 69–71
hunting trophies *see* trophies
Husserl, Edmund 211–12, 213, 227

icons 202–3
    see also objects
identification *see* classification
ideology 241
    see also religious subsystems
immortality:
    through collecting 63–6
Impey, Oliver 7
Indian life 178, 241
individual adjustment 147, 149–50
    see also sociology
Industrial Revolution 196, 238
information systems 167–8
    historical narratives 203–9
    message sets 170–1, 180
    see also language
institutional development 157–8
    see also sociology
interpretation 217–20, 255
    see also meaning
Inuit life 147–9, 179
Iser, Wolfgang 211, 218–19, 220
Isherwood, B 34

James, M R 45
James, William 55
Jameson, F 230
Jenkins, I 112
Jenkinson, Peter 78
Jesup, Morris 113
Jobst, Helga 73
Jones, Ernest 73
Jones, M O 212
Journal of the History of Collections 7
Judaeo-Christian tradition 2–3, 18–19

Kaltemarcht, Gabriel 93
Katriel, T 51–2, 53, 54
Kavanagh, G 122
kayaks 147–9
Kingery, D 8
Klein, Melanie 45–6
knowledge 116–17
    historical 260–1
    legitimacy of 234–5
    objective 258–62
    and power politics 231, 234–5
Konkretisation 218–19
Kristeva, Julia 46
Kuhn, T 116, 262
Kunstkammer see galleries

labels 249, 253
Ladurie, Le Roy 223
Laing, R D 217–18
Lambert, Daniel 57–8

Lancashire County Museums 203
language 22–3
　communication systems 167, 168, 177, 180, 211
　information systems 167–8, 180
　semiotics 26–9, 30, 38–9, 141–3, 168–71, 174
　vocabulary 169–70, 180
　langue 26, 27, 168–9, 170, 171, 174
　see also semiotics
Leach, Edmund 12, 27, 28, 71, 145, 174, 182, 184
Leicester University 82
Leicestershire Museum Service 69, 72, 216
leisure industry 230
Levi-Strauss, Claude 171
Lewes Museum 108
Lewis, R 56
libraries 99, 101
life-spans:
　of objects 16–17, 24–30
Linguistic Criticism (Fowler) 249
Linnaeus, Carl 101, 123, 125, 127
Literary Theory . . . (Eagleton) 81
locational relationships 16
Lord of the Rings (Tolkien) 43, 44
the Louvre, Paris 100, 101
Lowenthal, D 116–17
Lubar, S 8
Luce, Richard 237–8
Ludwig, A 213–14
Lyell, Charles:
　Principles of Geology 103

Macdonald of Keppoch, Alistair 24–30
MacGregor, Arthur 7
McManus, P 249
magic *see* talismanic objects
magpies 30–1, 32
Making of the English Working Class (Thompson) 196
Malinowski, B 145, 146, 197
Manchester City Art Gallery and Museum 107, 263
Manchester University Museum 111
Marx, Karl:
　Das Capital 83
Marxism 228–9, 230–1, 253, 255
material culture 5–6, 8–9, 17–21, 85–6, 131, 169, 195
　functionalist theory 144–65
　see also cultural development
material culture subsystems 154–5, 157–8, 161, 190
　see also sociology
material things *see* objects
materiality 146
　of objects 17–21, 139, 141
Mayer, Joseph 74, 81, 83
Mayo, E 115

meaning:
　definition of 259–62
　and functional analysis 144–65
　of historical past 192–209
　interpretation 217–20, 255
　and structuralist analysis 166–89
von Mechel, Christian 101
medals 149–50
the Medici 91, 99
memorabilia 49, 71
　see also private collections
men 82
　as collectors 60–3
　mentalités 222, 224
message sets 170–1, 180
　see also information systems
metaphorical relationships 38–9, 41, 43, 171, 172–80, 262–3
metonymic relationships 38–9, 41, 180
Miller, Daniel 23, 81–2, 87–8, 177
Miller's publications 76
miniaturization 58
models:
　for object study 265–73
modernity 2–3
　post-modern period 229–35, 264
Monte, C F 59
Montgomery, Charles 270
monuments 193–4
　gravestones 213–14
moon rock 5
Mouse Cottage 61, 62, 63
mummies:
　Egyptian 59
　musaeum 92–3
Musée de Cluny, Paris 194, 207
Museographia (Neikelius) 99
museum archives 120–2, 135
　see also collection management
museum buildings *see* architecture
museum collections 1, 2
　anthropological 38–41
　antiquarian 92, 94, 100, 103, 193–4
　archaeological 8, 44, 49, 103, 135
　definitions 48–50
　disciplined 119–20
　donated 65–6, 121
　ethnographic 103, 104, 111–12
　and gender 59–63, 64, 82
　natural history 30–1, 32, 69–71, 111–12, 132, 134
　nature of 36–47
　Polynesian 103, 104, 134
　private 7, 8, 48–66
　sale of 34–5
　selection process 7, 8, 38
　undisciplined 120–2
　Yoruba material 38–41
　see also collection management

museum displays 29, 87, 96–8, 105–9
  contextual 110–17
  dioramas 110
  exhibitions 136–43, 141–5, 147
  functionalist 155–61
  habitat groups 110
  heritage 11, 201–8, 230
  historical 192–209
  structuralist 180
  tableaux 110, 111
  wartime 208, 245
  see also collection management
Museum of London 205–6, 248, 251–2
museum practice 9–11, 13–14
museum theory 9–11, 13–14
museums:
  appearance of 105–9
  and capitalism 235–8, 242
  contemporary 109–17
  critical tradition in 7–14
  and cultural development 2–4, 8
  definitions 2, 92–3, 257–8
  future 256–64
  history 2, 90–109, 115–16
  intellectual rationale 89–117
  national collections 99–101
  open-air 110, 207–8
  and power politics 100, 201–2, 228–55
  as public institutions 89
  role of 3–4, 233–5
  social significance 116
Museums Association 2
myths 44–5, 47

names see classification
National Air and Space Museum, Washington 5
national collections 99–101
  see also museums
national culture 201–2, 244
National Maritime Museum, London 203–5
National Museum of American Art, Washington 201–2, 263
National Museum of American History, Washington 8
National Museum of Wales 248, 250
natural history material 30–1, 32, 111–12, 132, 134
  trophies 69–71
Natural History Museum, London 1, 84, 108, 109, 110, 137, 139, 140, 249
natural objects 95, 97, 99, 101
natural sciences 84–5
Neikelius, C F:
  Museographia 99
neo-functionalism 151–5
New Archaeologists 146
Newarke Houses Museum, Leicester 57–8
Nicholls, George 81
Nordiska Museet 110–11

North of England Open Air Museum, Beamish 207

object study 265–73
objectification 69, 87–8, 211
objective knowledge 258–62
Objective Knowledge . . . (Popper) 259–60
object-relations theories 45–6
objects 1, 4–6, 15–35, 66–88, 256–7
  accessioning 128–9, 134
  artificial 95, 97, 99, 103–5
  authentification 121, 237
  collectables 75–81, 114
  conservation 99, 121
  context of 83
  copies 24
  definitions 5–6, 15–17, 259–60
  departure from the norm 85
  durables 34–5
  fetish objects 73–84, 149
  as history 224–7
  as icons 202–3
  life-spans 16–17, 24–30
  materiality of 17–21
  medals 149–50
  memorabilia 49, 71
  natural 95, 97, 99, 101
  natural history 30–1, 32, 111–12, 132, 134
  object biographies 132
  organization of 41, 78, 87, 96–8, 101
  original 121
  perception theory 217–20
  personalia 49, 71
  physical nature of 16–17
  possession of 31–2, 34–5, 48, 51–2
  quality 75, 81
  rarities 75–6
  rarity of 33
  realization 218–19
  reception theory 217–20
  relics 197–202, 208–9
  rubbish 34–5
  selection process 7, 8, 38
  significance 38–9, 41, 46–7, 201–8
  as signs 27, 30, 31
  social significance 8, 21–4, 26–7, 210–27
  souvenirs 69–73, 149, 197–8
  structuration 221–2
  study of 7–14
  subject-object process 69, 83–4, 211
  as symbols 27–8, 29, 30, 31
  systematics 84–8
  talismans 43–7
  typicality 85
  value 32–3, 75, 236–7
  virtuality 219
  see also collecting process
obsessions 48
O'Neil, Mark 115

open-air museums 110, 207–8
organization:
    of objects 41, 78, 87, 96–8, 101
    see also collection management
original objects 121
    see also objects
Outline of a Theory of Practice (Bourdieu) 236
Owen, Jeff 76
ownership *see* possession
Oxford Museum 107–8

Panofsky, I:
    Studies in Iconography 265–6, 270
parole 26, 27, 30, 168–9, 171
    see also semiotics
patchwork 69
Pearce, S 177, 265, 272–3
Peckham, M 55
Peel Collection, Exeter City Museum 69–70
penis sheaths 8
perception theory 217–20, 261
performance theory 139, 141–3, 212–13
    see also exhibitions
personalia 49, 71
    see also private collections
phenomena 212, 227
phenomenology 211–12, 216
Philosophy of Money (Simmel) 32
Pierpoint, S 150–1
Pinto Collection, Birmingham City Museum 65–6, 67
plates 185–6
play:
    collecting as 50–3
    significance of 46–7
political science 83
politics *see* power politics
Polynesian material 103, 104, 134
    see also museum collections
Popper, Karl 262, 263
    Objective Knowledge . . . 259–60
pornography 244–5
possession:
    importance of 55–6, 81
    of objects 31–2, 34–5, 48, 51–2
posters 245–9, 250–2, 254
post-modern period 229–35, 264
post-structuralist analysis 229, 231, 255
    see also structuralist analysis
powder compacts 69, 72
power politics 100, 201–2, 228–55
    economic 236–7
    and knowledge 231, 234–5
    and meaning 232
prehistory:
    collecting process in 90–1
Principles of Geology (Lyell) 103
private collections 7, 8, 48–66
    see also museum collections

progress:
    concept of 3
provenance 121, 124, 269, 270
    see also collection management
Prown, J 265, 270
psychology 170
    of collecting 45–55
Punk style 214
purchase grants 238–9
Pye, David 270

quality:
    of objects 75, 81
Quiccheberg 95

Radcliffe-Brown, A R 145–6
rarities *see* curiosities
rarity:
    of objects 33
realization 218–19
    see also perception theory
Rebora, C 264
reception theory 217–20
reconstructions:
    of the past 207–9
Règles de la Methode Sociologique (Durkheim) 145
reification 39, 41, 42
relics 197–202, 208–9
    see also objects
religious rituals 177
religious subsystems 153–5, 157–8, 161, 190
    see also sociology
Rembrandt van Rijn 262
Remington, Frederic 201–2
research 124, 131–4
    see also collection management
resource centres 264
resource expenditure 135–6
    see also collection management
Rheims, M 51
Riegl, A 194
Rigby, D 60
Rigby, E 60
ring symbols 47
rituals:
    religious 177
    social 174–7
Rivers, Pitt 8, 85–6, 105, 145
    Evolution of Culture 86
Pitt Rivers Museum 86
Rochberg-Halton, E 55–6, 65
Roman society 155–61
romantic concepts:
    of collecting 69, 72–3
Royal Academy, London 244–5, 253
Royal Collection, Dusseldorf 99, 101
royal collections 99–101
Royal Ontario Museum 137

Royal Scottish Academy, Edinburgh 107
Royal Scottish Museum, Edinburgh 241–3
Royal Society, London 84, 92
rubbish 34–5
  see also objects
rule systems 169–70, 180

Saisselin, R G 66
sale *see* disposal
samplers 69
Sartre, Jean-Paul:
  Being and Nothingness 56
de Saussure, Ferdinand 12, 23, 26, 168, 169
Schiele, Egon 244–5
school uniforms 151, 153
  see also clothes
Schreyvogel, Charles 201
Science Museum, London 249, 271
scientific societies 101, 103
Scott, Gilbert 108
Scott, Walter 27, 29, 193–4
Scottish National Gallery, Edinburgh 107
Sedgewick Museum, Cambridge 101, 102
selection process:
  by individual collectors 7, 8, 38
  objects 7
self-image:
  and possessions 55–63
semiotics 26–9, 38–9, 141–3
  langue 26, 27, 168–9, 170, 171, 174
  parole 26, 27, 30, 168–9, 171
  see also language
    structuralist analysis
The Sense of Order (Gombrich) 23
series:
  of objects 48
service industries 229–30
shared understanding 212
significance:
  of objects 38–9, 41, 201–8
signifiers 26, 38–9, 41
  see also semiotics
signs:
  objects as 27, 30, 31
Simmel, Georg:
  Philosophy of Money 32
simple stimulus 59, 60
Skansen Museet, Sweden 110–11
Sloane, Hans 74–5
Smithsonian Institution, Washington 9, 115
Soane, John 194
social change 158–9, 229–35
social rituals 174–7
social significance:
  of museums 116
  of objects 8, 21–4, 26–7, 210–27
  see also material culture
social subsystems 153–5, 157–8, 161, 190
sociology 145, 146–7, 152, 153–5, 167
  comparative 145–6

cultural institutions 146–7
ecological adaptation 146, 147, 149, 153
homeostasis 153, 159
individual adjustment 147, 149–50
institutional development 157–8
subsystems 153–4, 157–8, 161, 190
Somerset County Museum Service 180, 181
du Sommerand, Alexandre 194, 207
Sorsby, B 249
Sotheby's 51
soup tureens 217–20
souvenirs 69–73, 149, 197–8
  see also objects
specimens *see* objects
Springburn Museum, Glasgow 115
Stevenage Museum 78, 79, 113
Stevens, Ted 202
Stewart, S 59
stimulus:
  and experience 59, 60
Stoke-on-Trent City Museum 248–9
Stokes, Adrian 46
Stone, Sarah 134
storage management 121–2
  see also collection management
structural history 222–4, 226, 227
structuralist analysis 12
  and aesthetics 188–9
  changes in 187–8
  and meaning 166–91
  post-structuralist 229, 231, 255
  problems of 180, 182–9
  see also semiotics
structuration 221–3, 227
Studies in Iconography (Panofsky) 265–6, 270
style 131, 132, 133
subject-object process 69, 83–4, 211
swords 24–30, 51
symbols:
  objects as 27–8, 29, 30, 31
systematic collecting 84–8
  see also museum objects
systematic functional analysis 146, 159
systems theory 151, 153–5, 159
  see also functionalism

tableaux 110, 111
  see also museum displays
talismanic objects 43–7
Tate Gallery, London 203
Tavistock School 217
taxidermy 58
taxonomical linguistics 124–7
  see also classification
taxonomy 84, 123–4, 125, 127
  see also classification
Taylor, L 215–16
tea drinking 174–7
teddy bears 51
temple sites 91

terminology thesauri 129–31
  see also classification
things see objects
Thompson, E P:
  Making of the English Working Class 196
Thompson, M 34
Three Age system 103, 105
  see also classification
Tolkien, J R:
  Lord of the Rings 43, 44
toys 51, 69
Tradescant Collection, Oxford 74, 81, 96
Tradescant family 91, 95
transients 34–5
  see also objects
treasures 44, 47, 90–1, 151, 203
Trevelyan, V 238
trophies 69–71
Tuan, Y 51
Turner, Victor 108
two-headed calf 59
  see also freaks
type classification 48, 50, 85, 87–8, 99, 109
  see also classification
typicality:
  of objects and artefacts 85

Ucko, P J 8
Uffizi Gallery, Florence 99, 101
UNESCO:
  Convention on the means of prohibiting . . . illicit
    import . . . cultural property 150
Universal Exhibition, Paris, 1878 111
University Natural History Museum, Cambridge
    84
Unruh, D 63
Upton, Del 212–13
Utah University 9

value 234, 269, 270–1
  of objects 32–3, 75, 236–7
Van Gogh, Vincent 237
Veblen, T 65
Victoria and Albert Museum, London 3–4, 69,
    114–15, 238, 239

Victorian Things (Briggs) 195–6
HMS Victory 198
Viennese Royal Collection 99, 101
virtuality 219
  see also perception theory
visitors:
  to exhibitions 137–9
vocabulary 169–70, 180
  see also language

Wagner, Richard 47
Walker Art Gallery, Liverpool 203
Wallach, A 108
Wallendorf, M 61–3
Walsall Museum 78, 80, 113, 216, 263–4
Walsh, William 52
war sourvenirs 72
  medals 149–50
Warhol, Andy 237
wartime images 208, 245
Waterhouse, Alfred 108
Waterson, C D 242
Watts, Alan 19
Welsh Folk Museum 129–30
Wernick, A 20–1
Williams, Charles Hanbury 75
willow pattern 185–6
Wilson, E 215–16
Winnicott, D W 46
women 82
  as collectors 60–3, 64
Woodward, John 101, 102
words see vocabulary
Worm, Olaus 96–7
Worsley, Richard 103
Wright, E 46–7
Wunderkammer see cabinets of curiosities

York Castle Museum 69, 87
Yorkshire Philosophical Society 101, 103
Yoruba material 38–41
  see also museum collections